D1563526

Autism in Film and Television

Autism in Film and Television

On the Island

EDITED BY
MURRAY POMERANCE AND R. BARTON PALMER

University of Texas Press ◆◆ *Austin*

Requests for permission to reproduce material from this work should be sent to:
Permissions
University of Texas Press
P.O. Box 7819
Austin, TX 78713-7819
utpress.utexas.edu/rp-form

♾ The paper used in this book meets the minimum requirements of
ANSI/NISO Z39.48-1992 (R1997) (Permanence of Paper).

Library of Congress Cataloging-in-Publication Data
Names: Pomerance, Murray, 1946– editor. | Palmer, R. Barton, 1946– editor.
Title: Autism in film and television : on the island / edited by Murray Pomerance and
    R. Barton Palmer.
Description: First edition. | Austin : University of Texas Press, 2022. | Includes
    bibliographical references and index.
Identifiers: LCCN 2021038216
    ISBN 978-1-4773-2491-2 (cloth)
    ISBN 978-1-4773-2492-9 (paperback)
    ISBN 978-1-4773-2493-6 (PDF)
    ISBN 978-1-4773-2494-3 (ePub)
Subjects: LCSH: Autism in motion pictures. | Autism on television. | Autism in
    motion pictures—Social aspects. | Autism on television—Social aspects. |
    Autistic people. | Autistic artists. | Autism spectrum disorders—Social aspects.
Classification: LCC PN1995.9.A845 A98 2022 | DDC 704/.0874—dc23
LC record available at https://lccn.loc.gov/2021038216

doi:10.7560/324912

To all those
who did not know

To be born is to be wrecked on an island.
—JAMES M. BARRIE

Contents

Autism in Film and Television

Two Meditations

Who Am I?

MURRAY POMERANCE

In a dramatized narrative, a character stipulated as autistic—until relatively recently, Aspergian—by the script's narration or by other characters may move through the story without impacting it at all, or may act in, possibly even affect, the plot, or be affected by it, principally in terms of the autism. The personality characteristic is sometimes a story link, sometimes mere decoration. Thus, being on the spectrum can be not only a personal but also a narrative circumstance, and it can appear on the screen in either way. But filmmakers have become more and more aware that one's being on the spectrum does not, with absolute regularity, emit telltale signs in the way that other human conditions may do: skin color, gender (often), age, even some talents. Extrinsic characteristics can be noted simply on inspection. Think of African American Sidney Poitier in *Guess Who's Coming to Dinner* (1967), female Jodie Foster in *The Silence of the Lambs* (1991), aged Ruth Gordon in *Harold and Maude* (1971), or dancing Sammy Davis Jr. in *Porgy and Bess* (1959). When, in a drama, we are given the chance to do extrinsic identification, all the following apply (when intentional disguise is not in play):

- Actor and character are, or are susceptible to being made up to seem, possessors and sharers with other characters of characteristics vital to the tale: skin color, gender, ability, age.
- But the story can play out without intending any particular indication *of* the signed category as a category. Moral valuation is not part of the formula. In *Guess Who's Coming*, Poitier's character John Prentice's point is

that skin color doesn't figure; but the filmmaker Stanley Kramer's point is that here we see how it does. Less important than what happens to the character in question or what the character makes happen in the story is the character's presence simply put. All kinds of people—to the extent that there are *kinds* of people—can be found populating all kinds of stories, their mere presence cuing action but not necessarily indicating an outsider's evaluation of them or any particular meaning inside the tale. (One often thinks of this as token inclusion.)

- Key characteristics can be rendered with or without explicit emphasis, depending on the shape desired for the work and the declarative power of the characteristics. Age doesn't always "tell" as well as skin color, and gender sometimes doesn't "tell" at all. Talent doesn't show until there is action.

- There is nothing inherently disparaging, insulting, demeaning, or degrading about producers reaching out to cast a somehow identifiable performer in a role congruent with the identification in play. Dramatic requirement does not prescribe that such casting be "authentic," nor need casting mean that the work overall is a signal or statement about any qualities or conditions portrayed. American Meryl Streep can play British Margaret Thatcher. Or: an onscreen murderer does not have to be portrayed by a real murderer for a murder drama to read as realistic.

When in visual storytelling a central character's telling characteristics are not available on inspection, however, it will be necessary that some definitive, cinematically relevant action take place before the camera in order to "show" them. In the interest of storytelling economy, it can be useful if visual identification is possible on the viewer's first exposure: a quick, almost instantaneous "read." The camera can "see" only what is on show, but a show can be made rather swiftly.

"Definitive action": there are many fascinating ways to handle this in film, and a performative tic that appears to "sign" a symptom is only one of them. Often when a character appears for the first time before our eyes, we have already been prepared by some other character to take a certain kind of view; or indeed, when a character is introduced to us, we gain insight less from that character than from other characters nearby who make significant reactions. Context is crucial. As we learn from Henry James: "When you've lived as long as I you'll see that every human being has his shell and that you must take the shell into account. By the shell I mean the whole envelope of circumstances. There's no such thing as an isolated man or woman; we're each of us made up of some cluster of appurtenances. . . . One's house, one's furniture, one's garments, the books one reads, the company one keeps—these things are all expressive" ([1881] 2002, 191). But also, as we learn from Thomas Szasz ([1974] 2010), there is a tremendous power of contextualizing residing in the persona and utterance of a relevant authority, such as a professional practitioner or the dominant social personality in a scene. What we think someone is, then, is partly, but only partly, inspired by what we notice them doing (and not doing). Yet notice we must. In the arts of visual representation, all is notice.

A further twist of the screw: "inspection" has a diagnostic meaning. An admitting nurse can look up from her desk and with the bat of an eye categorize a patient (for an admission form). This is a cheap form of identification, as such forms go, taking the least amount possible of the nurse's paid time (Garfinkel 1967). In film terms, a "cheap" identification is one that can be made swiftly enough that plenty of narrative space is left for developing the story rather than being used for spelling out a character's condition. Take Plato (Sal Mineo) in *Rebel Without a Cause* (1955) and note how instantaneously he is discoverable as "disturbed." Take Kristen Stewart's Maureen in *Personal Shopper* (2016) and see how in a flash she is shown as sensitive, perhaps clairvoyant. The uniqueness of such characters must be acted out, not merely "present," but the acting out can be in a shot or a gesture, a dramatic breath.

Autism being differentially visible across the spectrum, the autist must be *explicitly* shown as such for the viewer to effect a recognition. Some unequivocal performance of "autistic characteristics" is required for the storytelling. But audiences can see only what they already know how to see—what they expect should be there for them to look at. What features about autism can easily (quickly, cheaply, without undue study) be shown, then? And by implication, what is it that most viewers will instantly recognize (diagnose)? These considerations obtain no matter the intent to make *or not to make* statements about autism, and despite much of what viewers "know" being nothing but stereotype or myth in the first place, picked up, perhaps, from other dramatic presentations.

Questioning the "accuracy" of a dramatization of autism raises numerous seriously problematic questions: What is accuracy anyway? Who legitimates so-called accuracy? Whence comes the call for accuracy of representation in visual stories? Or in any stories? Stories are not social accounts, though they point to, and assume an understanding of, social visions. Film and television narratives are not forms of journalism.

And so we come upon the surely dramatized, often exaggerated, often awkward, often almost caricatured—but also often very easily read—image of the autistic personality onscreen. Dramatized, because autism need not present visible scars. Exaggerated, because the slight or only marginal extenuation of speech or gestural tic might be too small to be noticed in a richly organized shot. Awkward and easily read, because the writer wants to proceed *as though the autist is known and recognized now*, not as though it is necessary to spend the first act arranging recognition. Caricatured, at least in part, because the presentation must read at a great distance—sometimes around the world—for audiences not connected or familiar with autism at all.

Typically in screen portraiture of autism, we see some combination of the following techniques (which have struck me for their importance, much as they earlier struck other observers, such as Mark Osteen):

- Intensive but variable optical focus: the autist is searching for what to look at and how closely; or is looking at something that many people would consider trivially marginal and keeping his or her eyes away from what is apparently thought centrally important.
- Conversational one-sidedness coupled with supreme articulateness, shown in speeches longer than conversational partners appear ready to tolerate. (This is in part a "showing" of autism through supporting performances by other actors looking bored, irritated, antsy, and so on.)
- Informative fill: the tendency to give information others may find irrelevant, or more information than others think appropriate, or indeed arcane information most people don't have—answers without questions. Check out Will Hunting's (Matt Damon) NSA interview in *Good Will Hunting* (1997).
- General interpersonal clumsiness, shown in any number of ways, but typically physical: gaze aversion or staring forward, "declarative" walking or running styles, "odd" conversational silences.
- A tendency to operate outside teamwork situations, and so to spend more time than other characters working or relaxing alone.
- Difficulty with sensory extremes, especially sound, with notable withdrawals from loud, particularly treble sounds in the surround.
- High apparent intelligence, often linked with productivity, involving, often, replete technical knowledge of subjects that other characters never think about.

It is easy to see how these characteristics are amenable to an actor's screen work. They are easy to accomplish, readily recognized, and efficient from a scriptwriter's point of view. You can take a young man (statistically, autists are predominantly male) and have him look slightly away, or not so slightly away, from other people's gazes; do a lot of talking, more than a questioner thought was needed; lard the speech with details that from *some* point of view (not the autist's) have no direct bearing; be notably inept at managing casual encounters, certainly not realizing how to interpret what's "between the lines"; spend considerable time in unitary activities like scanning a screen or keyboarding or listening to music; writhe or withdraw in the presence of loud sound; notice small details of situations or persons that other people apparently miss—a cheap faux-diamond necklace, lipstick slightly smeared.

The purpose of showing characters this way is not stereotypy but economic efficiency in portraiture, especially when the character's autism plays a central role in the story. One very telling example is Michael Cristofer's *The Night Clerk* (2020), in which all these characteristics get notation of a specific and dramatically crucial kind.

Autistic Tropes

Some autists and non-autistic "supporters" of autism have openly cringed at particular screen portrayals, loudly excoriating a failure of "accurate" representation, as though there is one supreme version of autistic experience to which religious observance should be paid. It is easy enough to cringe when presentations seem exaggerated or awkward; but it is even easier, even mindless, to fail to wonder why one is cringing. I abjure considering the ins and outs of "liberal" identity politics, and the argument that some portraits misrepresent, because all portraits in any medium misrepresent in some ways and for some reasons of practical significance. Further, autism is so varied across its population—a population hard, even, to aggregate—that making any claims for identification rights, and thus claims that one or another representation violates or appropriates, would be spurious.

The camera requires some highlights to be stronger than others; the picture is composed. Sex being popular with mass audiences, generally speaking, a character's reticence about the body works nicely to shape an autistic character. The autist, unless very young, will tend to know this. In *The Night Clerk*, Detective Espada (John Leguizamo), in his first interaction with Bart Bromley (Tye Sheridan)—who has been giving a rather long account of what he did last night, step by step by step by step, including every street he used while driving home—suddenly asks the kid, "You have a girlfriend?" It's at once a rather blunt and awkward conversational intrusion, and Bart's silence shows that he picks that up. But also, from Bart's point of view, it's a typical query for him; he is young and knows that many young people talk about sex, even if he doesn't, but also that, partly because he doesn't, people easily wonder about him. "Ever have a girlfriend?"—"No"—(hesitantly) "Boyfriend?"—"No." The abrupt questioning and quirkiness in answering all helps us understand how the detective thinks, stereotypically, that autists are somehow notable in their relation to sex, and opens a pathway for the viewer to understand Bart in a similar way. But a more careful viewing shows how Espada's probing has nothing much to do with Bart's autism as Bart himself understands it, and as we may learn to. It's a probe that is entirely marginal.

One frequent trope in the dramatization of autism is to show a character uttering a statement of profound philosophical or intellectual pith, a kind of mini-lecture, in moments that other characters define as casual and everyday, that is, moments not suitably elevated for formalities of the brain (quite as though some situations are and some situations are not suitably elevated in that way): the grotesquely impromptu lecture. Another trope is to have a character played by an actor who either looks hale and healthy and vigorous and sensual, or has in some earlier drama played a character who is all these, now without warning move with hesitation, run awkwardly, have trouble maintaining balance, pause inordinately between phrases of speech, stare off—in short, very obviously *not* be uncompromisingly hale and healthy and vigorous and sensual, or at least not flawlessly coordinated. This actor's body should be hale, we think, but isn't, and the discrepancy is the readable clue. The gawkiness is being put on; and it becomes the performance.

There is also a mantra trope, involving the autistic character having, and numbly repeating over and over and over, some little verbal shtick (from early childhood, perhaps). This often occurs in situations defined by the powers that be as inappropriate or at least weird. Or doing the repetition strenuously in order to soothe the self (stimming): "I'm okay, I'm okay, I'm okay, I'm okay, I'm okay," Bart barks as he drives at breakneck speed to the hotel in the middle of the night. A "normal" character (as might be) might internalize such a chant, but the autist doesn't internalize. Or Bart goes to a convenience store to buy ice cream (five tubs, not one—he really likes ice cream, and why should he deny himself?), but when he looks up at the clerk, he says, perfunctorily, "That shirt is really annoying. The colors are really bright and the stripes are making me really dizzy." The clerk takes a quiet beat before quietly replying, "Fuck you." But the shirt has been designed in advance to give virtually anyone precisely that reaction of withdrawal; it is intended to look loud, even blaring; and Bart is being characterized by virtue of letting the words come out of his mouth. The autist, so we are often shown, has no self-monitoring phase. But think how, in terms of movie production, a little scene like this is very easy to stage and perform.

It is also very useful for dramatic production to lay upon the autistic character some behavioral "tell," a quirky or utterly individualistic way of doing something that audience members do routinely and unconsciously, and in a less marked way. Normal behavior, bizarre manner. Bart gets his dinner on the steps that lead from his mother's kitchen to his basement apartment, schleps it downstairs, sits watching her eat in the kitchen or dining room on his private monitor, and "eats with her." (Only late in the film do we learn why he may be doing this, a reason that is less about autism than considerateness or shame.) On *The Good Doctor* (2017), Shaun Murphy (Freddie Highmore) has to have as large a television as possible, one so large that in his apartment he can have almost nothing else. The eponymous physician Gregory House (Hugh Laurie in *House* [2004–2012]) bounces a ball against the walls of his office and limps with dramatic fervor, one of the walking wounded. Not just a limp, a suppurating war wound. And so on. In *The Tunnel* (2013), Clémence Poésy drops blunt and brilliant aphorisms, always muttered as asides. In her private life she shows ravenous hungers. Not just hungers. Sherlock Holmes as played by Jeremy Brett holds his tongue but then quickly releases long phrases in a single breath, losing many words in the shuffle. Raymond Babbitt (Dustin Hoffman) in *Rain Man* (1988) has to have all activity interrupted at five in the afternoon so that he can watch Judge Wapner on *The People's Court* (1981): "Five o'clock: Wapner."

Autists may or may not exhibit some or all of these quirky mannerisms, but mannerisms of this kind can believably be associated with autists and can therefore be used in visual dramas for quick character establishment. The autist's panic in social situations where the "rules of the game" are hidden is a much harder thing to show with clarity and is thus usually not shown, a principal difficulty being that most viewers, presumably not autistic, *do not recognize* that in the social games they themselves play the rules are indeed hidden—hidden in being categorically unexpressed. The hiding is not by intent. We all know the rules; we just don't *say* we know them, and why should we? After all, we all *know* them! Onscreen the audience sees simple normality, not a situation in which "normality" is being constructed in a power relationship. One can have a camera glide through a party (assuming the viewpoint of the autist) and in macro close-ups show the men and women in the margins forcibly smiling (perhaps smiling *too much*), and then intercut shots of the moving autist with eyes flicking back and forth without facial expression, as though lost in a Wonderland of human interaction. But this is an elaborate setup requiring plenty of actors on set and ample time for retakes, and doesn't get us any further than other, much easier tells do.

Another thing autists experience regularly is a kind of displacement when they notice that their own behavior doesn't fit, and they also notice that the reason it doesn't fit is that the behavior of others is in accordance with prevailing but uninteresting or incredible dictates. How did this patently insensible "normal" way of being come to prevail? On what merit? For the autist there is no merit in, or rationale for, the elusive rules of the game, except that they are recognized in the Authority of the Neurotypical as the rules of the game. Whose rules, however? And rules with what legitimation? In *The Night Clerk*, putting "normality" in the mouth of a somewhat brutal detective offers a nuanced but slight picture of the "normal" hierarchy of value. (The detective's open identity as a detective is no less telling of hierarchical power than the autist's open identity as an autist is telling of relative powerlessness.)

The autist knows that others find him strange. Strange, weird, peculiar, "different," heavy-duty, odd, abnormal, even—irony of ironies—"disabled." "There's the problem of being perceived as odd or unsophisticated. Naïve, clueless. Unfashionable. Or just plain stupid," Bart tells his friend Andrea. She says, "It's very difficult for people to know what's going on inside that head." To which he replies, "Yes, that's correct." The prevailing dictates "disable" anybody who doesn't go along, even permit that such outsiders be "disabled" situationally, both presumed lacking in ability and stigmatized as "disabled" to boot. Autists are not disabled, as a class or aggregate, although any one of them, like any one of the crowd generally, might see some disability in a self-image. There are plenty of tasks, attitudes, and operations at which autists are far more abled than people who "play by the rules" and constantly find "others" to point at. This is not to say that autists prefer flouting rules that seem to govern other people, or succeed by evading them; it may well be that they do not grasp rules or the legitimation behind them. That prevalent rationale: "Now, now: what if everybody behaved that way? What would happen if everybody did that?" "Yes," the autist could reasonably think, "but there is no conceivable way in which *everybody* could possibly do that. The rationale is nothing but a cheap way of preserving so-called 'normality,' a hegemony, in the face of human variability."

There is a beautifully illustrative little scene in Dawid Bodzak's *Tremors* (2018). A boy in a high school class (Natan Berkowicz) suddenly begins to have an attack while the teacher is prating in the front of the room. Leaning over his desk, shaking his arms and torso, putting his head down, grabbing the desk, and finally rattling it ferociously without cease, he is in patent agony and out of control. A kind of buried volcanic eruption. The teacher rushes the students out of the room, the very last one to leave being the girl who was sitting, stunned, next to him. The principal is called for, appears, acts ineffectively, and is barked at by the boy to go away. Then, while the teacher stands frozen, he rises, turns, and walks briskly out of the room. Out of the room, down the corridor, down another and another corridor, alone, except that his chum races to catch up. He looks at the chum and smiles happily. "I'm fine," he says. "But we're not really friends."

Abilities

Two genres of critique have coalesced around the represented autist onscreen. First, an argument has been mounted that the representation is, as it were, unrepresentative. Autists in everyday life, taken as an aggregate, are, it is put forward, distressingly not indicated by some or all of the tics the actor and writer embed in the character. Many autists are represented as quasi-savant, and although many autists in everyday life are intelligent, relatively few of them are savant. Dramatized autists are shown as avoiding others' gazes, but many real autists don't do that. And so on. The faults with this kind of critiquing are many, but principally these: in everyday life, in the real world that autists and others inhabit, there are no autists "in the aggregate." The spectrum contains legion personality combinations, and the autistic ones tend toward certain kinds of preferences, difficulties, discomforts, and work-arounds in order to "pass," but there is no general pattern of tendencies. For the autist, passing can mean either managing a performance in such a way as not to give off clues that would lead to an informal or formal naming. This is the sense introduced to sociological thought by Harold Garfinkel in 1967. It can also mean getting a sufficient grade on the secret invisible examination of the moment so that in spite of even clear autism, the autist is accepted socially in some desirable way. At any rate, regardless of who does and who doesn't pass, autists cannot be easily grouped or classed except, perhaps, in the very general sense many of them have that they "don't fit."

Beyond the absence of the aggregate that is used by critics as a basis for the negative assessment of screen portrayals, a great deal is being assumed when a screen characterization is treated as though by rights it *should* stand in for anything outside the work of which it is a part. This obligation is not laid on all screen depictions—heroin addicts, neurosurgeons, truck drivers, babysitters—and the dominant reason for laying it on the scripted autist character is a belief—taken on a false basis—that autists are among the disabled and therefore merit the kinds of "respectful," "gentle," "unabusive," "accepting" treatments that should be accorded in that case. The argument for disability is a huge boon to those who press for legislation and identity politics. But there is as much cause to wonder about the socially dominating abilities that autists presumably lack as there is to point at them being lacking. Nor—it should be said—are there spokespeople for the autistic personality. There is no "autist community," and there are no iconic examples (not even, as many claim, Temple Grandin or the fictive Raymond Babbitt). An autist could be willing to share, and be capable of sharing, aspects of a life experience with others who self-name in the same way, and the conversation might be pleasant or beneficial or entirely unhelpful. Autists can share their experiences with people who call themselves normal, too, and can find both sympathy at one extreme and intense incomprehension on the other. But the business of media production—television, film, novels in print, and so on—does not owe autistic persons any particular address beyond the very fundamental one we learned about thanks to Vito Russo's exposé (1987) of media treatment of homosexuals: a refusal to systematically dramatize autists as villains.

It is interesting to consider that in visual fictions, to the degree that it is taken wholly for itself as a presence, the autistic personality can be used egregiously or nonegregiously. (Mark Osteen has suggested to me how "catalysts" and "yardsticks," both functional in turning the course of dramatic events, can be autists, too; here I am not as concerned with what action an autistic character can commit in the story as I am with how fully, deeply, and touchingly that character can be treated quite outside of utility.) In what I would term the "egregious" portrait, a story at one point incorporates a character identified (but finally only identified) expressly as autistic; this character turns out to have no special merit *as an autist*, mechanically important though he or she may be, and the autism, however it is configured, is either disconnected from other, dramatically vital aspects of the story or has *only* a narrative, and not an expressive, function. We watch this character, perhaps with great enjoyment and curiosity, but never have the sense of a profound encounter. This kind of tokenism is hardly new to Hollywood or to Western culture and does not in and of itself constitute a problem. Here, the autist, in a kind of product placement, is used to decorate the story in some way that adds a frisson and, for some viewers, a pleasure of a decided and particular kind. But the story could have been produced without such a character—without a character who seems "strange," "marginal," or "unlike others." Even if the story needed one of Osteen's "catalysts" or "yardsticks," a non-autistic substitute could easily have been used.

"Nonegregious" usage puts the autist at the center of narrative happenings not only through action but also through a riddling of the viewer's fascination, and even ties particular experiences of the autist's life into the structure of the story. Consider a delicate arrangement in *The Night Clerk*: Bart has been working hard to overcome his social clumsiness and has given himself a little informal "education": he secretly films hotel guests and then watches his recordings over and over in order to learn from them how to behave socially: what to say, how to phrase his words, where to place verbal stress, when to use which expressions, what tone to use for embedding his words in discourse. And he does this even in private situations, when guests are in physically compromising positions. Bart's interest lies at first only in the way they behave, the nuances, the tics that can be imitated (like many autists, he is a secret actor of sorts); and we see and hear him working on copying what he hears and sees. But one of his hidden cameras inadvertently films a murder. The video files exist only because of Bart's autism and his desire to live with it successfully; but they also exist to complicate the murder plot. Here, there is really no way to separate the secret videos as murder evidence from the secret videos as the autist's self-created educational material.

It may well turn out that as representations of autists multiply on the large and small screen, audiences will become so accustomed to the tropes by which the autist is sketched that the person's presence on the spectrum, alone, will cease to have narrative value and social meaning, and plots will have to complicate identifications in order to be successful for viewers. Already in the 2010s, this is beginning to happen: *The Night Clerk*, *The Tunnel*, *The Big Bang Theory*, and *The Code* being examples as good as any.

More and more, autists in the everyday will recognize onscreen depictions working to express their experience, even if those depictions don't mirror their own lives. They will fill in the gaps, and viewers who know little about autism, who have more gaps still, will perhaps learn to do likewise as autism dramas become progressively more scripted in a shorthand that viewers come to know.

Who "I" Am

But the issue of knowing autism rather than just watching it—or, knowing it *through the experience of watching it*—can be fraught. To illustrate, I should take the one case I know better than any other.

I am on the spectrum. That is, as I like to say, I am autistic. To live through the days of my life, I am constantly thinking about this fact and its relation to circumstances: not thinking angrily or in pain, or thrilled, either, but being aware of certain, let's say, formulaic discrepancies or gaps that tend to pattern themselves and recur with some predictable frequency. The lives of many young autists are filled with possibilities for family and parental support and openings in clinics and therapy groups and discussion panels, and were I embedded socially in this way, I might think a lot about whether such a thing as "assistance" could benefit me seriously, and if so, how and where I might find some. But I never knew such embedding. I was born well before autism came into popular discourse. I found out about my autism in my seventh decade. When I was a kid, there was no such thing, at least not apparently in the crowd where, awkwardly, I moved; no parental support, and no discussion groups. What people thought of me I can hardly know, but I did hear words like "weird" or "different" used with some frequency. Other words were there, too, of course.

I found myself resonating very sympathetically with *The Night Clerk*'s Bart as he tells his chum Andrea that he is considered—that he is perceived as—"odd or unsophisticated. Naïve, clueless. Unfashionable." I can now flash back across vital moments in my life: as a child, as a young boy, as a teenager, as a young adult, as a grown man with a family: recalling flashes of moments in which I was treated by outsiders as though they perceived me like that. Perceived, Bart does not proceed to say—because, being twenty-five, he still doesn't have the courage—because the perceivers made the empowered decision to perceive that way, because they chose to use perceptual categories that were available to them (and they had made those categories available).

One aspect of my life that I know I share with others on the spectrum (because I have been told reliably) is that I tend to be a loner, especially as I work. And further, I cannot avoid noticing that I am sometimes labeled "productive." That makes me feel both odd and embarrassed, because I don't think of myself as notably productive; I'm a worker and I just work. Social class plays as much a role here as psychology: if you're in the working class and you work less than the managers would like, you're a slacker; if you work more, you're a workaholic. I have spent my adult—even my late-adolescent—life fielding jokes about working hard, being mocked, teased, pointed to, commented about, subjected to expectations made all too clear. One Monday morning a long time ago, a chum actually asked me, "How many books did you write over the weekend?" And as part of the fitting-in routine that I work hard to employ—please note: *routine*—I smiled amicably, "taking the tease," and responding with a pithy line like "Three" (big—too big—grin). In my own understanding, I work at the rate I work, and I both assume and seem to notice that people around me do the same. But many people are not openly evaluated for their speed of labor, as though somebody has decided on an optimal speed of work that everyone should keep to. Shades of the worker-efficiency studies at the Hawthorne Works between 1924 and 1932 (Mayo 1949) or of that truly horrifying scene in *Schindler's List* (1993).

The productivity measurement as applied to me, to autists more broadly, and to workers of every kind is of course a pillar of the capitalist endeavor, countable widgets finished per hour against profit per widget. I do not see the rate at which I write as related in any way to mass marketing, however. And I have no clue what benefit anyone else might derive by counting my pages per week, since I am not trying to "set an example" or "make a statement" or anything beyond concentrating on the text, sentence by sentence. Because I am a writer, I write, and when I've finished writing one thing, I go on to writing another. That is no more remarkable than an actor finishing one film and moving on to another; a carpenter finishing a kitchen in one house and moving on to a garage at another; a politician striving to get one bill passed and when it is, moving on to work on another.

Still one can be resented, and that makes for loneliness. I find myself craving friendship and warmth, yet from only a small number of persons at a time. I do not like parties. In fact, I abhor parties and do not go to them if I can possibly avoid it. (I also do not understand how or why anybody would, but that's none of my business.) Dinner with a friend or two, absolutely. But mass scenes are intimidating. I recall a dormitory dining hall where I had a most delicious breakfast, but only by sitting in such a way as to block out the many other people eating the same food at the same time. As to crowds and parties, I think I will never forget an experience I had when I was about sixteen. Word had gone around about a party on Saturday night, and I could not *not notice* that everybody I knew had been invited, but me. Saturday came, still no invitation. I moped. Why did I mope? Because I felt a signal had been sent my way that I was too weird, too unacceptable, too not-wanted, and it hurt profoundly—I've never again had a pang quite so stunning. About an hour before the party, an invitation came. I went. But once I was there, I felt (for me, quite predictably) like a bug in amber.

If I saw such a thing depicted onscreen, it would resonate with me, and I wouldn't ask or care how many other autists found it meaningful; whether or not it was "typical"; whether or not it was "accurate." In my chapter in this volume on *The Code*, I describe a scene that resonated with me very sharply and deeply, yet perhaps I speak only for myself. But perhaps, too, I speak for others as well. The self I would speak for is surely my musical self.

My training in classical music makes it possible for me to not only hear, but also to enjoy, loud and treble sounds, but only as long as they are part of a composition being performed. When in a restaurant (made of concrete) I hear reverberating high-pitched music or chatter, I go nuts and can barely taste my food. Music seems to me a paradigm of structure and form, and I do recognize in myself the need for repetitive structure and form, even to the extent that I will listen to one movement of a concerto or symphony over and over and over and over—no concern for the progression to conclusion in the overall work. I suppose what I am seeking is some mixture of complexity and surprise and the peculiar color that comes with sounds. Life is music, and music is not noise.

I am a little afraid of most other people.

A little afraid: I fear that I will not comprehend them, that what they say will be based on some axioms I do not understand or accept: that, as it were, I missed school the day these arcane principles were covered. (I was a religious attendee at school, but in my feeling, which is truer than my history, I missed a lot of classes.) I sometimes watch and listen very carefully—not unlike Bart Bromley, actually—so that I can memorize tactics and modes and later try them out and maybe use them. I practice a lot. I often find myself thinking about what a situation will be like before I am in it. When I write a sentence, I am thinking forward, too, imagining ways to turn it out with grammatical correctness and flow and wondering about other ways of saying the same or a similar thing.

Regarding the quest for structure: I notice that there are times when I not only seek to tease it out of circumstances but also work on the assumption that structure or order is to be found out there. That of course there's an order. Here's a situation of particular stress: at an outdoor café there's a window for putting in your order, and about twenty feet away a second window where you stand to pick it up. That much is really clear. But between these two windows are two things, side by side and in parallel: first, a patio, completely empty, decorated with lovely ferns among which you can walk or stand; and then a public sidewalk beside that. What people are doing is: lining up for the second window neither on the patio nor on the sidewalk, but *in both places*, and haphazardly, so that it is patently impossible to know where the end of the line is, there being, in effect now, two lines, but lines that do not signal themselves as lines, being so muddled that the end, if there is one, is invisible. No one but me, however, seems bothered by this: the other customers all know the *secret rule*, which is that there is no rule. Do whatever you like. Act arbitrarily. This rule—"Act arbitrarily"—being unknown to, and unsuspected by, me (I generally don't act arbitrarily), I stand around trying to figure out what these people must be thinking they're doing (when actually, I suspect, they're not thinking at all). The assumptions being made by those who casually, easily, effortlessly don't trouble to think are that *of course* any arbitrary action is fine, and that *of course* everybody knows that, that all this knowledge is automatically shared, and that there is no form. The pattern is, There Is No Pattern. Perhaps it's clear how confounding and distressing this could be for a mind seeking pattern and relationship and coherence. It is not hard, in a circumstance like that, to come to think of oneself as not being right-minded, since "the majority rules." Democracy may be a logical construct if it is thoughtful, if the polis thinks before acting, but it plays havoc when there is only behavior.

I have very little ability at visual imagination—that is, coming up with a vision, a picture, of something that does not yet exist. But when I see a painting, a film, a television show, or a photograph and walk away, I can be struck so powerfully that the image does not disappear, and I can call up minute points inside the image, often decades afterward. These are pictures, though. People's expressions I usually cannot read. I have learned workarounds for getting through conversations, but I almost never really understand anybody interpersonally, especially—noxiously—people who say one thing and mean another or who avoid saying what they really think. I have seen depictions of autists who cannot avoid saying what they really think—Bart is one of those—and I don't resonate with them. I can avoid saying things—in fact, I probably do that rather a lot—and can also express ideas when I am asked to, but very, very often when I watch or listen to someone, I simply don't quite know what they mean or where it's coming from. For example, if someone chatted with me amicably in order to have a conversation, I don't think I'd quite get that, and I would think they really did want to know something when they asked a question. I've learned that if somebody says, "How's it going?" he's merely using a tag and doesn't really need to know. But if a line comes my way like "How did you get interested in that?" I try hard to ponder and answer as though my questioner really is itching to know, and then later I sometimes think, "Oh, he was just being conversational, and I went on far too long for nothing."

One can harvest an impression of oneself that in this world one contributes nothing.

When an autistic character behaves volubly this way onscreen, I don't take the representation—which is not really inaccurate—as a slight, as an insult, as a mockery, as a diagnosis, or as a hand extended my way. I just think, "Oh yes, I understand that very well." And if an autistic character doesn't behave that way, I don't think, "Oh gee, autism isn't being represented well." I don't know what autism is in the general. I know what *my* autism is (a little, and more every day).

And yet I don't think autism boils down to a huge range of individualisms with no greater pattern. There is a greater pattern to one extent, one important extent. All of us are treated in some way by some people as though we don't fit, and while non-autists who are treated this way seem usually to understand why, I think we—I use "we" with caution—recognize the alienation but understand only that others feel they have the power and privilege to set us apart. I don't see why exactly they should or could feel that way: what rationale, what underpinning, what principle makes such exclusion rational. But I know that it does, that I am separated.

And in that way, surrounded by pretty creatures merrily going on their way in the sea, I feel myself, in ways I am only beginning to be able to speak about, on an island.

I Am, You Are

How peculiar it is to be found symptomatic! I finger a keyboard, and soon words are forming that I can order and reorder until there is a sensible line. Call it a poetic line. Fluttering fingers, letters, words, order, reorder, poetic line. And I do this all the time, trained from an early age to play the piano but then giving it up and now making words in a line, a kind of music. Since I was fifteen years old, over and over, many different kinds of lines, lines adding up to one thing or another, lines forming into paragraphs, paragraphs forming movements. And then quite suddenly, as when the clouds part, I learn that I am on the spectrum and am given the hint, in a movie about an autist, perhaps, that all my finger movement—*my writing*—is *stimming*. Now I must think I spent a lifetime assuaging a discomfort, feeling my own presence, assuring myself that I won't be lost in the crevices, something of a negative, icy thought.

Not to comprehend other people is to feel "not human" in the sense that they are "human" (or at least to think of oneself that way). And it is easy to find oneself involuntarily in a group. The minute the diagnostic mind has a "symptom," it has a mathematical set, a grouping of discernibly like items, no matter where they originated or are placed. "Trouble with relationships," for instance: over in Cornwall is a young woman who has it, too, and there is another woman in Uganda, and then a boy of fourteen in Los Angeles, all with the same "symptom." Diagnose the lot of them. That is nothing more than brutal, mechanical reductionism, leaching away the individual contextualizations of "relationship trouble," if one can even call it that in such a broad way.

Dove, a bird. *Dove*, Italian: where?

Ambiguity is all over the place, and if I can sniff it in the air, I am still not equipped to decode it. Situational and interactional ambiguity is the worst. It's almost impossible for me to grasp what someone else is thinking or feeling, and I would not be thought empathetic. Here's an illustrative case in point from *The Night Clerk*: To Andrea at a market, Bart says, "I talk too much"—this after giving a very long spiel not in reply to a question from her. "Yes," she agrees, but afterward. She doesn't look at him and say, "Hey, listen—you do talk too much, you know," even though we see that obviously this is what she was thinking. She's being polite and courteous, holding back a sincere response to an irritating moment. He knows he's always thought to be talking too much, and that he's being thought of that way now. This divergence rather nicely expresses the autist's conundrum, trapped outside conviviality by well-meaning others who assume that everybody assumes what they assume; and that holding back a response, out of etiquette, say, could be both good and helpful. And more: could easily be fathomed as good helpfulness. In that kind of case, for the autist there's no reaching out.

For my part, I take meaning to be what is said, not what is not said and "politely" held back. So very much is not said that could be said, after all, and even attending only to someone else's few words is a fraught experience. As my teacher Leslie Fiedler wrote a long time ago, "As if one could ever be understood too easily or too soon!" (1972, 164). Often we see this kind of thing portrayed in a drama when an autist interprets the literal meaning of what someone says rather than hopping eagerly, as all the "normal" characters do, to some "politely" unspoken truth. Usually, this trope is played for light humor, and the autist, typically stationary and without facial expression (because calculating), is taken as a momentary automaton, very funny.

I don't find such portrayals negative, but they are distinctly uninteresting. Not boring, un-interesting. They don't lure me into engagement. When in a comedy I hear (canned) laughter, I recognize and acknowledge the humor trope even if I'm not tickled myself. I am ticklish. Tickled by a great deal, I find myself laughing all the time, often at myself, aloud and in front of somebody else, but I do find it rare to be laughing and have a friend laugh at the same time, in the same way, so that it seems to be one laugh, choreographed.

Perhaps in my withdrawal or my distance, I am drawn in by and become attached to only art. When a performance or a script or a setting or a vision or a pacing or a tonality or a framing device offers art, I become fascinated, maybe even surrender myself to it, and the notion that a portrait of an autistic person conveyed in this way—say, in a movie or a television drama—could possibly offend, disgust, chagrin, or otherwise elicit negative comment from me is unthinkable. I recognize that offense seems sometimes to have been produced for some viewers, because they claim so, and I try without success to understand their rational framework so that I can at least comprehend how, given what they are looking at, they can deem themselves reasonable in complaining. Perhaps it is a general thing that I don't grasp the point of complaining. For my own part, rather than complaining, I work hard to get through situations and moments, so hard that I come not to feel myself working. I think I have learned over the years not to expect too much. And thus not to be as often disappointed at not finding.

Perhaps, even, I get so carried away by what I do find that for me there is *no* not finding.

Maybe I have come to understand Caliban:

Be not afeard; the isle is full of noises,
Sounds and sweet airs, that give delight and hurt not.

Before Neurodiversity

R. BARTON PALMER

The essays in *On the Island* engage with various connections between autism and screen representations of the condition, which has become an increasingly prominent subject of televisual and cinematic fiction during the last two decades, for reasons that require some explanation. In addressing this subject, however, this book first confronts an inconvenient and dismaying, if essential, truth. The morally problematic origins of autism as a diagnosis deployed in the labeling and pathologizing of certain forms of human behavior have been too easily downplayed or, more commonly, ignored in the present cultural moment, dominated by the thankful flourishing of neurodiversity, in which sweetness and light tend to hold sway (Blume 1997, 1998; and especially, Silberman 2015). Only one filmmaker—Costa-Gavras—has explored, in his *Amen* (2000), the horrific way in which modern medicine, in service to the National Socialist German state, identified and then went on to (mis)treat those with the condition.

To be sure, in the spirit of contemporary thinking about autism, the discussions in this book all promote a nonjudgmental neurodiversity, with the contributors focusing on texts that, minimizing discontents, showcase the accomplishments of high-functioning autists and treat what is remarked on as their quirkiness with wit and understanding. High-functioning autism, as the authors demonstrate, constitutes material with an obvious appeal for positive screen representations, which usually reflect the view that, as Barry Prizant puts it, autism is not an illness or pathology, "but a different way of being human" (2015, 4). This issue, as well as others raised by representation of so-called autistic behavior, has been usefully broached in Mark Osteen's multiauthor volume, *Autism and Representation* (2008a). Stuart Murray's contribution to that volume, which anatomizes Hollywood's fascination with autism as a narrative device, should be regarded as a particularly useful prolegomenon to the present volume. The contributors to *On the Island* do not intend their work to be included in, or judged by the criteria deployed in, the field of disability studies, though everything included here roughly follows what has become known as the "social" model in that field. All involved in this current project hope that what the reader finds here is the "sympathetic" approach (including the avoidance of offensive, ableist discourse) to the representation of autism that Osteen, who is one of our contributors, has forcefully promoted.

The reader of this book will notice an unusual feature in what follows: the absence (except in some specific instances that could not be altered for technical reasons appropriate to the context in each case) of any references to Asperger's Syndrome (AS) or to Hans Asperger, after whom it was named. Instead, the term of art used here is Autism Spectrum Disorder, or sometimes simply autism. Autism, or ASD, is conceived by most within the medical field as including AS. The precise relationship between AS and ASD is considered unclear by most in an area where such taxonomic disputes are far from uncommon. In any event, as revealed by recent research into Hans Asperger's connections with the eliminationist policies of Nazi medicine, there is good reason not to continue memorializing in a positive way Asperger's indispensable role in the furthering of research on a condition first identified and named by a Swiss psychiatrist, Eugen Bleuler, in 1911. Any book now addressing autism, however, should acknowledge the dark side of its emergence as a diagnosis, offering a necessary corrective to the otherwise brilliant and quite detailed historical account offered in Steve Silberman's *NeuroTribes* (2015).

Present disciplinary politics aside, discussing autism means engaging with an aspect of psychological-psychiatric thought whose intellectual contours emerged in a quite different and much less tolerant society than our own, if such an understatement might be permitted. The intellectual climate of interwar and wartime Austria in the 1930s and 1940s was profoundly shaped by Social Darwinist theorizing as well as by the increasing prominence of eugenics and the morally problematic practices of reproductive control and population "culling" to which such an evolutionary conception of human perfectibility gave rise. Contemporary controversies about autism as a cultural concept (a subject on which some of the chapters express views) refract something of the collision in early twentieth-century thought between the increasingly prominent practice of eugenics, with its technologizing approaches to human nature, and traditional humanist or religious views of the sanctity of human life.

The purpose of this introductory commentary is to touch on key points in the history of how autism took shape as a pathologizing way of understanding (and evaluating) certain forms of human behavior that at other times had been conceived and treated rather differently. In her recent study of this early history, *Asperger's Children*, Edith Sheffer observes that "the extent to which diagnoses can be shaped by social and political forces" is often underestimated; autism, she suggests, is a signal example of the resulting blindness (16). Yet how to explain, except by reference to such forces, why a diagnosis that developed in response to one particular set of conditions has found such fertile ground in quite different cultural surroundings, with ASD becoming, like Attention Deficit Disorder (ADD), a popular touchstone for describing certain styles of behavior (Sheffer 243)? The Norwegian medical researcher Ketil Slagstad points out that a search of Google Books and the Norwegian National Library reveals "an exponential growth for the terms Asperger's Syndrome and autism through the 1990s and 2000s" (2019, 14). Surely there is something quite remarkable in that fact, and the contributions to this volume, all published for the first time, testify to the remarkable popular resonance of the subject.

Autism is deeply connected with Hans Asperger (1906–1980), the Viennese physician and researcher whose work has often been celebrated as the most significant influence on subsequent inquiries into the nature of autism and the therapies devised for its treatment. That one particular manifestation of the "spectrum" was named in his honor speaks to the importance initially accorded his work by colleagues in the discipline. Asperger rose to prominence not through any advocacy of his own, but through resurrection by an ardent admirer—the British researcher Lorna Wing—in the first years after his death of the substantial work he had done during the war in Austria (then part of Greater Germany). His papers were subsequently edited and translated into English by Uta Frith, a developmental psychologist associated with University College London, who found that they spoke to her own observations and theorizing (Frith 1991; Wing 1981). The amazing growth of interest in, and the exponentially expanding clinical concern with, autism during the 1980s and after can be traced directly to this presentation of his ideas and practice. If a diagnosis can have a father, then in regard to autism, Asperger has no real rivals for the title.

It is certainly the case, as Sheffer observes, that for about thirty years after the war, history was especially kind to him. He passed easily through denazification protocols in occupied Vienna and was able to resurrect his career, rising to prominence once again in Austrian medicine when the country regained its independence in 1955, even though he had been professionally associated with the National Socialist medical establishment. Nazi medicine, in which he was a well-known figure, was universally condemned after the end of the war in Europe in May 1945, with many of the principal physicians involved charged with medical crimes against humanity and put on trial in Nuremberg. When, after his death, Asperger's work on autism became more familiar to the medical world at large, his connections to Nazi *Rassenhygiene* (racial hygiene) were mostly forgotten—the reflex of the general European disposition, after earlier spasms of revenge taking, to forget about the horrors perpetrated by the Third Reich (on this general question, see Proctor 1988). As Sheffer ironically observes, Asperger has been celebrated since the 1980s as a "champion of neurodiversity" who had supposedly opposed from within the darker eliminationist practices of Nazi medicine (15). He developed an image of himself as something of a *résistant*, a pose often adopted after the war by many *fonctionnaires* and professionals in the former enemy homelands or occupied territories.

The truth about Asperger's involvement in what was a multifaceted plan to restore the *Volk* to racial purity and rid society of those deemed "unworthy of life" was something quite different from what he presented to the postwar world as his wartime work with adolescents. Traditional medicine, adopting the ethos of Hippocrates, proclaims that the physician should always act to benefit the patient (the first principle being "do no harm"), and Asperger was such a practitioner, but only to a carefully limited degree. To be sure, he was the widely respected founder, during the interwar period, of the Curative Education Clinic at the University of Vienna. He was solicitous and diligent in the care he provided for those adolescent autists who in his view could be claimed for a normal life. Yet he was also complicit in those involuntary euthanasia (or genocide) programs that became what is arguably the central feature of the Nazi state. His involvement in this deadly business seems not to have been *done against his will*, since he agreed with the goals of racial hygiene, however much he might have found distasteful the practices instituted to achieve them. An examination of the historical record, Hedwig Czech (2018) reports, reveals that Asperger was by no means "a principled opponent of National Socialism" even though he refused Party membership. He did not defend "his patients against Nazi 'euthanasia' and other race hygiene measures" after determining they could not be turned into productive individuals who might fit into society in an acceptable fashion (1). At the same time, he was especially attracted to high-functioning, quirky autists, among whom he would certainly have counted himself (ibid.). Asperger developed a detailed clinical account of what he saw as a morbid form of self-absorption.

When much of Asperger's substantial publications on the subject were translated into English, a fuller picture of his work emerged, resulting in yet another taxonomic innovation, the identification of so-called Asperger's Syndrome, which is at present recognized as one of the conditions contained in the spectrum of autistic disorders (Frith 1991). It is worth noting that Asperger referred to the conditions he found in his patients as autistic psychopathy. This term distinguishes between autism as an orientation beneficial in some sense to those who might benefit from its energies, and autism as a disability. Crucial to Asperger's practice was the difference between those aspects of behavior and personality that, however troublesome, might be altered by forms of treatment, including cognitive therapy, and those others that adversely affected sociability and productive engagement in the world, usually proving to be incurable. In general, Asperger was not optimistic that psychiatric or other therapies could in most cases do more than ameliorate symptoms whose cause, he thought, was likely genetic.

In committing himself to the service of *Volksgesundheit* (public health), Asperger followed in the path of many of his Austrian and German colleagues in pediatric medicine. Like them, he promoted "first-rate care for children who might be redeemed for the Reich and excision for those they believed to be irredeemable" (Sheffer 17; also see Lifton 1986). Excision meant euthanasia, and the research of Sheffer and others establishes beyond any doubt that Asperger participated in the child euthanasia programs (the T-4 program, Aktion T-4, directed from number 4 Tiergartenstrasse in Berlin).

Himself a sufferer from the condition whose manifestations he took such pain to describe (some of his research writings are frankly autobiographical), the accomplished doctor, one of whose eccentricities was always to refer to himself in the third person, stands as an example of how autism need not stand in the way of considerable professional success (on Asperger's autism, see Lyons and Fitzgerald 2007). With the advocacy of both Wing and Frith, Asperger's writings became the center of ongoing debate, in both the discipline and the wider culture, about the key concepts for autism studies of the "normal" and "individual difference" or, put another way, the relationship between the individual and the group, with a notably valorized personal quality for Asperger being sociability.

This approach is quite consonant with the needs-based analysis of human development promoted by Karen Horney, which was at this same time achieving preeminence in psychiatric thought in the United States (Horney 1950). In other words, Asperger's framing of the issue of "normality" had a wide resonance, since it was arguably at the center of the revisionism that characterized the work of the neo-Freudians, who dominated psychiatric theory and practice in the postwar era, especially in the United States.

A book on, say, the representation of infantile paralysis in the cinema would need to confront a terrible illness, but not the darkest of moral issues. A book on autism is another matter entirely, requiring confrontation with ideas and practices that are beyond disturbing. The last stop of this increasingly barbarous journey is, of course, the final solution, whose goal was a "racially pure" and "healthy" *Volk*, unhampered by the continuing presence of those needing costly long-term care and who were therefore unable to contribute to the collective good. Among this group would be many of the more seriously autistic, whose excision from the body politic seemed to Nazi doctors like Asperger not only a moral necessity but also a political imperative. As Czech reports, Asperger used "lectures and publications to signal his fundamental accordance with the Nazi state's programs concerning race hygiene and public health" (31). Distressingly for proponents of neurodiversity today, his complicity was shared by a great number of other doctors practicing under National Socialism, most of whom, like Asperger, escaped any reckoning after the war. (For a useful overview of National Socialist medicine, see Lifton 1986.)

The "fashion" for autism (what else to call it?) must have something to do, Sheffer suggests, with the perdurable nature of the modern condition, with its dread of alienation and "anxieties about integration into a perfectionist and fast-changing world," qualities that the globalizing present shares with then-rapidly Nazifying Greater Germany (246). In the Third Reich, integration meant merging individuality into the collectivist spirit of the people that one lived with and for. Thus, an individual failure to be properly sociable and function well with others could appear as nothing other than an illness, as a psychopathy that, like all disabling mental conditions, put the sufferer beyond the social pale. It was as such a psychopathy that these behaviors appeared to Asperger in the course of his work with troubled children (Asperger [1944] 1991).

In postindustrial consumerist society, the same self-centered disposition might well seem a developmental problem—with the neutral term "syndrome" marshaled to describe this reluctance to "fit in" at a time when social normality has come to designate the desire for connection in an increasingly atomized lonely crowd. In her meetings with Asperger, Wing suggested "syndrome," which he may have liked, but in any case did not dispute. Today, supporters of neurodiversity would contest the use of the terms "disorder" and "disability" to describe what might be thought in many cases as a rather benign form of social or psychological diversity, something less than the largely tragic "endogenous constitutional damages" that Asperger believed were at its root (quoted in Czech 28). It is noteworthy that Asperger, when promoting his work in the postwar era, did not insist on his earlier view, first published in 1944, that autism was a pathology, a designation of harmful deviance that suited National Socialist understandings. As Sheffer shrewdly observes, when "Asperger's work went mainstream, it was cleansed of its historical context" (2018, 241). And yet he never distanced himself very far from the "genetic determinism typical of Nazi race hygiene" (Czech 28).

In the closing decades of the twentieth century, the development of a greater knowledge about autism was celebrated as a major accomplishment of medical science. That this discovery resulted ultimately from research and practice conducted under the Third Reich was considered irrelevant, if this history was known at all to many. Memory had faded of the Nuremberg trials, which had resulted in a thoroughgoing condemnation of Nazi medical science and practice; twenty of the twenty-three accused doctors and administrators were found guilty, and several executed, including the head of this department of the Nazi state, Karl Brandt, who maintained to the end that he had done nothing wrong. The principal charge against Brandt was that he had conceived and managed the numerous domestic euthanasia programs, which had begun before the outbreak of hostilities, and in which Asperger, along with many other physicians, was complicit. These practices were thought so heinous that they were designated "crimes against humanity," a new category of criminality that was made prosecutable by the occupying powers even though these crimes had been committed—legally—against citizens of the Reich (Schmidt 2007). In the early 1950s, however, most of the doctors serving long sentences were released, in resigned acknowledgment that any doctor practicing during the Third Reich found it difficult to refuse participation in practices that were manifestly immoral, but illegal only from an extra-national point of view.

A more important truth is at stake, however. The conceptualization of autism by Asperger as a condition to be differentiated from childhood schizophrenia had much to do with Nazi theories of the supposedly genetically superior Aryan *Volk* and the culture they had created. The autistic were thought by Asperger and others to be suffering from an absence of *Gemut*, a hard-to-define spiritual quality best understood perhaps as the disposition to be sociable, that is, to subordinate oneself cheerfully to the needs of the collective. As a psychopathic diagnosis, autism provided a set of criteria by which this disposition could be identified and judged.

Rehearsing this history raises what are undoubtedly the most distressing aspects of twentieth-century experience. To some degree, these are reflected in what we might call the disciplinary politics of the understanding of Autism Spectrum Disorder produced by the dehistoricizing efforts of the medical establishment to accommodate it. Psychotherapy's indispensable reference tool, the *Diagnostic and Statistical Manual of Mental Disorders* (*DSM*, first published in 1952), reflects in its various iterations, each larger than its predecessor, a seemingly ever-expanding repertoire of treatable mental conditions that continuing human experience (and more cynically, the increasing profitability of psychiatric practice) reveals. What is therein listed as a treatable disorder, of course, is subject to cultural politics, of which a useful example is homosexuality, listed as a disorder beginning in 1952, but then removed in 1974 after years of often-bitter dispute. Autism was first listed in *DSM-3* (1980) and has been included in subsequent editions.

Diseases or disorders might have "natural" histories (but perhaps not always—consider the cases of demonic possession or "cast spells"). The point is that they have cultural histories as well—as, indeed, does "nature"—and that these sometimes point us toward insistently problematic issues. In this case, autism as an identified condition raises two linked questions. What is "normal" in the always surprising repertoire of human behavior? And, more difficult, what should be done about supposed deviations from the normal, especially if these are seen as in some sense a threat to some identified collective good of the social body? Does everyone "need" to be sociable and submit to social norms?

This question was forcefully raised in America during the 1950s when autism was first coming to prominence on the national scene, even as the notion that behavioral norms were too restrictive was also very much in the air. Consider, for example, the widely influential writings of the psychologist Robert M. Lindner. Even if in his earlier and more famous work, *Rebel Without a Cause: The Story of a Criminal Psychopath* (1944), he had promoted the notion that criminality (a legal term, not a psychological one) resulted in part from an inability to do for others, Lindner was among those who called for what has since been termed neural and behavioral diversity. He answered with an emphatic no the question about sociability posed in the title of his book *Must You Conform?* (1956). Lindner exemplifies the rejection of conformism (and the pathologizing or stigmatizing of difference) that, beginning with the work of Harvey Blume and others, has in regard to autism developed into exhortations for patient toleration and understanding, as well as, in terms of political action, the autism rights movement (Blume 1997, 1998).

As far as autism is concerned, a further issue arises, one that figures centrally in a number of chapters. What is the role of treatment, if any, for those who display a neurodiversity that, on the scale of seriousness, seems little more than an essentially harmless manifestation of human variety, recognized as a fact (perhaps welcome) of our collective experience and not as a disorder that damages individuals or society itself? Consider the following formulation of the issues involved from Barry Prizant, one of the most prominent advocates for the neurodiversity movement: "The behavior of people with autism isn't random, deviant, or bizarre, as many professionals have called it for decades. . . . Autism isn't an illness. It's a different way of being human. Children with autism aren't sick; they are progressing through developmental stages as we all do. To help them, we don't need to change them or fix them. We need to work to understand them, and then change what *we* do" (2015, 4). The films and TV series discussed in this volume, especially those produced in the last two decades, engage in a variety of ways with this rejection of the pathologizing approach to autism first advocated by Hans Asperger.

As an anti-pathologizing approach to autism, neurodiversity interestingly shares much with the humanist-oriented psychiatry, the neo-Freudianism that dominated the American psychiatric scene in the 1950s and 1960s. These practitioners and thinkers were, to be sure, strong advocates for collective psychic health, but *contra* Asperger, they also stood for a vibrant individualism that offered "freedom" to mankind from religious or political regimes that would deny the Enlightenment promotion of inherent, unalienable, *individual* rights. Consider the work of perhaps the most influential of American neo-Freudians, the Frankfurt school émigré Erich Fromm, who promoted the view that National Socialism led to a denial of essential human liberty (in *Escape from Freedom* [1941]), even as he argued for political and psychological humanism (*Man for Himself* [1976]), with an emphasis on the "orientation of character." He was also an advocate for collective wellness in *The Sane Society* (1955), which offers an analysis of the hyperindividualism produced by postindustrial capitalism. To be sure, the turning inward identified by Fromm could manifest itself as a morbid self-absorption that begged for a collective restructuring. Importantly, his view was that this trend was *not* a psychopathy, but rather a deviation from the sociability that made for a more productive society and happier individuals.

What is complex about Asperger's legacy is the hardly uncontradictory resonance of his work with the neo-Freudian project, and its twin humanist goals of individual and collective mental health. Asperger was undoubtedly a Darwinist discoverer (and taxonomist) of a form of human behavior that had previously gone unnamed. He is to be credited with formulating the origins of the discourse that has been adopted by all those who discuss what we now understand as autism, including the contributors to and editors of this volume. He valorized an exclusively collectivist approach to human nature, with certain exceptions (legitimated by his own sense of himself) that should be made for those savants whose extraordinary talents marked them out as socially useful.

Writing in 1944, Asperger provided a definition of autism that, as Sheffer observes, became the basis of the description in the *DSM*, whose influence on the identification and treatment of mental deviations can hardly be exaggerated. The crucial element is that "the fundamental disorder of autistic individuals is the limitation of their social relationships" (quoted in Sheffer 15). This definition is of course incredibly question begging. What exactly is "limitation," a much-vexed term, redolent of ableist discourse, that is extensively discussed in disability studies? And exactly what interpersonal connections qualify as "social relationships"? Most crucially, how are these to be constituted so that they permit the individuality necessary to human happiness? By its very nature, autism as a purported defect has everything to do with the tension between individual behavior and group norms, which is foundational for all societies.

The Films and Television Series: Images and Stories

As my coeditor has shown in the commentary that precedes this one, very often the autistic personality seeks to arrange the world in ways that can seem arbitrary or mysterious to those who are not autists. Part of our intent in this book is to step outside the conventional (non-autistic) wisdom of lining up chapters either by coherent, repetitive "themes" or in some way that divides the book's overall subject into "parts." We have made a book that, aside from this preface, is really not divided. Or: a book that is divided in a way that conventional (rational, neurotypical) wisdom would not discern.

Can an android character, Lieutenant Commander Data (Brent Spiner), in a science fiction–fantasy narrative, *Star Trek: The Next Generation* (TV, 1987–1994), provide an interesting analogue for an autist, shedding light not only on human diversity but also on the "nature" of robots? In her multifaceted analysis "Autistic Android? The Curious Instance of *Star Trek*'s Data," Ina Rae Hark argues, "Data's uniqueness among artificial intelligences in the *Star Trek* universe provides a better metaphor of autism than does his contrast with humans. With them, he buys into ableist discourses, insisting on his lack of emotions as a defect and wishing only to be human." For Hark, the series's play with the intersection between human and android qualities speaks to "real-life autists who see themselves reflected in Data," especially in his discovery that "he can't read his own feelings as feelings but that doesn't mean the feelings are inauthentic."

Rebecca Bell-Metereau draws a similar conclusion in her analysis of the Disney documentary *Life, Animated* (2016), which focuses on the experiences of Owen Suskind, who develops autism. It is through animated films that Owen finds the means to express love, loss, kinship, and brotherhood. As Bell-Metereau concludes in "*Life, Animated*: Adapting a Book about a Hero with Autism," Owen's "courageous perspective invites all viewers to find our place on the spectrum, to locate what we have in common with each other, regardless of our abilities or language skills."

The breaking down of the supposed barriers between autism, on the one hand, and "normal" social and emotional life on the other is a perhaps unexpected main focus, as Dan Sacco argues, in Barry Levinson's *Rain Man* (1998), famed for its sympathetic presentation of the "disorder." *Rain Man* enjoys a reputation that, as Sacco reveals in "Where Is the Autism in *Rain Man?*," is problematic because of the film's medical inaccuracy. More interesting, he suggests, is the relationship between the autistic Raymond and his brother, Charlie, a young man with great difficulty expressing and controlling his emotions. It is this contrast between the "disordered" and the "normal" that *Rain Man* relentlessly deconstructs. In the end, as Sacco suggests, "the film is a thoughtful exploration of communication and emotion, of barriers and entryways for meaningful and wholehearted interpersonal exchange."

In *Rain Man*, the autist savant's mathematical abilities (turned to a profit at Las Vegas gaming tables) are enthusiastically displayed, and *The Good Doctor* (TV, 2017–) offers a medical version of the same gifted sprezzatura in its unusual depictions of the mental world of Dr. Shaun Murphy. The series, as Burke Hilsabeck discusses in "*The Good Doctor*: Images of Autism and Augmented Intelligence," tells us that Shaun possesses "a powerful and highly visual cognitive process that allows him to think in unusual ways, and he uses this ability to locate inspired and novel treatments for his patients." The series, in Hilsabeck's reading of the character and his extraordinary nature, and the production's high-tech mode of illustrating his interior, allows for a view of the mental diversity of the exceptional physician, aided in his profession by the autism that for him is both a blessing and an inconvenience since it affects his personal relationships.

In the depiction of the autist in *The Good Doctor*, neurodiversity is "good" in the sense that it "augments" intelligence. *The Big Short* (2015, Adam McKay) is yet another triumphal story, actually a biopic, about a high-functioning autist, a hedge fund manager who was able to see the fatal flaws in the global finance system before the Great Recession in 2008. But as Jason Jacobs demonstrates in his study of the film's focus on the connection between "oddity" and "catastrophe," the release cut deletes scenes that suggest the downside of autism when the heroic hedge manager, Michael (Christian Bale), if one pursuing self-interest can be "heroic," learns that his son also suffers from the personality qualities associated with autism, which for the young man hardly seem an advantage.

As Jacobs suggests in a passage worth quoting at length, "The rise of the

'medicalized self' over the past few decades, and the adoption and elasticization of fluid notions of mental conditions (viz. 'spectrum creep'), raise
troubling questions about normality and the distinction (call it the aristocracy) of illness and victimhood. . . . Morally, it seems to me to be troubling
to pose 'illness' or 'affliction' as a kind of magical gift that allows superpowered perception or moral insight." Jacobs identifies an important question to be asked of the ultrapositive promotion of autism as a "quality" and
not a "disability," recalling the two poles of Asperger's foundational research, with its championing of the savant and its acquiescence in the excision of the chronically disordered.

Unsurprisingly, as Christina Wilkins argues in "Diagnosing the Detective: Sherlock Holmes and Autism in Contemporary Television," representations of autism reflect genre conventions and rhetorical choices. Sherlock
Holmes has long been understood as a savant whose unconventional affect
and behavior were highlighted by the "normal" manner and mien of his
companion, Dr. Watson. Wilkins analyzes how this balancing act, essential to the effect of the original stories, is reconfigured in the CBS television
series *Elementary* (2012–2019). As she argues, "*Elementary* softens elements
drawn from recent Sherlock characterizations that are seen by audiences as
'Aspergian,' in order to help mold the show for the police procedural genre,
within which it clearly fits. This is helped by the presentation of supporting
characters who make the figure of Sherlock here empathetic, and the introduction of an explicitly and definitively ASC [Autism Spectrum Condition]
character, Fiona Helbron."

Given the tendency of media productions to be characterized by stock
characters and generic patterns, it is hardly surprising that, as Brenda
Austin-Smith observes, most movie autists are young men with intellectual
talents. The TV series *Stranger Things* (2016–), however, features a continuing character who, though not explicitly identified as autistic, is "the mysterious Eleven (Millie Bobby Brown), a young girl who speaks in monosyllables, and has telekinetic and biokinetic powers." In fact, she probably counts
as "the first female autistic superhero of the small screen," an explanation
for specialness more intriguing perhaps than being born on a distant, dying planet.

If, as Elliott Logan observes, the "mindedness" of many screen autists
simply escapes us, then a certain challenge is presented to viewers by the recent trend of films offering portraits of those in whom "autism is less profound, who sit nearer to the high-functioning end of the autism spectrum."
One answer, as he writes in "Autism, Performance, and Sociality: Isolated
Attention in *The Social Network*," is that such films engage with issues im-

plied in the term "sociality." In that regard, what better cultural phenomenon to examine than the invention and flourishing of social media, and the representation of that fundamental change in David Fincher's 2010 film, which, in its characterization of Mark Zuckerberg, centers on the desires, energies, and vision of a high-functioning autist?

Film, as Daniel Varndell reminds us, is fundamentally a performance art, meaning that the representation of autism onscreen depends on actorly techniques. Building such a performance has conventionally meant resorting to "the mimicry of stereotypical behavioral gestures and movements— casual stimming (self-stimulating repetitive movements, verbal tics, repeated phrases and gestures), avoidance of eye contact," and so forth. But since autism in women manifests itself differently, particularly through a "camouflaging" of the condition, how is an actor to create a female autist and convey the "hidden grace" that is the inner experience of this condition for many? In "Hidden Worlds of Female Autism," Varndell offers a carefully detailed analysis of Sally Hawkins's performance in *The Shape of Water* (2017) and Sofia Helin's performance as Saga Norén in the Nordic noir crime series *Broen* (Danish), or *Bron* (Swedish) (TV, 2011–2018), in order "to explore how camouflaging in the series is dominated by the exigencies and limitations of narrative cohesion."

Varndell's analysis of those performances is provided with further context by a close reading of the American version of the series, *The Bridge* (2013–2014), in Douglas McFarland's chapter "Eye Contact in Juárez: Borderline Empathy and the Autistic Detective," in which he argues that "autism is used to bring into sharp focus the challenges that we all face in both large and small ways." Especially noteworthy are the literary parallels that McFarland adduces, including Shakespeare's comedies and Umberto Eco's *The Name of the Rose*, works in which the mysteries of identity are probed. The presentation in the series of the liminality of autism, its bordering position relative to both normality and pathology, is reflected in its casting, acting style, and even its setting in the border town of Juárez, Mexico.

For Christine Becker, the Netflix production *Atypical* (2017–2021), because it "untypically" features an autistic character as the protagonist, foregrounds a question that is broached in one way or another by all the chapters in this book: What are the "forms" of autism to be presented by characters designated as suffering from this condition? An issue of authenticity arises. Because autism exists in "readily apparent heterogeneity in the manifestations and personalities of those identified by it, autism in film and television fiction has consistently been represented by a mere handful of key signifiers." If films treating autism aspire to be considered realistic representations, then such stereotypical features of performance should be avoided or nuanced. Becker's "The Creative Evolution and Reception of Netflix's *Atypical*" explores this issue in considerable depth. Her assessment is that the show is disappointing because of the limited involvement in its production of those with disabilities or those with detailed knowledge of them: "Without having people with autism in the writers' room, portraying autistic characters, standing behind the camera, and making decisions from the executive suite, autistic voices still will be marginalized and their representations limited."

The sitcom *Community* (2009–2015), as Joshua Schulze points out, has a gallery of diverse, kooky characters but features one, Abed, who, as a neurodiverse pop-culture obsessive, is an autist—or so it is strongly hinted. If, for Schulze, the series aims to present itself as the kind of good televisual object that offers representations of cozy fellowship, it does so largely through its foregrounding of Abed's metafictional consciousness, his consciousness of "living in a sitcom" that figures as a kind of mise en abyme for the experience of the viewers at home. Schulze provides a compelling analysis of Abed's specialness as his presence in the world of the story becomes a key element in the viewer's experience of his sociability, even if he is only one character in an ensemble dramatization.

Since its televisual debut in 2007 and its continuing presence worldwide through syndication, *The Big Bang Theory* has featured the best known "aspie" in popular culture, Dr. Sheldon Cooper, the unofficial leader of a gang of highly educated science nerds. Sheldon is, as Fincina Hopgood describes, a living, breathing repository of stereotypical aspie qualities, especially "his strict adherence to routine and his distress when his routine is disrupted; his difficulty relating to other people and understanding their emotions; his physical clumsiness and social awkwardness; his lack of affect in vocal and facial expressions; and his obsessive interests in science and 'geek' popular culture." Hopgood's "Portrait of the Autist as a Young Man" provides a fascinating glimpse into the understanding of ASD within the culture at large, as Sheldon, not furnished with an official diagnosis of his specialness by the show's writers, becomes the object of taxonomic debate. The issue of "normality" is usually at stake, but the positivity of the show's portrayal of neural diversity also very much comes into play. As Hopgood observes, "For preteen and adolescent viewers on the spectrum, such as my son, Sheldon Cooper offers a rare point of identification and aspiration in popular culture: a heroic protagonist whose superpower is his brain."

In his discussion of autism in two fairly recent feature films, *Nightcrawler* (2014) and *The Accountant* (2016), Dominic Lennard likewise argues that narratives focusing on high-functioning autists like Sheldon Cooper provide interesting insights on issues and difficulties that everyone faces in negotiating social connections. As he suggests, it is "unsurprising then that the appearance of high-functioning autistic characters in fiction might have a strong 'exploratory' focus, evoking uncertainties in our strategies of social interaction, especially our ability to read and predict the moods, thoughts, and intentions of others." If Hollywood films are traditionally narrative driven, with characters that are functional rather than interesting in their own right, those that focus on high-functioning autists usually rely on the "characterological ambiguity" of dangerous males. The two films discussed here in detail, Lennard suggests, "invite us to exercise a kind of due diligence around highly capable neurodivergent protagonists, ultimately arriving at different perspectives on the relationship between neurological difference and social belonging."

Alex Clayton reminds us that "the need to imagine how the world manifests 'through' autism is pressing for those of us with friends and relatives on the spectrum, where conversation may not yield the vividness of insight we crave into the condition as lived." In other words, the representation of the experience of autism is an important social function that the cinema is best equipped to provide. In "Mind the Gap: Autistic Viewpoint in Film," Clayton explores several related issues of neural atypicality in order to provide a grid for reading the realization of autism as a mode of perception and understanding, especially in *Stand Clear of the Closing Doors* (2013), a film in which, Clayton argues, the sensitivity of the filmmakers to providing the "manifestation of the world through autism" is effected.

Being There (1979) and *Phantom Thread* (2017) can both be regarded as films responding to the need, identified by Clayton, for autism to be represented so that it can be understood by those outside its ambit. In his engagement with these two films, Matthew Cipa focuses on the need for actors to subtract from their presence, to exercise a "performative restraint" in realizing the "externalization" of the minds of the autistic characters. As Cipa demonstrates, mise-en-scène must, in each case, make up for the gap in character depth, enabling an empathetic response from spectators for such a protagonist "in his habits of life, the structure and design of his local environment, and the objects and people in the surround."

Living with an autistic child, Mark Osteen suggests in "'A Spoonful of Sugar': Watching Movies Autistically," has given him insight into the condition and, appropriately for a film critic, provided an understanding of what kind of movie appeals to an autist—and why. As he writes, "A truly autistic movie, then, would appeal to a neurodivergent mind on its own terms by using repetition and musical structures." Osteen discovered this because his son Cam developed an especial attachment to Disney's *Mary Poppins* (1964). And this was "because it is organized around musical structures—emotional crescendos and diminuendos, repeated melodic motifs that offer sameness with variation—and because, as I discovered when I viewed the movie one more time, it celebrates neurodivergent ways of thinking, feeling, and communicating."

Frank Perry's *David and Lisa* (1962) imagines a residential treatment center that can accommodate the needs of a high-functioning autist with exceptional intelligence who is troubled by compulsive behavior and a refrigerator mother who squashes his independence, and those of an adolescent girl suffering from schizophrenic paranoia and trapped by a need for repetition. The treatment center, set up as an alternative family home, provides therapeutic relief for both. As I point out in "*David and Lisa*: The Healing Power of the Group," "The developing, unplanned connection between David and Lisa also emphasizes the healing energies of residence-centered group therapy, in which the authoritative, professional voice plays a smaller role than it does in traditional psychotherapy (and in screen versions of traditional psychotherapeutic practice)."

Like a number of the chapters, Murray Pomerance's "Jesse: Torture That Autist" concerns itself with the question of how autism is performed onscreen. His intention is "to point out some interesting features of a visual narrative in which a collaboration was made to give a portrait of a central autistic character over and above the already exciting plot. The plot is a conventional type, but the autist is not; the point of the program material I analyze is, bluntly, that the distinctive qualities of the autist are at least as important to consider, if not more so, than the overall story—that this person comes first." His analysis offers a detailed engagement with the performance in particular, and presentation in general, of autism in the six opening scenes of Shelley Birse's Australian police thriller *The Code* (2014–2016). So authentic is the film's portrayal of the atypicality of the character named Jesse that he never becomes merely a "story-relevant" character, reflecting, even on the level of story, his divergence from the normal as it can be measured by storytelling conventions.

If, as the contributions to this volume make clear, the high-functioning autist has proved irresistible to screenwriters as a model for characters with unusual abilities and intriguing forms of quirkiness, what Pomerance reminds us is that these representations, even when purportedly antijudgmental, engage complexly with the issue most insistently raised by autism: difference.

CHAPTER I

Autistic Android?
The Curious Instance of *Star Trek*'s Data

INA RAE HARK

Christopher Boone, the autistic-savant narrator and protagonist of Mark Haddon's *The Curious Incident of the Dog in the Night-Time* (2003), muses that most people misunderstand the nature of consciousness. They view it as if it were some sort of "homunculus" dwelling in the human head, looking out on the world "like Captain Jean-Luc Picard in *Star Trek: The Next Generation* sitting in his captain's seat looking at a big screen" (117–118). But, he explains, this metaphor masks the fact that the human brain operates according to electrical impulses the way a computer does. Humans are in denial about this equivalence and "think they're not computers" (118).

Although Christopher does not articulate the connection, this discussion invokes the character of Lieutenant Commander Data (Brent Spiner), the android second officer and science officer of the *Enterprise*, who sits on the bridge with Picard (Patrick Stewart) in *Star Trek: The Next Generation* (*TNG*, 1987–1994). Christopher resembles Data in several ways. He is a mathematical prodigy planning to become a scientist, and Data, in an alternate future glimpsed in "All Good Things," the *TNG* finale, holds the Lucasian Chair of Mathematics at Cambridge. The two have treasured pets, difficulties in reading the emotions of others, and a tendency toward undiplomatic frankness. Both are fans of Sherlock Holmes. Data designs a Doyle-inspired holodeck program where he plays Holmes to Geordi LaForge's (LeVar Burton) Watson ("Elementary, Dear Data," 2:3). Christopher names *The Hound of the Baskervilles* his favorite novel and concludes: "I like Sherlock Holmes and I think that if I were a proper detective, he is the kind of detective I would be" (Haddon 2003, 72). He sets out to solve the murder of a neighbor's dog in a novel that refers to another of Holmes's canine adventures, "The Adventure of Silver Blaze," in which Holmes points Inspector Gregory of Scotland Yard to "the curious incident of the dog in the night-time." Holmes has often been diagnosed or performed as an autist. (See the chapter by Christina Wilkins in this volume.)

To be sure, Data's resemblance to two other fictional characters that are confirmed or suspected to be autistic is hardly sufficient to analyze him as an analogue to someone with Autism Spectrum Disorder. But a real-life autist, the livestock management expert Temple Grandin, has affirmed her personal identification with the *TNG* android: "I am like Data, the android man, on 'Star Trek, the Next Generation.' As he accumulates more information, he has a greater understanding of social relationships" (1995b, 147). To see Data's interactions with humans as an analogue for the interrelationships between autistic people and the neurotypical world therefore makes sense. The analogy is far from perfect, however, and Data sometimes allies himself with humans whose traits must combine with his in order to give a fuller picture of those with ASD. Indeed, I argue, Data's uniqueness among artificial intelligences in the *Star Trek* universe provides a better metaphor of autism than does his contrast with humans. With them, he buys into ableist discourses, insisting on his lack of emotions as a defect and wishing only to be human. Seen as the traits of a particular and unique android, Data's differences from other cybernetic beings receive far more affirmation.

Star Trek androids who gain the equivalent of human emotions frequently suffer terrible consequences, so his pure roboticism proves a saving grace.

Autists and Robots

Science has launched a number of studies about the effectiveness of using robots in therapies for children with autism. The robot interfaces have anthropomorphic designs and cute names such as Kaspar, Milo, Nao, or Probo. Nicole Kobie (2018) in *Wired* reports on the European Union–funded DREAM (Development of Robot-Enhanced Therapy for Children with Autism Spectrum Disorders) initiative, wherein a consortium of universities evaluated robots' success in teaching autistic children the skills of joint attention, imitation, and turn taking. Obvious advantages include relieving therapists of repetitive, time-consuming feedback, providing a tool for children who cannot frequently meet with a therapist face-to-face, and sparing the child the need to "read" another human's expressions and emotions.

But a number of researchers Kobie interviewed warned that the assumptions behind using robots to teach autists may derive from the view that people on the spectrum are *like* robots. Kathleen Richardson of De Montfort University, in Leicester, England, said, "I think this idea that children with autism are mechanical, they prefer systems, and they lack empathy is what really provided the basis for the thinking about autism and robots." Damian Milton of the University of Kent added: "The idea that it's like a computer brain is dehumanizing. Due to popular understanding—or misunderstanding—of what constitutes autism, it's often incorrectly seen in such terms that autistic people are somehow less than human, animalistic or machine like, only capable of compiling and broadcasting strings of information." By contrast, Richardson asserted, "The reality is some people with autism can't speak, are withdrawn and beset by anxiety and obsessive compulsive issues."

As an android, Data by definition displays only the robotic characteristics of ASD, not the overwhelming emotional overloads that can lead to meltdowns. The closest analogy to a meltdown would be his vulnerability to being hacked, but that experience comes from malign outside actors, not an intrinsic flaw in his brain's wiring. He does not depend on repetitive rituals, avoid eye contact, or have sensitivities to stimuli like bright lights or loud noises. He does misread social cues, speak with undiplomatic candor, have an odd affect, and speak in a stilted manner, the last due to a ludicrous glitch of his programming that does not permit him to use contractions. Like many autists, Data has consuming specialized interests whose minutiae he articulates in numbing and overwhelming detail. (These do not tend toward the scientific and technical, as might be expected, but rather to classical arts and letters: his expertise regarding the Holmes stories, his painting, his violin playing, and his performances of Shakespeare plays. These preferences reflect on his desire to better understand and emulate humans rather than to achieve any self-actualization inherent to a cybernetic life-form.)

Data's portrayal equates the distress his differences from organic beings cause him with how his behavioral tics annoy his crewmates. This depiction parallels those in other media texts that treat autistic humans as a source of humor and frustration among neurotypicals, even those who have sincere affection for them. But *TNG* invokes such emotional distress in humanoids who think synthetic beings are comforting companions who minimize their mental turmoil. For these individuals, artificial intelligences are soothing complements rather than objects of identification. One of them is the Betazoid negotiator Tam Elbrun (Harry Groener) in "Tin Man" (3:20). Prodigiously empathetic even in a race of empaths, Tam regularly employs brutal honesty and defies social niceties, not because he doesn't understand emotions but because the cacophony of thoughts that assault him constantly leaves him in a state of perpetual meltdown, often leading to psychological collapse. Data's positronic neural net emits no such emotional clamor. To Tam he is a blank, almost as if he "weren't there." Data's company is "restful," Tam tells his friend, Counselor Deanna Troi (Marina Sirtis), who smiles at the idea of her android colleague, with his stream of verbalized technical factoids, relaxing anyone. When Data confides in Tam about his sense of inadequacy over his lack of human emotions, his fears that he has only mechanisms and algorithms inside his brain, Tam assures him that all forms of consciousness are valuable.

Lieutenant Reg Barclay (Dwight Schultz) is that rare Starfleet human who suffers from crippling insecurity; eyes often downcast, inarticulate, unable to assert his conclusions, Barclay seems to have some sort of anxiety disorder. Other crew members, including La Forge, Will Riker (Jonathan Frakes), and teenage Wesley Crusher (Wil Wheaton), admit that he makes them nervous and anxious to leave his company. Wesley coins the cruel nickname "Broccoli," which spreads throughout the ship. Although Data questions the use of this epithet and defends the soundness of Barclay's scientific theories, the two don't interact one-on-one. Barclay instead finds his confidence in the company of another sort of AI: the versions of his fellow crew members that he has programmed for a holodeck simulation. His first appearance, in "Hollow Pursuits" (3:21), immediately followed "Tin Man" in the original broadcast of the series. Coping strategies for the non-neurotypical were clearly on the minds of the writers at this time. Were they reading the results of the experiments with robot-autist therapies, they would clearly interpret them as demonstrations of the value of such interactions, because AIs have a calming effect on ASD individuals, but not because ASD individuals are themselves robotic (Kobie 2018).

For many autists, *Star Trek* in all its manifestations serves as one of those nerdy obsessions they can immerse themselves in. When the autism activist Meg Evans decided to solicit for her website stories about their lives from those on the spectrum, *Star Trek* fan fiction was a logical choice:

> Inspired by Aspergia's use of fiction as a catalyst for discussion of autism in the context of disability rights—a concept that was becoming more commonly known as neurodiversity—I decided to create a page on Ventura33 for that purpose. I put out a call for stories featuring autistic characters and others with neurological differences in the Star Trek universe. . . . I had in mind that the stories would promote reflection and constructive dialogue as a counterweight—if only a small one—to society's unthinking repetition of autism myths. (2020, 127)

The many outsider characters that populate the *Star Trek* franchise, serving to view humans from another perspective, provide a point of identification for people with autism. For example, Jeri Ryan commented upon the appeal of her cyborg character Seven of Nine, in *Star Trek: Voyager* (1995–2001), to fans with ASD:

> Personally, with Seven of Nine, I've heard from so many people who are on the autism spectrum, that they appreciate seeing a character who has the same struggles that they did. Because she didn't have social skills. She didn't know personal space boundaries. She didn't understand social norms. So she had to learn all of that. And that's very much the same kind of experience that a lot of those people have. And I know this because my son is on the spectrum. (quoted in Yehl and Collura 2019)

The outsider in the *Star Trek* universe who has become a particular locus for autists' fascination is Mr. Spock (Leonard Nimoy), the half-human, half-Vulcan first officer of the original series's *Enterprise*. Many assume that the factors that lead to such identifications are similar to the ones that compel attachment to Data. In his book *An Anthropologist on Mars*, the neurologist Oliver Sacks, a *Star Trek* fan, points out that "a surprising number of people with autism identify with Data, or with his predecessor, Mr. Spock" (1995, 275). Yet as is the case with Tam Elbrun or Reg Barclay, their departures from neurotypicality are of complementary types. *TNG* makes this clear in a dialogue exchange between the two in "Unification, Part 2" (5:8), which features a guest appearance by Nimoy as Spock. He is amazed at Data's desire to become more human: "You have an efficient intellect, superior physical skills, no emotional impediments. There are Vulcans who aspire all their lives to achieve what you've been given by design." Data replies: "You are half-human . . . but you have chosen to follow the Vulcan way of life? In effect you have abandoned what I have sought all my life." Given that *TNG* privileges humanity and humanistic ideology, it is hard not to read Data's disregard for his inherent strengths while pursuing the impossible goal of becoming what he is not as the autist hating his own way of being while worshipping the neurotypical.

Like Spock, most of the other outsider characters—Odo (René Auberjonois) on *Star Trek: Deep Space Nine* (1993–1999), the Doctor (Robert Picardo) and Seven of Nine on *Voyager*, T'Pol (Jolene Blalock) on *Star Trek: Enterprise* (2001–2005)—regularly critique human failings and hypocrisy. Data does at times express curiosity about why a given human behaves in ways inconsistent with human ideals, but his insistence that humans at their best are the best life-forms in the galaxy renders him the only sycophant among these beings who otherwise cast a skeptical eye on the species. (See Rashkin [2011] for an analysis of Data's pursuit of being human in psychoanalytic terms.)

Data versus Lore

Data's atypical status within the *Star Trek* universe becomes more complex when one views him in the context of other androids rather than that of humanoids. In *Star Trek: The Original Series* (*TOS*, 1966–1969), distrust of all artificial intelligence is the norm. Androids look far more human than Data but lack his sentience. Capable of some independent thought, they cannot deal with situations that set up logical conundrums within their programming, as in "I, Mudd" (2:8). The episode "What Are Little Girls Made Of?" (1:7) depicts androids' inevitable inferiority to biological life forms but also their danger to those life forms. The *Enterprise* discovers a scientist named Roger Korby (Michael Strong), long missing, on a remote planet where his research vessel crashed. The planet's dead civilization created a race of androids that eradicated them when the creators grew fearful of their powers. Korby recovered the technology and can now transfer humanoid consciousness into perfectly copied android bodies, granting them immortality and liberation from physiological needs. When Kirk (William Shatner) refuses to embrace the idea, Korby moves to force the issue; an ensuing struggle reveals that he has performed the procedure on himself. Pressed to prove that he is still the same man, he can offer only equations and theories and, realizing that his ideals and emotions have been compromised, he kills himself. Kirk's final report: "Dr. Korby was never here."

TOS is at great pains to warn against the temptation for humanoids to inhabit synthetic bodies, stressing the loss of sensory pleasure and a moral compass (besides "I, Mudd," see "Return to Tomorrow" [2:20]). Persuading biological life-forms to surrender their organic existence is their main threat, and focusing on this threat is the primary interest in androids in the first series, although the series does depict some androids who are pure AIs. *TNG*, with Data, provides an extended immersion in the android point of view. This point of view, however, is singular. Data at the outset is one of a kind, a "curiosity" ("The Measure of a Man" [2:9], "The Most Toys" [3:22]), the only known sentient android in the galaxy, as atypical as it is possible to be. (This is the reason the acquisitive, sadistic collector Kivas Fajo [Saul Rubinek] goes to such lengths to possess him in "The Most Toys.")

As *TNG* progresses, two other androids that Data's "father," Dr. Noonian Soong, created, plus one offspring of Data himself, appear, revealing that those things that set Data apart from humans are not limitations of android technology but, as Spock notes, are there by design. The most important of these is Data's older "brother," Lore, who first appears in "Datalore" (1:12). (Spiner plays both Soong and Lore.) Soong gave Lore the ability to feel and express emotions and to speak colloquial English, contractions intact. Were it not for the yellow eyes and golden skin he shares with Data, he could easily pass as human. Unfortunately, Lore turns out to be a narcissistic psychopath. Skilled in lying, deception, and manipulation, he repeatedly appropriates Data's identity and conspires with aliens the Crystalline Entity and the Borg to commit mass murder. Deactivated and disassembled many times, Lore has not reappeared in the Trek universe after *TNG*. But he still lurks there like the repressed of the android species.

In building Data, Soong withheld emotions and realistic human behavior, suggesting that being more robotic means being less inclined to make immoral choices. Thus, if some find a robotic affect characteristic of autists, then Data is the autist of androids, and that difference is a positive, not a negative. He may aspire to emulate humans, but has no desire to become his duplicitous brother. His self-loathing because of his lack of humanity does not transfer to his lack of some android capabilities, although he does envy those androids who experience emotions. But when Lore deactivates Data's ethical subroutine while sharing some of his own emotions, rendering Data capable of committing atrocities, Data for the first time questions his pursuit of these emotions and is relieved when his "emotion chip" is damaged ("Descent, Parts 1 and 2" [6:26 and 7:1]). Yet he still blames an incompatibility of android nature with the moral exercise of emotions for what has gone awry. That many humans ignore their ethical subroutines, more like Lore than Data, is a contradiction that *TNG* chooses to wave away.

In naming the *Enterprise*'s resident android, Roddenberry and *TNG*'s other creators emphasized Data's "just the facts, ma'am" consciousness and its concomitant tendency to make him regale others with streams of, well, data. The contrast with Lore expands the significance of Data's devotion not just to facts but also to truth. The spellbinding tales told with verbal facility that we define as lore are often fanciful and, harmless or not, a lie. Once again, autistic traits such as amassing expertise and speaking with sometimes unwelcome candor are valorized as morally superior in androids. Recently, the attacks on science from the likes of anti-vaxxers and climate-change deniers have spawned an internet meme featuring the brothers: Trust Data, not Lore.

The two other Soongian androids to appear on *TNG* also experience the emotions Data lacks, without becoming homicidal maniacs but not with a fully happy deployment of them either. In "The Offspring" (3:16), Data uses his positronic neural net and design specifications to build another android, which he considers his child. He tells no one until the project is complete, infuriating Picard. Do other crew members have to ask permission of their commanding officer to procreate, Data counters, shaming the captain, who argued passionately for Data's personhood and free will in "The Measure of a Man." As in that episode, however, Starfleet claims ownership of the new android, named Lal (Hallie Todd), and moves to take her away from Data for observation. Lal, like Lore, can use contractions and comes to feel emotions, abilities that Data did not knowingly program into her. Instead, they spring from a defect in her positronic brain that causes a cascade failure that destroys her.

The second android results when Soong transfers a human consciousness—that of his wife, Julianna (Fionnula Flanagan)—into a synthetic body ("Inheritance" [7:10]), as was the case with Roger Korby. This time there is no loss of humanity associated with the procedure; however, Soong did it

while the real Julianna was in a coma, dying. The android Julianna has no
idea that she is not fully human. Her programming deactivates her when an
accident reveals that fact. Data, who spotted the signs of her true nature before the mishap, decides not to tell her when he reboots her. Once again, he
believes that to be android is to be *less than*. If one can pass for human, then
staying in the closet is desirable. This is hardly a positive message to send to
high-functioning autists and others with silent disabilities.

Love and Robots

Unlike Data, Lore, and Korby, Julianna and Lal are gendered female. Because Julianna was a woman before her consciousness resided in an android
body, this is not remarkable. But the idea of fully synthetic beings adher-
ing to gender paradigms that correlate with biological sex raises many questions. Lal's creation documents how arbitrary the process is. The android
activates as a metallic humanoid blank, what Michael Chabon in the spin-
off series *Star Trek: Picard* (2020–) calls a golem; it functions perfectly well
in that state. But Data insists that his offspring adopt both a gender and a
race-species identity, asking his humanoid colleagues to comment on the
pros and cons of each of four finalist permutations and combinations. Lal
eventually makes the choice, deciding to be female and human. (As Data's
child, what other species would she select?) Again, androids on *TNG* cannot be what they are but must define themselves against a very narrow range
of normative possibilities for recognized sentient life forms. The show often marks those with prejudices against Data by having them use "it" rather
than "him" as a descriptor. Ostensibly, such usage defines androids as things,
mere mechanisms; the judge in Data's personhood hearing declares that
without a demonstration of sentience, he is de facto a "toaster" ("The Measure of a Man"). Yet the subtext implies that to be a person, one must have
a binary gender designation. No one, not even androids, got to choose alternative pronouns in the late 1980s. (For a broader discussion of gender in
TNG, see Roberts 1999.)

Furthermore, the *Star Trek* universe does not treat these gender choices
as arbitrary. The gender identity that androids present seems to predict their
behavior upon the development of emotions. Those coded male, like Lore
and Korby, easily become murderous. Data's first felt emotion, induced by
Lore, is anger and pleasure at killing an enemy. Those coded female, like
Lal and several androids in the original series, express love but then their
brains short-circuit. Usually expressed as a mechanical failure, true love

from robots, it is implied, is not only an aberration but also a perversion. When his android companion Andrea (Sherry Jackson) tells Korby that she loves him, he is appalled, insists that she cannot love, and then vaporizes her along with himself.

These divergent behaviors stem from human gender stereotyping and from the examples of iconic androids and robots in film and television that preceded Data. Robby the Robot from *Forbidden Planet* (1956), his later incarnation as the robot in *Lost in Space* (1965–1968), C-3PO (Anthony Daniels) and R2-D2 (Kenny Baker) in the *Star Wars* films (1977–2019), Yul Brynner's robotic gunslinger in the original *Westworld* (1973), the Terminator (Arnold Schwarzenegger), and Roy Batty (Rutger Hauer) of *Blade Runner* (1982) do not spend time pursuing intimate relationships. By contrast, female-coded robots and androids, beginning with the evil temptress (Brigitte Helm) in *Metropolis* (1927), are eroticized and created to be sex toys—a "mechanical geisha" as Nurse Christine Chapel (Majel Barrett) calls Andrea—or less eroticized mates for their Pygmalion creators. Even female android protagonists in twenty-first-century feminist narratives, such as Ava (Alicia Vikander) in *Ex Machina* (2014) or Dolores (Evan Rachel Wood) and Maeve (Thandie Newton) in the rebooted HBO *Westworld* (2016–) television series, begin with that purpose, only to transcend it.

Like robots, fictional autists tend overwhelmingly to be male. This follows from real-life data that show boys are four times more likely than girls to be diagnosed with ASD. The prominent autism researcher Simon Baron-Cohen (2010) has theorized that autism is in fact a syndrome characterized by an "extreme male brain," that men and autists are "systemizers" while women and neurotypicals do better than men and autists at empathy. Needless to say, this theory, which hews closely to entrenched gender stereotypes, has come in for much criticism. Nidhi Subbaraman (2014) reports a response by David Skuse, the chair of behavioral and brain sciences at University College London: "The idea that people with autism lack empathy is wrong. . . . People with autism can feel others' pain, but they are slower to process this emotion." Data is obviously a great systemizer, but he also seeks out intimate relationships with others, whether as friends, family, or romantic partners, working hard to understand their emotions in the supposed absence of his own.

Women in particular connect with Data. Rhonda Wilcox believes his appeal is "to women who are drawn to the exotic," to racialized Others (1993, 265). He has sex with his crewmate Tasha Yar (Denise Crosby) when she initiates it while under influence of a disease that releases inhibitions ("The Naked Now" [1:2]); Data is "fully functional" and programmed with many erotic techniques. Robin Roberts, however, sees him as "a feminine stand-in" (1999, 92). His less masculinist traits, however, also seem to contribute to his allure for women. He is a good listener, even if that trait is driven by his interest in how human emotions work. Keiko Ishikawa (Rosalind Chao) uses him as a confidant, and he facilitates her romance with Miles O'Brien (Colm Meaney), giving her away at their wedding ("Data's Day" [4:11]). Ard'rian McKenzie (Eileen Seeley), in "The Ensigns of Command" (3:2), bonds with him over their shared scientific interests, and is disappointed when he doesn't want their friendship to be more than that. With "In Theory" (4:25), the series explores what it might mean for Data to have a mutual romantic relationship. Lieutenant Jenna D'Sora (Michele Scarabelli) confides in Data about her recent breakup, and his sympathetic response prompts her to suggest they date. The android is game, researching all possible permutations and combinations of human love affairs. But the experiment fails. The episode suggests that because Data lacks passions, he can avoid jealousy and possessiveness and can, without being prey to controlling anger, let a woman be herself rather than what he wants her to be. But that advantage is also a detriment. Jenna ultimately doesn't matter to him in any profound way. Who wants an intimate partner who does not passionately desire them, who values them no more than anyone or anything else?

Can Data never love, then? This is what he tells the dying Lal as she professes her love for him. She replies: "I will feel it for both of us." In the *TNG* pilot "Encounter at Farpoint," Riker dubbed Data "Pinocchio," after the puppet who yearns to be a real boy. The character from children's literature most like the android, however, may be the eponymous one whose name Starfleet gives to the organic alien vessel in "Tin Man." In the classic 1939 movie version of *The Wizard of Oz*, the Tin Man sought a heart from the Wizard, who expressed sentiments similar to Lal's: "A heart is not judged by how much you love but by how much you are loved by others." At the same time, though, the Tin Man has been the most emotional of all the travelers; he mistakes the absence of an actual organ as the absence of the feelings it connotes. Data may not have human emotions, but there are many indications that he has android equivalents. Despite his beliefs to the contrary, he adores Lal. When he laments that he cannot grieve for the terminally ill Dr. Soong, his creator responds: "You will, in your own way" ("Brothers" [4:3]). Likewise, in "The Most Toys," his contempt for Fajo, whom he is on the verge of killing in cold blood, is apparent.

So, as *Curious Incident*'s Christopher notes in comparing computer brains, and by implication autists' brains, to humans', feelings are simply a particular way of classifying information: "Feelings are just having a picture on the screen in your head of what is going to happen tomorrow or next year, or what might have happened instead of what did happen, and if it is a happy picture they smile and if it is a sad picture they cry" (Haddon 2003, 119). Autists may have to study images of human facial expressions and learn how to interpret the emotions they signify, but that doesn't mean they don't experience similar emotions, even if they don't signal them in this way. Data, that most atypical android curiosity, can't read his own feelings as feelings, but that doesn't mean the feelings are inauthentic. In Tam Elbrun's words, "Perhaps you're just different. It's not a sin, you know, though you may have heard otherwise" ("Tin Man"). Those autists who see themselves reflected in Data may respond to this subtext, but the android's stubborn insistence on striving to be as neurotypical as possible tarnishes that identification.

CHAPTER 2

Life, Animated: Adapting a Book about a Hero with Autism

REBECCA BELL-METEREAU

When I first viewed Roger Ross Williams's *Life, Animated*, I was flying to Strasbourg, France, watching movie after movie to pass the time on a twelve-hour flight. I knew this film had earned an Academy Award nomination for best documentary in 2016, but I had not seen it, in part because the subject was Disney movies. While they have many adoring fans, they also receive scathing criticism about elements of sexism, racism, and other cultural biases. Somewhat skeptical, therefore, I started *Life, Animated*, and was soon drawn in, resisting making sappy sentimental responses to the Disney snippets and at the same time feeling deeply moved by the real-life drama of Owen Suskind—the hero of the story. Owen develops autism,

and his parents, Cornelia and Ron, and his big brother, Walter, all struggle to cope. Ron's voiceover explains how, almost overnight, their laughing
and talkative three-year-old became mysteriously unreachable and inarticulate. At one point, a doctor asks Owen to walk to his mother, a task he finds
practically impossible as he zigzags his way into his mother's arms. While
I watched this scene, I let out a sudden sob. In the swell of my emotions, I
didn't want to lose sight of the real Owen—whose life revolves around Disney movies—or lose track of exactly what bothers me about the facile way
the Disney clips in this film manipulate our emotions until we can hardly
see the social, commercial, and gender dynamics through our tears. By the
closing credits, I was convinced this film could teach people not just about
autism but also about how all of us learn, adapt, and create meaning in our
lives. After reading Suskind's book, I hoped the movie would drive viewers to discover the details in the written story that provide nuance and backstory, which are instructive for families of children with autism and for anyone who loves movies.

I apply the term "hero" to Owen rather cautiously, because in the film's
source—*Life, Animated: A Story of Sidekicks, Heroes, and Autism*—the author,
Ron Suskind, explains that his son identifies more with sidekicks than with
lead characters. Owen shows his father a sketchbook filled with drawings of
Disney sidekicks, with the closing captions: "I Am The Protekter Of Sidekicks" and "No Sidekick Gets Left Behind" (Suskind 2014, 101). Traveling
with Owen on his journey from miserable mute to expressive young man,
Williams uses the "Interrotron" method developed by Errol Morris to allow "documentary subjects to feel as though they're talking to the director through a television screen" (O'Falt 2016). He illustrates how Owen's
desperate parents discover that the best way for him to escape the overload
of a confusing and frightening world is to watch Disney movies. One day
while Owen is watching *The Little Mermaid* (1989), he keeps repeating the
sound "juicervose," which Cornelia assumes is a request for juice until she
suddenly realizes it sounds like Ursula telling Ariel, "It won't cost much—
just your voice" (Suskind 2014, 24). She and Ron wonder whether this has
significance for Owen, who finds himself mysteriously unable to locate the
voice he had begun to develop as a toddler. The psychiatrist they consult
dismisses Owen's repeated phrase as echolalia, just parroted sounds, but
later they come upon more examples to bolster the claim that the boy knows
what he's talking about. After Walter's ninth birthday party, Owen delivers
his first clear sentence in years to his dumbstruck parents: "Walter doesn't
want to grow up like Mowgli or Peter Pan" (53). Ron has the brilliant idea
to use Owen's beloved hand puppet of Iago, Jafar's parrot sidekick, to ask

Owen how it feels to be him. He answers, "Not good. . . . I don't have any friends" (54), and they proceed to have a real discussion. At another point, Owen watches *Beauty and the Beast* (1991) and repeats "bootylyzewitten"; Cornelia eventually realizes it is a phrase from the film, "Beauty lies within," a major theme of the story (37). Gradually, by using Owen's memorized dialogue and drawings of his favorite characters as entry points into his thought process, his parents grow to understand why their son identifies with sidekicks, whose function he eventually defines: "A sidekick helps the hero fulfill his destiny" (104).

Competing Sources and Taboo Topics

Most viewers find multiple points of identification in Disney films, but Owen takes this process a step further. By memorizing the dialogue and the lyrics of every song in every Disney film he sees, Owen struggles to understand a suddenly bewildering world and its complex web of social situations through the stock—some would say stereotyped—characters and their stories. Disney films, marketed and remarketed in savvy ways, perennially renew people's demand for these universal stories about characters that might have otherwise ended up forgotten or been viewed as dated, culturally insensitive, or irrelevant. Instead, they live on through the decades, in the hearts and minds of devoted viewers. Suskind's book explores the negative aspects of the Disney entertainment juggernaut more than Williams's film does, although he maintains that the Disney Company put no restrictions on the film or the use of clips for it. As a director, Williams was also careful to follow fair-use copyright rules regarding the length of clips. Perhaps he consulted Eric Faden's "A Fair(y) Use Tail" (2007), which explains the rules and history of copyright law by using tiny snippets of Disney films.

As I considered patterns in Disney films and in films about autism, I considered the accuracy of the depiction of Owen and his family. Although *Life, Animated* is a documentary, it shares territory with the often-undervalued subgenre of biopics, many of which contain inaccuracies that pander to viewers. Most autism films favor brilliant people such the Nobel Prize winner John Nash (Russell Crowe) in *A Beautiful Mind* (2001) or Temple Grandin, portrayed by Claire Danes in Mike Jackson's 2010 television biopic. As a character and real person, Owen is more ordinary than the subjects in Dave Wagner's *Rainman Twins* (2008) and Petra Höfer and Freddie Röckenhaus's *Beautiful Minds* (2015), documentaries that focus on the unusual occurrence of autistic savants with special mental powers, who constitute a much larger percentage of subjects in films than they do of the general population.

Owen represents a fairly rare occurrence of delayed or late-onset autism, but he does not appear to be a hidden genius. He was fortunate, however, to be born to a special set of parents. Williams's depiction of Owen's experience is set against a social class that is atypical in many ways, but any family with a child on the autism spectrum will recognize their experience in the sense of fear and anxiety that the boy's family members express as they adjust to a new and inescapable reality. Families of children with Autism Spectrum Disorder find themselves learning by trial and error as they recognize their child's condition and discover ways to cope with the resulting challenges. It is useful to look for other people who have experienced similar difficulties, and it also doesn't hurt to throw money at the problem if a family has enough to spare. When Ron and Cornelia first receive Owen's diagnosis, they quickly enlist experts to help. They look hopefully to the case of Temple Grandin, famous for being a person with ASD who became a renowned scholar and researcher, growing up before most people were familiar with terms for autism. Unlike Grandin, who scored 137 on the Wechsler IQ test, Owen scored 75 when they first tested him (Grandin 1995a, 104).

Most films about autism feature gifted statistical anomalies, and researchers have asked whether such portrayals of autism in film and television increase or decrease viewers' misperceptions about individuals with ASD. Researchers such as Anders Nordahl-Hansena, Magnus Tøndevolda, and Sue Fletcher-Watson observe that the size and variety of the test sample influences answers to that question, so they call for "the community . . . to encourage larger numbers of incidental characters with ASD on screen, in order to present a more nuanced picture of the multiple facets of the condition" (2018, 352). They observe that ideally "screen representations would not only be diagnostically accurate but also do justice to the obstacles faced by people on the spectrum, while illustrating how people with ASD can achieve great things in a supportive environment" (251). This element of verisimilitude is a strength of *Life, Animated*, showing its willingness to look—even if not squarely, at least with a solid sideways glance—at issues that make some people uncomfortable. The most poignant revelation is the sadness and concern of Owen's family when they receive his diagnosis, and the continuing, nagging worry the parents and brother express when they consider what will become of Owen once his parents are gone.

Suskind's book gives more small details behind the broad and inspiring story than the film does, as is inevitable in a book-to-film adaptation. When the family moves to Northwest DC, where seven-year-old Walter begins Lafayette Elementary, he insists on being dropped off a few blocks from school. Eventually, he rides his bicycle to school, a habit the parents interpret and explain to their friends as Walter being "independent." Years later, he confesses that he did this because he was worried about what people at his new school would think of Owen, who was always in the car with his mother. Another time, the family attends a library showing of *The Page-master* (1994), and Owen ends up crawling between the bookcases, an embarrassing moment that prompts Walter to flee outside and ask his father why Owen has to be this way. A more costly and rather humorous episode of family discomfort arises when Owen sees and falls in love with *Song of the South*, which caused controversy over racism during its original release in 1946. When it was briefly rereleased in 1986, "the film still resonated with audiences 40 years later," netting "more than $17 million when it toured theaters a second time" (Lattanzio 2019). To surprise Owen for Christmas, the parents swallowed hard and bought a $100 British videotape of the hard-to-find original movie, only to discover that they would have to pay another $400 to have it converted from British PAL to an American VHS format. As the family watches it, young Walter groans about the film's racism. To placate his older brother, the parents try to explain the evils of slavery to Owen by comparing it to a scene in which Jafar, as a genie, locks Aladdin in chains. Owen pauses a moment and then asks whether they can all sing "Zip-a-Dee-Doo-Dah," which they do. This story is followed in the book by a more layered description of Owen's direction and casting of a Thanksgiving family performance of Roald Dahl's *James and the Giant Peach* (including members of the Kennedy clan, distant relations of Cornelia). In this production, Owen played the Earthworm, who confessed that he was "jealous of the Grasshopper and Centipede and characters who can do things that he can't. And that's why I'm the Earthworm" (Suskind 2014, 90). Ron Suskind looked around the room and saw that all the parents' cheeks were wet. By deleting such touching or embarrassing incidents, the film scrubs a great deal of profundity from Owen's story, but this streamlining also created a ninety-minute film that would be more palatable to a mass audience.

To maintain a lively pace and appeal to contemporary audiences, Williams skillfully weaves together past and present in the opening sequence, to establish the family's backstory, interspersing fantastic animated sequences with serious comments from family members about how their family is coping. He follows the next rule for a film's success by avoiding issues that might offend members of the target audience. One of the most important topics that most films on autism skirt is sex. Like a Disney movie, both Owen and the filmmaker take pains to ignore the icky details of human sexuality. Walter takes a stab at explaining French kissing, but Williams does not play it humorously, perhaps because he refuses to exploit cheap laughs about the subject. When Walter talks about the situation, his unspoken anxiety about Owen's future shines through. He observes that Owen learns everything from Disney films, which do not deal with sex very well, an understatement indeed.[1] The montage of close-mouthed concluding kisses speaks volumes without being heavy-handed or critical. Nonetheless, the director's reticence about exploring this element in Disney is part of what makes the film frustrating for media scholars. A trend toward film prudery may end up being more significant than people realize, given the sobering effects of the Me Too movement, which makes everyone—but particularly politically correct film teachers—hypersensitive about invoking disturbing emotions, often signaled by common buzzwords such as "trigger," "microaggression," feeling "uncomfortable," or finding a discussion, topic, or character "inappropriate" or "creepy." While film teachers want to address controversial subjects, they don't want to face criticism or lawsuits for creating a hostile work or classroom environment, causing emotional trauma, or committing sexual harassment. Filmmakers may be similarly skittish about portraying sexual topics, particularly in films about people on the spectrum who may be viewed as pure or naïve in such matters.

Money Matters

Another common feature of documentaries about people with ASD is the invisible privilege of many of the families depicted. Children on the spectrum from poor families rarely appear in such narratives, whether documentary or fictional. Temple Grandin, for example, had a governess, and her mother was able to devote herself exclusively to helping her daughter speak and read at an early age, before people were aware of the existence of autism. To portray Owen's story, Suskind, a Pulitzer Prize winner, was able to work with the Oscar-winning Williams because they had known each other for fifteen years. Their pairing points to interest in disability and outsider status, combined with personal insider status as award-winning artists. Williams explains why he feels for people who are marginalized, noting that his own background was anything but privileged, having grown up with a mother who worked as a maid in South Carolina. As the first person in his family to attend college, he describes his brother and sister as "left behind, addicted to crack cocaine."

In spite of his achievements, Williams continued to face situations where he found himself left behind, even when he received his Oscar for Best Documentary Short Subject, *Music by Prudence* (2010). This film documents the life of Prudence Mabhena—a girl whose disfiguring arthrogryposis was seen as a sign of witchcraft in her home country of Zimbabwe—showing her triumph as a singer, songwriter, and bandleader. When Williams, the first Black director to win in this category, was just beginning his acceptance speech, the producer Elinor Burkett barged up, grabbed the mic, and talked over the rest of his speaking time. Ironically, this attempt to steal his thunder gave him even more publicity when news outlets publicized how the Black director, Williams, was "'Kanye'd' by Burkett" (McDonald 2016). Although Owen may look similar to Prudence in his outsider status, he comes from a much more affluent background.

Suskind writes about the math behind the family's attempt to get Owen into the best possible private schools in order to help him catch up with his peers and develop as quickly and fully as possible. In tandem with the family's struggles to place Owen, Suskind as journalist seems to find some escape as he becomes enmeshed in the lives of students at Ballou Senior High School, in one of the poorest Black neighborhoods of Washington, DC. In a piece for the *Wall Street Journal*, Suskind focuses on the story of Cedric—a gifted outcast whose father was in jail—recounting how Cedric struggled for acceptance to a summer program at MIT. The story ends with him receiving his acceptance letter, but as his mother reaches to embrace him, he holds "the letter against his chest, his eyes shut tight. 'This is it. My life is about to begin.'" Suskind admits that he cried as he wrote those words. One can imagine that he was crying at least as much for himself as for Cedric or his mother, who gets left behind by a son who views his life as just beginning. When Suskind wins a Pulitzer Prize for this piece, the money and fame put his family in a better position to afford the expensive schooling their son will need in order to have any chance of functioning normally, let alone making it into an elite program at MIT.

The Suskinds' financial status is glossed over in the film, but the book shows how it is a central factor in the lives of any family with a loved one on the spectrum. Suskind describes a workshop that explains legal ways to protect Owen from exploitation or poverty once the parents are dead. The closest the film comes to economics is a scene showing Owen interviewing for a job as ticket taker at a theater. Only thoughtful viewers will notice that a salary for this job would not come close to paying for housing and supervision. In contrast, Suskind's book returns repeatedly to financial considerations in a variety of ways, the most amusing being a description of what Suskind calls the "Owen Economy":

> A country of Owens would halt rampant consumerism. He still doesn't watch television, and ads on the Internet, where he trolls sites for movie-related memorabilia, have no effect on him. Their come-hither tone, that some purchase will make the buyer a better person, or at least more content, wash [*sic*] right over him. The equation that someone could be changed or enlivened by what they buy—a birthright of just about everyone except Burmese Buddhist monks—never took root. (2014, 304)

The pleasure that Owen takes in repetition and familiarity is, indeed, counter to the spirit of a capitalist nation whose economy and ethos are rooted in novelty, constant growth, waste, and expansion, and founded on planned obsolescence. At the same time, Disney capitalizes on the desire for familiarity and repetition as yet another convenient way to make a buck, a widespread taste for the familiar shown by the success of the reboot of *Beauty and the Beast* in 2017. This live-action film remake, which repeats practically every song from the 1991 version, surpassed $1 billion worldwide gross.

Who Are the Sidekicks?

As the film *Life, Animated* moves from having "Team Owen" tutors and trainers come to his home, to his attending a series of schools that accept students on the spectrum, Owen seems to progress seamlessly from one situation to the next. Suskind's book paints a more complicated picture of school settings, particularly at the Katherine Thomas School, which accepts a range of different learners. Here, for the first time, Owen develops a cohort with two other devoted film fans, who call themselves "The Movie Gods," forming a real friendship. All goes well until a fellow student in music class tells Owen that his parents no longer love him and are therefore going to abandon him. If Owen mentions this incident to his parents, the bully threatens to burn down their house. Over time, his tormentor manages to enlist others in this harassment, and in response Owen develops a fascination with the dark Tim Burton *Batman* movies. Eventually, he pokes a fellow student with a pencil, a warning signal that alerts his counselors and parents to his desperation. Ron Suskind pieces clues together, wringing the story out of Owen, and the school expels the bullies. Through therapy, Owen recovers from his trauma. Williams condenses this incident considerably, having Walter give an abbreviated version of the story.

Another part of Owen's life is acknowledged in the book but underplayed in the film—the support and patient teaching provided by his mother, Cornelia. Ron Suskind describes her economic contribution in devoting herself to coordinating Owen's early care, structuring one-on-one education, and chauffeuring him to various lessons and therapy sessions—quite a demotion, considering her earlier status. Before marriage, she had been a reporter for *People* magazine and an associate editor for *Family Weekly*; her father was a senior vice president at Shearson Lehman Brothers; and her late grandfather was Martin J. Kennedy, Democratic congressman for Manhattan. After marrying Ron, she took on the role of stay-at-home mother for their first son, Walter, while he continued to write. After the diagnosis of Owen's autism, Ron went on to publish a Pulitzer Prize–winning article while Cornelia made Owen her new and largely thankless career.

As the film enters its final third, the narrative introduces Owen's friend Emily, showing their tentative steps toward romance, which Suskind fashions as a happy ending in the book. Going beyond the events and time frame of the book, Williams's film adds the complication of Emily breaking up with Owen, who is heartbroken. After a time, Owen regains his footing, shown in a scene that has him shining as a resident of a semi-independent group-living situation at the Riverview School on Cape Cod, where he leads discussions for a Disney Club he started. Participants watch and analyze dialogue, and Owen performs as a deft teacher who brings out his students' enthusiasm and emotions. In one of the final scenes of the film, while Owen and his club members discuss *Aladdin*, we witness one of the most obvious signs of the connected-insider status of his family and friends. One assumes that his father, a Pulitzer Prize winner, was the one who arranged for a visit from Jonathan Freeman, whom Owen describes as "a great actor" who "does the voice of the evil Jafar and is now my official buddy, pal, and friend of the family." Intercut with reaction shots of a young woman with her hands clasped in front of her in awe, the documentary has Owen explain, "Jonathan and I first became pals and friends for my nineteenth birthday when me and my mom and dad went to New York to see Disney's *Mary Poppins* on Broadway." He is interrupted by applause and murmurs of approval from his film group, and then Freeman begins to read the words of Jafar as Owen plays Iago. In the midst of this exchange, who should arrive but Gilbert Gottfried, speaking the lines of Iago (as he does in the film), with Owen slapping his head in obvious surprise, saying, "I can't believe it!" after which Gottfried repeats the same line as Iago: "I can't believe it!" while the crowd explodes with laughter, clapping at this intertextual event in which a movie turns into real life. The reaction shots of Owen's film club companions showcase him as having special status, a heartwarming climax to a feel-good documentary, typical of the arc of practically any Hollywood film in which the little guy triumphs—or in this case, as the sidekick becomes the hero.

But the film avoids answering the questions that hover over Williams's portrayal of the life of Owen Suskind. Will his depiction simply join the preponderance of film figures on the spectrum who magically conquer their many challenges and overcome all obstacles? Will the character revealed in this film give viewers new insight into autism, or will this depiction encourage people to have unrealistic expectations for people living with ASD? Does the film glide too readily over the economic realities that the author explores with more depth and complexity, or did Williams create a Goldilocks film, not too depressing and not too unrealistically cheery?

In the book, Suskind repeats several common assumptions about people on the spectrum—that they cannot lie, that they have little sense of privilege or hierarchy. Some of the details and actions seen in the film contradict this image, perhaps to show that Owen is adopting the coloring of neurotypical people he takes as his models. His introduction of his friends Jonathan Freeman and Gilbert Gottfried displays this disconnection, since he demonstrates some awareness of the prestige of having famous friends. To become popular is one of Owen's fondest wishes, an elusive goal that seems unattainable throughout much of his childhood. His position of authority among his peers and his association with celebrities satisfy this desire for social status.

Disney films avoid certain unspoken truths, such as the virginity of a particular character or the socioeconomic status of sidekick or servant characters who seem to function like slaves. In a similar way, Williams's film focuses on the success story of Owen's transformation from living as a frustrated and lonely child to thriving as a well-adjusted and nearly independent young man. Lurking in the background of this inspiring tale, however, is the more complicated narrative of selfless family members who have subjugated their own desires and freedom to help ensure the success and growth of Owen. This emotional sacrifice is performed willingly and with love, and their generous acceptance of their roles as a support team is both moving and uplifting. Nonetheless, at second glance, one wonders what the life of Owen's brother or mother might have been if they had not focused so much of their energy and attention on his well-being.

Reconfiguring Disney Ideology

Viewers love a happy ending, and the film provides that. Owen is a celebrity who manages to meet Freeman and Gottfried, and his neurotypical big brother is the one who plays sidekick. Meanwhile, if Cornelia and Walt look like forgotten sidekicks in the background, Ron could also be seen as a father who recognizes an opportunity when he sees one, writing a book about his son and producing a film that practically makes a cottage industry of their family's interesting case. This impression would be the furthest thing from the truth. In the book, Suskind revels in how Owen envisions ways of being that differ from the standard hero model. Owen's plan for a screenplay includes twelve sidekicks who cooperate with one another rather than supporting a traditional lone hero, and the motto for this group is, not surprisingly, "No Sidekick Left Behind." In spite of the pervasive influence of American ideologies of commercialism, capitalism, competition, individualism, racism, sexism, and exceptionalism, *Life, Animated* posits a new paradigm—a model for social interaction that helps people figure out how to find their passion and use it to do something good in the world. What is important and innovative about this film is that it promotes a kind of therapy that may work for educators and family members, for students of all stripes and not just for learners on the spectrum. Following in the footsteps of Temple Grandin and her teachers, the Suskinds recognize Owen's Disney obsession as a possible tool, and the book and the film adaptation portray escape from isolation as a story of learning how to leverage that affinity to communicate with their son. The concept may not be original, but the film provides one of the strongest and most accessible articulations of the theory to date. Obsessive fascination is a common feature of people on the spectrum, but it has traditionally been viewed as a symptom to be overcome. The Suskind family was able to recognize Owen's attachment to Disney as a tool, described in the *Autism Speaks* blog as more "pathway than prison" for learners like Owen, who can use such affinities "like an enigma machine to crack the codes of the wider world and find their way forward" (quoted in Neufeld 2016).

Temple Grandin and her mother also recognized the utility of this pattern once they understood that she thought in pictures, perceiving the world in a way that made it easier for her to understand the experience of animals. By observing the responses of animals, she was able to develop environments for livestock that made the trauma of transit to market less harmful and dangerous. Although the end result for animals is still the slaughterhouse, her recommended methods of moving animals physically through the process is more humane and has the benefit of preventing the flood of harmful toxins produced by fear and anxiety, thus keeping these chemicals out of the meat that humans will consume. When the Suskind family learned about Grandin's experience, they were immediately fascinated and inspired by her example. *Life, Animated* promises to be another beacon for people who work with students on the spectrum or those who are alienated and disengaged because of other factors in their lives that are beyond their control.

By the concluding scenes, I was watching Owen ask his Disney Club members the same kinds of questions that I often ask my film classes. I was struck by connections between Owen's efforts to engage fellow members of the autistic community and my own attempts to get my students to connect emotionally with characters and events onscreen and then step back and analyze how films create those emotions. Students are fascinated by movies, but some fall silent when asked to analyze them in historical or technical terms. Watching Owen, I learned new ways of understanding identification and viewer engagement without narrowing the discussion to film jargon and theoretical concepts. *Life, Animated* teaches viewers about challenges and solutions for people on and off the spectrum who use movies and art to discover their own language and powerful voices.

Owen's worldview offers a counternarrative to critics who focus solely on the negative aspects of portrayals of people who learn differently. In analyzing the depiction of characters with mental disabilities in Disney films, Karen Schwartz, Zana Marie Lutfiyya, and Nancy Hansen (2013) point to Dopey (*Snow White and the Seven Dwarfs*) and Gus (the mouse in *Cinderella*) as negative stereotypes that undermine the self-esteem and social reputation of people who learn differently. Looking at these depictions through Owen's eyes, however, focuses on the image with a new lens. Rather than viewing these portrayals as demeaning, Owen sees such characters as kind, well-meaning, courageous figures with whom he can identify. He refuses to abandon his positive interpretation of events, an important part of his persistent spirit. Even Owen's disturbing flirtation with the more negative figures in the *Batman* films during the period of being bullied actually helped him work through his anger and fear and come out on the other side of being deceived and pushed around. Owen's family calls him their best teacher, and I see what they mean. His courageous perspective invites all viewers to find our place on the spectrum, to locate what we have in common with one another, regardless of our abilities or language skills, in a world where no sidekick is left behind.

Note

1. Calling to mind Peter Sellers in Hal Ashby's *Being There* (1979).

CHAPTER 3

Where Is the Autism in *Rain Man?*

DANIEL SACCO

In an early second-act moment in Barry Levinson's acclaimed Hollywood drama *Rain Man* (1988), Charlie Babbitt (Tom Cruise) and his brother Raymond (Dustin Hoffman) are speeding along an interstate highway in a classic Buick Roadster convertible. Raymond, who, we have been told, is an "autistic savant," is growing anxious at the realization that the pair are driving farther and farther away from the Cincinnati Kmart where his underwear is typically purchased. Charlie tries to reassure his brother that underwear purchased elsewhere will be every bit as adequate for its designed purpose. This assertion clearly fails to assuage Raymond's concerns. With this lack of communication regarding (what could be considered) a fairly trivial point, Charlie's frustration, which has been building for some time now, reaches a tipping point. He slams on the breaks and exits the vehicle, swiping at the air around him and cursing at the sky. "What difference does it make where you buy your underwear!?" he shouts at the top of his lungs. "Underwear is underwear! Wherever you buy it!" This is not the first time we have seen Charlie express his frustration with Raymond, but we have not seen it reach this level of intensity. Charlie is clearly approaching the end of his rope. Here, the dialogue takes an interesting turn as Charlie— not an especially efficient communicator when it comes to emotion—bares his true thoughts. "You know what I think Ray?" he begins, turning to face his brother, who is sitting calmly in the car. "I think this autism is a bunch of shit!" We hear the exasperation in his voice. "Because you can't tell me you're not in there somewhere!"

For Charlie, as his tirade makes clear, Raymond's idiosyncratic behavior, monotonal style of communication, and expressions of anxiety are little more than an act. To be fair, at this point in the narrative Charlie has spent just over twenty-four hours with Raymond, who before this period was institutionalized and totally estranged from him. Until the previous day, Charlie was not even aware that he had a brother. For the viewer, Charlie's diatribe takes on a peculiar extratextual significance. What we, along with Charlie, have been watching in Raymond thus far is, indeed, an act: an impressively naturalistic but, at the same time, obviously meticulously crafted and calculated performance by Hoffman, already considered by this point in his career one of Hollywood's finest actors. More precisely, he had been widely regarded for his "realistic" work in films such as *The Graduate* (1967), *Midnight Cowboy* (1969), and *Lenny* (1974). Hoffman is noted particularly for his versatility, his ability to disappear into the wide range of rolls he took on throughout the 1970s (Lenberg 2001, 110). In *Rain Man*, Hoffman's performance is perhaps the most consistently resonant feature of the film, at least for pop-cultural reference points today. But in his televised review on *Siskel and Ebert at the Movies*, Gene Siskel made a compelling point about *Rain Man*—one that bears repeating: "The greatness of it is *Cruise*'s performance—his best role to date." Siskel elaborated: "He goes through a slight change, and you see it honestly earned." His colleague, Roger Ebert, chimed in: "The rule is that fiction is about change, so here's a two-character piece in which one of the characters *cannot* change and will *never change*" (Siskel and Ebert 1988).

As the formatting constraints of a four-minute network television segment no doubt required, Siskel and Ebert's brief exchange boiled a rather complex 175-minute dramatic screenplay down to its core essence—one I do not necessarily seek to dispute. Indeed, the fundamental crux of the fictional "hero's journey," as identified in ancient myth by Joseph Campbell (2008, 30), is the transformation (for better or worse) of the story's protagonist. According to this paradigm, *Rain Man* is unquestionably Charlie Babbitt's story. Further to this point, it is an exceedingly conventional story. Charlie is introduced to us as the classical "self as child" mythic archetype, whose greatest virtue is his (yet unrealized) potential for positive self-transformation and growth. He is a twentysomething sports car dealer whose entire existence has been hitherto darkened by the shadow of his apparently tyrannical (but perhaps simultaneously wise and benevolent) millionaire father. Over the course of *Rain Man*'s runtime, we see Charlie transform from an unfeeling, pathologically self-centered "child," brimming with anger and resentment, to a reasonably well-adjusted, sensitive, and communicative "hero" whose virtue is no longer the potential, but rather the fully realized capacity, for love (manifest in this case by a newfound willingness to put the interests and well-being of another person before his own). This transformation takes place entirely via his weeklong "ordeal" (dramatically speaking) with Raymond, the result of which is the "connection" that, by the film's climax, Charlie insists has formed between them.

Beneath this veneer of remarkably conventional dramatic storytelling, however, something more fascinating takes place. From a narrative standpoint, we do indeed see a connection formed, gradually and incrementally, between the brothers. As Ebert's comment astutely observes, this is all the more compelling given the unlikelihood of such a connection, given Raymond's inability to partake in the transformation and meet Charlie "halfway" (Raymond's interaction with the world around him being largely based on routine and consistency). But as I attempt to highlight, remarkably nuanced elements of Levinson's staging, Hoffman's and Cruise's performances, and the screenwriters Ronald Bass and Barry Morrow's dialogue suggest that the growing "connection" between Charlie and Raymond within the narrative merely builds on connections that, even before meeting each other, the two men seemingly and unknowingly already shared. These subtle parallels, elusive correlations, and abstract links between the brothers run much deeper (thematically and conceptually) than the connection that Charlie vocally identifies in the film's climax. I hope to address a rich but oft-neglected dimension of *Rain Man*'s complex dramaturgy. To conceive of the film primarily as a clash between, and eventual reconciliation of, two distinct characterological "types", namely, the "autistic" Raymond and the "neurotypical" Charlie, is to gravely oversimplify what the film was rather carefully structured to communicate. *Rain Main*'s primary achievement is its subtle and nuanced, indeed easily missed, undermining of any such clearcut binary dynamic.

In the decades since its release, *Rain Man* has proved divisive in the matter of its representation of autism as well as in the lasting implications of this representation on popular perceptions of the condition. In an article in the *Guardian* in 2018 marking the thirtieth anniversary of the film's release, the psychiatrist Darold Treffert (who served as a script consultant on the film) is quoted as calling it "the best thing that ever happened to autism," adding that "no gigantic public education or PR effort could have produced the sensational awareness that *Rain Man* brought to the national and international radar screen" (J. McCarthy 2018). Given Treffert's work on the film, we should perhaps take his claims with a grain of salt. Furthermore, for viewers (such as me) who were too young to possess an empirical understanding of autism awareness in the late 1980s, it is somewhat difficult to divorce the film's content from the (at least presumably) greatly expanded contemporary field of knowledge surrounding differential development. *Rain Man* does, however, effectively dramatize this presumed lack of general awareness. For example, Charlie is patently unfamiliar with the term "autistic" when Dr. Bruner (Jerry Molen), Raymond's in-house physician at Wallbrook Hospital, first uses it during their initial meeting in reference to Raymond's condition. So too is a nurse at a small-town clinic that Charlie and Raymond visit midway through the film. She mistakes the term for "artistic" when Charlie uses it to describe Raymond's symptoms. If we are to believe (as I am inclined to) that the unfamiliarity of most of the film's characters (including even some who work in the field of medicine) with autism is a reasonably accurate reflection of the general public's limited familiarity with the condition in 1988, we may indeed imagine that the phenomenally popular success of the film (the highest-grossing of that year and the Oscar winner for best picture) played no small part in the expansion of that familiarity.

At the same time, critics have challenged the film's depiction of autism on the grounds that its authors, in particular the screenwriter Barry Morrow, perhaps somewhat carelessly conflated details from the two real-life cases that served as inspiration for Raymond's character. While the relationship between Charlie and Raymond is said to resemble Morrow's relationship with a developmentally disabled man named Bill Sackter (whom Morrow effectively "kidnapped" to prevent him from being institutionalized), Raymond's extraordinary capacity for memory and mathematics was inspired by an American savant named Kim Peek, who was similarly adept in these areas (J. McCarthy 2018). Although Bruner refers to Raymond as an "autistic savant" upon Charlie first meeting his brother, the script makes no further mention of savant syndrome, and Raymond's condition is thereafter referred to with the blanket term "autistic." This simplification has led to (perhaps quite justifiable) concern that the screenplay of *Rain Man*, whether deliberately or carelessly, conflates the broad, general category of autism with the far less common identifiers of savant syndrome, at least in the popular imagination. In so doing, the argument continues, the film perpetuates a potentially stigmatizing stereotype, that is, that all autistic individuals possess extraordinary cognitive abilities.

Furthermore, the unnamed doctor at the previously mentioned small-town clinic (Kim Robillard) identifies Raymond as "very high functioning," adding that "most autistics can't speak or communicate." This assertion, of course, runs contrary to more contemporary understandings of autism as a condition that, in fact, incorporates a very wide "spectrum" of developmental difference (Rapin 2011, 3), in which Raymond is more likely somewhere in the "middle." While gauging the potential positives and negatives of the film's depiction of autism—relative to both the period of its release and the significant subsequent developments in the field of cognitive research—is certainly important and worthwhile as a critical exercise, it is somewhat beyond the purview of this study. Since my objective is primarily to analyze the film from a purely dramaturgical standpoint, retroactively highlighting its outdatedness from a cognitive research standpoint risks becoming a more perfunctory exercise. No one would question that the film was made more than thirty years ago, after all. For the purposes of this analysis, it is perhaps better to use the film's own definition of Raymond's condition—however we might choose to classify it. When Charlie asks Bruner to elaborate on his diagnosis of Raymond, the doctor tells him that "there's a disability that impairs the sensory input and how it's processed." Charlie implores the doctor to rephrase in "English." Bruner continues: "Raymond has a problem communicating and learning. He can't even express himself or probably even understand his own emotions in a traditional way." Emphasis, then, is on what Raymond *can't* do, in lieu of noting what he *can*, thus the importation of the then-popular category "disability." Bruner continues to explain how disruptions in Raymond's routine or "rituals" produce tremendous anxiety—a phenomenon manifested repeatedly throughout the remainder of the film. But it is the doctor's previous statement that warrants closest examination here: Raymond's "problem communicating" and inability to "express himself or probably even understand his own emotions in a traditional way." Charlie learned a day or two earlier that his extremely wealthy father, Sanford Babbitt, had passed away. He then learns, from the executor of his father's will, that a used car (which figured prominently in the estrangement between father and son) and a set of "prizewinning" rosebushes are the only assets that Sanford wished for Charlie to inherit. The rest of Sanford's wealth, totaling three million dollars, has been left in a trust, of which Raymond is to be the sole beneficiary. Feelings of frustration and rejection, and the dire consequences of the news (he has incurred serious debt related to his dealership business), are likely, and understandably, swirling through Charlie's mind at this moment. But were he to be thinking more clearly, and with a higher level of self-awareness, something in Bruner's description of Raymond might have struck a familiar chord with him, as indeed it may well have with us. We have known Charlie for only a short time, having seen him briefly at work and then en route to Sanford's funeral, and eventually heading to Wallbrook with his girlfriend, Susanna (Valeria Golino). We know very little about him at this point, midway through the film's first act, but what we do know could be articulated as something like this: Charlie has a "problem communicating" and an inability to "express himself or probably even understand his own emotions in a traditional way." This realization raises the question, what are we to make of this conspicuous, and perhaps startling, textual connection between the eventual diagnosis of Raymond and the observations of Charlie we have already made as viewers of the film?

To suggest that Charlie, like his brother, exhibits symptoms of "disability that impairs the sensory input and how it's processed" may seem a drastic conclusion to leap to (see the chapter by Alex Clayton in this volume). But his inability to express himself emotionally is undeniable. Indeed, Susanna crystallizes this fact in a piece of astute and observational dialogue. She tells Charlie, shortly after his first meeting Raymond, "They tell you today for the first time that you have a brother, I don't see in your face one reaction." Charlie responds defensively: "Take it easy, you don't know what I'm going through here." She responds aggressively: "No, I don't know what you're going through. What are you going through? Because I don't know, because you don't tell me anything!" Like Susanna, we have seen nothing resembling a traditional emotional response from Charlie regarding either his father's death or the discovery that he has an older brother. The screenplay offers superficial reasoning for this: Charlie is thoroughly distracted by his money problems and, we are told, never got along with his father. Furthermore, Charlie sees Raymond, with whom he has no relationship to speak of, first and foremost as an obstacle to his "birthright," the three million dollars of potential inheritance. In other words, Charlie has been bombarded with stress and life-changing information, which he has barely had the chance to process. His inability to address his own feelings, let alone express them to his girlfriend, can be read on some level as purely circumstantial. But the phrasing of Bruner's diagnosis is not the only significant connection between Charlie and Raymond that the film alludes to, quite beyond the screenplay itself.

What follows are three additional instances in which Morrow and his cowriter, Ronald Bass, but also Cruise and Levinson, make this connection palpable. First, when Charlie and Susanna arrive at the home of Charlie's deceased father, they encounter a classic luxury automobile in the garage. Charlie tells Susanna, "It's a 1949 Buick Roadmaster convertible. Only eight thousand production models made, straight eight / fireball eight. It was the first full year of the Dynaflow transmission." Later, during Charlie's first encounter with Raymond, which takes place in that same vehicle, Raymond recites a near identical technical description: "1949 Buick Roadmaster. Straight eight / fireball eight." Both men, it would appear from the stark similarity in dialogue, have an impressive recall for technical details—indeed, the same technical details in this case. In another instance, the executor of Sanford's estate (Jack Murdock) has just read the will to Charlie. He detects Charlie's disappointment. Charlie responds: "Disappointed? Why should I be disappointed? I got rosebushes, didn't I? I got a used car, didn't I? This other guy. . . . He got $3,000,000 but he didn't get the rosebushes. I got the rosebushes." In Cruise's performance here, we see another parallel to Raymond's style of communication as he continues, "I *definitely* got the rosebushes." Cruise's slight but detectable emphasis on the word "definitely" is echoed in Raymond's near constant use of the word in various contexts: "We're *definitely* locked in this box with no TV"; "That's *definitely* my book"; "If the syrup is on the table after the pancakes, then it will *definitely* be too late." Finally, in at least one instance, Levinson's camera direction also points to an unstated connection between Charlie and Raymond, this time concerning Raymond's autism. The small-town doctor asks Raymond, "Are you autistic?" As we anticipate the answer, the camera slowly dollies in from a medium to a close-up shot, not of Raymond as we might expect, but of Charlie.

Toward what are these subtle but unmistakable connections, via screenwriting, performance, and camera composition, working in unison to point us? Could one reasonably take these cues to infer that the neurological divide between Charlie and Raymond is not as pronounced as a surface reading of the story might suggest? We see a much starker interpersonal contrast in emotional expressiveness and communicativeness between, for example, Susanna and Charlie, or between Susanna and Raymond, than we do between Charlie and Raymond. Susanna seems to have no difficulty whatsoever showing her feelings to both Charlie and Raymond. Whether expressing her frustration with Charlie's coldness or her affection for Raymond, she makes her feelings clear, plainly, sensitively, and articulately. Charlie, on the other hand, for all his presumed "neurotypicality," seems no better able than Raymond to express, communicate, or even understand his own emotional drives and impulses. Of course, this statement must be qualified with specific reference to the Charlie Babbitt we meet in the first act. Returning to Siskel and Ebert's assessment of Charlie's character development, we do indeed see a marked change in Charlie's interactions with both Raymond and, equally important, Susanna, as the story progresses into its second and third acts. This change is gradual but is marked, I would argue, by four distinct moments in the script, corresponding to Raymond's four (to use the phrasing of the court-appointed psychiatrist [Levinson himself] who appears in the film's climax) "outbursts."

The first of these outbursts, which takes place in a Cincinnati airport, marks quite clearly the end, in dramatic terms, of the film's first act. Determined to have Raymond return with him to Los Angeles, Charlie tries to coax Raymond to board a departing flight. Raymond begins to riffle aloud through his encyclopedic mental database of airline crashes, repeatedly insisting on the danger of air travel. Charlie, growing weary of Raymond's protestations, attempts to take physical control and force his brother onto the plane. Raymond is instantly and severely overcome with panic. He begins to scream at full volume while striking himself in the head with his fist. Charlie, stunned and shaken by the sudden explosion, relents, suggesting that they drive to Los Angeles instead. For Charlie, this moment acts as the first in a series of significant realizations regarding how Raymond interacts with the world around him. The outburst, rendered very powerfully by Hoffman's performance, clearly denotes Raymond's pure and irreparable anguish at the prospect of flying. Ironically, it is a *much* clearer expression of emotion than anything we have seen from Charlie so far. In this moment, Charlie first realizes the need to adopt significantly more flexibility in his accommodation of Raymond's needs.

A second outburst, which occurs rather unexpectedly in a motel bathroom, is triggered by a seemingly much more innocuous act. Through a somewhat labored conversation with Raymond, Charlie has just learned that his brother was the "Rain Man" whom he had always thought was an imaginary friend from his youth. While processing this revelation—that he and Raymond indeed do share a brief and distant past together—Charlie begins to run a bath. Seeing the hot water gush from the tap, Raymond is overcome with panic. He begins to shout: "Scary! Scary! Hot water burn baby!" Charlie, instantly identifying the hot water as the source of Raymond's fear, shuts off the tap and reassures his brother. In an instant, the significance of the outburst's trigger and timing dawns on Charlie. He, in fact, is the baby that Raymond fears the hot water will injure. Once again, the moment acts as a significant turning point in Charlie's understanding of Raymond—but of a distinctly different sort from the moment in the airport. Assured that Charlie has not been injured by the hot water, Raymond becomes calm. He reaches out and softly pats Charlie on the head. It is a minor physical gesture, but also the first time we have seen Raymond willingly initiate physical contact with anyone. For Charlie, the significance of the moment is deeply felt. Raymond cares deeply for Charlie's well-being, despite his clear inability to communicate it via traditional means of interpersonal interaction.

In the second act, Charlie begins to reciprocate and to care for Raymond's well-being, signaling a growing fraternal bond between them. On a certain level, Charlie is still exploiting his brother: by the opening of the third act, he has hatched a scheme to use Raymond's extraordinary mathematical abilities in the service of monetary gain at a Las Vegas casino. This plan proves a tremendous success—Charlie and Raymond win upward of eighty thousand dollars in a single session of blackjack, and are rewarded with a free night in a "high-roller's suite." Raymond, who was earlier approached in the casino bar by a prostitute, now believes he has a date with the woman—for which he will *definitely* need to learn to dance. Charlie, feeling grateful for the casino winnings, and guilty about his continued impatience with Raymond, obliges, leading Raymond in a slow dance. Pleased with Raymond's cooperation in the dance lesson, and no doubt processing a newfound fraternal compassion for his brother, Charlie embraces Raymond with a sincere and affectionate hug. Raymond suddenly recoils and darts backward. Clearly, he is uncomfortable with the sudden and intimate physical contact. Charlie, startled and dejected, lowers his head: "I just felt like giving you a hug, Ray." Far from a throwaway line, this is the first time we have heard Charlie make any attempt to articulate his own feelings.

A final outburst, midway through the film's third act, is perhaps the most significant for Charlie's character development. Having returned from Vegas, the brothers take up residence in Charlie's LA home. While Charlie is sleeping, Raymond prepares himself a breakfast of frozen waffles. His incorrect use of the toaster oven results in a billow of thick gray smoke, which sets off a ceiling smoke detector. Raymond plugs his ears to shield himself from the detector's piercing ringing. Significantly, the staging and photographing of the scene marks a clear departure from the distantly captured, objective style of Raymond's previous outbursts. Instead, Levinson captures this moment in a highly stylized fashion—a crash zoom on the smoke detector, a quick succession of close-ups (the toaster oven, the lock on the door preventing Raymond's escape), frenetic handheld-camera work as Charlie rushes in, a diegetic soundtrack dropping in and out. Despite his often opaque emotional states, Charlie is undoubtedly the character with whom we have most readily identified along this journey. In this moment, however—more than two hours into the film—the camera, for the first time, shows us the scene as Raymond experiences it. We, like Charlie, no longer view Raymond's outbursts as indecipherable or alien. Insofar as it is possible, we now *understand* them.

The significance of the incident with the smoke detector is not lost on Charlie, who realizes what could have happened had he not been there to calm the situation. Raymond, who reacts to the danger by banging his head against the glass of the locked door (the only available exit), requires care and supervision if he is not to inadvertently harm himself. Furthermore, Raymond's repetition of the phrase "Main man Vern" in the incident's wake, a reference to his primary caretaker at Wallbrook, signals to Charlie that Raymond's residency at the institution is perhaps the best thing for his brother's safety and well-being. This poses a moral dilemma for Charlie, however, who finds himself in a mutually caring relationship, perhaps for the first time in his life. We can certainly imagine the Charlie Babbitt whom we met in the film's first act erring on the side of self-interest. His initial decision to (effectively) kidnap Raymond from Wallbrook for ransom—what he perceived as his right to half of the three-million-dollar inheritance, indeed suggests something more troubling than mere selfishness—verging on what could very easily be construed as sociopathology. The Charlie of the film's first act sees those around him—Sanford, Susanna, Raymond—as little more than means to his own selfish ends. Susanna tells him as much—outright and angrily: "You use me, you use him [Raymond], you use everybody!" But that Charlie is decidedly not the Charlie of the film's third act.

The change in Charlie's priorities and outlook is ultimately signaled most transparently by his decision to drop his planned custody suit and let Raymond return to Wallbrook. In this action, we see the archetypal heroic "sacrifice"—in this case, Charlie learning the virtue of putting the interests and well-being of someone else before his own, as adequate a definition of love as one is likely to come up with. But we see another marked change in Charlie when Susanna rejoins the narrative. Of his and Raymond's upcoming meeting with the court-appointed psychiatrist, Charlie tells her, "I'm nervous," then adds: "Listen, I'm glad . . ." He catches himself, pausing to refine his statement: "Happy. I'm *happy* that you came to Vegas." Once again, this marks a subtle but unmistakable change in Charlie's communicative abilities. To the best of his ability, and through no small effort, he is now attempting to articulate and express his feelings clearly and earnestly, and he is succeeding. As he embraces Susanna, we see rather plainly that his hard-earned capacity for love, cultivated and fostered through his tireless and sincere efforts to accommodate Raymond, are translating to an openness and warmth in his other relationships. In effect, he is reborn, having discarded his previous cold and calculating tendencies and replacing them with a genuine desire to be a source of warmth and light in the lives of others. It is undoubtedly the culmination of a profound transformation, captured rather beautifully in Cruise's exceedingly nuanced and touching performance.

But what resolution is to be found for Raymond, the character whom Ebert identified as one who *"cannot* change and *will never* change"? What resolution beyond his satisfactorily functioning in the story to redeem someone else? It is a testament to the screenwriting skill of Morrow and Bass that in accordance with a delicate sensitivity to Raymond's condition, the screenplay does not necessitate the kind of dramatic change we have witnessed in Charlie to be reproduced in Raymond, in order to facilitate a satisfying dramatic resolution. That said, a final stylistic flourish in the screenplay is, to be sure, worth noting. Throughout the film, we have seen Raymond launch into a verbatim recitation of Abbott and Costello's famous "Who's on First?" comedy routine as a defensive coping mechanism:

ABBOTT: Who's on first?
COSTELLO: Yes.
ABBOTT: I mean the fellow's name.
COSTELLO: Who.
ABBOTT: The first baseman.
COSTELLO: Who is on first.
ABBOTT: I'm asking *you* who is on first.

We have also heard Charlie—perplexed by this behavior—try his hardest to impress on Raymond the comedic value of the routine, Raymond's exposure to which came in the form of a passage in a "sports trivia" book that he memorized. In the final scene, however, as Charlie is preparing to say good-bye to Raymond—who is boarding a train back to Cincinnati—a curious exchange takes place. Dr. Bruner, who is also present, asks Raymond how he enjoys being back in familiar "Kmart" clothes? Charlie chimes in: "Tell him, Ray!" Raymond announces, "Kmart sucks!"—a callback to his and Charlie's earlier conversation about where to buy underwear. Charlie laughs: "You made a joke, Ray!" Raymond, in turn, also laughs. In this moment, we see that Charlie and Raymond's connection is not unilateral.

What seems at first glance like a story of a neurotypical yuppie redeemed by his autistic brother may be something altogether more complex. When the small-town doctor asked Raymond, "Are you autistic?" Raymond paused before responding, "Definitely not!" Charlie, the one who seems redeemed, would likely have given the same answer to that question, yet appears in some ways no less autistic than his brother. *Rain Man*, it would seem, may simply be a story of two autistic men, neither of whom sees himself that way, forming a deeply felt connection.

Ironically, while *Rain Main* predates contemporary understandings of autism, not as a monolithic and disabling condition but rather as a wideranging spectrum—incorporating many forms of differential development—the logic of this discovery is not wholly absent in the film's drama. Charlie indeed finds himself somewhere "in the middle" of a spectrum—of ability in, and style of, heartfelt communication and emotional expression—being situated somewhere between the demonstrative Susanna on one end and the diffident Raymond on the other. While the film's contribution to evolving understandings of autism—for better or worse—remains debatable (and it is a debate that, by any measure, should be had), at least one thing is certain: the film is a thoughtful exploration of communication and emotion, of barriers and entryways for meaningful and wholehearted interpersonal exchange. For that, its critical and commercial success seem well deserved.

CHAPTER 4

The Good Doctor: Images of Autism and Augmented Intelligence

BURKE HILSABECK

As with many critics and scholars who were trained in English departments, my antennae perk up when I come across interesting features of style. This can make watching network television pretty boring because unlike even many middle-of-the-road fiction films, television shows tend simply to repeat the styles of the shows with which they share a genre and an audience. Sure, the style of the television drama has changed a bit over the decades, but these changes have occurred at what, in the arts, is a glacial pace, not the "make it new" speed of modernist literature. Network television is the *People* magazine of cinema: a fun way to pass the time, but you don't pick it up looking for experimental prose.

Is *The Good Doctor* (2017–) the rare show that issues radical experiments in form and style, ratings be damned? Definitely not. For the most part,

The Good Doctor is simply another medical drama. Its twist on an old (and successful) formula is that its protagonist, a resident surgeon named Shaun Murphy (Freddie Highmore), is an autistic savant. This is likely the way that *The Good Doctor* was pitched, and it is more or less the way that it is marketed. Its tagline on the ABC website puts this pretty succinctly: "A young surgeon with autism and savant syndrome uses his extraordinary gifts to save lives and challenge skepticism."

Yet *The Good Doctor* does have one stylistic device that stands out, both because it is relatively unusual on network television and because it is plainly different from the rest of the show. From the beginning of the first episode, *The Good Doctor* tells us that Shaun possesses a powerful and highly visual cognitive process that allows him to think in unusual ways, and he uses this ability to locate inspired and novel treatments for his patients. The show represents these feats of memory, analysis, and interpretation in the form of computer animations that overlay images of Shaun at work. These animations, which do not depict anything in the "real" world of the show but instead represent thought itself, feature prominently but briefly in most episodes. They also tend to suspend the show's story midair, giving us time simply to experience a sense of fascination with Shaun's unusual mind. As one reviewer described this process, "When he's cogitating on a diagnosis, he goes blank, like a computer app in spinning-wheel mode, and the show suspends the tension long enough that you, like his colleagues, wonder if something's gone wrong" (Poniewozik 2017).

Style always has a subtext, so how might we explain this fascination with cognition? Why, relative to the efficiency with which *The Good Doctor* tells its stories, is such time and effort expended on the representation of Shaun's thought processes? Why do these animations tend to put the brakes on the story in order to make a spectacle of thought? After all, *The Good Doctor* is not terribly interested in the rest of Shaun's subjectivity. It is sympathetic, certainly, to his struggles, and it frequently aims to teach the audience about them, but it doesn't spend thirty seconds elegantly illustrating his difficulty in exiting a San Jose bus. Why are his cognitive powers given such pride of place?

It is easy to feel that these questions are obvious. Are not many people fascinated by strange and wondrous powers of the mind? Are there not innumerable television shows and films dedicated to the representation and performance of feats of mental cognition, of wild and romantic imaginations, of the experience of magic? My feeling is that this stance dodges the question. It is undeniable that neurodivergence, autism in particular, occupies a place of prime fascination (and fear) in our culture. But we have a very limited understanding of the depth and contours of that fascination. *The Good Doctor* tries to harness this fascination. Why, and to what end?

Let me first sketch the show in broad strokes. Shaun Murphy is a resident in the surgery department at the prestigious (and fictional) St. Bonaventure Hospital in San Jose, California. The hospital's chief of surgery (Hill Harper), the surgeon on whose team Shaun serves (Nicholas Gonzalez), and the hospital's board initially disapprove of Murphy's appointment, but with the advocacy of the president of the hospital (Richard Schiff), Murphy proves himself to be a capable and worthwhile member of its staff. He does so through what the show's promotional materials call "his extraordinary medical gifts," a prodigious, photographic memory for medical literature and his ability to form inspired diagnoses that elude the neurotypical doctors around him.

I hesitate to apply the word "disability" to his condition, or to what the show calls his "gifts." The character does not seem to understand himself as disabled, and although he struggles with aspects of everyday life that do not trouble the people around him—he speaks in ways that his colleagues perceive to be too blunt, for instance—it is hard to see how the designation applies. Especially in early episodes, however, *The Good Doctor* makes it clear that some of Shaun's colleagues perceive him as disabled, and the show, at least implicitly, places him in a narrative role that has traditionally been occupied by the disabled. For that reason, it is helpful to put the show, and the character of Shaun, in the context of a larger history of representations of disability.

Indeed, *The Good Doctor* largely follows a pattern common to narrative representations of physical and cognitive difference in which characters with these differences serve to contain the threat of difference or warm the hearts of the normals. In their seminal study of literary representations of disability, David T. Mitchell and Susan L. Snyder (2000) argue that narratives that feature disability nearly always do so as a kind of prosthesis. That is, across boundaries of time, nation, and genre, writers have used disabled bodies as one means of telling stories about bodily, cognitive, and cultural ideals. Far from seeking to represent or acknowledge the lived experiences of persons with disabilities, the action of narrative prosthesis forces disabled persons and bodies to serve "as the raw material out of which other . . . communities make themselves visible" (S. Murray 2008b, 122). In some cases, writers and audiences construct what amount to fetishized and exoticized images of disability that simply enact disavowal, while in others they enact a sentimental mode in which disabled persons serve as the fulcrum for feelings of inspiration and hope.

Writing around twenty years ago, Mitchell and Snyder were mostly concerned with physical disability, but in his survey of the representation of autism in Hollywood cinema, Stuart Murray sees the same action in portrayals of cognitive difference. The films that Murray looks at "present a constant invitation to look at the person with autism, and this look is, ultimately, a moment in which the audience is encouraged to speculate on the very nature of the human condition" (2008b, 129). These narratives are often characterized by what Murray calls "the sentimental savant"; they are texts in which an "emotional story becomes folded into the broader wonder generated by the savant skill" (88; on the "sentimental savant," see also Murray 2006 and Moore 2019). Most film and television representations of autism, Murray says, "use the refraction narrative of paired impaired/non-impaired characters not only to explore ideas of difference, but also to illuminate for majority audiences questions of individual responsibility, behaviour and knowledge" (2008b, 123). In other words, Hollywood uses cognitive disability to set up a figure-ground relationship: neurological difference creates a space out of which the real story emerges, the personal growth of neurotypical people.

This description applies pretty fully to *The Good Doctor*. In the first episode of the series, for instance, we learn that the president of the hospital has hired Shaun as a resident surgeon over the objections of the hospital's chief of surgery and its board, and in an impassioned speech he explicitly compares Shaun's neurological difference to differences of race and gender, implicitly placing this difference within a larger narrative of civil rights. "We should hire him because he is qualified," Dr. Glassman says, "and because he is different. How long ago was it that we wouldn't hire Black doctors in this hospital? How long ago was it that we wouldn't hire female doctors at this hospital?" In this sense, the show occupies the sentimental mode that Rosamarie Garland-Thomson describes in her account of photographic representations of disability: "Sentimentality makes of disabled people occasions for the viewers' own narratives of progress, improvement, or heroic deliverance and contains disability's threat in the sympathetic, helpless child for whom the viewer is empowered to act" (2002, 63). Or as Allison Moore has written of *The Good Doctor*, "The narrative function of the 'sentimental savant' is to shine a light on the behaviour, attitudes, and relationships of the non-autistic and expose *their* deficits in communication, interaction and empathy" (2019, 300). Thus, Shaun becomes an alien, a bright eyed E.T., here to teach the normals about what ails them (on autists as aliens, see Moore 2019 and Hacking 2009a).

So is *The Good Doctor* not actually interested in Shaun or his unique powers of cognition except as a means of framing these other conflicts? While it is undoubtedly true that *The Good Doctor* is prosthetic in just this way, this explanation doesn't account for my initial problem, that is, the show's fascination with neurological difference. If Shaun were there simply as the ground out of which a norm emerges, it is hard to understand why the show is specifically fascinated by his condition. Shaun's cognitive difference is certainly made prosthetic, but it isn't just the fuel for an ideological payload.

Of course, the condition with which *The Good Doctor* is fascinated is not autism per se, but a doubled condition, autism plus savant syndrome. Although very small numbers of people with autism also exhibit savant syndrome, the figure of the autistic savant looms large in film and television representations of autism. *Rain Main* (1988), to pick a particularly germane example, was partly based on Kim Peek, an autistic savant who was known as the "human Google" for his remarkable memory (S. Murray 2008b, 83–88). As Moore has argued, *The Good Doctor* draws a picture of Shaun that places him squarely in this tradition. And just as the savant in *Rain Man* is valuable for his ability with numbers (he helps his brother win money by playing blackjack at a casino), it is Shaun's savant syndrome that makes him valuable to his hospital.

And it is unquestionably the presence of savant syndrome that lends *The Good Doctor* the stylistic invention with which I began: the computer animation that visualizes Shaun's cognition. In one scene (in "Pipes," 1:4), he works alone, at night in his apartment, to fix his sink. We see him in medium close-up from the back of the sink, the camera positioned where the wall would be and the plumbing interposed between him and us. The image is so dark that we can see only small sections of the pipes, Shaun's face and hands, and the spaces where his flashlight picks out the space. As the camera dollies closer toward him, his face in "spinning-wheel mode," animated lines of yellow light trace paths across the plumbing, wrapping themselves around the disposal and following the hot-water line. (In other instances, these animations include words and graphics pulled from his medical textbooks, which are presented for our view before receding and dissolving into the background of the image.)

In this particular case, Shaun has been treating a patient who has a tumor that is wrapped around a nerve in her thigh. Shortly after this experience under his sink, Shaun runs into the patient's room, yelling, "Nerves are like pipes!" He then proposes an obscure idea for a surgery that will save feeling in this patient's nerve: "We can connect the distal end of the pudendal nerve to the branch of the femoral cutaneous nerve from her inner thigh!" Thus, Shaun's mind draws an original connection between the plumbing in his apartment and the nervous system of a patient. More importantly, he produces a solution that has escaped his neurotypical colleagues.

Like *The Good Doctor*'s narrative use of cognitive difference (which it misidentifies as a disability) to articulate a message of human progress, these animations are recognizable as a form of prosthesis. "A prosthetic intervention," Mitchell and Snyder write, "seeks to accomplish an erasure of difference all together; yet, failing that . . . the minimal goal is to return one to an acceptable degree of difference" (2000, 6–7). In the case of physical prostheses, disability is first hidden (a prosthetic limb beneath the leg of one's pants) and then, failing that, made acceptable (a wheelchair that allows for movement in space). But a similar operation is true of literary and visual representations of disability in which physical and cognitive differences are not declared or made visible but are instead used as engines for metaphor and narrative meaning. In the first case, prostheses mediate the relationship between difference and "normality"; in the second, they mediate between the realms of the real and the imaginary.

Interestingly, these moments of visualized cognition in *The Good Doctor* often occur in moments of solitude. If they do not occur in physical solitude, like the example above, they occur when Murphy is separated from the people around him by a kind of trancelike absorption. Murray notes that "the idea that autism is a condition of withdrawal and solitude . . . prompts photographs in which the subject is framed as though overwhelmed or lost in the surrounding environment" (2008b, 108). And in just this way, the visualizations in *The Good Doctor* separate Shaun, both physically and subjectively, from the characters around him.

So the narration presents Shaun to us as autistic, but his colleagues and patients find value in his abilities as a savant. And this allows *The Good Doctor* to understand cognitive difference as productive. The show imagines Shaun as a uniquely valuable participant in economic life because he possesses an ability that neurotypical people do not. As Maria Neicu writes of Aimee Mullins, a sprinter and fashion model with prosthetic legs, she transformed "the category of *unable* into *superable*" (2012, 42).

There is a kernel of reality here. The philosopher Ian Hacking has noted that the unique abilities of certain autistic people are indeed suited to an economy that prizes the production and organization of information. But in fictional representations of autism, the phenomenon of superhuman neurological ability encourages "the image of the autist as gifted with a secret knowledge or wondrous powers":

> Yes, there is a simple fact that some high-functioning autistic people are good at some tasks that many neurotypical people find arduous or boring. Paradoxically, the tasks are often the ones that may have special uses in our logocentric era, in which the formal codification and structuring of information plays an ever-increasing role. . . . But this fact, plus a lust for strangeness in stories, can lead some novelists in search of a plot to create the child, the adolescent, or the adult with whimsical or mysterious powers. (Hacking 2009b, 504)

Shaun is often just this, an autist gifted with "wondrous" or "mysterious" powers—in Murray's phrase, a "sentimental savant." But unlike earlier representations, *The Good Doctor* understands its savant as someone who contributes to the knowledge economy.

The Good Doctor isn't really about the experience of living with autism, and its meaning isn't exhausted by a new, feel-good approach to the inadequacies of the neurotypical, but it may be a story about work. Consider the following scenario. A sixty-year-old woman has symptoms that lead her physicians to diagnose acute myeloid leukemia. Her doctors prescribe a standard treatment, chemotherapy targeted to kill the cancer cells. While the chemotherapy does indeed destroy the cancer, the woman's recovery is unusually slow. Her frustrated doctors order another round of tests, but the tests fail to change their initial diagnosis. Enter another doctor with an encyclopedic knowledge of the literature on leukemia, a doctor with a memory so powerful that it can combine this knowledge with an assessment of vast quantities of the patient's genetic data. Surprising the first doctors, he comes up with a diagnosis of a rare, secondary type of leukemia caused by myelodysplastic syndromes. This inspired diagnosis leads to a change in therapy, the woman's condition rapidly improves, and she is discharged from the hospital (Otake 2016).

This would be wholly recognizable as the four-act structure of an episode of *The Good Doctor*. It follows a familiar plotline from the show: a patient suffers from a rare disease; her earnest physicians misdiagnose the disease because it fails to conform to the cases with which they are most familiar; finally, a doctor with a photographic memory and an unusual neurological condition reviews the data, pulls a new diagnosis from his hat, and cures the patient. This incident described in the previous paragraph is not, however, the description of an episode of television. It actually occurred in a Tokyo hospital in 2015. And the doctor who performed the inspired diagnosis was not a neurodivergent human being but an intelligent computer, IBM's Watson, the machine that went to medical school (Wakeman 2011).

Is Shaun a machine? Yes . . . and no. Since they are the only obviously digital animations in the show, those that visualize Shaun's thought processes represent his cognitive difference as a *technology*, and they specifically imagine these thought processes as superhuman—not in the sense of being fantastical (although they are sometimes this) but in the sense of being exceptional. To be sure, *The Good Doctor* thus picks up a long-standing (and false) metaphor of "autism as computer or machine" (Moore 2019, 305). But in this case, it connects this metaphor with a specific anxiety, the worry that not simply blue-collar labor in warehouses and factories, but even the most prestigious, white-collar, brain-heavy work will be replaced by automation.

In her essay on prostheses and organ transplantation, Margaret Shildrick writes, "It is in the nature of prostheses to effect powerful transformations to the embodied subject that move beyond mere modification towards the far more radical step of rethinking the limits of the human" (2013, 217). Shildrick extends earlier work on physical prostheses that showed them as having destabilizing effects on the wholeness and integrity of the body, in order to ask the question how organ transplantation might do the same, on the "inside" rather than on the "outside" of the body. But cognitive difference immediately raises the question not of bodily integrity but of the wholeness of the mind itself. This is an important part of the cultural fear of autism—particularly around suspicions that it might be caused by a larger, poisoned environment. Autism has presented to a neurotypical majority a sense in which the mind might be nonidentical, less than unified, in flux. But if that altered view of human consciousness is one way to describe a general fear of autism, it is also a source of its fascination. This fascination emerges in narratives in which autistic subjects are understood as, in Hacking's phrase, having "wondrous powers" or as uniquely suited to the economic and cultural moment.

Of course, Shaun's consciousness is not literally prosthetic. He is not the result of human-germ-line engineering, nor does he take supplements or pharmaceuticals that alter his cognitive functioning. And he does not, like many people with more severe forms of autism, use a technological prosthesis to speak or write. Yet in its animations, the show imagines the consciousness of this autistic savant as prosthetic. Like the computers that diagnose real patients in actual hospitals, Shaun exhibits a kind of augmented intelligence. Crucially, *The Good Doctor* does not represent these animations, and hence his cognition, as the dreams, fantasies, or *effects* of consciousness, but rather as a kind of augmented sight in which an object before the mind is made more perspicuous by means of an overlay and organization of data or information. The visual rhetoric of the show seems to suggest that we are being given not a translation of a fundamentally nonvisual process that occurs beyond our grasp—inside Shaun's mind, as it were—but that thought process itself.

When Shaun is alone in a dark office, his insight is visualized as an inspired combination of definitions, schemata, and illustrations from medical textbooks, pulled together as if by powerful software. But the sense in which Shaun's disability is a kind of augmented intelligence is even clearer when the animations occur in the midst of dramatic action, when the images in Shaun's mind are overlaid directly onto the bodies of his patients. In "Hurt" (3:1), for instance, Shaun rushes into a bar where several people have sustained injuries in an earthquake. As firefighters prepare to transfer a woman with a back injury to an ambulance, Shaun stops them so that he can size up the case. On top of her prone body, the show visualizes first the bones of her skull and torso as well as a handful of nerves; then the skull, neck, and vertebrae are lifted up and away from her body and held suspended in the air. A series of numbers describes the names of these vertebrae, which then appear in a second animation in close-up, in which one of the vertebrae glows red. Shaun then emerges from this trance to announce, "It's not just a fracture—something is pressing on her spinal cord!"

Thus, the movements of the animation figure Shaun's consciousness—hence his neurological condition—as being akin to the powers of a sophisticated electronic device. His consciousness, which can call up photographically accurate representations of the human body, is seen to possess a power of memory more like that of a computer than that of a neurotypical brain. He is also seemingly able to manipulate the spatial orientation of this information in something like the way that visual representations can be lifted, turned, and skewed on a touch-sensitive device. And crucially, the show imagines Shaun's intelligence not as a mere repository of information, however dynamic, but as a process capable of overlaying this information on the world in ways that allow him to read and respond to that world more quickly and accurately. This is a fantasy of autistic consciousness as augmented intelligence.

The Good Doctor participates in a long history of fictional responses to the automation of labor, but it does so from a perspective that speaks to a new kind of automation. Whereas the first machine age led to the automation of jobs that had previously resided in the hands and simple tools of individual workers, the second machine age, it has been argued, is digital in nature and involves the automation of more strictly cognitive tasks (Brynjolfsson and McAfee 2016). In the first case, a machine automatically shapes wheels that would previously have been forged by a blacksmith; in the second, an artificial intelligence diagnoses cancer patients who would previously have relied on doctors' human intelligence. And just as the fictional heroes of the first machine age astounded and relieved audiences through feats of physical resilience and grace, acts that redeemed the place of the human being and human body in a mechanized economy and world, it makes sense that the feats of the second machine age would be not physical but cognitive in nature. Thus, *The Good Doctor* imagines the experience of an autistic savant not as that of a human encyclopedia but as fundamentally that of an advanced technology. Shaun's mind is prosthetic, a kind of Google Glass of the brain.[1]

In this sense, *The Good Doctor* imagines cognitive difference as a posthuman condition, one in which the rounded, unitary, uniquely human body and mind are instead considered malleable, nonidentical, and prosthetic (Murray 2017; on disability and the posthuman, see Murray 2020). And while disability continues to serve as a metaphor through which "the audience is encouraged to speculate on the very nature of the human condition," as Murray puts it, the human condition is no longer imagined as unitary or closed off, a whole toward which disability represents a (containable) threat. Just as in older instances of narrative prosthesis, the subjectivity of the person who is understood to have a disability remains almost entirely submerged, but his condition is leveraged for a different end: the conceptualization of a posthuman experience.

At times in *The Good Doctor*, this sense of Shaun, and of neurological difference as posthuman, dovetails with other representations in which humans are combined with machines. While "Heartbreak" (3:18), for instance, is largely about the emotional pain that Shaun experiences after the breakup of a romantic relationship, it also follows a farmer who has mangled both of his arms in a combine and who is eventually forced to have his arms amputated and replaced with prostheses. This man initially rebels against his condition, making it plain that, for him, the stakes of this operation are precisely the difference between being human and something monstrous. ("I want to be a farmer," he says, "not a cyborg!") And later, just before he agrees to the surgery that will replace his arms, he invokes a similar rhetoric: "I don't want false limbs. I don't want to be that guy. I want to be who I am." Here, a simple phrase ("who I am") evokes the desire for a fixed, permanent, unitary self, a humanness that this man has hoped the miracles of modern medicine might help him to save. And of course, one of the surgeons assures him that even with prosthetic arms, he will remain human: "You are the toughest, most tenacious person I've ever met," she says, "and that's not going to change because we replace your hands with titanium." But all this is belied by a final scene in which he learns to use his new arms and hands. The show displays an obvious fascination with their soft silicone and tight gearing, dwelling on their movements for what is, on network television at least, a long interval.

Seen in this light, the heart of *The Good Doctor* is an imaginative though problematic attempt to overcome some of the fears associated with artificial intelligence and its intrusion into the workplace. Through the representation of his difference as dual, the figure of Shaun Murphy enacts a magical reconciliation in which the human coexists with intelligent machines.

Why are bodily and cognitive differences so often forced to serve a narrative function? Perhaps somewhere deep in the culture is the feeling that difference must somehow be made to *work*. Of course, this relentless drive to make people and things work, from welfare recipients to neurodivergent brains, is a kind of fetish. It disavows reality for a fantastical image of wholeness. In the case of automation, it is not just work and livelihood but a sense of human culture that is threatened. The presence of artificial or augmented intelligence practically screams from the rooftops that one sense of selfhood, a sense of the coherence of the mind and body, is false. But this truth is too painful. The figure of the autistic savant is an obvious choice to fill this void. He—and on television and film, it is almost always he—fills it like a totem. He fashions a new image of wholeness: he may not be "normal," but he does the work of an intelligent machine while at the same time preserving the wholeness of his person.

Have I simply turned Shaun Murphy into my own prosthesis? Perhaps I have made him the engine for another kind of narrative, a scholarly one that again denies his difference, this time to make an argument about the representation and experience of automation. Is this character a cipher for my own fears? I find myself in a double bind: if I take representations of difference at face value, I am left with facile pictures of real subjectivities; if I reveal them to be false, I instrumentalize them as the engine of academic argument. Perhaps we need to grasp both sides of this dilemma at the same time. Murphy is not a real human being and needn't be treated as such, but the signs that *The Good Doctor* mobilizes do point toward real people in the real world. And real people are not metaphors.

It is sometimes said that we fear that machines will replace us. But what do we mean by "replace"? Our fear is that we will disappear. Not that our bodies will vanish but that they, and we, will be made superfluous. So what is to be replaced is not *us*, but a particular sense of ourselves, a sense of the human.

How much more comforting to believe that there is a person—even an entire kind of person—who will not vanish, a person who performs the functions of our machines better than the machines themselves. In this sense, Shaun Murphy is both human and machine, and for that he is a kind of hero. If this is because he is a savant, the presence of autism here makes this wish fulfillment more realistic by suggesting that the human being who is equal to these machines has sacrificed something in the process of becoming a machine. What is lost is a more exclusive sense of what is human, say, or an ability to more easily share forms of life with family and colleagues. But this hardly matters: in the figure of the "good doctor," the human itself is preserved. *The Good Doctor* is frequently praised as abjuring cynicism and irony, as being earnest and full of feeling. But perhaps the feelings that the show generates are not experiences of hope and progress, but of mourning.

Note

1. Google Glass is a display in the form of a pair of eyeglasses.

CHAPTER 5

Oddity and Catastrophe in *The Big Short*

JASON JACOBS

There is a deleted scene from *The Big Short* (2015) in which a hedge fund manager named Michael Burry (Christian Bale) and his wife (Jae Sue Park) take their son, Nicolas (Colin Lawless), to a children's psychiatric center for testing. When Burry arrives late because "everything's falling apart at work," his exasperated wife informs him, "They think it's Asperger's syndrome." By this point in the film (if the scene had remained part of it), we know that Burry is a skeptic about received authority and an obsessive about detail, and we see him research the symptomatology of autism, reading various guides for parents. The film gives us close-ups of the text he is reading, and we hear him saying the words we can see, most of which describe *him* as we have seen him so far: "Many parents will report that their child will stay at the computer for hours not breaking to go to the toilet, to eat or to sleep"; there is a common fascination "with numbers from an early age." The words "social isolation" and "lack of social understanding" are given prominence in the calibration of extreme close-ups of the text he reads. When the text tells him that "especially the fathers" of such children share "some of the personality characteristics of their child," he puts his thumb to his lips as if to suck it. This is the moment he realizes that he may share this condition with his son and may therefore be responsible for passing it to him. A kind of transaction quite different from the strictly economic ones we see in the film. Except the following scene (also deleted) shows us that Burry's concern is rather with himself: we see him outside, on top of his office building, where a man in a white coat, smoking, presumably a doctor (he has "MD" stitched on his front lapel pocket), tells him the following:

> MD: I don't know, man. Diagnosis like this, as an adult? It's pure upside. You don't have to feel like something's wrong with you anymore. I mean, now you know.
>
> BURRY: What's the upside of having Asperger's?
>
> MD: Come on, Burry. I mean who other than an aspie actually reads entire bond prospectuses? Your entire life, your brain's been telling you one thing, society's been, kind of, telling you another. Well, fuck society. Fuck us. Don't you get it? We're normal. We can't keep up.

The Big Short seems to want to let us know here and elsewhere that the only way one would see the world as Burry, in his skewed vision, does is to have skewed vision oneself. And more: in a painful way, to fail to see like that—which for Burry is to fail to see at all—is a colossal moral failure. *The Big Short* seeks to tell the story behind the US housing market crash of 2007, which triggered the global financial crisis of 2007–2008, and it does so by following three groups of people who, in historical reality and in the words of Jared Vennett (Ryan Gosling), the film's "narrator" (who is also a character in it), were the only ones who bothered to "look" at the evidence clearly pointing to an imminent catastrophe. Each of these groups contains a character who is in some way odd: Burry, whose hedge fund, Scion Capital, was named after Terry Brooks's fantasy novels, in particular *The Scions of Shannara*; Mark Baum (Steve Carrell), who runs a hedge fund called Frontpoint Partners; and Ben Rickert (Brad Pitt), a retired securities trader who is recruited by two young financial parvenus, of which more later.[1] Burry, Baum, and Rickert are odd in very different ways, but it seems it is their peculiarities that enable them to use a kind of canted cunning not only to perceive the looming disaster baked into the housing market but also to exploit it for financial gain. And this makes what I believe wants to be a very moral film, a film that wishes to be a warning to its audience, very odd, too.

Before I address each group, and the film in turn, I want to describe my moral and ethical problem with the ever-blurring distinction between odd-ness and illness. The rise of the "medicalized self" over the past few decades and the adoption and elasticization of fluid notions of mental conditions ("spectrum creep") raise troubling questions about normality and the dis-tinction (call it the aristocracy) of illness and victimhood. As the doctor on the roof with Burry says, the rest of us "can't keep up." Morally, it seems to me to be troubling to pose "illness" or "affliction" as a kind of magical gift that allows superpowered perception or moral insight, and it does enormous disservice to those who suffer greatly at the sharp end of what used to be a fairly discrete spectrum. As Dr. Michael Fitzpatrick (who is the father of an autistic son) put it in 2004:

> The tendency to label as autistic every absent-minded professor and eccentric scientist, and every obsessive engineer, train-spotter and stamp-collector (compounded by the vogue for identifying historical figures and even contemporary celebrities as autistic) carries the risk that the spectrum becomes stretched so wide that autism loses its distinctiveness. "Normalis-ing" autism may reduce stigma, but at the cost of diminishing recognition of the extreme aloneness that results from the social impairment of autism even in higher functioning individuals. Temple Grandin is a professor of veterinary science at Colorado State University and the title of Oliver Sacks' account of her life—*An Anthropologist on Mars*—is Grandin's own description of what she feels like when trying to engage with other people, and clearly expresses the profound sense of alienation experienced by even the highest-functioning people with autism. (Fitzpatrick 2004, 71)

The decision to delete the sequence in which Burry confronts the fact that he may be autistic is a wise one in this respect. Social awkwardness, eccen-tricity of manner, saying the wrong thing at the wrong time, oversensitiv-ity, and other painful but benign aspects of social interaction are left, with-out this diagnosis, as markers of a difference of perception and cognition rather than a pathology that gives one insight without having to go through the business of looking hard to acquire it. That would have diminished Bur-ry's achievement: there are happy, good ways to be odd—even rude—with-out being bizarre and eccentric as well. And if pathology is somehow part of that oddness and there is no way to treat it, is it better to acknowledge it, to socialize our pathologies, or just to accept them as part of who we are? If we can function socially, however clumsily, then that sets us apart from those whose condition separates and distances them from the ordinary nourishment of human community. This is not a film about that more extreme kind of problem. Vennett's narration describes them this way at the start of the movie: "As the whole world was having a big old party, a few outsiders and weirdos saw what no one else could. Not me. I'm not a weirdo. I'm pretty fucking cool. . . . These outsiders saw the giant lie at the heart of the economy. And they saw it by doing something the rest of the suckers never thought to do. They looked."

We first see Burry interviewing a prospective employee. The scene begins with him playing drumsticks on his legs (he is barefoot, wearing cargo shorts and a T-shirt, with earbuds), regaling the aspirant with a story about the collapse of the housing market in the 1930s. We have already seen Vennett address us direct to camera as he describes the transformation of banking in the late 1970s, but here an over-the-shoulder shot of Burry seems to be doing the same thing: who is he talking to—the interviewee or the camera? This is a matter further confused by the fact that Burry has a glass eye (in real life, but computer generated here in postproduction), so even his direct-to-camera gaze is off-kilter. Midway through his historical lecture, Bale adjusts his performance, turning more toward the still-unseen face of the person sitting opposite him, and at this point the camera zooms directly into an extreme close-up of Bale's face before cranking into slow motion and cutting away to a group of young cheerleaders at a football game: this is a flashback to when he was a child playing a group sport. Then we hear Burry talk about himself as we watch him swim in a pool from an angle deep in it, below him: he says he has always been more comfortable alone, and that he believes that was because of his glass eye: "It separates me from people." Back again now in the football flashback, we see that the young Burry's glass eye has fallen to the ground and his peers are looking on—distant, slightly repulsed perhaps.

Back in the present interview, he explains that social interactions are awkward for him and for the people he is having them with: what he says comes out "wrong." And as if by magic, he provides an example: "That's a very nice haircut. Did you do it yourself?" It is not clear whether this is a line to test the interviewee's understanding of Burry's disclosure, or whether Burry has just spontaneously asked it: Is it cunning or symptom? Or some alloy of both? And in either case, is it a compliment or an insult? Again we are treated to a remarkable shot of Bale looking toward his guest and then turning, "directly" looking at us, and gleefully grinning (in a way not too far from his version of Patrick Bateman in *American Psycho* [2000]);[2] by contrast, all through this the interviewee plays it straight, keeping his eyeline directed toward where we know Burry is seated opposite him. But Burry/Bale and the camera's twitching zoom-in/zoom-out motions unsettle us, allowing us to share the strangeness of this encounter visually. A caption appears telling us the date is March 2005. Then Burry offers the man the job and tells him to get the top twenty mortgage bonds in the country (each bond is made up of thousands of mortgages bundled together) so that he can read them. He turns up the heavy metal music in his headphones (which we share via the soundtrack).

Many of the early scenes of Burry involve him reading numbers on a spreadsheet, intercut with flash still images of ordinary scenes of US life and popular culture icons. Isolated in his office, he discovers that embedded in the bonds are mortgages in desperate arrears, that is, mortgages that are not as valuable, in aggregate, as they appear to be. Only someone with his peculiar patience, perception, and capacity to tolerate extreme repetition (partly visualized by his workout routine in the office: push-ups and crunches) could have achieved this insight, so the film seems to assert. Hedge funds like Burry's are basically funded by investors who trust his superior judgment (the real Burry was a neurologist who blogged on financial markets as a hobby before he became a full-time finance guru): as Lawrence Fields (Tracy Letts), one of his biggest investors, tells him, "Whenever you find something interesting, we all tend to make money." But Burry's discovery that the housing market is likely to soon collapse is so counterintuitive—"Who doesn't pay their mortgage?" is the palpably ignorant refrain we hear a few times in the movie: those who can't afford it anymore, of course—that for the rest of the film he is faced with his own catastrophe: the increasing social pressure of investors wanting to withdraw their funds because Burry has bet them against ("shorted") the continuing success of that mortgage bond market. What Burry has seen in the webs of dense spreadsheet numbers is that many more people are defaulting or behind on their mortgage payments than the value of the mortgage bonds indicates, that the bonds' purported value is a fiction. His capacity to "look," to perceive this, is his "superpower," but also the very thing that brings intense pressure on him. (The deleted scene would have occurred at the crisis point when many of his investors were trying to withdraw.) His investors are losing money until their magic man's prophecy comes true.

Our experience of Burry/Bale throughout the rest of the film is pretty much this: his stonewalling of investors wishing to get out. But this is not a matter of mere stubbornness. It appears more as a form of conviction derived not from allegiance to a decision but from sheer empirical facts (the "markers," as he calls them) as he perceives them. That is why when Lawrence Fields charges into his office and aggressively demands his money back, Burry's refusal seems less like courage or bravery than a kind of holy virtue born of a deficit: the cost of seeing the truth is that he cannot see other aspects of the world. As he says to Fields: "I don't know how to be sarcastic. I don't know how to be funny. I don't know how to work people. I just know how to read numbers." Even when the value of the bonds does not fall as he predicts, he cannot understand how he could have been mistaken: "I guess," he tells one of his employees, "when someone's wrong, they never know how." At the peak of the crisis of his uncertainty, we see him playing drums in his basement while listening again to heavy metal music, finally throwing the drumsticks aside. This is a picture of chaos and confusion: we hear his version of the drum section, and the metal track is far lower in volume, providing a weird sense of synchronized discombobulation; it is as if his distress manifests itself in a desire to order his body to a set soundtrack. Shortly after this scene he bans his investors from making withdrawals. Part of the problem for the holy man is that the bankers' deceit really has no rationale or order. The film's premise is that the bankers built the housing market's value on sheer lies, involving the collusion of many institutions in overvaluing assets that, when they began to fail, would demand further deception to offset disaster. Bankers' lying to their public is absolutely incomprehensible to Burry, a numbers man whom numbers never deceive.

As is by now obvious, the film's ideological foundations are precarious, because its putative heroes, like Burry, are betting *against* the economic stability of their nation and its people. In each case, they have to be seen to have a redemptive side, an inner life that is in some—albeit always odd—way virtuous. For we might think that had Burry the capacity to persuade potential investors in a sociable, inspiring, and honestly influential manner, perhaps something might have been done earlier to at least mitigate the crisis that he rather passively awaits. He updates the value of his company on a whiteboard only once a day. In his final email to investors, he shares something of his inner life: that he met his wife via an online dating service and that she agreed to date him because he was honest about his one eye, his student debts, and his awkward social manner. (Notably, in the released version of the film she appears only as a photo on his desk; in the deleted scene, she is clearly exasperated with him, and the marriage hardly seems to be on solid ground.) He goes on to write about the financial industry in a way that seems to disavow his fascination with it: "This business kills the part of life that is essential, that part that has nothing to do with business. For the past two years my insides have felt like they're eating themselves. All the people I respected won't talk to me anymore . . . People want an authority to tell them how to value things, but they choose this authority not based on facts or results. They choose it because it seems authoritative and familiar. And I am not and never have been 'familiar.'" The problem then, is with us: the people who lazily, perhaps even greedily, rely on the faux charm of the corrupt mortgage salesmen we see depicted throughout the film, and who eschew the hard work of checking facts. This is not a picture of people I recognize (although I certainly recognize it as a view held by many), and I don't think it excuses Burry, however regretful he sincerely is about his limitations ("honesty" not being one of them). At one point we glimpse a paperback copy of Adam Smith's *The Wealth of Nations* on his bookshelf; if only he had read *The Theory of Moral Sentiments* instead!

Burry's insight into the imminent failure of the housing market is the propulsion that activates the other two groups in the film that eventually short that market. Jared Vennett gets wind of one of Burry's trades and takes the intelligence to Mark Baum's Frontpoint Partners (a subsidiary of Morgan Stanley). Using a set of Jenga game blocks, he illustrates the fragility of the mortgage bonds, and despite the skepticism of his team, Baum is attracted both to Vennett's transparent self-interest ("I kind of respect him") and to the opportunity to punish banks that have charged extortionate rates on credit card interest and student loans. He sees virtue in the "short," the virtue of punishing clumsy, overreaching greed. And this is part of his oddity, too. We first encounter Baum blundering into some kind of trauma therapy session, interrupting an already hesitant speaker midconfession and complaining loudly about some incident at his workplace. He is rude, ill mannered, and hotheaded. Later we learn that his oddity lies on another kind of spectrum, that of trauma: his brother committed suicide by jumping from the top of a skyscraper. Baum later confesses to his wife that he had offered the brother money as a palliative for his depression and has suffered from crippling guilt ever since.

As with Bale's depiction of Burry's autistic personality, Steve Carrell theatricalizes Baum's aggressive and often obnoxious repugnance at the fraudulent and corrupt activities of the industry of which he is a part, with relish and exuberance. He is by far the most attractive figure in the movie because he makes it easy for the viewer to align with a knee-jerk repulsion against the vulgarity of those who, as one of Baum's associates puts it, "prey" on ordinary people simply wanting a better life (as anyone would). Baum's capacity for sociality, like Burry's, has been compromised, not by a neurological condition (like Burry's) but by the fact that he is a banker. When he tells his wife, Cynthia, that he fears the entire economy may collapse, she reminds him that he has been predicting that for years and asks why he should be "shocked" now:

BAUM: It's more twisted than I could have imagined.
CYNTHIA: You love to be the virtuous one.

BAUM: I'm a banker. I'm part of it.

CYNTHIA: You always have, Mark, like you're untainted.

BAUM: It changed me. It changed me into a person who is not able to reach out to someone. . . . He was in pain. My brother was in real pain. . . . He told me that he was having bad thoughts.

CYNTHIA: Just feel the feelings like the rest of us.

BAUM: My first response was to offer him some money. I offered him fucking money. . . . His face was so smashed.

My linear transcription of the dialogue does not do justice to the very peculiar way we hear it, sometimes as voiceover, overlapping with shots of Cynthia and Baum either not speaking or saying something else, in shots that are occasionally overlayered with other shots, as if the whole moment of confession and breakdown has been compressed, pressurized into this pinpoint of release. But again, as with Burry's email to his investors detailing how his insides have been "eating themselves," we ought to be surprised at the blurring between the professional and the private, as if one thing—autism or tragic trauma—somehow compensates or excuses how both men are profiting from a catastrophe that will happen to others.

Finally, Brad Pitt's performance as the former securities investor Ben Rickert is arguably the one that causes the film the most problems in reconciling its depiction of honor and virtue in people who are relying on financial catastrophe for their success. We meet Rickert when two young investors, Charlie Geller (John Magaro) and Jamie Shipley (Finn Wittrock), unceremoniously shut out of Lehman Brothers, accidently discover in the firm's lobby one of Vennett's prospectuses detailing the advantages of shorting the market. They contact Rickert, who introduces them to the right contacts and tutors them in how to make their version of the short a success. Pitt depicts Rickert as a bearded recluse, a kind of eco-prepper, someone who hates not just Wall Street but modernity itself. As Shipley narrates the postcard snapshot of Rickert: "Ben was dark. He didn't just think the whole system would fail. He thought the whole world was going down." We then see a short scene of Rickert cooking for Shipley and Geller, boasting, "Every one of these vegetables is fresh from my garden—you guys should start your own garden. What you got to do is get your soil off the petrochemicals . . . Seeds are going to be the new currency, and not those Frankenseeds from Monsanto . . . Learn to live off the land."[3] Like a lot of virtue-spouting egotists, he is well able to afford to hold these luxury beliefs: it is not as if he lives in a yurt somewhere in the forest. When he organizes the short trades with the banks, we see him arrive in Manhattan wearing a medical mask, later pulling the price tag off his newly bought tie, and patting a large belly indicating a life no longer lived between the luxuries of corporate life and an ab-affirming gym. And when he finally secures substantial shorts for Shipley and Geller at the American Securitization Forum in Las Vegas, he curtly and pompously reprimands them for their obvious delight: "Do you have any idea what you just did? . . . You just bet against the American economy . . . which means if we're right, people lose homes, people lose jobs, people lose retirement savings, people lose pensions. You know what I hate about banking? It reduces people to numbers. Here's a number: every 1 percent unemployment goes up, forty thousand people die. Did you know that? Just don't fucking dance."

Once again, Rickert's oddity has a doubleness, his disgust with the very industry from which he will profit by betting against its success. Later we see him as the housing market collapses, making his trades in an English pub: "I'm trying to sell $200 million in securities. In a pub. Smells like sheep." The sheep are really the poor sods we glimpse behind him, one of whom, overhearing his trade, observes, "If you're a banker you can fuck right off." After Rickert completes a trade for over $80 million, he cleans his hands with a liquid sanitizer; he has already told Shipley and Geller, "Greece and Iceland are finished. Spain is teetering," in an even voice that—at least to my ears—is unresponsive to what that means, despite his command of the consequences of mass unemployment expressed earlier. In the background, we can hear a football match playing on the television for the patrons, and Pamplona has just scored. And this is the problem with the film and its odd characters. It wants to be virtuous, but it also wants to be clever and witty, and to somehow clarify an important aspect of recent Western history. (The global financial crisis did not have as much impact outside the Western world, so it was not truly "global.") It does so by deploying a range of formal techniques familiar to any student of counter-cinema or third cinema: direct address to the camera; real celebrities explaining "complex" financial instruments (Margot Robbie, drinking champagne in the bathtub of a luxury beachside condo, explains mortgage bonds; Anthony Bourdain uses a catering analogy to clarify collateralized debt obligations [CDOs]; Richard Thaler and Selena Gomez at a blackjack table in Vegas tell us all about "synthetic" CDOs, a mixture of historical figures and fictional characters; formal and narrative experimentation, including onscreen titles, animated graphics, and rapid flash-montages of historical cultural icons (Ali G, Cartman, Tom Cruise in *Top Gun*); and so on. At one point, one of Baum's team complains of a lump on his testicle, and we get a medical diagram, upper screen left, of a teste. But none of this formal complication and showiness adds clarity. The basic assumption that runs through the movie is established in the first few minutes: bankers are greedy, seedy, and unscrupulous. No shit, Sherlock. (An early scene shows a bunch of them in a strip club as if such places were exclusive establishments for the newly wealthy; but the moral point about the connective tissue between wealth and depravity is what is being made.)

What the film fully elides is the role of elected politicians who, after all, are tasked with overseeing the nation, including its economy. But that would implicate the Clinton dynasty, with its notoriously close ties to Wall Street, and the tepidly ineffective response of President Barack Obama in the aftermath of the 2007–2008 catastrophe, which avoided any reform of the financial sector's practices. The film tries so hard to socialize us into the world of what it sees as a complex industry that it utterly fails to clarify the real reasons—beyond the technical and formal ones associated with the financial sector—for the catastrophe that it is so keen to depict. For example, we are shown Burry at Goldman Sachs, uncomfortable in a suit. He cuts a deal to short the mortgage bonds in return for paying the bank a monthly premium if their value rises. This is one of the deals that made him over $100 million, and $700 million for his investors. And the real reason for people's not paying their mortgages—unexplored by the movie or by Burry—is that while it was easy to get a mortgage with zero financial credentialing, real wages in 2005 had not risen significantly in the West for over twenty-five years (and have not since). At the same time, the rate of productivity in the West has stagnated since the early 1970s, leading to what Phil Mullan (2017) calls the Long Depression, culminating in national economies trading in massive amounts of cheap debt while avoiding investment in productive capital entities, a practice that continues to this day.

But depicting *that* would require a quite different approach, and it could not be sustained by the idea that only the odd, only those distant from the corrupt sociality of the financial sector, only paragons out of synch with the everyday world the government shaped and controlled, could perceive or accept the inevitability of catastrophe. In its very form, charming though it wants to be, the film feels awkward and fails to familiarize us with the very topic it wishes to explain. We can't keep up, not because the movie is complicated—and it is!—but because it does not grant us the capacity to see beyond its own narrow interests, to see further toward politically contentious matters. The film, like the autistic personality at its center, is wholly bound up in its own mystery and magic, quite without intending malevolence, delving into arcana only some can explain, and paying little heed to the politics secretly setting the scene. In that sense, *The Big Short* is itself on the spectrum.

Notes

1. A hedge fund permits an investor to make "hedge bets" against other investments by essentially betting against their success. To "buy short," or simply "to short," is to lower a purchase in one commodity while going "long" in another.

2. Derived from Michael Caine's performance to the camera in *Alfie* (1966).

3. For some time, Brad Pitt was an avid gardener in Los Angeles.

CHAPTER 6

Diagnosing the Detective: Sherlock Holmes and Autism in Contemporary Television

CHRISTINA WILKINS

"You really are an automaton—a calculating-machine!" I cried. "There is something positively inhuman in you at times."
ARTHUR CONAN DOYLE, *THE SIGN OF THE FOUR*

There is a temptation to classify characters that we are familiar with, as if doing so will allow us to see them in a new light or reach a new understanding of how they function. Our classifications border on diagnoses as we try to categorize people's key traits as aspects of a type. Once they are neatly squared away, we have the function of the characters and can reuse the types in stories when called for. Famous characters have been diagnosed, increasingly so, as the boundaries of classification stretch to include more elaborate descriptions and definitions of conditions and states. Interestingly, characters whose actions and attitudes confound us or break away from the norm are the ones most commonly put under examination. Hannibal Lecter, for example, or our case for this chapter, Sherlock Holmes. The question of Sherlock's classification has been argued over since his literary inception. On more than one occasion, Arthur Conan Doyle likens him to a machine, emphasizing his status as something beyond human. This has led some critics to retroactively diagnose the character as being on the autistic spectrum (similar to how some past historical figures have retroactively been diagnosed with various conditions). Later in this chapter, I engage in more detail with the retroactive-diagnostic minefield and the stereotypes of autism being relied on for this. For now it is pertinent to note that this diagnosis has not just been applied by a few rogue psychologists but has also been introduced into the cultural milieu and the Sherlock mythos.

Recent iterations of the Sherlock Holmes figure in particular have been discussed most animatedly as displaying signs of the form of autism known until 2013 as Asperger's Syndrome. Both of these iterations have been televisual creations: BBC's *Sherlock* (2010–2017) and CBS's *Elementary* (2012–2019). The aim of this chapter is to explore the American construction of the figure in *Elementary* and the presentation of autism in that show. Specifically, I argue that *Elementary* presents the figure of Sherlock not as an adaptation of Conan Doyle's texts but as a web of different iterations, and was particularly influenced by the BBC series. But unlike the BBC's *Sherlock*, *Elementary* softens the elements drawn from recent Sherlock characterizations that have been seen by audiences as autistic, to help mold the show for the police procedural genre, within which it clearly fits. This reconceptualization is helped by the presentation of supporting characters who make the figure of Sherlock empathetic, and the introduction of a character explicitly and definitively on the autistic spectrum, Fiona Helbron.[1] She functions within the narrative as what may be considered a comparatively more "authentic" portrayal of autism, albeit a more complex one, given the nature of autism's presentation in women.

Autism Onscreen

Autism presents complex issues of representation for those portraying it and in ways of physically manifesting a neurological difference. Mark Osteen (2008a) begins to tackle these issues in his collection *Autism and Representation*. The collection falls into the category of disability studies, although as he discusses, what can be included within this area of inquiry is contested. Film and television representation is crucial; for many people, it is their primary encounter with the condition, creating a template of behaviors and characteristics labeled "autistic." The difficulties come in how characters are portrayed. According to Osteen, "Autism has been represented over the years mostly by non-autistic people" (2008a, 6), including most actors. Prominent autistic characters are often played by neurotypical actors who don the mask of autism, highlighting its constructed nature onscreen as a collection of easily recognizable gestures. Since autism is a spectrum, there are difficulties in classification, leading to what Osteen calls the disability-difference conundrum. It is "plausible" to argue that the difference between autists and neurotypicals lies largely in "matters of style or adjustments," whereas severe autism would be defined as a disability (7).

When autism is presented onscreen as a disability, it is often tempered by certain stereotypes that give it a "useful" function by neurotypical standards. In film, *Rain Man* (1988) "serves as the primary definitional text for autistic spectrum disorders," notes Anthony Baker (2008, 229; see also the chapter by Daniel Sacco in this volume). The autistic-savant characterization (by Dustin Hoffman) in *Rain Man* is a pattern followed in other films. Baker outlines a "formula" for a typical film with an autistic character, which is disappointingly easy to identify in texts that feature such characters. Perhaps this is because of the value assigned to such characters. Particular stereotypes are played to, like savantism, which serve to further the plot or act as a narrative device. But such stereotypes strip autistic characters of agency and position autism as spectacle. They enable a clear visualization of difference, although identifying the autistic body can be difficult, as Stuart Murray states: "The autistic body, unlike certain physically impaired bodies, frequently does not signal its disabled status. It can however suddenly move from such a situation to generate—through excessive physical movement—an obvious behavioural difference" (2008a, 248).

The autistic body onscreen is required to operate in contexts that will trigger the display of these behavioral differences, signaling difference explicitly. These actions then reflect on the other behaviors of the character, which we re-view for signs of difference. How dissimilar are they to our own? What behaviors do we share? Disability and difference, as Osteen notes, help us center our own identities by showing us what we are not. As he notes, autism in particular is presented in such a manner as to "validate neurotypical experiences" (Osteen 2008a, 9). This explains the pairing of autistic characters with a neurotypical protagonist to give an anchor of identification for the (primarily) neurotypical audience, which is part of the formula that Baker identified. The neurotypical character acts as an onscreen comparison, confirming our own difference from the autistic character. As noted, the autistic body requires particular contexts in order to elicit difference. The most common situation associated with autistic characters is a social one—audiences search for the frequency of eye contact they make and their distinctive patterns of speech. Whether this is due to an overall cultural awareness of autism and its attendant behaviors or to increased cultural representation is unclear. But recent years have seen an increase in autistic characters beyond film, moving into the often long-form medium of television.

With television series comes increased screen time. Autistic characters are often put into a wide variety of scenarios that showcase their difference and distinctiveness. The autistic "formula" for film has a function. The autistic character is primarily an instrument of the plot rather than the subject of a sympathetic portrayal. But with television, producers and audiences often create long-running arcs that depend on investment in, empathy for, and, in some cases, identification with characters. Recent autistic characters onscreen are especially prone to being marked as "different" rather than "disabled." Autistic characters are found in long-running television series such as *Bones* (2005–2017), *The Big Bang Theory* (2007–2019), *Community* (2009–2015), and *Hannibal* (2013–2015). In the BBC series *Sherlock*, the titular character is situated similarly, and this is true as well, to an extent, in *Elementary*. But the positioning of characters as autistic comes mostly from an audience's understanding and recognition of what constitutes autists' behavior, and from subsequent classification by reviewers and audiences. In each of the shows mentioned above, the characters are not explicitly defined as autistic within the show. The autistic protagonist or character on television becomes a web of intertextual references that rely on understood fictional representations of autism, thereby strongly leaning toward stereotypes. Perhaps this explains why the careers of these characters are linked with the computational autistic stereotype.

Autism as a computational or machinelike condition has long been noted. In particular, savantism is primarily associated with this stereotype, and this association grounds prominent representations of autism onscreen, despite the fact that savants comprise just 10 percent of the autistic (Treffert 2009, 1351).

Savant characters are structured as computational beings, processing the world around them as data, which, says Baker, "offers a reductive definition of autism as . . . [an] inhuman condition" (2008, 237). Doyle's use of the term "inhuman" is similarly linked with the idea of the machine, and authors and producers relying on computational stereotypes when retroactively diagnosing a character as autistic are working from a very reductive idea of autism. The televisual representations of autistic characters are reductive in that way. These autistic characters are most commonly depicted as problem solvers; or as being able to see patterns that other people cannot; or as offering commentary that is deemed socially insensitive (but factually correct and often used to reveal information between characters). By virtue of their depictions, these characters become, beyond individual selves, a type, a distinctive element of the show's dynamic. Screen autists are usually part of a larger set of characters rather than lone protagonists (in line with Baker's formula). But in the recent portrayals of Sherlock, the focus is unquestionably on him. Stereotypes of autism that are evident in both the BBC and the NBC series (though more in the former than the latter) emerge from this web of representations, furthering an idea of the characters as being on the spectrum. As Paul Howell notes: "In Sherlock, the ability to store incredible amounts of data, to systematize and retrieve, whilst at the same time to discard useless data is portrayed as a three-dimensional touchscreen as the character processes data and makes conclusions. But, in keeping with the 'intelligent agent' of AI, the data which Sherlock is able to analyse stretches beyond simple information to the gathering of information from 'other agents.' He is able to read gestures and intonations of voice, and deduces 'obvious reasons' for complex sequences of action" (2015, 149).

Yet, says Howell, Sherlock's perspective functions as redemptive, humanizing the computer rather than mechanizing the person. While this observation may be Howell's attempt to show autistic representation as being less reductive than we might assume, it still relies on repeated stereotypes. Here he is discussing the BBC version, which was hugely popular with audiences, both in the UK and the United States (where it was shown on BBC America). Benedict Cumberbatch's portrayal of Sherlock as computational is perhaps more explicit than earlier performances of the Sherlock character, given the frequent onscreen matching between computer screens, information labels attached to people, and his intensely concentrating (often expressively blank) face. He sees as if he is scanning the visible surround and his memory for information. Perhaps this is an update to the Sherlockian method reflecting our society's general computerization, but Cumberbatch's approach (with the express help of Danny Hargreaves and his team) is markedly more extreme. Although the fascination with Sherlock as machinelike is something that goes beyond the recent versions, its explicit linking with computers, along with certain behavioral traits, has situated him on the spectrum for many audience members. In *Elementary*, however, the need for certain changes speaks to an awareness of what these stereotypes and representations mean, instantly and already, for audiences.

Arguably, the "softening" in *Elementary* is a tactical move that nods to the BBC version while also shying away from an explicit diagnosis. In both recent portrayals, audiences have seemed to need to categorize and diagnose Sherlock Holmes as autistic.

Retroactive Diagnosis and Understanding Sherlock

What do we know about Sherlock as character? Does his neurological state matter? Perhaps giving a name to it enables us to explain his astounding ability to see things missed by the rest of us, as well as his vast (obsessive), virtually encyclopedic knowledge of categories and types of things, such as cigar ash or bees. He becomes a repository for data and a filter for processing the world around us. He is often portrayed without a human relationship to distract him, and his character is solely as a case solver extraordinaire. Crucially, it should be remembered that this understanding of the Sherlock character extends into a variety of representations in film, television, and literature. Thomas Leitch's exploration of this commodification centers on the idea that any adaptation of Sherlock refers to "the franchise as a whole" (2007, 213). The understanding of Sherlock as a case solver, the brains to his sidekick Watson's heart or (comparatively) emotional perspective, is thus a collective understanding. It is principally because of this classification of Sherlock as a walking, talking brain that the recent onscreen portrayals have toyed with the stereotypes of autism. Sherlock is clearly behaviorally different, and his attendant behaviors and mannerisms that could be seen as indicative of autism offer a form of explanation for this. Speculation online has been rife for both *Elementary* and *Sherlock*. In the UK, the National Autistic Society has "claimed" Cumberbatch's Sherlock as autistic, despite the series not explicitly categorizing him as such. The same occurs with the character as a whole, with internet discussions focusing on a cluster of behaviors seeming to confirm his condition. But to be clear: the writing of the character of Holmes, and Doyle's imbuing of it with certain obsessive traits and markers of social difference, and his description of him as machinelike, all occurred before autism was identified as a developmental condition. Sherlock Holmes's first public appearance was in 1887. Autism was first diagnosed in the early 1940s.

The classification of conditions is culturally specific. Our understandings of which appearances and actions constitute the symptoms and behaviors of a condition shift with increased knowledge about and changes in social attitudes toward difference. Stuart Murray argues that autism can be seen as a constructed idea, a way of grouping people via a collection of symptoms. Films and other forms of representation aid in this construction, which gives us a set of observable behaviors or markers for classification. In this way, we are armed with a framework to apply to characters who fit these symptoms or behaviors, which may be especially inaccurate. Working from such a framework, audiences increasingly identify certain characters as autistic; these types all share similarities in their differences, and labeling them as being on the spectrum provides a way to understand that difference.

It is pertinent to highlight the separation between difference and distinction. In keeping with Osteen's idea of autism embodying elements of difference and disability, the autistic characters discussed here are classified as different. But how they are used in the series is as an element of distinction, bordering on the eccentric. Distinction here moderates difference and packages it in ways palatable to audiences, which is explicitly what occurs in *Elementary*.

What should also be considered is the repeated hesitancy among the creators of these televisual texts to explicitly diagnose characters as autistic. The filmic cases (which are the ones most often addressed in scholarship) are often more extreme portrayals of autism, ones labeled as disability rather than difference. But with the current television Sherlocks there is no element of onscreen diagnosis. This is particularly evident in *Sherlock*. Steven Moffat, the writer of the BBC series, defines the character as a "psychopath" or a "sociopath" in interviews and in series dialogue. Yet fans and critics frequently return to the idea of him being on the spectrum. Similarly, with *Elementary*, the writer Robert Doherty explains the relationship of the character to a categorization as autistic:

> What I was really starting from was . . . was the idea of an addict. Someone who is, who has spiraled out of control, and is trying to get better, but is too proud to accept help, at least in the beginning . . . [It was] what was important to me about, about this Sherlock Holmes. . . . I think some of the quirks of personality that people respond to or, or the quirks or the behavior that, that get people thinking in that direction, you know, as far as the possibility that he is autistic, or at least on the spectrum. . . . For me, I think that's just being true to the character that Conan Doyle wrote. I also wouldn't want to, to mislead anyone and say, "It's all very deliberate and that was my plan!" (Baker Street Babes 2015)

The retroactive diagnosis of the character of Sherlock is enabled here by Doherty's claiming that these traits emerge from Doyle's creation and are somehow embedded in Sherlock's core. The need for Doherty to explain this, and also for Stephen Moffat to address Sherlock's perceived autistic status, speaks to how audiences are reading these characters. Yet we cannot claim Doyle intentionally framed his character this way; and it is impossible to effectively diagnose someone at a distance, especially a fictional character designed to function narratively in a particular way. Such "diagnosis" only enables audiences to compare Sherlock's behavior to common understandings of autism, which serves to further particular (rare or unrealistic) stereotypes of the condition. It is also limited by sociohistorical changes that affect not just the conditions for a diagnosis but also the manner in which the diagnosed characters are portrayed.

US Context and Changes

What becomes evident is the "glamorization" of autism, or the use of it in a spectacularized way. Mat Greenfield (2014) argues that the recent portrayals of Sherlock Holmes present "romanticised, distinctly pop-culture version[s]" of autism. Like established filmic portrayals, these televisual approaches, specifically in the case of *Sherlock*, are used to evoke amazement at the character's almost superhuman abilities, despite the creators denying any explicit diagnosis. To enable a more productive discussion, a closer examination of the presentation of Sherlock in *Elementary* is necessary.

Elementary is a particularly interesting case when it comes to adaptations of the Sherlock Holmes figure. Like other adaptations, it retains some of the details associated with the figure as whole, including name, nationality, and familial relations (his brother Mycroft). But it introduces significant changes that challenge most interpretations of the figure. First is the relocation of his adventures to New York from London. Second is the characterization of his sidekick, Watson. Rather than Dr. John Watson, an Englishman, *Elementary* offers Dr. Joan Watson, an Asian American (Lucy Liu). This is explained in part by the American setting and the American police genre, in which the show is positioned. Watson here is a sober companion to Sherlock, a recovering addict. Yet when in episode 1 we first encounter Sherlock (Jonny Lee Miller) through Watson's perspective, he is surrounded by a vast array of blaring TV screens, and is staring at them catatonically. There is immediately something "otherly" about this person. After she interrupts him, he recites, word perfect, a speech that had played on one of the screens. This ability to sort and repeat large quantities of information further marks him as different. Throughout the episode, we are shown other distinct behaviors that appear out of place socially, including a lack of direct eye contact, often associated with autistic characters. Sherlock is clearly different and has a lack of concern with social cues or standards. He has a desire, says Watson, to "solve people." In the following few episodes, in which the character is established, we witness his functional views on sexual intercourse and his literal approach to relationships and cases. The relationship between Watson and Holmes is central to the show. Watson is more typically emotional and socially smart. Tensions arise from Holmes being too logical, too detached; but after a few episodes, he appears to soften this approach. By episode 3, the sparseness of eye contact has gone, and Holmes appears to act in a much more neurotypical manner. What marks him as different is not so much his gestures as his speech and the perspective that emerges from it.

Holmes's perspective is compared to neurotypical standards throughout the series. Whether or not he is defined as being on the spectrum, his behavior is still held up alongside norms to highlight the difference. From his detached approach to romantic relationships (seeing the body as having needs to fulfill) and his functional view of food as "fuel," the series appears to veer toward presenting neurological difference as stereotypically machinelike, common in portrayals of autists. Yet his difference, which is not explicitly defined or categorized, is somewhat softened by the emergence of the character of Fiona Helbron (Betty Gilpin) in season 4. Fiona is crucial in establishing Sherlock as not-Other in the way of neurological differences, and she is principally there to claim that she *is* different and that Sherlock is not like her. This presents a reductive view of autism, particularly in the way it is portrayed.

Fiona is introduced in an episode as part of a case, and later becomes Sherlock's romantic interest. The dynamics of her introduction and her relationship with Sherlock are of particular concern here, since they enable both an exploration of the presentation of autistic characters and a subsequent reconsideration of Sherlock's neurological state. At first she is a coder involved in a murder ("Murder Ex Machina," 4:9), but we know of her autism before we see her face. As the scene cuts to the boardroom where she, Sherlock, and Watson are placed, we hear her voice: "Autism is a spectrum." Several earlier mentions of her have been linked with her difference, such as "She's kinda weird." Her boss, when questioned whether she could have been involved in the murder, argues that "she can't hurt anyone" and that he "knows what's in her head." His description is initially unclear to us, since we haven't been directly introduced to her yet. Her autism is positioned as an alibi, with her boss again repeating how it makes her innocent: "Her *con-*

dition makes it virtually impossible for her to lie." This assessment relies on particular stereotypes of the autistic condition that are reflected in her behavior. She avoids eye contact, maintains very closed body language, and speaks in the matter-of-fact way we have become used to seeing with screen characters associated with autism. In some ways, she functions as an on-screen educator for audiences as she explains key aspects of autism and terminology useful for categorizing difference. She is neuro-atypical, whereas Joan Watson, she states, is neurotypical. When it comes to Sherlock, she "doesn't know what" he is. Yet she recognizes his efforts to appear "normal," telling him at the end of the episode, "You have good manners, you must try hard."

Fiona's presentation—she spits information out in a robotic way—is in line with that of other autistic characters onscreen and notably in line with machines such as a car with which she is closely connected in her initial introduction. As a coder, she works *within* the machine, a condition echoed later in the episode when her voice comes through the car speakers as she controls it. Here she is merged with the machine and *acts as* a machine. This machine-human union is further compounded by how the series positions her character and gives it limited development. We are shown Fiona in contexts meant to facilitate our understanding of her as an autistic character. Her behavior modulates slightly when she is placed in a cat café, for example: she is comfortable there and makes increased eye contact. But any story-line recaps for her arc always begin with Fiona's explanation of autism, stressing her condition before describing other aspects of her. Thus, she functions primarily as a signifier of autism—and one beset by stereotypes—rather than a character in her own right. Sherlock's treatment of her also marks her as someone needing to be protected, since, he argues, she is "more sensitive than the average woman." A relationship with him would "not be good for her," and as with her boss, Fiona's decisions as an autistic woman are taken away from her, which further defines her as vulnerable or incapable.

The Fiona story line continues as Sherlock grapples with the difficulties of dating someone neuro-atypical. He undertakes research on how to approach his relationship with her, and she accuses him of acting differently around her because she is different. She states that he sees her as a puzzle or a project to be undertaken. Here, *Elementary* seemingly attempts to atone for its limited portrayal of autistic characters, with Sherlock claiming that his stilted behavior is due to his difference, not hers. This attempt at leveling difference relies on the audience's acceptance of Sherlock's eccentricity, a characteristic modulated differently in the UK and US shows. It is clearly stressed that Fiona is an Other, given the mentions of her as sensitive, different, innocent, special, and weird. Sherlock's move to making her the "normal" one in their relationship cannot obscure the caricatured way in which her character functions.

It is also useful to note her gender, given the ways in which women present autism. Women receive diagnoses later than males, and at a lower rate. In discussions of female autism, researchers note that "females require more severe autistic symptoms and greater cognitive and behavioral problems to meet ASC criteria" (Bargiela, Steward, and Mandy 2016, 3281). Thus there is research into a female autism phenotype, a particular presentation of a condition that is altered by gender. Women with autism are less likely to have externalizing behaviors, it was shown, and popular representations influence how quickly young women are diagnosed, by affecting perceptions of them as autistic. Fiona's behaviors and markers are those more commonly seen in male representations, which are currently the most common on television. The characters mentioned earlier here who are coded as autistic are all male. Fiona's characterization stands out.

The presentation of Fiona relies on stereotypes broadly recognizable as associated with an autist, and they are used to mark out Sherlock's veering toward the neurotypical end of the spectrum. This connection is in line with the way female characters are used in BBC's *Sherlock* for normalizing aspects of the principal character. Here we find a response to the frequent understanding of the relationship between Holmes and Watson in the series as homoerotic. Fans have speculated about whether they have a romantic attachment, as has been noted in recent scholarship on the series (Porter 2013; Stein and Busse 2012). The talented schemer Irene Adler, then, is introduced as a heterosexual foil for the perceived queerness of the relationship between Sherlock and Holmes. An indication of Sherlock's heterosexual attraction works to neutralize audience speculation. With *Elementary*, this isn't necessary, because of the (convenient) gender switch of Watson; heterosexuality becomes the clear norm onscreen. But the Sherlock-Joan relationship is never made sexual, so what needs "normalization" in the US version of the character is not his sexuality but his neurological state.

Theorizing Change

In attempting to outline the reasons for these shifts in *Elementary*, we cannot ignore the format in which we find the character. Unlike *Sherlock*, which was shot in three hour-long episodes per season (and for airing in North

America, sliced into slottable pieces), *Elementary* follows from the start a traditional pattern for US prime-time TV, of twenty-four forty-five-minute episodes a season. The series falls generically into the crime-procedural category, with every episode focused on the solving of a particular case, overlaid by longer, season-long story arcs, for example, a murder plot against Sherlock's father. The adherence to this formula illuminates how Sherlock Holmes is presented as a more toned-down—as in less transgressive or familiar—version of the character in the BBC version. US crime procedurals are awash with eccentric leads who break the rules and are attached to (often) female sidekicks, as with *Law and Order* (franchise; 1990–) or *Castle* (2009–2016). Terrence Rafferty (2012) notes that the gender switch of Watson allowed for *Elementary* to fall in line with other shows featuring "eccentric male investigators." This trope is so prevalent that it is known widely as the "defective detective," and is seen as well in series such as *CSI* (franchise; 2000–) and *House* (2004–2012). In *Elementary*, Sherlock's difference needs to be a "quirk," as Doherty describes, not a diagnosable condition; otherwise, it risks altering the formula of the procedural. Hence the introduction of Fiona, who serves to reduce Sherlock's characterization to one of eccentricity or quirkiness. The confluence of the Sherlock Holmes character with the genre results in a hybrid version of the figure that appears to be defined more by format than by audience expectation. Holmes has been molded to fit a particular narrative, and instead of being marked out by difference, his character becomes like others that typically front crime and problem-solving procedurals.

Jonny Lee Miller is coded as autistic far less strongly than Benedict Cumberbatch, but the audience reads the autism clearly, principally because the character is Sherlock Holmes. That subsequent portrayals of autism contribute to and are subject to this framework complicates the understanding of what autistic viewers would consider "authentic." Although Fiona's portrayal in *Elementary* may edge closer toward realism, it remains the figure of Sherlock in recent adaptations that audiences are inclined to see and understand as a representation of autism. Like the filmic stereotypes of autism invoked by *Rain Man*, Sherlock has become a repository for televisual stereotypes. Although *Elementary* makes an attempt to distinguish Holmes as different rather than autistic through the inclusion of an explicitly autistic character, the attempt is fleeting. Fiona is given much less screen time than Sherlock Holmes or almost any of the other main characters, and is shown in reductive terms. What these recent versions of the Sherlock figure have done is to encode in modern terms our understanding of the character as autistic, coloring the perspective of Sherlock's past, present, and future. The positioning of *Sherlock* and *Elementary* in the web of Holmes texts serves to strengthen the audience's ability to diagnose the detective, rightly or not.

Note

1. I refer to people on the spectrum with the term "Autistic Spectrum Condition," rather than the more common "Autism Spectrum Disorder." This usage is in line with that of other scholars who refuse to situate autism as a disorder.

CHAPTER 7

She's So Unusual: The Autist in *Stranger Things*

BRENDA AUSTIN-SMITH

Some boys take a beautiful girl
And hide her away from the rest of the world.
CYNDI LAUPER, "GIRLS JUST WANT TO HAVE FUN"

Unsurprisingly, film and television have a complicated relationship with autists as characters. Depictions of those with Autism Spectrum Disorder have been part of both big and small screen productions at least since *Run Wild, Run Free* (1969), starring Mark Lester (from *Oliver*) in the lead role of a noncommunicative child searching for a white horse on the English moors. Characters with symptoms suggestive of ASD have become more prominent onscreen, moving from the uncredited periphery of a film such as *Change of Habit* (1969), in which Lorena Kirk plays an autist named Amanda, to influential star turns by Dustin Hoffman in *Rain Man* (1988) and Tom Hanks in *Forrest Gump* (1994). On television, characters exhibiting autistic behavior have appeared in several otherwise standard television medical and detective shows such as *Sherlock* (2010–2017) and *The Good Doctor* (2017–). Just as legal dramas and police procedurals often feature a protagonist with a disability (obsessive-compulsive disorder in *Monk* [2002–2009]), gambling in *Cracker* [1993–1996], alcoholism in *Prime Suspect* [1991–2006]), occupying the autism spectrum is often treated as an entertaining complication for a character whose place and agency in the story line is largely determined by genre. Behaviors associated with autism such as attachment to routines or attention to detail are worked into plots as advantages for those who can solve a murder mystery or legal problem by detecting patterns others do not see. Rarely is an autist associated with a talent that is not intellectual in nature.

Main characters on television associated with autistic behaviors also tend to be white and male. Noting the absence of other identity markers in the best known of these screen autists, Malcolm Matthews writes of them as exemplars of what he calls an "aesthetic of autism" that links "technocentric intellect" with whiteness (2019, 57). It is easy for such characterizations to slip into stereotypes of the awkward genius—Sheldon Cooper in *The Big Bang Theory* (2007–2019) comes unavoidably to mind. The symptoms these characters exhibit are usually those of savant syndrome, as well as discomfort with group activities, crowds, and emotionally charged situations. Anthony D. Baker sees most films about autists as following what he calls "The Autistic Formula," and his checklist has relevance for television as well. Among Baker's narrative boxes (which are typical of film narratives in general) are the introduction of a non-autist hero; the appearance of someone with traits credibly read as autistic; the autist's passivity and reliance on a neurotypical caregiver; the treatment of ASD as spectacle; the separation of the autist from a parent; and the rescuing of the vulnerable, engaging, and endangered autist by the hero, who often becomes a replacement parent (Baker 2008).

But one of the most popular television series currently airing stars a young girl whose presentation in the show refreshes elements of this formula as well as the media characterizations of someone who can be read as autistic. Neither a numbers whiz nor a human compass with no other purpose than to guide other characters along the route to personal growth, Eleven in *Stranger Things* (2016–) is, without being diagnosed by the script or others as an autist, what Christina Belcher and Kimberly Maich call an "incognito" autist (2014,

104). In combining the otherworldliness found in *E.T. the Extra-Terrestrial* (1982) with the powers seen in *Carrie* (1976), El may be the first female autistic superhero of the small screen.

The Duffer Brothers' Netflix series *Stranger Things* has entranced viewers and critics for its film and pop-cultural references. The horror-comedy, something of a nostalgia basket, is chock full of rummagings through the cultural filing cabinet of film nostalgia, weaving bits of *Star Wars* (1977), *Blow-Up* (1966), *The Conversation* (1974), *Jurassic Park* (1993), and *Poltergeist* (1982), among others, into everything from its title design to its plot points. Though focused on a group of young boys, the series's most important figure is the mysterious Eleven (Millie Bobby Brown), a young girl who speaks in monosyllables and has telekinetic and biokinetic powers. Here, I discuss the first and second seasons of *Stranger Things* to argue that Eleven's characterization as socially awkward and nearly nonverbal suggests that she may be on the autism spectrum. El has superpowers, limited language skills, and an inordinate fondness for Eggo waffles (a quirky, specific attraction that suggests the kind of fixed attachment associated with autism spectrum disorder). She is magical and marginal at once, transforming the savant qualities of other autistic characters audiences have seen in media into those of an action hero through her translation of thought into strength.

At the same time, what makes El (as she is nicknamed by her friend, Mike [Finn Wolfhard]) distinct in the depiction of autists on television is her central role in conquering the evil that threatens her town, in this case, the monstrous forces of the Upside Down. While the show observes Baker's formula in many ways, and endows Eleven with abilities that are indeed spectacular, the series also handles her atypicality in ways that diverge from the exclusively spectacularized moments that Baker and others criticize. The show does not depict autism in realistic ways, and does not undo misunderstandings and misrepresentations of ASD in the media, but it does offer an unusual take on the autist as hero that is worth exploring.

El's appearance in the town of Hawkins in 1983 follows the disappearance of Will Byers (Noah Schnapp), who crashes his bike after encountering something terrifying on the road near the Hawkins Lab while riding home with his friend Dustin (Gaten Matarazzo) after a game of Dungeons and Dragons. The camera in "The Vanishing of Will Byers" (1:1) focuses on a pair of bare feet walking hesitantly through the dead leaves of a forest floor and then pausing. A tilt travels up the body of a child wearing a partly torn, dirty institutional gown and settles on the child's face and shaven head. This is El. We see her enter a diner, where she is caught stealing food by the owner, Benny (Chris Sullivan), who then feeds her and calls social services to report her as missing and likely abused. Benny's supposition is correct though incomplete, as flashbacks show El in the Hawkins Lab, subjected to traumatizing situations and experiments. What no one knows yet is that El and the monster that abducted Will escaped from the lab at the same time. Used as a test subject by Dr. Brenner (Matthew Modine) in experiments on astral projection as a form of Cold War spying, El accidentally makes contact with another realm, later dubbed the Upside Down. Encouraged by Brenner to make physical contact with the monster in a subsequent experiment, El screams in terror when the monster turns to face her after she touches it. The contact between them and the reverberations of El's cries shatter the wall of the lab, allowing the Demogorgon access to the world of Hawkins. In the confusion, El runs away from the lab, but is pursued by those she calls "bad men" throughout the first season of the show.

Eleven's escape from the lab carries with it a host of other associations, many of them filmic and some more historically significant. She arrives at the diner without shoes, and with numbers tattooed on her forearm. The allusion to a concentration camp survivor is obvious, as is the initial impression that she may be a resident of a psychiatric institution, given media clichés about the dirty hospital gowns that such residents wear. There are also muted references to El as a kind of Frankenstein's monster: powerful, misunderstood, and excluded. In the episode "Trick or Treat, Freak" (2:2), for example, we see her watching *Frankenstein* (1931) on television in Sheriff Hopper's cabin. Like that literary and cinematic creature, El has been damaged by scientific hubris, in her case by Brenner, the man she refers to as "Papa" and who has deprived her of a conventional childhood by using her as a point of contact between Hawkins and a strange, malevolent force that inhabits an underground labyrinth of squelching tunnels. At one point in "The Flea and the Acrobat" (1:5), Lucas (Caleb McLaughlin), one of the four friends who discovers El hiding in the woods, points accusingly to her: "Maybe she is the monster!" before being thrown against a bus by El's telekinetic powers. And after saving Mike from the bullies who make him jump off a cliff, El lies exhausted on the ground in despair, telling him that she has inadvertently opened the gate to the Upside Down: "I'm sorry. I'm the monster." As with Mary Shelley's creature, the greatest risk to El is being misunderstood as indiscriminately dangerous, even though her intentions are not malevolent but protective. Mike shelters her in his basement, exactly the way Elliott hides the abandoned alien in *E.T.*

El's atypical characterization in season one leads to misinterpretations and even prejudice against her. She presents as ambiguously gendered, and is identified as a young boy in early reports to the Hawkins police force.

She seems to be merely distrustful and excruciatingly shy when Benny finds her stealing food in his diner, but her social discomfort persists throughout the series, as does her difficulty with verbal communication. While El does speak, her vocabulary is very limited and shows evidence of echolalia, her words repeated from the speech of others. "Pretty," "promise," she repeats after Will in "Holly Jolly" (1:3). El struggles with concepts such as friendship and seems to lack what is called a "theory of mind"—it is difficult for her to imagine other people thinking beyond what she herself thinks and does. Like many other media dramatizations of people with ASD, El cannot stomach withholding or dishonesty of any sort. She repeats what Mike has told her: "Friends don't lie." This intolerance results in significant conflict between El and Sheriff Hopper (David Harbour), who deceives El in order to protect her from discovery and persecution in season two. It is impossible for El to reconcile what for her are opposing intentions, or to imagine a situation in which lying in order to keep someone safe could make sense for someone else.

Another mark of El's characterization as someone with atypical tendencies is her oversensitivity to certain sensations. We see the first sign of her telekinesis when she is eating in Benny's diner in the first episode of the series. As the sound of a warped electric fan begins to dominate the soundtrack and become ever more irritating, the noise interrupts El's enjoyment of her fries. She pauses, looks up and over at the fan, lowers her head, and directs a concentrated frowning gaze in the direction of the offending gadget as the camera moves in to a medium close-up of her face. A cut to the fan shows it suddenly coming to a stop. Later in this same episode when she is given a place to stay by Mike, she flinches as he reaches out to touch her tattooed arm, starts at the sound of thunder, and strokes her cheek with the clothes Mike hands her from a nearby laundry basket in a gesture suggestive of stimming, comforting herself and soothing her anxiety through the feel of the fabric.

That someone, especially a child, would experience profound oversensitivity to sound and touch after the deprivations of the Hawkins Lab is not a surprise. But as season two reveals, El is not the only survivor of Brenner's experiments. In "The Lost Sister" (2:7), El takes a bus to Chicago after learning of another girl who was subject to the same mistreatment. Arriving alone in the city, El uses her visionary ability to locate Kali (Linnea Berthelsen), a young Black woman who leads a crew of self-described outcasts who rob in order to fund the assassinations of those they deem responsible for what happened to Kali at the lab. Kali and El initially bond and share experiences not just of their horrific years at the hands of Brenner (signaled by the numbers tattooed on their arms—Kali is "008"), but also of their extraordinary gifts. Kali uses her ability to make people hallucinate when she and her group need to escape capture after their crimes. Fleeing from a heist in a van with her friends, Kali makes the pursuing police slam on their brakes and swerve to avoid what seems to be a collapsing road tunnel in front of them. Kali encourages El to draw on her reserves of rage to develop and hone her telekinesis, and invites El to join the group in their vigilante crusade. Up to this point, El has not demonstrated much control over her gift. Her terror inadvertently opened the gate for the Demogorgon in season one, and in season two her frustration at being confined provokes a tantrum that smashes all the windows in Hopper's cabin. What she learns from Kali is the strategic value of emotional self-regulation.

Though El comes along on one of the group missions to kill a former security guard at the lab, and uses her powers to begin choking the man when they have tracked him to his house, she falters when she catches sight of a photograph of the target with his family members. As it turns out, his two daughters are in another room of the home, and El cannot continue with the mission. The resulting confrontation clarifies the differences between El and Kali. While El is willing to harm and even kill to keep herself and her friends safe from immediate threats (we have seen her dispatch several agents who worked for or with the Hawkins Lab), she is not willing to use violence to settle past scores. Kali's focus on revenge clashes with El's focus doing no more harm than is necessary to ensure her and her friends' survival. "They cannot help you," says Kali as El prepares to go back to Hawkins. "No, but I can help them," says El.

Although the loss of this connection is registered in a match cut that shows both El and Kali gazing sadly out the windows of vehicles moving in different directions—El heading back to her small town, and Kali returning to the hideout—the episode confirms more than the moral direction of each of these characters. Though each has been damaged by Brenner, and each has experienced deprivation and manipulation in the lab, Kali does not exhibit symptoms that would lead a viewer to conclude that she is an autist. She does not demonstrate the same social discomfort, physical awkwardness, and stilted verbal communication that El does. And Kali's gift for making others see things is effective precisely because she has a theory of mind and can imagine other people's worries and fears. That's why she gives her friend Axel (James Landry Hébert) a vision of spiders crawling up his arm in order to stop him from menacing El. What Kali's verbal and social skills, and her ability to understand the emotional states of others, show (as when she senses El's hesitancy to kill the guard, or urges El to set aside her loyalty to the band of friends back in Hawkins) is that El's time in the lab was not the sole cause of her symptoms. If it were, Kali would share the same or similar ones. El's atypical symptoms are not, then, explained by post-traumatic stress disorder, though there is no denying that her time in the lab was traumatic.

The "Lost Sister" episode has received a fair degree of criticism. Some viewers felt it was a narrative misstep, cut off as it was from the supply of cultural nostalgia that fueled season one's depiction of children battling evil while negotiating preadolescence in a small town. But others observed that the episode did equal disservice to Black characters in the series, effectively relegating them to urban spaces and refusing in particular to give Kali any real characterization aside from being a supernatural angry Black woman who trades in the kind of violence stereotypically associated with Black people. The absence of any obvious ASD symptoms in Kali (other than an overemphasized lack of empathy with her targets) also does nothing to disturb Matthews's aesthetics of autism.

The community of children into which El wanders as the series begins is oddly suited to receive her. In the first episode of season one we see a group of middle-school boys play Dungeons & Dragons (D&D), the role-playing board game that dominates basement rec rooms in the cultural imaginary of the 1980s. As the scene progresses, we learn that Lucas, Will, Dustin, and Mike have been playing for ten hours in a row. Mike, as dungeon master, dramatically announces that the Demogorgon has come for their characters, putting pressure on Will to do something to save the other players in the campaign. Will launches an attack on the game figure of the Demogorgon by rolling dice, but the number he throws is obscured when the dice fall off the board. As the boys pack up to leave Mike's house, Will confesses to Mike that he threw only a seven, which wasn't powerful enough to stop the attack. "The Demogorgon—it got me," he says before riding away on his bike into the darkness and, only moments later, being captured by the real-world version of a Demogorgon, a monster escaped from the Upside Down by way of the Hawkins Laboratory.

The four friends gathered in Mike's basement are total nerds—geeks, even. They obsess over D&D campaigns, belong to the school's AV Club (their equally nerdy teacher refers to them as the "nonathletic kids"), and stick largely to themselves. They are mocked and bullied for their looks and interests, and in Dustin's case, for the way he speaks. (The actor who plays Dustin has cleidocranial dysplasia, which was written into the script as a reason why other kids torment him on the school grounds.) Mike's immediate fascination with El when they meet her in the woods is a threat to the group's closeness and a distraction from their primary mission. "We went out to find Will, not another problem," says Lucas, making an argument for leaving El out in the rain where they found her. El's appearance on their social horizon allows Dustin and Lucas to pull rank in their closed and gendered social hierarchy, subjecting El to a grilling as insensitive as anything they have likely suffered. "Do you have cancer?" asks Dustin. "At least she can talk," says Mike. "She said 'no' and 'yes,'" says Lucas. "Your three-year-old sister says more. There's something seriously wrong with her. Like, wrong in the head." Lucas in particular is suspicious of El and resistant to admitting her into the group. He refers to her repeatedly as a "psycho" and guesses that she is "an escapee" from a local institution called Pennhurst. As a Black kid, Lucas has probably endured a lot of racism, and Dustin knows what it feels like to be teased for having a disability. The presence of El gives these characters someone to feel pity for and anger at, in a complex response to her differences from them and to their anxieties about their own contingent status in a social landscape that privileges neurotypical white kids.

Kayla McCarthy observes in an article on the role of geek culture and nostalgia in *Stranger Things* that the term "geek" can be both pejorative and complimentary. The archetypal geek in media, usually "a white, straight male, exhibits primarily three qualities: (i) propensity for science and technology; (ii) social awkwardness; and (iii) near-obsessive interest in science fiction and fantasy genres" (2019, 664). The geek is also associated with nonhegemonic and "uncool" white masculinity (664). Mike, Lucas, Dustin, and Will embody all of these geek markers, and in their geekdom lies their strength. As McCarthy notes, the knowledge the boys have of ham radios and D&D allows them to save their hometown from the Upside Down, validating their obsessive interest in technology and complex board-game campaigns. At their school, the senior dreamboat Steve "The Hair" Harrington (Joe Keery) may be popular with girls like Nancy (Natalia Dyer), but it is the geek group of Lucas, Mike, and Dustin who realize that the Upside Down poses an immediate threat to their world and who use their knowledge of ham radio technology, supersaturation, and D&D to fight the Demogorgon.

Whenever the boys need access to something usually off-limits—such as the key to the AV Club room or more library books on lizards—they invoke the AV Club teacher's inspirational phrase that they are on a "curiosity voyage." It is in this spirit of scientific discovery that the boys encounter El as something intriguing and mysterious, kind of like Dart, the baby Demodog that Dustin finds and temporarily adopts in "The Pollywog" (2:3). As both an autist and a girl, El presents differences from the boys that they have not encountered before. They are surprised, for example, that she can use one of their walkie-talkies to make contact with Will in the Upside Down. In a way, El's special powers embody the boys' own interests in electricity, conduction, and radio waves, which suggests an affinity between them, especially given the boys' marked social exclusion. El is eventually accepted into the group and even admired—Dustin says at one point, "We never would have upset you if we knew you had superpowers." But more than anything else, El is safe with them. The nerdy boys who are by turns fascinated by and wary of her would never turn her over to the "bad men" from the lab or expose her to danger. And though they are impressed by her telekinesis (Dustin says to a pair of bullies thwarted by El, "She's our friend, and she's crazy"), none of them try to force her to use it in their interests. In fact, after her escape from the Hawkins Lab, El is never again exploited for her power, and she uses her telekinesis when she wants to, not when someone else wants.

El is the most important character in *Stranger Things*, tracing a developmental arc in the narrative that nods to Baker's "Autistic Formula" but that also departs from it in crucial ways. El exhibits enough visible symptoms of ASD to be credibly labeled autistic, and she conforms to some of the other formulaic depictions of autists in film and television. For example, she was separated from her mother by Brenner, who kidnapped El because of her telekinetic power. Though El calls Brenner "Papa," it is unthinkable that he is her biological father. He is, though, another manifestation of monstrosity in the series. El is also naïve about complex social situations, as when we see her walk through a rough area of Chicago as she searches for Kali in "The Lost Sister." But her obliviousness of those around her is also a function of her determination to find her sister from the lab. El consistently acts with agency and focus throughout seasons one and two, setting her apart from many other onscreen autists. Media autists are often characterized as passive and as needing constant instruction, guidance, and protection from a non-ASD person such as a doctor or a reluctantly conscripted family member like Charlie Babbitt in *Rain Man*. El begins the series effectively parentless and alone, but she does not remain dependent on a neurotypical caregiver to complete her tasks or care for her. She is neither cute nor quirky, qualities that Baker highlights as typical of film autists, and has none of the makings of the savant sidekicks whose sole purpose seems to inspire non-ASD characters to become better people.

We see El assert her independence first when she runs away from the boys after stopping Lucas from attacking Mike in "The Flea and the Acrobat" (1:5). Mike shouts at her, and El takes off into the woods in remorse for having hurt Lucas in a moment of emotional overload. She then steals Eggos from a local store and smashes the doors with her powers as she leaves. In season two, El chafes under the confinement that Hopper has imposed to keep her safe, and leaves the cabin first to find her mother, Terry Ives, and then to look for Kali, traveling to Chicago and back again on her own. We also learn in one of El's flashbacks in season two that after escaping the Upside Down, she lived in the woods on her own, hunting for food and stealing a warm jacket from a hunter after knocking him unconscious. El is self-sufficient and steadfast, fixed on her own goals. She is also angry and defiant—her tantrum in "Will the Wise" (2:4) breaks all of the windows in Hopper's cabin—and by no means fits the conventional media image of the autist as passive and incapable.

El's telekinetic powers are so visually and narratively extraordinary that they threaten to turn her into a spectacle, a tendency in many films about autism that associate the condition with fascinating card tricks, mathematical abilities, or even miraculous cures (Baker 2008). But El's identity as an autist is incidental to her powers, as her reunion with Kali demonstrates. El's ASD symptoms coincide with her telekinesis but are not the source of it. Her powers are desired by the villainous Brenner and his henchmen, but after bolting from the lab, El decides when and on whom to use her gifts, learning over the course of the first two seasons how to control her energy. Baker's formula for what he terms the autism plot of film and television concludes with the endangered autist's rescue by a non-ASD hero, and the hero's replacement of the autist's missing family. This is not the path taken by *Stranger Things*. Sheriff Hopper shelters El in season two and becomes her adoptive father, but he is not the hero of the series: El is the hero. In her ability to discipline and direct her powers, and in her bravery in facing the Demogorgon in season one and closing the gate under the Hawkins Lab (2:9), she is the one who summons all her physical and mental resources to save her town and her friends.

El's role in the first eighteen episodes of *Stranger Things* is tinged by excesses reminiscent of melodrama. She is a victim of horrendously cruel treatment by Brenner, and each flashback of her time in the Hawkins Lab emphasizes the physical and psychological suffering she endured there. As the series progresses, El gains more and more control over her powers, and as her relationships with Will and Hopper grow and deepen, her sense of how best to use those powers takes shape. This character arc has much in common with that of other superhero figures who must learn to discipline their extraordinary gifts in the name of something other than personal vengeance. The extremes of these dramatizations at times leave little room for

El's atypicality to express itself in more ordinary ways, threatening to diminish our sense of her personhood and reduce her to a plot device.

There are, though, moments that offer viewers something other than El suffering punishment in the lab after refusing to harm a caged cat, or El demonstrating visually extravagant displays of telekinetic wonder as she pins the Demogorgon against the wall of a classroom. These more mundane scenes are critical in undoing the flattening and dehumanizing effects of the spectacular aspect that Baker identifies in many films about autists, and they restore to us a sense of El's idiosyncratic personality. There is El's delight in making Mike's dad's recliner move back and forth, and her curiosity about Mike's sister's room and the ballerina figure that decorates the jewelry box on the dresser. There is also her love of waffles and her inability to resist Hopper's description of the "Triple-Decker Eggo Extravaganza" that he is going to have without her if she doesn't come out of her room in "The Pollywog" (2:3).

Perhaps even more than her love for Eggos, El's attraction to Mike, and his to her, is one of the most genuine things about *Stranger Things*. Like other preteen girls, El becomes concerned about her looks and about whether Mike still likes her: "Still pretty?" she asks him nervously, having decided to ditch the blonde wig in "The Bathtub" (1:7). Without infantilizing her or waving away her differences in a gush of puppy love, the first two seasons forgo a recovery narrative for El, crediting her desire and affection for Mike, and his for her, as no big deal. She may be autistic, and may also be a superhero, but as she and Mike try to figure out how to slow dance in the school gym, El is just a girl who wants to have fun.

CHAPTER 8

Autism, Performance, and Sociality: Isolated Attention in *The Social Network*

ELLIOTT LOGAN

I don't want friends.

MARK ZUCKERBERG IN *THE SOCIAL NETWORK*

The lasting impact of David Fincher's *The Social Network* (2010) surely has its deepest source in Dustin Hoffman's performance in *Rain Man* twenty-two years before. As Jason Jacobs notes in his appreciation of Hoffman's work, the actor inhabits a character "who is both human and apparently without a legible interior, a mindedness that most of us watching any other film would recognize in a character even if we did not share it" (2018, 213). Raymond's mindedness, however illegible, is nevertheless and undeniably there. It is in front of us to be seen. Raymond's "is a face that demonstrates continuous activity just below the edge of blankness," thus evoking a "unity," Jacobs argues, "between the rapid-yet-droning urgency of his voice and the laser-sighted notice of order disrupted that is communicated by his eyes" (218). Through Hoffman's performance, *Rain Man* achieves its power as a picture of autism by presenting us with a person whose individuality we might come to identify and cleave to even as it remains impossibly distant—even alien—from our own.

Increasingly, however, films and television programs present characters whose autism is less profound, who sit nearer to the high-functioning end of the autism spectrum, and whose expressiveness and interiority is therefore more legible, less impenetrable, less alien. How is our fascination with spectacles of profound autism linked with performances of less severe autistic behavior, or with those that evoke autistic qualities without explicitly depicting autism as such? What attracts us to these performances, and what does that attraction speak to or reveal?

The performance of autism—or of behaviors we associate with autism—offers a way to dramatically amplify the difficulties and risks of sociality, those of confronting and responding to other people, of negotiating the claims that others make on us, along with our potential failures of them. They may also point to a fantasy of immunity from those claims. In doing so, performances of autism offer more than developed images of the condition, whether accurate or not. They can also give expression to the deeper concerns that autistic conditions evoke among some neurotypicals, and thus reveal the hidden nerves that are touched by our ideas of autism. *The Social Network* offers a rich example of this kind of portrayal, in which the suggestion of autism is used to picture a more widespread cultural condition. Fincher's film tells the story of Mark Zuckerberg's (Jesse Eisenberg) invention of Facebook during his time at Harvard University, where he started the website with the help of his roommates at Kirkland House, especially his closest friend, Eduardo Saverin (Andrew Garfield). Interwoven with the events of Facebook's origin are the legal conflicts that ensued in its aftermath: Zuckerberg is sued not only by Eduardo but also by Cameron and Tyler Winklevoss (both played by Armie Hammer), who claim the website was stolen from them. The film thus moves back and forth between the energetic creation of a new kind of social space and the static, acidic environment of hostile legal depositions. At its core, then, *The Social Network* is about the psychological forces that corrode and destroy Mark and Eduardo's friendship: forces expressed in behavior that we might describe as autistic and that is performed and given significance through motifs of isolation and attention. These motifs, I argue, speak to a desire for masterful remove from the social world, a desire that paradoxically emerges as a response to one's need for a full and satisfying inclusion in it.

Breaking Up

The Social Network opens on sounds of community. Over the Columbia Pictures logo, we hear the opening guitar chords of the White Stripes track "Ball and Biscuit," music that we soon place in a crowded bar as the song mixes with the clink of beer glasses and a hubbub of background chatter. The film thus calls for our attention before we likely expect it to. We might have been caught off guard, but we now tune our ears to the noise, searching its blurred shapes for the clear outlines of meaningful talk—looking for a way in, a way to share in what others are saying. This readies us to receive the film's opening line, which, as the Columbia logo fades to black, is spoken by Jesse Eisenberg at a quick clip: "Did you know there are more people with genius IQs living in China than there are people of any kind living in the United States?" His female companion, who we still do not see, the screen remaining black, replies in disbelief, "That can't possibly be true." Eisenberg's response is immediate and final: "It is." The line is swift and flat in its declarative tone, his words cutting off room for consideration of hers. In its opening moments, then, before we see any sights from the film's world, *The Social Network* asks its viewer to listen for conversation. But we might question whether it is true conversation that we hear.

The tempo and tenor of Eisenberg's vocal delivery come to be a defining feature of his performance as Mark Zuckerberg, and this is crucial to the film's treatment of attention as a key to social connection. The actor's frequently rapid and arrhythmic speech patterns—together with, in this role, his generally muted range of facial expression and his twitching, spasmodically blinking eyes, which often wander as they avoid contact with others—inflect Mark's manner with traits that some would read as autistic. In the opening scene, these qualities of expression introduce Mark's tendency to talk at, or past, people rather than to speak with them. The film thus opens on a social failure in which the risks of interacting with others are laid bare.

Just after Mark flatly declares his own correctness—"It is"—the image fades in to join the opening sounds of the bar and its sights. We see Mark sitting opposite a young woman, Erica Albright (Rooney Mara), who asks what would account for this scarcely believable number of Chinese geniuses.

> MARK: Well, first, an awful lot of people live in China. But here's my question: How do you distinguish yourself in a population of people who all got 1600 on their SATs?
> ERICA (LOOKING AROUND): I didn't know they take SATs in China.

MARK: They don't. I wasn't talking about China anymore. I was talking about me.

It is not that Erica speaks substantially more slowly than Mark. She is trying to keep up with her date, so Rooney Mara plays her line about SATs as part of a sharp back-and-forth. But Eisenberg doesn't have Mark simply speak quickly. Here as elsewhere in the film, he talks like a living telex machine, automatically stamping out the words he speaks. Eisenberg thus suggests Mark's single-minded focus on the transmission of what he has to say, without interest or concern for its reception or its receiver.

Yet Mark's reception by others, their concomitant perceptions of him, become the subject of his words as he and Erica go on to discuss how he can "distinguish" himself in the Harvard population, whether by singing in an a capella group, inventing a twenty-five-dollar PC, or rowing crew. Erica, knowing what is on Mark's mind, teasingly warns him that a capella singing might be seen by some women as slightly less than masculine, and suggests that he could "get into a final club"—final clubs being the all-male fellowship societies that, in Mark's world, represent the most exclusive route to social distinction. Erica's teasing manner when she suggests membership in a final club and Mark's echoing response in agreement ("Or I get into a final club") appear to put them on the same page. But as they continue to talk, they continually get their wires crossed. When Mark mentions that he obviously can't row crew (while also doubling back to answer her earlier question about his SAT score—"Yes, I got nothing wrong on the test"), Erica asks whether he has ever tried. "I'm trying right now," he says. "To row crew?" she asks. "To get into a final club," he corrects her, and then goes on, incredulously, "To row crew?! No. Are you, like, whatever, delusional?" Not only do the two of them not always know what the other is explicitly referring to, but Eisenberg also plays Mark as, for the most part, oblivious of what Erica's observations and questions implicitly mean.

Erica tries to share with him, through shadings and adjustments of her eyes, brow, mouth, and voice, playful insinuations about him and what he's saying. Mark is largely blind and deaf to her. Note how, while highlighting the low-wattage sex appeal of a capella singing, she relaxes back into her chair, smiling as though the idea of using membership in an a capella group to get girls is preposterous, and then flicking her gaze sideways, a sign of bored distraction that offers him a hint to drop the idea (and the subject?) but also, perhaps, gives an unconscious nod to her wandering eye, whose attention cannot be held by such unimpressive pursuits. It is a moment of performance in which Erica has fun telling the truth. So is the next moment, although the truth it conveys, and the fun in it, is badly mistaken by Mark. "This is serious," he tells Erica after her a capella quip, correcting her again, trying to force her point of view to fall in line with his own. He isn't in a mood for jokes or is unable, perhaps, to spot one. "On the other hand," replies Erica, not skipping a beat, turning her gaze back to Mark's and then lowering her eyes as though to confess a weakness, "I *do* like guys who row crew." With that, her eyes deliberately roll upward to meet his with a droll irony, as though to silently convey her complete lack of interest in guys like that, perhaps her lack of interest in types at all, and instead to signal her desire to spend time and attention on whoever can earn it. "Well, I can't do that," Mark replies. In contrast with Erica's playful irony, Eisenberg speaks the line with earnest regret, tinged by Mark's bitter, swallowed frustration at being unable to occupy a prestigious and exclusive spot in the social order, a spot for which he is not built. Erica nearly bursts out laughing as she tells him she was "kidding," in disbelief at the blatancy of his misreading. What kind of person could miss those kinds of cues, she wonders (and leads the viewer to wonder, too)?

It is only now, having admitted to this lack of athletic ability—he could never conceivably be the kind of guy who rows crew—that Mark circles back to admit that, yes, he got nothing wrong on the SAT. But the line is not offered as an inflating boast. Mark looks down and away from Erica, to his right, his eyes on some featureless point on the floor. And Eisenberg forces the words out as though asked to say anything but to say it as quickly and blankly as possible. Mark's attention here is not introspective. His mind doesn't seem to turn inward. Instead, it seems to dart away from the person in front of him and momentarily alight on some distant sphere of remove, even as he continues to converse. Yet it remains hard to avoid the impression that Mark's present aversion to Erica is a defensive response to being rejected. Her ironic line about being attracted to guys who row crew was not meant as a refusal of Mark. Obsessed with how he might be seen, however, Mark cannot appreciate how Erica actually sees him. He is missing the fluency that she easily intuits, and that will cost him.

The Social Network's opening exchanges thus contrast Eisenberg's performance with Rooney's to highlight Mark's difficulty with interpersonal interaction. In this way, they establish the film's interest in sociality as a sometimes challenging effort, fraught with potential for misunderstanding and confusion and thus overlaid with a burden of risk. Of course, these are considerations that we navigate in almost any social encounter, and they are all the more treacherous as we grow closer to people. Our everyday social gambits, challenging to begin with, are made even more challenging—like an obstacle course of invisible tripwires—if we do not easily share in the un- spoken cues of those around us, if crucial signals sent via subtle undertones go unheard and thus unheeded, and if we are equally out of tune with the potentially injurious impacts of blunt-force fact (see the chapter by Murray Pomerance in this volume).

It is this last dimension of his social insensitivity that breaks Mark's re- lationship with Erica. The loose threads of their fledgling romance start to pull apart when Erica asks him which of the final clubs it is easiest to get into. He takes this as a slight, a noxious hint that she thinks him generally mediocre. Perhaps someone with a more confident sense of his relation to others could let the (unintended) implication—that is, what he reads as an implication—slide. Erica's question might say more about her than it does about him: that *she* is the kind of person to naturally look for the easiest or most likely path to a passable outcome rather than to seek out the hardest climb to the most intimidating heights. But it is telling that Mark, who we might expect to be secure in his vast intelligence, takes Erica's remark as a comment on *him*. He struggles to escape his own viewpoint—to understand and accept that others might see the world differently from the way he does. For Mark, Erica's question is like the raised edge of a tempting scab, and so he picks at it: "You asked me which one was the easiest to get into, because you think that that's the one where I'll have the best chance." They parry over her question's meaning, Mark finding offense in what he takes to be Erica's low aspirations for him, Erica recoiling from Mark's suggestion that through his membership in a final club he would introduce her to "a lot of people you wouldn't normally get to meet"—in other words, that he could conceivably be her best route to a new and better social world. Erica's clearly feigned appreciation of his gallantry ("You would do that for me?" she asks, in a sarcastic impression of feminine gratitude) is another joke that Mark fails to recognize. Looking Erica dead in the eye, but without so much as a smile, Mark shrugs: "We're dating." It is this moment, this expression from Mark, or perhaps this lack of fitting, suitably responsive expression, that moves Erica to break up with him.

At first Mark thinks this is another joke, but then, as the reality dawns, he scrambles to recover. As she moves to leave, he grabs her hand across the table. "Okay," he says, "then wait, I apologize," shaking his head in con- fusion, his furrowed brow and eyes searching the tabletop. Erica says that she has to go home to study, so Mark tries once more. "Erica," he says, "I'm sorry—I mean it." The moment is a centerpiece for the inflections of au- tism in Eisenberg's performance. As he says Erica's name, Mark appears to be drowning in muddled confusion, unsure of what he will do or say next. He is clutching at whatever might give him some hold on a rapidly dissolving situation. In the slight space that opens up after he regains Erica's attention, Mark's mouth stutters silently as he searches for words that aren't there, his eyes closed, eyelids twitching, head tilted away from Erica at an odd angle. And then, in a flash, he remembers what you are supposed to say in moments like this and how you are supposed to say it. Eisenberg snaps his stare back up to meet Erica's, his eyes and face held still, a snapshot of forced deliberateness. His "I'm sorry—I mean it" is rattled out all at once, the words coming out simply one after the other, their monotone leavened not by emotion but by their oddly rapid pace. Whatever feeling there is behind his words, he cannot find a route to its surface expression. The moment passes quickly—Erica insists that she is leaving to study, and Mark further fluffs his lines when he blurts out that she doesn't need to study, because "you go to BU." (Boston University isn't Harvard, in other words.) Erica walks out, leaving Mark at the table.

But Eisenberg's performance of Mark's earnest attempt at apology lingers. In that frozen, stilted moment, we glimpse something of the core qualities that draw our interest to him as a person whose expressive manner bears an autistic shading. Like all of us, Mark lives in a world where one's social success and acceptance depend on the effective negotiation of performance, on being able to read and respond to the slightest expressive subtleties with immediacy, accuracy, and agility. And in Mark, we see a person who is not beset by any clear disorder, but who is missing the skills of social interpretation and navigation that we might all fear, at any moment, could abandon us and leave us stranded—adrift and alone.

Embracing Isolation

Beginning with a breakup, *The Social Network* uses the origin story of Facebook to stage a drama about the desire for social standing as a marker of inclusion, and about the attendant pains and rewards of exclusion. Across the film, Mark pursues entry into a series of exclusive spaces where belonging will confer distinction and prestige, even as we see him increasingly retreat within spaces of isolation from the social world around him. The desired spaces of longed-for, imagined acceptance and recognition are the final clubs, especially the most out of reach among them all, the Porcellian. It is the Porcellian to which Mark gains teasing, partial access through his engagement with the Winklevoss twins, paragons of the eastern elite to whom he is drawn because they row crew. They invite him to discuss their idea for an online social network while standing in the club's "bicycle room." Harvard is one of the more exclusive spaces in American society, and Mark is continually invested in exclusivity as a value. For Mark, worthwhile belonging is demarcated by boundary lines that either admit people into a privileged sphere or prohibit them from consideration and entry, thus consigning them to invisibility. After moving to California to grow the website with venture capital funding, and coming under the tutelage of the charismatic Napster pioneer Sean Parker (Justin Timberlake), we see Mark in a San Francisco nightclub, again sitting across a table in conversation, but this time in the bottle-service mezzanine, perched above the masses of other people below.

The key spaces of exclusion in *The Social Network*, however, are not physical settings—they are mental ones. It is by cutting himself adrift from others—or by looking and stepping away from them—that Mark finds insulation from the risks of social encounter. In the opening scene, when he takes offense at Erica's question about the easiest final club to get into, her frustration with his incessant focus on their exclusivity boils over. "You're obsessed with finals clubs!" she says. "You have finals clubs OCD! You need to see someone about it who'll prescribe you some sort of medication. You don't care if the side effects may include blindness!" During Erica's outburst, Fincher cuts from Rooney to Eisenberg as he absorbs the impact of her words. Mark sits back from Erica, his head in a downward, sullen tilt. His eyes seem downcast even as they continue to stare at Erica, unmoving and seemingly unmoved. Then, as she tells him to see someone, he looks away from her, not out to the people or spaces around him but down to the fingertips of his own right hand, which he now extends to examine as though in disinterested consideration of a specimen or in pleased admiration of his own neat cuticles. It is at once a withdrawal and an extension of attention, a pulling of focus that draws Mark apart from Erica and that pushes her away from him. Eisenberg displays coolly controlled focus as a measured response to hidden hurt and rising humiliation. The actor's gesture thus resonates with Aaron Sorkin's writing as a deliberate display of uncaring "blindness," one that protects Mark from the pain of being seen. Against the communal hubbub of the Cambridge bar in which he sits, he thus carves out a space of self-isolation by refusing to pay attention to the person before him. And it is this ugly mood that seems to propel him as he leaves the bar in hurried embarrassment at the breakup and then—traced from on high and far away by Fincher's stalking camera, and ghosted by the buzzing melancholy of the film's brooding score—walks alone through the bustle of Harvard Square, back to the privacy and security of his dorm.

More than his programming skills, the film shows us that Mark's gift lies in his ability to so narrowly focus his attention that the world and the people around him are effectively blocked out. This gift is first on powerful display in the hacking montage that follows his return to his room at Kirkland, and it is here that Fincher connects Mark's capacity for both attention and inattention with the larger tendencies toward anonymity, isolation, and distance that characterize the contemporary, online sociality he designed.

Arriving at his dorm, Mark begins pouring out his thoughts in an online blog. As he types, we listen, Eisenberg narrating Mark's thought process as he first publishes juvenile putdowns of Erica and then turns his attention to women in general. Mark proposes a website that compares a woman's attractiveness to that of various farm animals before his stoned roommate suggests a direct comparison of girl to girl, and Mark sets to work hacking the Face Books of each Harvard college—their online repositories of student photographs. As Mark builds the Facemash website, Eisenberg's voiceover, in concert with the pulsing score by Trent Reznor and Atticus Ross, conveys the character's relentless, irresistible focus and invites us to take the same enjoyment in that form of control and command as he does. Around him we see Mark's roommates drunk or stoned, idly distracting themselves. They play video games and half watch "Shark Week" on the Discovery Channel, occasionally gaining Mark's attention for a moment before he halfheartedly smiles and turns back to his online quarry.

In parallel with these scenes, we are shown inside one of the physical and social spaces Mark covets—the Phoenix Club's first party of the fall semester. There we see young women participating in dark rituals of social admission, spectacles of sexual performance as the price for earning and keeping the attention of this select group. These are disturbing images of objectification. But as far as we are shown, they are, nevertheless, images of consenting social engagement in which the participants understand and agree to, as it were, the rules of the game. (It is no accident that the partygoers are shown playing strip poker.) In the privacy of Mark's dorm, by contrast, his attention is paid not to people but to lifeless, unresponsive images, pictures of women recruited without permission into a disembodied social sphere where there is no one to return his gaze, and so no one from whom he feels the need to avert his eyes.

Across the film, Mark develops his capacity for blinkered focus of attention as a defensive tactic against exposure to others. In this regard, we see him explore his talent for absorption in his own world, testing its strength and power as a social shield. Sean Parker's being one of his guides in this exploration is improbable: as played by Timberlake, he represents a fantasy of pure, unencumbered social confidence. If our introduction to Mark shows him confounded and hapless in the face of what others mean, Sean stands for natural fluency in the language of gesture, look, and tone. In contrast with Eisenberg, Timberlake inhabits a mode of approaching others that exhibits a bounty of welcoming ease and pleasure at having their company as well as a cocksure grace some of us are happy to admire without having the confidence to try on for ourselves. For example, his entrance to the film, and into Mark's life—sauntering into a restaurant meeting twenty-five minutes late but unhurried, giving cheerful notice to everyone he walks by—is one that viewers might envy but never imitate. For those of us who feel that twinge of envy, its provocation lies not only in Sean's gregariousness but equally in his neglecting to apologize for his lateness. He is unselfconscious *and* performative, unconcerned about censure by others without keeping an aloof distance from them. In other words, Sean embodies a masterly command of social conduct while seeming indifferent to the claims of society. Fincher thus offers Timberlake's performance as a normative image of social inclusion and expressiveness that we are expected to desire over Eisenberg's embodiment of the autist outcast. But perhaps Sean's lure to Mark consists less in that effortless charm and more in his confident embrace of separateness—not as exile, but as freedom.

Sean thus reveals himself to share a trait with his protégé, one that allows Mark to harmonize Sean's performative command with his own tendency toward self-absorbed withdrawal. While in conversation at the San Francisco nightclub, on the mezzanine above the crowd below, Sean confesses that he invented Napster (the original online music file-sharing program) to compete with the lacrosse-playing boyfriend of a girl he liked at high school. After Sean encourages him to take single-handed control of Facebook, as Mark's creation is now called, and to not rely on or bend to others who might constrain his aspirations, Mark asks whether he ever thinks about the lacrosse captain's girlfriend. Moments before, Sean asked Mark for his trust. "Look at me and tell me I don't know what I'm talkin' about," he says, holding Mark's gaze. The camera shows us Timberlake's face in close-up, underlit by the colored lights from the dance floor below. His handsomeness still shines even as it takes on an ugly and distorting twist. In this moment, in his tempting offer of access to the charismatic power he wields, Parker appears as something like a devil. And it is a kind of devilishness that comes out as he answers Mark's question about the girl from his years at school. His response is a desiccated inversion of Everett Sloane's great scene in *Citizen Kane* (1941) when, as Kane's abandoned associate Mr. Bernstein, he remembers the girl on the ferry who didn't even see him notice her but of whom he has thought every day since. "Do you ever think about her?" asks Mark. Sean laughs. It is hard to tell whether he is amused or disgusted by Mark's romantic sentimentality. "*No*," he says. To be deeply moved by someone, to let them make such an impression, is—in the world that Sean and Mark inhabit, and the one they are building—to be a figure of scorn, to be trapped by something not worth paying attention to.

We cannot say whether any particular viewer of *The Social Network* will be attracted to Eisenberg's performance as Mark, with its arrogance, its aloof coldness, its frequent rigidity and mannerisms, or whether they will be repulsed by it, or feel bored and indifferent. But we can more reliably say how we are invited to see and respond to certain qualities of the performance. I have tried to show that we are invited to see in Mark an amplification of our own buried anxieties about the challenges and risks of social interaction, of engaging in the social world itself. In its depiction of Zuckerberg, then, perhaps *The Social Network* discovers a source of our collective attraction to his Facebook world, which—much like the interactions of the Facemash montage early in the film—offers sociality at a safely disembodied, anonymized remove. Eisenberg's performance evokes what we might recognize as autistic features of behavior in a way that gives some anchor to his frequent confusion and discomfort with others, and to his envy and resentment of those who are able to more smoothly steer past the rocks of interpersonal exchange. But in contrast to his inept encounter with Erica that opens the film, during the deposition scenes in the lawsuit we see the matured Mark in stronger command of the qualities that set him apart from others, and that also push others away from him. In the section of the film during which Mark's friendship with Eduardo starts to fray, we cut to his interrogation by the lawyer for the Winklevoss twins (David Selby). He asks Mark about emails sent between the two parties during their time at Harvard, but Mark's answer is not any kind of meaningful reply. Mark has slowly turned away from the questioning. The lawyer and his clients blur into soft-focus background as our attention is pulled toward Mark's gaze, aimed into an unseen space past the camera, past us.

"It's raining," he says.

"I'm sorry?" the lawyer asks.

"It just started raining," Mark states, his stare still trained away from the room, out the small window that we now see, through which the Golden Gate Bridge lies in the distance, a gray silhouette in the rain falling across the bay.

"Mr. Zuckerberg," the lawyer intones, his patience already thin, "do I have your full attention?" There is a beat of silence in which Eisenberg's face remains still. Only the smallest tweak of his brow shows any sign of a thought or a deliberate plan. He does not turn around or flinch or waver. "No," he says, even and calm. Soon the scene descends into more elevated theatrics as Mark, in a moment, turns and excoriates those suing him for their lack of courage and inventiveness. This he does without fear and without need to excuse or moderate himself.

Regardless of how we judge these moments, they offer—especially in Mark's gaze out the window—a picture of distraction, of blindness, that holds within it an achievement of focused attention. In its most attractive and disturbing moments, Eisenberg's Mark Zuckerberg embodies the fantasy of fully directing one's mind without the burdensome claims of others, without their worlds impinging on one's own. In its closing moments, *The Social Network* leaves us with an image of that condition as Mark sits alone in the glass box of an abandoned conference room, slumped listlessly in front of his laptop, waiting, hoping to reconnect with a frozen-smile picture of Erica that stares from his screen. Outside the windows, the night is dotted with the lights of the community, shining but far away through the glass.

CHAPTER 9

Hidden Worlds of Female Autism

DANIEL VARNDELL

O brave new world,
That has such people in't!
SHAKESPEARE, *THE TEMPEST*

Since the 1980s—and increasingly in the late 2010s—studies of Autism
Spectrum Disorder have stated that females "present," in the medical sense
of the word, differently from males. In her critical review of the fifth edition of the *Diagnostic and Statistical Manual of Mental Disorders*, Jolynn
Haney (2015) goes so far as to call it a "gender bias in autism diagnosis."
The issue pertains to the general problem of diagnosing autism, described
by Stuart Murray as the difficulty of "witnessing": if "looking *for* autism—
the processes of assessment and diagnosis—is complex, then looking *at* au-

tism—seeing it in the world—is equally a far from straightforward activity" (2008b, 104). This problem is exacerbated in diagnosing females by what Meng-Chuan Lai and his coauthors call "compensatory camouflaging," an idea that has been described for some time in clinical and autobiographical material but remains underresearched (2019, 1220). Carrie Grant discusses "camouflaging" in her young girls as involving both "blending" and "masking," the former referring to attempts to blend in with neurotypical people (maintaining eye contact despite not wanting to, for example), and the latter referring to an ability to hide or suppress one's anxiety in order to appear calm (holding an honest opinion back to avoid embarrassing others, for example) (2019, 32). Hence, while girls on the autistic spectrum might have the same level of behavioral symptoms as boys, camouflaging makes it much less likely that they will be diagnosed, thereby leading to delayed diagnoses, if any. Moreover, as Francesca Happé points out, classic autistic behaviors may appear more neurotypical in girls than in boys: showing narrow special interests—focusing on horses rather than electricity pylons, for example—or a "clingy" rather than an "aloof" style of interaction (2019, 13). In their study, Meng-Chuan Lai and his coauthors noted that camouflaging was neither exclusive to nor always present in females on the spectrum, but they observed masking and blending to a much higher degree.

The link between camouflaging and acting might seem immediately obvious to a film scholar, and Rachel Townson and Carol Povey observed that "autistic females often describe themselves as actresses" (2019, 172). As with the actor who practices her technique in order to move her body in ways that appear to audiences completely natural—lifting or tilting her head in a certain way in response to a question, raising a cigarette to her lips in a way that conveys contemplation (or irritation)—masking and blending involve training and practicing to take control of one's social performance in order to imitate and reflect the actions of one's neurotypical peers. "An actor's technique," to take Robert Speaight's classic definition of stage acting, "is the outward and visible sign of her inward and spiritual grace" ([1937] 1947, 71, pronoun altered). Except that for autistic girls, the outward and visible signs of their performance must last as long as they are in the presence of those with whom they don't feel intimately comfortable (which could be a number of people), and their inward and spiritual grace is often described by them as something closer to "compensation." It is little wonder that when Paul Collins draws attention to the well-known fact that autists are often described by others and themselves as "aliens among humans," he qualifies this by adding, "It is as much about what is abundant as what is missing, an overexpression of the very traits that make our species unique" (quoted in

Murray 2013, 53). Camouflaging is not just covering for the "untoward" absence of something; it is also covering for something supplemental, an excess. One of the key issues is to understand the association between camouflaging techniques and well-established neurodiverse constructs such as "imitation, introspection and social anxiety," as well as the connection between blending and neurotypical social behaviors, for example, "impression management, or 'performance' as described by the sociologist Erving Goffman" (Lai et al. 2019, 1220). In any case, autistic "acting" points to an increasing sense of "heterogeneity in autism" (1219).

It is here that a forked problem emerges for neurotypical actors performing autism onscreen. If an actor cannot understand the way someone with ASD sees the world, how can she perform an autistic character without simply reducing the performance to the mimicry of stereotypical behavioral gestures and movements—casual stimming (self-stimulating repetitive movements, verbal tics, repeated phrases and gestures), avoidance of eye contact, and so on? And if female autistic experience is a kind of performance to begin with, a "camouflaging" of that experience, how might an actor convey not only the effort required to mask and blend, but also the autist's interior world, her inward and spiritual grace? This problem is exacerbated by Mark Osteen's point that despite the general upsurge in autistic diagnoses in the twentieth century and a marked increase in stories about autism, those stories have not tended to follow the increasing sense of diversity in medical circles regarding ASD. By contrast, Osteen bemoans what he calls the "narrative problem of autism," the degree to which stories tend to rest on formulaic representations that "display a tension between the demands of narrative cohesion and the obligation to tell the truth" (2013, 261).

To tackle first the problem of representing camouflaged female autistic experience onscreen, I look at the nuances of Sofia Helin's performance as Saga Norén in the Nordic noir crime series *Bron/Broen* (2011–2018; English: *The Bridge*) to explore how camouflaging in the series is dominated by the exigencies and limitations of narrative cohesion. And second, to explore the possibility for discovering a properly visual expression of female autism onscreen, I look at the shifting dynamics in Sally Hawkins's performance in *The Shape of Water* (2017) as Elisa Esposito, a character who uses the movies playing in a cinema underneath her apartment to negotiate the tensions between outward presentation and inner feeling. Both characters have been embraced in online forums by autistic female viewers who see in them images of the expressive potential of autistic Otherness. That said, I want to stress that this chapter does not presume to "diagnose" camouflaged performances as autistic. One must remain wary, as Susan Sontag (1978) put it in a different context, of using metaphor as a means to "provide control" "over the experiences and events . . . over which people have in fact little or no control . . . [which] undermines the 'reality' of the disease" (55); or worse, placing blame on sufferers and leading them away from treatment (47) or, for the autist, from some kind of acceptance and understanding. The problem is acute with ASD, writes Shirley Dent (2007), who implores critics not to pretend that they are psychiatrists and "'diagnose' fictional characters." The result is all too often reductive, she writes, when critics look "outward towards the individual's relationship with the world and society, however confining or crushing that society may be," or diminish it by "looking inwards and reducing our relationship with the world to our own unfathomable neurology." While Sofia Helin has explicitly stated in interviews that she played Saga as autistic, having engaged in extensive research to prepare for the role, no such evidence exists in the case of *The Shape of Water*. While I remain somewhat skeptical of Osteen's praising of visual media over written media as better suited to portraying the heterogeneity of autistic life, he is not wrong that film is a powerful medium for exploring the rich worlds of neurodiverse females.

Sofia Helin in *The Bridge*

A corpse is dumped from a moving car in the middle of the Øresund Bridge exactly on the border between Sweden and Denmark. Two detectives are drawn in, one from Malmö, Saga Norén (Helin), and one from Copenhagen, Martin Rohde (Kim Bodnia). Together they must work to solve the murder (see the chapter by Douglas McFarland in this volume). Despite their being detectives of equivalent superiority, Saga swiftly assumes command of the investigation (Swedish victim, Swedish car: her authority, she reasons). Her brusque manner is easily brushed off by Martin, whose strained smile breezily conceals his annoyance. After all, they have only just met. But when Saga imperiously tries to apply strict protocols to protect the integrity of the crime scene, Martin bristles. He polices by instinct, she by the book, which she has read and can quote verbatim.

This introduction to Saga appears to uphold the (now outdated) notion initially proposed by Simon Baron-Cohen (2010) that those with "high-functioning" autism tend to have "extreme male brains"—that is, a high IQ and an advanced capacity for systematizing knowledge but a low capacity for empathy (regarded by him and many others as a female trait). Such a view has more recently come to be seen as unhelpful, writes Sarah Bargiela, because "someone with a high IQ might become non-verbal in a stressful situation" (nonverbal and hence low functioning), and also because an "extreme male brain" might in females be concealed by using social mimicry (2019, 4–5).

In the case of Saga, we are presented with a somewhat mixed picture. She is clearly very high functioning and has many of the "extreme male brain" attributes—a high IQ, encyclopedic knowledge, and so on—making her an incredibly effective detective. But although clearly not very good at it, Saga also clearly demonstrates a capacity to camouflage. For example, she demonstrates her recognition of the danger of giving offense when, shortly after securing the crime scene, she phones her commanding officer, Hans Petterson (Dag Malmberg) while driving to break the news to the victim's next of kin. Alarmed at the prospect that Saga's social skills might lead her to be unintentionally insensitive, Petterson urges caution. "Tread *lightly*," he stresses, pointing out that there may be children present, to which Saga confusedly replies that there aren't too many ways to say that the victim was "chopped in half." Saga clearly understands that "tread lightly" means "be sensitive," but equally she struggles to fathom how she might speak other than directly. This tension in Saga is illustrated in the next scene when the victim's husband, still reeling from the bad news Saga has just delivered, asks rhetorically why someone would do such a thing. Saga is momentarily thrown. She has been answering his questions with sensitivity but has now been asked to comment on, even speculate about, a motive. Drawing on her statistical knowledge of such cases, she tentatively suggests that the motivation might be personal until, finding that the husband hasn't asked her to stop (because he is too meek to do so), she begins listing all the reasons such murders occur (debt, drugs, affairs). The husband is left dumbstruck as Saga simply drives off, happy in the thought that she has succeeded in "treading lightly."

The moment offers a key insight into Saga's social decision making: a tension common to female autists who camouflage, which Helin communicates through the gesture of blinking twice, as if searching for the rule for how to handle the husband's question, which has brought an unanticipated turn to the conversation. On one hand, Saga clearly knows she ought not say what is on her mind, but on the other hand, she has misinterpreted his rhetorical question as a question requiring an answer, an answer from her—indeed, a social cue. A second example of Helin's gestural nod to Saga's social processing occurs later in the episode when Martin, now officially assigned to work the case with her, imposes himself on her place of work in an effort to break the ice with his new partner. To Saga's rising irritation, he deliberately paces up and down, prompting her to finally complain, at which he takes the opportunity to engage in small talk. After announcing that he has five children, he asks Saga whether she has any. "No, why would I want to?" she frostily replies, to which he playfully points out that no one has ever responded to that question that way. Saga fires back that perhaps more fathers ought to question parenthood, puncturing her attempted camouflage, prompting him to shake his head in resignation and look down at his feet for strength. Noticing his reaction, Saga again blinks and shakes her head ever so slightly before attempting to recover by qualifying her remarks: "Not *you*. I'm sure you're a wonderful dad." Blinking again, she perfunctorily returns to her paperwork.

In these two moments from the first episode of the series, Helin elevates such minor gestures—pauses, head movements, and blinking—without exaggerating them, into performative signs indicating the minute adjustments required of, and tensions experienced by, the camouflaging autist. Hence, while some might argue that Saga is another example of a high-functioning "extreme male brain" type with little self-awareness, one can point to such gestures—her rapid uninterrupted blinking—as exhibiting the more nuanced behaviors typical in female autistic experience, as illustrative of the tendency to mask and blend (or at least attempt to do so). It is little wonder that Saga was lauded by critics and reviewers for more than simply existing (as a rare example of female autism onscreen). Rosemary Collins writes that Saga is "the best reflection of myself I've ever seen in fiction, but she is me as I know myself *to be inside*, and not remotely like me as I present to people in my life" (2016; emphasis added). The effort of masking and blending, Collins adds, is about minimizing the emotional and sometimes physical harm that might arise from living in a neurotypical world filled with a dearth of understanding and compassion. The effort required to "semi-pass as neurotypical," she writes, "doesn't exactly help me make friends because the effort it takes can make me seem cold and fake." Critically, however, Collins points out that Saga does not attempt to "pass" but "act[s] out" what for Collins has to be suppressed. One might even say that while Saga attempts to mask, by failing at it she makes herself unable to blend.

And yet, in her we nonetheless discover a detective who is not just intellectually but also morally superior to her male neurotypical colleagues. She is generally mocked by her colleagues, aside from her commanding officer, and is treated with bewilderment, teasing, and occasional irritation by her new partner. But as the series unfolds, she increasingly appears to possess not only superior investigative skills but also superior social skills, since she alone keeps the investigation from spiraling out of control when Martin's own idiosyncratic shortcomings come to the fore. He is revealed to be a serial philanderer whose weaknesses threaten to undermine the investigation and become an integral foil to the murderer's twisted games. By the series's end, Saga is hardly a mere atypical to be measured against neurotypical male standards. In exposing hypocrisies, she is the standard against which so-called neurotypicals should be evaluated. However insensitively she might sometimes communicate her thoughts to others, it is her personal integrity that ultimately keeps the department (and the show) functioning.

To draw on a (somewhat extreme) view of the idea that certain autistic traits can afford one a moral and intellectual superiority, we might compare this view of Saga with the words of Alan Kirby, who wrote that "autism's contrasting embrace of exhaustive knowledge, its love and recall of facts, its rich and grammatically correct use of language, its insistence on rationality, truth and rigor; all of this constructs autism as an incapacity to accept the sub-intellectual barbarism of its age" (quoted in S. Murray 2013, 62). While Stuart Murray is perhaps right to regard this "near-vitriolic" assessment as "throwing up a number of challenging, and potentially contradictory, complexities" (62), its emphasis on autistic integrity and the value of knowledge and reason in a world of ignorance and stereotyping suggests that Saga is more than just a sorely needed representation of female autism. In addition to introducing the complexity of female camouflaging into what is principally a male type, Helin offers a richly complex performance that, following Murray (69), might even be said to revise the standards to which neurotypical human behavior might be held.

Sally Hawkins in *The Shape of Water*

In Guillermo del Toro's *The Shape of Water*, Elisa Esposito (Sally Hawkins) is a cleaner who works night shifts at a secret government facility at the height of the Cold War in 1962. Her life revolves around a precise routine: she wakes for work, masturbates in the bath for (exactly) eight minutes as her eggs hard-boil, and delights in the sounds (and the lights) coming up through the floorboards from the movie musical playing in the cinema below. Elisa, who is entirely mute—mysterious scars run across her vocal cords—communicates with her best friend and neighbor, Giles (Richard Jenkins), and her coworker Zelda (Octavia Spencer) by using sign language. She finds her routine unsettled one day when she and Zelda are ordered to clean a chamber containing a mysterious water tank in which a top-secret military asset is being held for testing. The cleaners soon learn that the asset is an "Amphibian Man" (Doug Jones), a creature captured in a South American river by a sadistic military careerist, Richard Strickland (Michael Shannon), who confronts them and warns that the "monster" is an "affront" to God and the natural order. Against Strickland's explicit instruction to leave "it" alone, Elisa forges an intense, eventually sexual bond with the creature, teaching him basic sign language and bonding over a shared passion for hard-boiled eggs and Glenn Miller records. But when she overhears Strickland arguing with his superiors for the Amphibian Man to be vivisected, Elisa convinces her reluctant friends to help her rescue the creature, planning to keep him in her bathtub until the tide is high enough to return him to the ocean. (The story here is informed, at least a little, by *E.T. the Extra-Terrestrial* [1982].) When her mission succeeds, an enraged Strickland discovers that his career rests on being able to relocate this sensitive military "asset" (lest it fall into the hands of the Russians). The film ends with Elisa mortally wounded by a vengeful Strickland and plunging into the ocean with the Amphibian Man, whose touch not only heals her wounds but opens up the scars on her neck to reveal gills enabling her to breathe underwater and live there (we are left to suppose) with her amphibian lover. The strong implication is that she has had gills all along.

On its release, several viewers identifying as being on the spectrum quickly took to internet forums to discuss what they felt were strong links between Elisa's mutism and heightened sensory awareness, and traits associated with autism. Kit Mead (2018) experienced Elisa's musical stimming (tap dancing, finger drumming, masturbation), as well as her movements and initial interactions with the Amphibian Man (who also cannot speak), as a mirror of her own experiences of living and communicating in an "alien" world. While Mead expresses reservations about aligning autistic experience with Otherness, especially a monstrous Otherness (which, as Murray points out, has become something of a standard when discussing autism [2013, 53]), she acknowledges the power of cinema to represent "those of us who struggle with feeling human in the face of the world, who sometimes identify with the Other and embrace it as a tool to survive, whose narratives and relationships . . . are messy and muddy the waters," and to render neurodiversity in ways that might otherwise be overlooked (2018). Another reviewer echoed this sentiment, writing that as someone "for whom speech did not come easily and never will," the film's embrace of muteness and resistance to the stereotypical denouement in which an atypical character is "cured" of her impairment was "empowering" (*Chavisory's Notebook* 2018).

Cinema has often drawn on the trope of the woman held in the grip of a monstrous romantic passion: Fay Wray in the clutches of a marauding *King Kong* (1933); Julie Adams stalked by *The Creature from the Black Lagoon* (1954); Belle consenting to be a guest in *Beauty and the Beast* (1946; 1991). A metamorphosis tends to result in the death of the monster or else his transformation into a prince. It was *The Shape of Water*'s resistance to this cliché that led Chavisory (a pseudonym) to defend the film's alignment of mutism and monstrosity: "There are ways in which identification with the monstrous can be protective, defiant, or represent a stand for personal integrity" (*Chavisory's Notebook* 2018). As Sarah Kurchak (2017) put it in her review of the film, "When the world sometimes tells you that you're a monster, and when you love movies but can't see yourself in the heroes, you might start to find yourself identifying with the monsters." Just as Helin's performance of Saga Norén's autistic camouflaging paradoxically comes to represent a (very female) personal integrity in a world full of (very male) hypocrisy and moral relativism, Hawkins's portrayal of Elisa Esposito's mutism transforms the idea of monstrosity by turning on its head our conception of what is human. Before I look at two key moments in her performance, it is worth stating that *The Shape of Water* begins with a voiceover narration (by Richard Jenkins, in the character of Giles) offering to tell Elisa's story, describing it as a story of wonder and triumph despite the "monster who tried to destroy it all."

The first moment I draw attention to comes shortly after Elisa overhears Strickland gloat that the Amphibian Man is to be vivisected. Desperate but determined, she pleads with Giles to help her rescue the creature, but he dismisses the notion as folly. The scene is poignant for Elisa's double failure: first, in not being able to convince Giles to help her, and second, perhaps more woundingly, in her struggle to make herself understood. As she signs to him, he seems barely attentive, loosely interpreting her meaning while hardly looking at her as he translates only the literal meaning of her signs. This scene shows the difference between knowing what a sign signifies and understanding to what use it is being put by the signer. For example, after (somewhat pedantically) quibbling over semantics when she describes the Amphibian Man as a "thing," Giles doesn't see the implied quotation marks and seizes her statement as blunt proof that a rescue mission is not worth the risk. "Say what I *sign*," she implores, frustrated, "you're not *hearing* me." Here we get a sense of the problem that Kristina Chew describes as the "task of the translator," in which neurotypical folks find they must translate the speech of autists through the prism of neurotypical expressions (2013, 305). We also get a sense of what Carrie Grant, in describing the experience of a mother with autistic girls, means when she writes that "one of the keys to understanding our girls is to try to hear what they are saying *beyond the words*" (2019, 26; emphasis added).

When Giles finally pays attention to Elisa's signs and repeats what they mean rather than translating them, Jenkins turns his body to face Hawkins and really looks at her. Del Toro uses subtitles to translate the sign language in order to demonstrate this shift in concentration and focus. Elisa continues, "What am I? I move my mouth like him. . . . I make no sound, like him . . . What does that make me?" When Giles seizes on her pronoun use ("You said 'he'!") she smacks his arm sharply ("You hit me?!" he bristles—more from the shock than the pain). Elisa attempts one last time to communicate her message as Giles, more carefully now, interprets: "The way he looks at me," Giles says, beginning to see the significance of Elisa's heart-rending plea, "he doesn't know what I lack or how I am incomplete. He sees me for what I am, as I am. He's happy to see me, every time, every day. Now I can either save him or let him die." Moved but still reluctant to help, Giles tries to leave while huffily defending his decision: "We are nothing . . . We can *do* nothing . . . This . . . this . . . this is not even human." As he walks away, Elisa bursts with rage and slams her fist into the wall, then signs, "If we do nothing, neither are we." The moment is a powerful reminder of the Cartesian doubt at the core of what it means to *be*, and it reflects what Bargiela describes as one of the biggest issues for female autists: being told, "You're not autistic" (2019, 18).

In another scene, one that has been celebrated, scorned, and even ridiculed in reviews, Elisa's frustration that she cannot communicate her love to the Amphibian Man drives her to fantasize a breathtaking means to express what she feels. Elisa sits at the breakfast table with the Amphibian Man, having succeeded (after finally convincing Giles to help) in rescuing him from the facility. As they eat, she tries to sign that she "loves" him, but he cannot understand the meaning of her hand gestures. While the Amphibian Man understood the sign for "egg," he seems unable to comprehend the sign for an abstract emotion like love, prompting Elisa to move into a different medium. It is here that she passes from the frustration of finding her language lacking to the language of pure film. She begins to silently mouth words we can't hear. The room falls into shadow, and a spotlight illuminates her. As she continues with some difficulty to move her mouth, we begin to hear faint words—the words of Alexandre Desplat's rendition of Harry Warren and Mack Gordon's "You'll Never Know," performed sumptuously by Renée Fleming with the London Symphony Orchestra.[1] The faint strains of Elisa's voice strengthen until, standing and throwing her arms in the air, Elisa finds her voice and belts out the lyrics, which give expression to the pathos of being unable to communicate ("You'll never know . . .") what one feels (". . . how much I . . . love . . . you!") to another person. As her voice finds its strength, the kitchen falls away and she is joined by the Amphibian Man on a starlit art deco stage, recapitulating Carroll Clark's iconic rooftop set design on which Fred Astaire and Ginger Rogers performed Irving Berlin's "Let's Face the Music and Dance" in *Follow the Fleet* (1936). She sings and they dance. Finally, as she perches on the Amphibian Man's knee, the dreamy lights fade, leaving the single spotlight. They are back in her kitchen.

The power of cinema is invoked here to give voice to her voicelessness. Earlier in the film, Elisa is shown walking into a room and chancing upon Alice Faye singing "You'll Never Know" on the television in Giles's apartment. As she stands there entranced, her eyes sparking with emotion, we recognize that for her this song is an aching expression of longing and loss with which she identifies. Faye's performance entrances Elisa precisely because it *can* express the inexpressible, movingly, even sublimely. For her, there is perhaps no stronger form of communication than the musical number in cinema, bittersweet though it may feel. As Elisa springs into the world of film to find the means to express her love, one might draw a parallel with the well-documented use of alternative media by autists seeking alternative communities for emotional and intellectual outlets when traditional institutional frameworks, such as schools, seem too overwhelming and stimulating. As Sonya Freeman Loftis writes, "Autism is disruptive to notions of consciousness and perception, destabilizing the very idea of a shared reality. Sensory activities (e.g., intense reactions to bright lights, loud noises, or crowded places) can mean that two people (one autistic and one neurotypical) can stand in the same space but have completely different perceptions regarding the activity in that space" (2016, 12). For a number of young girls with autism interviewed by Sarah Hendrickx, the internet offered a range of new possibilities for neurodiverse interaction (89, 148), and Felicity Sedgewick and Liz Pellicano point out that online forums offer opportunities to communicate in ways that suit neurodiverse needs, including giving autists time to think about how to respond to posts, and enabling them to keep track of who said what and when in a discussion thread (2019, 129). For Charlotte Amelia Poe, the "outside" community she embraced was online fandom, especially around tattooing and piercing (2019, 89, 107). Before the internet, Liane Holliday Willey expressed a preference for imaginary friends (2015, 19). For Temple Grandin, it was horses (Grandin and Johnson 2006, 6).

It is far from unusual for film and television viewing to be the object of intense interest or the repeated activity through which autistic girls calm themselves down (Hendrickx 2015, 59). But my aim—in keeping with my intention to avoid "diagnosing" Elisa—is to emphasize something different in her expression of love through cinema.

The choice of musicals generally—but also of this musical, this number, and these performers—points to a layering at a textual level both for, but also in excess of, Elisa's memory of *Follow the Fleet*. On one hand, the example is somewhat clichéd, having been used before to express romantic frustration (and not necessarily in a good way), for example, in the scene from *Pennies from Heaven* (1981) in which Steve Martin sits in a cinema lip-syncing to Astaire before launching into a fantasy musical number of his own. Whereas *Pennies* uses the "Let's Face the Music" number to subvert and flatten its own expression of musical form, Del Toro niftily inverts the musical moment from *Follow the Fleet* to punctuate a more sophisticated comment on escapism than *Pennies* ever manages. Treading a fine line between the ridiculous and the sublime, Elisa's dance sequence with the creature transcends the cliché, since, in the end, the transformative moment is not the metamorphosis of the frog into a handsome prince, thereby facilitating a happy ending—the equivalent of the autistic "cure" and the seamless integration of a neurotypical couple into society; it is the elevation of the already atypical couple into a moment of sublime exceptionality experienced as something far from malign. In fact, it is (at least for this viewer!) divine. After all, is this viewing experience not what musical numbers intend to invite? One's aspiration to dance like Astaire and Rogers among the glittering stars would hardly constitute a desire to pass for normal. They embody a moment of *exceptionalism*, even virtuosity. As Astaire and Rogers dance and their characters' romance begins, writes Murray Pomerance, "the two figures continually mirror each other in physical moves; their commonality is based in an ability, and willingness, to stretch themselves towards the visible" (2019, 96)—as well as, in this case, the audible.

And if we find ourselves in such a world, as Rosemary Collins (2016) hopes for in writing of Saga Norén that "sometimes you want to see yourself as you could be in an ideal world," might this film quotation not itself be a form of stretching toward the visible? Giles's shock when Elisa hits his arm, and his astonished reaction as she slams her fist into the wall in frustration, are born from her ordinarily reclusive being in the world. With Astaire, writes Pomerance, "the signal use of the polished limb extension or attenuation of pose, the pointed foot, the perfectly calculated spin, the embrace stretched for noticeability," is about making visible that which is ordinarily hidden (2019, 96). Is the image of Elisa and the Amphibian Man not, if just for these brief moments, an image of an atypical ideal? After all, when ethologists define the worlds of animals, they do so, wrote Gilles Deleuze, poetically, by "showing that an animal responds to a certain number of stimuli, sometimes very few, that amount to little glimmerings in the dark depths of a vast nature" (1995, 158). It is for such glimmerings in her Amphibian Man that Elisa is searching. And while he seems oblivious of her cinematic reverie, nevertheless she returns to her kitchen full of hope.

As with Temple Grandin's realization that "autistic people can think the way animals think," and that "autism is a kind of way station on the road from animals to humans, which puts autistic people like me in a perfect position to translate 'animal talk' into English" (Grandin and Johnson 2006, 6–7), the autist does not merely adapt to the neurotypical way of seeing the world, but also finds ways to adapt the neurotypical world both to seeing autism and (what is infinitely more difficult) to *seeing autistically*. "Who tells our stories?" asks Charlotte Poe rhetorically, and then answers, "Neurotypical people. . . . It's their narratives we are forced to conform to, and their narratives the public sees" (2019, 150). After all, the word "monster" is, as Jeffrey Jerome Cohen points out, etymologically derived from "that which reveals" (2007, 199). True, Elisa and the Amphibian Man end up ostracized from society, but so too were John Wayne and Claire Trevor at the end of *Stagecoach* (1939). What is crucial about these two performances by Sofia Helin and Sally Hawkins is that they invite us to think otherwise about normality, just as John Ford invited us to think otherwise about civilization. The point was made by the actor Michael Shannon when Del Toro helped him realize that "back in the day, when Hollywood was making these kind of creature movies, Strickland would have been more like the hero" (quoted in Miller 2017). In this film, Strickland is nothing less than hateful, and it is no accident that Elisa's friends—who get to speak most of the dialogue in the film—are from marginalized groups. (Giles is a closeted gay man; Zelda is African American.) The "monster who tried to destroy it all," referred to in Giles's opening voiceover, is, we come to realize, Strickland.

"Finding yourself in popular culture is invaluable," writes Poe. "We need to be seen. And we're not, or at least, not in the way we should be" (2019, 152). As the medical world begins to adapt and become more creative in identifying and diagnosing the hidden worlds of autism, especially in light of dynamic new developments in gender transition and redefinition, perhaps it is time that film critics looked again at hidden representations of neurodiversity onscreen. While Sofia Helin's performance as Saga in *The Bridge* drew important attention to female autistic experience, and explored nuances gesturing to its camouflaging characteristic, it might be more accurate to think about that experience as generally more concealed (sometimes in plain sight), as already constitutive of an extremely accomplished form of acting in itself. And to risk stretching the point, is this not the experience of many women diagnosed with ASD who, having felt the need to mask and blend in a neurotypical society not set up to recognize them (because it was unable or perhaps simply unwilling to), find new communities within which they can flourish? Let me end with an observation from a review of *The Shape of Water* by Sarah Kurchak (2017), whose essay moves on from an eloquent defense of the film's celebration—as she sees it—of a distinctively autistic representation to embrace the power of cinema in expressing autistic experience more generally: "But if you happen to have had a long-term unrequited relationship with the cinema, there's a certain joyful rush that comes from having the object of your affections finally turn around and notice that you've been there all along."

Note

1. The song was recorded first by Alice Faye in *Hello, Frisco, Hello* (1943) and then in the same year by both Vera Lynn and Frank Sinatra.

CHAPTER 10

Eye Contact in Juárez: Borderline Empathy and the Autistic Detective

DOUGLAS MCFARLAND

I have never doubted the truth of signs, Adso; they are the only things man has with which to orient himself in the world. What I did not understand was the relation among signs.

UMBERTO ECO, *THE NAME OF THE ROSE*

In this chapter, I cite passages from William Shakespeare's *The Comedy of Errors*, Umberto Eco's *The Name of the Rose*, and Roberto Bolaño's *2666*, even though these works make no direct references to autism. But they speak to the condition and have aided me in understanding *The Bridge* (US version, 2013–2014) and specifically its central character, Sonya Cross (Diane Kruger), an autistic El Paso homicide detective. I use these three passages to provide a loose structure for the chapter. I am not a clinician; I have not analyzed data or conducted interviews; I am not familiar with the secondary literature; I have not published in the field. But in some sense, my lack of expertise provides me with an advantage. The mother of an autistic child recently wrote an opinion piece for the *New York Times* in which she judged the accuracy of the depictions of autistic characters in works of fiction. For me to make such judgments is neither possible nor helpful. I cannot assess anyone's success or failure in depicting a particular autistic figure. I want to avoid any preconceived set of expectations; my intention is to encounter the subject of this chapter for who she is as she negotiates the world, interacts with others, and comes to understand herself. Moreover, the condition of this autistic character addresses problems intrinsic to the human condition: How can we cross borders separating self and other? How can we see from the perspective of others? How do we truly express empathy? How do we fashion self-narratives, and why is it essential that we do so? How do we change over time? And finally, most broadly, how do we navigate the ambiguities that inform our world? I do not mean to suggest that autism should be treated as a metaphor. But I do mean that in *The Bridge*, autism is used to bring into sharp focus the challenges that we all face in both large and small ways.

The Bridge is a thirteen-episode series that appeared on the FX network. A second season followed, but it did not generate sufficient interest for a third to be undertaken. *The Bridge* was based on a Swedish-Danish coproduction (2011–2018; see the chapter by Daniel Varndell in this volume) with multiple episodes and multiple seasons, and led to a British-French coproduction, *The Tunnel* (2013–2018). I have adopted the strategy of ignoring the second season of the American production, the Swedish-Danish production, and the French production. The first season of *The Bridge* focuses intensively on an autistic protagonist and her emotional evolution rather than on the investigation of a crime. While the narrative arc of emotional change parallels the arc of the investigation as it proceeds, it reaches a significant climax (however qualified) at the end of the season. Moreover, the substitution in the American version of the dysfunctional landscape of Juárez, Mexico, for the Copenhagen of the Swedish production provides a critical environment for staging the final struggles of its central character to bridge the gap between herself and others. By comparison with Juárez, Copenhagen is a highly developed urban environment, European in flavor, and neither as squalid nor corrupt as Juárez is shown to be.

To See through the Eyes of Another

The Comedy of Errors points to the primary concern of *The Bridge*. In Shakespeare's play, two sets of twins, "pretty babes" (I.i.72) separated soon after birth, unknowingly meet many years later. Confusions of identity lead to a multiplicity of comic misunderstandings until identities are finally revealed and the twins reunited. In the final lines of the play, one twin looks into the face of the other and says, "Methinks you are my glass, and not my brother" (V.i.418). In short, one twin sees himself when he looks at the face of his brother. But this is more than a witty resolution. The ability to see oneself as others see us, to exchange perspectives, and to cross the boundary that separates one person from another is critical to understanding Shakespeare's body of work. In *A Midsummer Night's Dream*, this is stated explicitly by a daughter responding to an overbearing and intolerant father: "Would my father look'd but with my eyes" (I.i.56). When this relationship between self and other is fulfilled, the genre is comedy; its failure leads to tragedy, and hence to soliloquy, by its very nature a psychological collapse into a linguistic solipsism, a retreat across a bridge into self-confinement.

As a show title, *The Bridge* reflects the many liminal boundaries that permeate the series. The narrative begins on the bridge separating El Paso and Juárez with the discovery there of the halves of two bodies placed together to create the appearance of a single corpse (1:1). This literal and grotesque corporeal division is accompanied by other divisions—geographic, cultural, social, and psychological. These include the borders separating the United States and Mexico; parent and child; wife and husband; one detective partner and another; gay and straight; male and female; FBI and the local police. Above all is the division between our detective, Sonya Cross, and the world that surrounds her.

Let me begin with Diane Kruger's performance as Sonya. Her task is a difficult one. How to portray someone who appears essentially inaccessible to others? To varying degrees, this is an issue with any performance. Can Marlon Brando convince us he works on the docks? Can Toshirô Mifune convince us he is a medieval samurai warrior? But in this instance the difficulty is striking. Autism offers an extreme example of the barrier between an actor and her role. Kruger's performance must take the audience beyond behaviors that would merely objectify her as different. As genuinely as possible, she must turn inward into a particularly private subjectivity and then convey that to the viewer. It would be rather easy to adopt the stereotypical mannerisms of an autistic character, but much more difficult to lay bare her inner life. Kruger understood the challenge that she faced as an actor.

She worked daily on the set with the series consultant, Alex Plank, a well-known advocate for autism rights and himself a filmmaker. Her efforts resulted in a performance remarkable for its nuances.

The casting of Kruger as Sonya has subtle yet pervasive consequences. The creators of the series (Elwood Reid, Björn Stein, and Meredith Stiehm) exploit a common prejudice regarding how an autistic individual should physically appear. They chose a stunningly "beautiful" actor, one whose exteriority would instantly be read by the mind of any observer who thought that to be the most important kind of observation to make. In the series, Kruger's iconic beauty works to help her frame the character. She began her career by representing Germany in the Elite Model Look contest and went on to become a professional model. At this point in her career, her looks were all Kruger had. She brings her celebrated fashion appearance to her role as Sonya. And within the context of the series, her beauty is acknowledged by others. In fact, her physical appearance provides an element of the plot. The wife (Catalina Sandino Moreno) of Marco (Demián Bichir), the Mexican detective who becomes Sonya's partner, asks him whether his new partner from across the border is "good looking," afraid that Sonya's physical appearance might be a temptation for her husband. When his wife finally meets Sonya, she is taken aback by her looks and is immediately wary. And Marco's son (Carlos Chalabi), before even speaking to her, falls in love with her looks, not her character. When Sonya enters a bar in which she intends to find a sexual partner, she has little trouble ("Calaca," 1:2). Her exterior beauty renders her an object of desire and works against the audience's ability to see beneath it. I believe the creators of the series had two things in mind in casting Kruger: to use her iconic beauty to objectify her in the eyes of other characters as well as in the eyes of the audience; and to very subtly turn this objectification back on the audience in order to expose its proclivity to dissociate beauty from what is perceived as a mental disability. This strikes me as a daring move by the creators. Beauty becomes a barrier, and thereby another bridge to be crossed.

In more overt ways, Sonya is objectified by other characters. She is not referred to as autistic but as "different . . . strange . . . a bona fide wack job . . . an interesting gal." Her behavior often seems inappropriate and unanticipated. Most references to her are demeaning, and are often uttered with raised eyebrows and a smirk. Kruger's performance defies these characterizations, however. Her primary technique, one that nicely fits into my thematic approach, involves the movements of her body and, especially, her eyes. In medieval romance, the eyes were considered windows into the soul. Kruger uses her eyes to draw us into the interior life of Sonya: she stares off, not to turn away in discomfort so much as to process or struggle with a thought.

Three early scenes provide an overture to the ensuing narrative. The show begins with the discovery of what appears to be that single severed body placed with exactitude across the boundary line dividing Juarez and El Paso. The arrival on the bridge of Marco, the Mexican detective, is shot from his point of view, the camera positioned in the front seat of his car and peering out through the front window. A quick cut to the side and then back again reveals Marco's face so that we see whose perspective we are sharing. His point of view continues as he leaves the car and approaches the crime scene. The camera is set very low, so the viewer seems to move along with him. But the depiction of Sonya's arrival avoids her point of view. The camera is a few feet behind her and at shoulder height. Her blond hair falls over her shoulders and draws our attention. When she arrives at the crime scene, the camera cuts to a profile of her face, almost as if she were posing for a fashion shot. We are struck by a photogenic beauty that overwhelms her personal identity. She is, in short, immediately distanced from the audience. In addition, she is wearing white earbuds connected to her telephone, subtly suggesting that she is comfortable and perhaps even needful of a self-enclosed space. No one else is wearing them. And their color highlights her face and hair. They seem almost to be a fashion accessory. We are curious about what Marco will find, but of Sonya our curiosity is about who she might be. We are drawn to her precisely because she seems distant.

When Sonya addresses others at the scene, this distancing becomes more pronounced. She asks "inappropriate" questions and makes unexpected assertions, apparently oblivious of the body parts on the bridge. On first meeting Marco, she asks in a clipped impersonal manner, "Who are you?" Her tone of voice and inclination to avoid engaging him with her eyes precedes the arrival of an ambulance from Mexico carrying the victim of a heart attack and his wife. With some urgency, the wife asks that they be allowed to cross. Sonya blocks their passage even though the victim might very well die unless he reaches a hospital for treatment. Sonya adamantly refuses, citing the rule against letting anyone or anything come near a crime scene. "There are rules," she emphatically declares. Having made this pronouncement, she turns back to the body on the bridge. Without her awareness, Marco tells the ambulance driver to cross over into the United States. When Sonya sees the ambulance passing by, she chases it, pounding on its side and shouting for the driver to stop. Her aberrant behavior draws all eyes toward her. Her identity becomes its own mystery. She is foregrounded relentlessly through this opening scene as somehow different from the people around her. The divisions of the severed body on the bridge are symbolic of the division between Sonya and her external environment.

Our understanding of Sonya begins to expand in the scene that follows. Hank, the sheriff who is her superior officer and mentor, accedes to her request to contact the husband of the "top" murder victim, rather easily identified because she was a well-known judge in El Paso (interestingly little attention is paid the "bottom" victim). Sonya will conduct a preliminary interview. Hank tells her, "Remember eye contact," flagging an inability of many autists. Evocative of Shakespearean comedy, *The Bridge* is all about the eyes. Sonya turns her head and eyes aside, not to retreat into an enclosed space but to struggle to understand what it means to express empathy and how she might accomplish this. Her eyes also suggest her personal need to satisfy Hank, and the fear that if she cannot do this properly, she might lose her job. Moreover, the audience sees her commitment to her occupation and recognizes that her personal identity rests on it. Closing off a crime scene to the public is relatively straightforward; one must simply follow a procedural rule. Demonstrating empathy is a much more difficult task. Kruger subtly uses her eyes throughout the series to draw us into Sonya's subjectivity and to trigger our desire to know her. Her eyes offer the audience a bridge that might be crossed into her world.

But Sonya's encounter with the husband proves to be a disaster, an almost comic failure. Although she asks typical questions that might help in the investigation, she asks them in a mechanical manner that shows a complete lack of empathy. A few minutes into the interview, before the shock of his wife's murder has quite taken hold, she coolly asks, "Affairs?" She holds a pencil in her hand, apparently prepared to write down a simple yes or no. When she asks whether his wife used drugs, the husband says, "She was a mother," as if mothers were necessarily excluded from the ranks of addicts. Sonya responds, "My mother used drugs." She is pointing out the husband's false logic rather than sharing her own experience: if her mother was a drug addict, then it stands to reason that any mother could be a drug addict, too. Almost immediately Sonya's eyes show the recognition of her failure and befuddlement over how to proceed. She responds to failure with a formulaic utterance: "Would you like a glass of water?" When she leaves the house, she knows she must try one final time. With her eyes turned aside, failing one final time to remember eye contact, she says, without a trace of empathy, "I'm sorry if I didn't exercise empathy." The husband scoffs and closes the door behind her. The scene fluctuates between a comic distancing and our own empathy for her failure. On one hand, to put it figuratively, she gets a pie in the face; on the other, in large part because of our experience in the previous scene and Kruger's continued use of head and eye gestures, we are able to sense her vulnerability. The audience fluctuates between pity for Sonya and empathy for her struggle. Pity turns subjects into objects; empathy requires that one enter the consciousness of another.

The Narrative of the Rose

Umberto Eco's *The Name of the Rose* (1984) is a murder mystery set in the fourteenth century at a secluded Franciscan abbey in northern Italy. A monk has been killed, and Brother William, known for his powers of deductive reasoning, has been summoned to solve the case. His method adheres to Aristotelian empirical analysis, the collection of data in order to construct a narrative that leads to a conclusion. But his method ultimately fails to lead to the murderer. As he puts it, "I have never doubted the truth of signs . . . they are the only things man has with which to orient himself in the world. What I did not understand was the relation among signs" (492). William is left with a fundamental question: "Whether there is a design that goes beyond a natural sequence of events" (501). He also understands that to uncover that design, one must "reconstruct in one's own mind the thoughts of others" (465). In other words, the accumulation of external data must be accompanied by the probing of interior worlds of consciousness. These tandem methods speak to Sonya's growth as a detective as well as to her deepening involvement with the world beyond her.

There are multiple mysteries to be solved in *The Bridge*: the identities of the two (half) victims discovered on the El Paso–Juárez border bridge; why and how the killing was done; the death of Sonya's sister; the murders of some young women of Juárez; and most importantly, the mystery of Sonya herself. Can Sonya assemble the parts of her life into a linear narrative? Can she see herself through the passage of time in the context of others and their narratives? Can she engage the complexities and vagaries of self-consciousness? And, critically for the overarching narrative, can Sonya evolve over time? In other words, can she discover the design contained in the parts?

As with Brother William, Sonya's great strength lies in collecting and analyzing evidence. She displays her skill several times in the series, first on the bridge when she insists on preserving the crime scene, lest any evidence, any sign of the crime be compromised. In the morgue later in that episode, she shows no reluctance in examining the halves of the severed bodies. She moves her face and eyes so as to almost touch the skin of the lower half of the second corpse, another female. Through her analysis, she ascertains what the pathologist has already discovered: that the two halves come from different women and were placed together on the bridge. Through the rigorous examination of a live video, she identifies the precise location where an immigrant was staked to the ground ("Maria of the Desert," 1:4). She studies hydraulic systems in a *Popular Mechanics* magazine in order to determine where Marco's son Gus is being held by the killer ("Take the Ride, Pay the Toll," 1:11).

But she is less adept at probing the evidence contained in the minds of others. Places are not people. Her flaw is made painfully clear when she questions a reporter in the police interrogation room ("Calaca," 1:2). As we expect, she has trouble making eye contact, and her questions are ineffective. She gives away more than she receives, and is later admonished by Hank. The scene resembles her earlier questioning of the victim's husband. But that earlier interview also showed her skill at the logical analysis of data. When she is asked later by Hank whether she believes the husband is the killer, she says no: she had noticed his ineptitude with his phone and concluded that his ignorance of technology would prevent him from shutting down the electrical grid in order to place the bodies in darkness on the bridge. She failed at reading the husband's eyes but succeeded in reading his signs. She confidently tells Hank that the husband could not have done it.

Sonya's response to the sudden death of her sister, some time before the beginning of this show, further reveals her attraction to signs and symbols when she fixates on tokens of the departed. Her repetitive engagements with these signs are ritualistic and do not move her beyond the barriers of excessive mourning. She has taken her sister's pickup and made it her own. She repeatedly plays her sister's favorite cassette tape. Her investment in this "sign" is made clear when Marco ejects the tape in her car and Sonya immediately and angrily inserts it back into the player. Her sister loved horses, so she drives a Bronco (her sister's vehicle) and wears a jacket on whose back an image of a horse has been woven. She has placed a miniature horse inside the aquarium conspicuously displayed in her apartment. The aquarium is symbolic of Sonya's own self-enclosed world. And by placing the figure in the aquarium, she reveals a need to contain a symbol rather than exploit its meaning. In the final episodes of *The Bridge*, Sonya moves closer and closer to seeing beyond a sign to its place in a larger design.

How Long Can El Paso Look Away?

In *2666* (2008), Roberto Bolaño creates a fictionalized version of Juárez. It is a modernist, dysfunctional landscape: "factories, maquiladoras . . . a cocaine cartel, a constant flow of workers from other cities . . . money and poverty . . . an urban infrastructure that cannot support the level of demographic growth . . . equal parts lost cemetery and garbage dump" (286). More importantly, this fictionalized landscape has been the site of more than two hundred murders of young women. For Bolaño, these unsolved, barely investigated killings signify the destructive underpinnings of capitalist exploitation. Bolaño's Mexican border city is the bad dream of modernity but also the place—as a character enigmatically asserts—"where the secret of the world lies hidden" (348). For Sonya, the mission that she must undertake, not simply to solve a crime but to evolve as a character, transpires in the landscape of Juárez.

The Juárez depicted in *The Bridge* is the bad dream that threatens Sonya's reliance on rules and repetitive rituals. In an early episode, she adamantly asserts, "I do not dream." Her categorical denial suggests defensiveness. What is it about dreams that causes Sonya such disquiet? And how might it be associated with Juárez? The dysfunctional Juárez landscape in the American version of *The Bridge* is the most distinct change from its European predecessor. The juxtaposition of Sweden and Denmark pales in comparison with the radical contrast between El Paso and Juárez. The Mexican city's landscape of brothels, garbage, crumbling foundations, violence, and unsolved killings is prominently displayed in the American version. In the opening montage, El Paso and Juárez are visually contrasted, but images of the Mexican border town outnumber those of El Paso. A striking aura of otherworldliness informs the Juárez depicted here. Diego Rivera colors collide with images of material corruption. The opening montage concludes with an image of a cemetery at night, the graves marked with crosses lit by candles. We realize as the narrative unfolds that the graveyard is filled with the bodies of the many murdered women of Juárez. At one point the killer sends the message to Sonya and Marco: "How long can El Paso look away?" Juárez is a nightmarish dreamscape across the border that haunts El Paso and poses a threat to Sonya's strategies for containment. She is threatened by Juárez as she is threatened by dreams. They are extremely difficult to analyze; it is extremely difficult to discover a narrative pattern within them, extremely difficult to avoid ambiguities and contradictions.

When Sonya tells Marco they need to go to Juárez because that is where the truth about the murdered women lies, Marco responds that it is not the place for her ("Calaca," 1:2). And at this point he is correct. Juárez is a dysfunctional zone, lacking discernible rules and cultural practices. Communal rituals seem tenuous at best. The Catholic Church has little presence, and burial rituals are both overwhelmed by the sheer number of bodies and tainted by police indifference to solving the murders. Sonya tries to gather evidence in Juárez concerning the young Mexicana whose body formed the lower half of the double corpse. At the Juárez police station, she requests the box of evidence, which is carelessly stored along with the boxes of other unsolved cases. When it arrives, she adamantly demands that it be opened, and seems puzzled by Marco's evident anxiety. On the table is a photograph of the top half of the other bridge victim. His superior enters and Marco quickly hides it under the box, knowing full well that the local police have no interest in pursuing this case. Sonya cannot understand why there might be a need for apprehension and duplicity. Marco later explains to her, "It doesn't work like that." Sonya will need to learn how it works in Juárez. To put it bluntly, she must learn how to accept the innate duplicity of a locale depleted of rules. Marco tells her later, "All things are not black and white." The landscape of Juárez, the world on the other side of the ridge, proves to be the environment in which much of her evolution as a character transpires.

Juárez is a place of lies. This is subtly expressed at the beginning of the first episode. An odd and suspicious-looking man (Thomas Wright) has forced a young woman of Juárez into the trunk of his car. When he arrives at the border stop, the guard asks him why he was visiting Juárez, suspecting that he is carrying drugs across the border. He sheepishly responds that he has been there for the "señoritas." His lie is an ironic one. He has been there for *a* woman, but for a woman he means to rescue from the street life, not one he visited in a brothel. The guard knowingly smiles and sends him on his way. To deal with Juárez, to confront its environment and cleanse it in some small way, requires a lie, requires that she look, as Shakespeare puts it, with a "parted eye" (*A Midsummer Night's Dream* IV.i.188).

The complicated nature of lies envelops Sonya as the narrative continues until it reaches a dramatic and psychological climax on the bridge. To lie requires the circumvention of rules, and hence lies are anathema to Sonya's disposition. Her initiation into them begins in a small way. When Marco's wife is abducted by Kenneth Hastings, aka Tate (Eric Lange), who, we learn later, is the killer of the two women on the bridge ("The Beetle," 1:9), Sonya tells him that the kidnapper is smart and that therefore a rescue will be problematic. She says this without making eye contact, almost as if her eyes were turned inward and she were talking to herself. Marco reacts angrily. Sonya is confused by his anger: "What did you want to hear?" He replies, "I need to hear my wife is okay." Sonya apparently failed to see that there are people who don't always express what they are thinking or feeling. Empathy, in this case, requires a lie and, for Sonya, a new kind of vision.

The stakes rise in subsequent episodes. Marco asks Sonya to take Gus to a safe house, but along the way Hastings crashes into her car and takes the boy ("The Beetle," 1:9). Afterward, Sonya apologizes to Marco for failing to protect his son ("Old Friends," 1:10). "It was my job and you asked me," she says. This marks a significant change. She failed to meet the obligations that her identity as a police officer dictates, but now, more importantly, she also failed to fulfill a personal obligation. Marco then receives a phone call from Hastings ordering a meeting, apparently to negotiate his wife and son's release. Marco asks Sonya not to tell anyone where he is going. She responds, "I can't lie to Hank." Marco says, "Do it for me." And so she does lie to Hank. When asked where Marco has gone, she says, "He got a call and left." At best a half-truth. Sonya thus becomes entangled in a world that cannot be contained by prescribed behaviors. She has stepped into an environment where personal relationships complicate life, a world of contingent circumstances, divided loyalties, painful ironies, and the needs of others. She can no longer turn a blind eye.

Sonya's initiation into the complexities of lies and human relationships comes to an excruciating climax on the bridge. While Marco has been pursuing Hastings, Sonya has been desperately attempting to discover where the kidnapper took Gus. She deduces where he is being held, but arrives too late to save his life ("The Beetle," 1:9). She rushes to the bridge, where Marco has meanwhile been threatening to kill Hastings ("Take the Ride, Pay the Toll," 1:11). In a frenzy, he demands that Sonya tell him whether Gus is still alive, the implication being that unless his son is alive, he will shoot Hastings. Sonya's loyalty to Marco cuts in contradictory directions. She knows she has a personal obligation not to lie to her partner. And yet she knows that if she does not lie, Marco will be ruined. He will kill Hastings and become lost in the darkness of revenge and surely go to prison. But the cost to Sonya will be extraordinarily high if she lies. She will alienate Marco. He will blame her for taking from him the chance to take revenge. The pain in her face is concentrated in her eyes. We can see through them to the struggle she is enduring. The confusions that life can generate, the costs of personal sacrifice, the disruptions caused by contingent circumstances, and the debilitating ironies that inform human relationships: these cannot be reconciled by a blind adherence to rules.

The bridge clearly, neatly, and legally separates two worlds. But on that bridge Sonya discovers that the world cannot be so neatly divided. She finally lies, telling Marco what she believes he needs to hear: that Gus is alive. Marco relents, but almost immediately knows from her eyes that she has lied to deny him his revenge. He falls to the ground in abject pain over the death of his son. Sonya takes him in her arms, attempting to console him and genuinely sharing in his loss. It marks the first time in the series that she has been in any way physically intimate with another person. She weeps along with him. Her actions, in my opinion, are truly heroic. She did not put her life on the line, but rather her psychic condition. She has emphatically and willfully crossed over into a space where she can no longer be separate and private, where she violates the boundaries that were established around her from the beginning of her life.

The final three episodes focus on the relationship between Sonya and Marco long after the discovery of the bodies on the bridge. It is here, as one might say, that the real work for Sonya begins. Hank tells her, "He [Marco] needs a friend" ("All About Eva," 1:12). Sonya quietly responds with a single word: "Friend?" She says this to herself, not to merely turn away from Hank and his observation but also to draw the concept of friendship and the need for friendship into a space where she can struggle over their meaning. When she visits Marco, she discovers the pitfalls of establishing bonds with those who reside beyond oneself. She immediately makes eye contact with him and holds it throughout much of the encounter. It is Marco who turns away, literally and emotionally. He utterly rejects her for lying to him. She answers with a vulnerable innocence, "We are friends, and I did what friends do." This is still the Sonya who still needs logical and fixed guidelines. Friends do this; we are friends; so I acted that way. But then, in a demonstration of her growing ability to read the minds of others, she tells Marco that Hastings wanted to be killed by him. It would have been his way of exacting revenge on Marco. She read the mind of Hastings and recognized the design he had crafted. She goes on to say, showing that she knows who Marco really is, "You're not that person," meaning a killer. Marco bitterly responds, "Yes I am," and then cruelly tells her, "We are not friends. We were partners. . . . That's over." Another irony: Sonya breached a wall that had figuratively separated her, and now Marco has retreated behind it.

Marco returns to Juárez, refusing to testify in Hastings's trial. Sonya crosses into Mexico and goes to Marco's house ("All About Eva," 1:12). Once again she has made herself vulnerable, now in a landscape alien to her. She brings pastries, emulating Marco who brought breakfast rolls to Kitty (Diana-Maria Riva), the receptionist at the El Paso police station, to ingratiate himself with her. Has she done something similar? Has she done this to soften Marco so that he might agree to testify? Or does she truly care for him? Is this a sign of empathy for Marco's loss? Or is it simply a rule that one should bring an offering to one who mourns? These questions point to how remarkably nuanced and subtle is the learning process whereby Sonya moves closer and closer to engaging others. Marco tells her, "A normal person would not come here." She no doubt has been treated as abnormal most of her life, but here her abnormality is the uncommon strength she displays in taking what is for her an enormous risk. She has crossed over alone into the alien landscape of Juárez and into the elusive and bedeviling landscape of human relationships. Her eyes tell us that she needs Marco not only to testify but also to acknowledge her as a friend. She movingly reveals herself to him: "I wanted to check on you." He responds with bitterness, "You don't know me." Herein lies the crux of the series. To paraphrase Shakespeare: how difficult it is in all human relationships to see through the eyes of another. Marco utterly and cruelly rejects her: we were "only two people working a case." He tells her to leave Juárez and return to El Paso.

But she returns the next night to Juárez, where solving a case seems less difficult than solving the human heart ("All About Eva," 1:12). She finds Marco in a bar, drinking himself into oblivion. She takes him to his home, and once again he rejects her categorically. You can't understand, he tells her, what it is like to lose a child. But of course she does understand, because she has lost her sister. Marco at this moment fails her and fails himself. Once again her eyes speak to us: she recognizes his blind spot and knows that this moment cannot be shared; it must be reserved for herself alone. She responds that she doesn't find people very often and says, "Don't send me away." They sit in Gus's room on his bed. He tells her that he can still smell his son. And of course, Sonya has done the same thing. She can feel her sister's presence whenever she plays her tape and sits in her car. She tells Marco that Gus was "a sweet boy." She then looks up and sees Gus in the collage that he pinned to his bedroom wall. And now they are remembering Gus, not together but separately. In the morning, Sonya cooks breakfast for Marco. She reveals that her mother always liked eggs in the morning after a "rough night." Unlike the earlier revelation of her mother's addiction, which she used to point out the logic of her questioning, she is now attempting to share her world with Marco.

The next day, Marco does show up at the trial of Hastings ("All About Eva," 1:12). Sonya looks down from the top of the courthouse steps. She sees him and her eyes brighten. He comes up the steps, and she says simply, "You came." She reaches out to Marco with the hand in which she is holding an ornament that hung in her sister's car. Marco reaches out and puts his hand over hers. They look at one another, their eyes locked together, and he almost whispers, thereby making it more intimate, "Thank you." Sonya's worship of the sign of her sister has now been relocated as part of a larger design. This is, I argue, the true climax of the series. It represents a profound moment for Sonya, an act of communion, of grieving together, the experience of sharing with another person a common tragic loss. The moment resembles the ending of *A Comedy of Errors*, cited earlier, when one characters sees himself in the face of his twin. But in *The Bridge* there is none of the playwright's lighthearted cleverness. The encounter between Sonya and Marco is moving and yet, as we soon discover, a fleeting achievement.

That night Sonya returns again to Juárez and to Marco's house ("The Crazy Place," 1:13), fearful that he still intends to kill Hastings even though he is incarcerated. "I know what you are thinking," she tells him, "You want to kill Hastings." She tells him he can't do it, not because he would be breaking a rule but because it would erase himself. He would no longer be a "good man." He responds that he will not do anything stupid, and although they make eye contact once again, he is lying to her. After she leaves, Marco turns to the refrigerator door and sees a drawing by Gus that expresses love for his father. Earlier, on the wall of Gus's bedroom, Sonya saw the collage he had made. Marco and Sonya are both thinking of Gus, and seeing him, but not together. This missed opportunity hangs out there, qualifying the end of the series and exposing the precariousness of all human relationships.

That qualification is made explicit in the final scene of *The Bridge*. Marco goes deep into the Juárez of his past. He asks his childhood friend Galano (Ramon Franco), something of a crime lord, whether he can help kill Hastings in prison. Galano can. Marco replies, "No, I want to kill him myself." The camera then moves to a close-up of Marco's face and slowly moves closer and closer toward his right eye until it almost touches his pupil, and freezes there. In this final shot, we pass through his eye into the heart of his darkness. For Marco, we realize that the loss he has been nursing will never fade.

Afterword

By way of conclusion, I offer an experience of my own. I am a retired college professor. Before my final semester of teaching, I received a letter from a student enrolled in one of my spring classes. He explained that he was autistic and requested that during the semester I not make eye contact with him or directly address him in class. The letter, polite and straightforward, came through official channels. Although it was signed by the student, there was little to suggest that it was specifically addressed to me. It read like a form letter. He had given nothing away of himself other than his autism, and he wished to keep it that way. I diligently honored his request. At the end of the semester, he came to my office to turn in his final examination. It would be the last I would see of him. I expected he would drop his paper on my desk, avoid eye contact, say little more than "here is my paper," and leave. At no time during the semester did I know what he was thinking. And so I was taken aback when he lifted his head toward me and said, "I hope you have a good retirement." Did he see that expressing congratulations was to be expected in this context, almost as if it were a rule? Or did he mean this personally? Was he genuinely expressing himself to someone whom three months earlier he had asked to avoid all direct interaction? But the student and I were not finished. As he spoke these words to me, his eyes began to move upward until he was looking directly at my face and making eye contact. Then I took a chance and extended my hand, and he briefly took it into his own before quickly pulling it back and leaving my office. I was deeply moved. I had experienced a remarkable moment of intimacy, however short-lived. Remarkable because the border between us was powerfully guarded and very difficult for my student to cross.

I end with this because *The Bridge* is informed by mysterious moments big and small, successful and failing, of the interactions between Sonya and the world of others. At the end of the series, she and Marco come tantalizingly close to my experience at the end of that semester. But such relationships between all of us are often ephemeral and soon relegated to memory. *The Bridge* is ultimately profound and daring in that through Sonya, that "interesting gal" whom no one seems to fully understand, it explores a subject germane to us all.

CHAPTER 11

The Creative Evolution and Reception of Netflix's *Atypical*

CHRISTINE BECKER

Atypical (2017–2021), a coming-of-age story on Netflix about a teenage boy with autism and his coping family, is one of very few series in US television history to center on an autistic character rather than just featuring one at the periphery. This distinction puts considerable representational pressure on the show to deliver in one character what might be considered an accurate depiction of a condition defined by a spectrum of manifestations as well as by elements that are not readily visible and that are experienced differently by different people. Accordingly, the question of authenticity is at the core of many critical reviews of the series, particularly ones written by those with a personal investment in how autism is depicted in popular culture. Many who assessed season 1 found fault with the depiction of *Atypical*'s main character, Sam (Keir Gilchrist), identifying it as deeply inauthentic and thus highly problematic. The show's creative team, led by the showrunner Robia Rashid, responded with a handful of creative changes in season 2, some of which directly responded to the perceived criticism, and the result was both increased critical appreciation and richer storytelling. Through dissecting the creative decisions and critical reception of *Atypical*'s first two seasons, this chapter illustrates how the demands for authenticity in the fictional representation of autism go well beyond what is visible onscreen, and also illuminates the challenges of journalistic criticism applied to the series.

The Authenticity of Fictional Autism

Issues of authenticity in regard to any representation of "disability" or "difference" are always up for questioning in terms of their accuracy, but the particulars of autism make for an even more acute debate. A significant factor complicating the demand for authenticity in representing autism is that it is a nebulous condition presenting persistent clinical and cultural questions about definitions of and differences between related conditions such as Autism Spectrum Disorder, and even the extent to which such conditions point to nonnormative behaviors (Loftis 2016; Nadesan 2005). Because of these factors, Anders Nordahl-Hansen (2017) cites "the slightly worn-out saying that 'if you have met one person with autism, you have met *one* person with autism.'"

Despite such heterogeneity in the manifestations and personalities of those identified as autists, autism in film and television fiction has consistently been represented by a mere handful of key signifiers, such that characters tend to be collections of quirks rather than fully dimensional beings. These markers, traditionally classified under a so-called triad of impairments, include "communicative problems, lack of self-awareness, missing of social cues, no eye-contact and avoidance of emotionality, both mentally and physically" (Reichelt 2020, 184). These are not the only behavioral traits that the fifth edition of the American Psychiatric Association's *Diagnostic and Statistical Manual of Mental Disorders* (*DSM-5*) identifies as characteristic of autism, yet they are the ones most consistently represented in fictional visual media (Dowdy 2013). Similarly, consistent plots and topics appear tied to characters with autism, such as "hypersensitivity to environmental stimuli, problems in school and struggles with academic success . . . severe bullying . . . difficulties regarding dating, sex and relationships . . . also more overarching existential issues and general difficulties with social communication that leads to feelings of social ostracism" (Nordahl-Hansen and Øien 2018). Most disproportionate is a sizable gap between the number of autistic characters in mainstream entertainment with savant skills and those in real life. Douwe Draaisma writes about feature films:

> Actors insist that they invest months of preparation to study the movements and reactions of autistic persons, script writers read scientific articles on autism, directors call on consultants, they all want an absolutely sincere and truthful rendition of autism; what they come up with is an autistic character with freak-like savant skills, unlike anything resembling a normal autistic person. The stereotype of autistic persons being savants is without doubt one of the most striking discrepancies between the expert's view and the general view of autism (2009, 1478).

Because of its predominance in popular culture, this "general view of autism" sets the standard for the average neurotypical person's sense of "authentic" autism, whether it precisely matches any given autistic person's reality or not. In fact, some of these tropes have become entrenched not because they are authentically representative but because they fit the industrial storytelling demands of mainstream film and television. They are more easily visualized than other internal elements, and sensationalistic characteristics like savantism satisfy demands for compelling drama more than instructive characterization does (Dowdy 2013, 9). Reliance on stereotype also makes evident how autism can quickly become a plot device rather than an organic basis for characterization, especially when a narrative needs its most fundamental component: conflict (Baker 2008, 231). Avery Holton explored autism as plot device in the television series *Parenthood* (2010–2015), finding in the autistic son, Max, a common representation of strife and struggle that suggested "to society that ASD individuals are a cumbersome bunch with little to offer aside from emotional distress and unending anxiety—all of this while pressing the mute button on ASD individuals, in essence promoting a fear of ASD individuals without ever considering the individuals themselves" (2013, 12). The last part of Holton's comment refers to the fact that Max's parents don't initially inform him of his diagnosis, but it also fits with the casting of the series and many others featuring autistic characters, since Max is played by an actor, Max Burkholder, who does not self-identify as autistic.

Here we must shift behind the screen to account for additional components of authenticity, as when minority race, disability, and such Othered identity representations are in play. As the amputee actress Katy Sullivan (2018) explains, when able-bodied actors "play at" living life with a disability, it is not just an employment opportunity but also a "genuine, authentic perspective" that is lost.

Miscasting extends into the area of creative authorship and the realm of normative writers penning screenplays about Othered characters, in which a gap in experience and knowledge must be overcome not just for one character but also for the whole narrative world (Bishop 2003, 47). The outcome is likely to be stories that lean on the same general view and tropes described above, despite the best intentions. Holton advances just such an argument via his analysis of *Parenthood*, whose creator and showrunner, Jason Katims, self-identifies as neurotypical but has an autistic son: "Parents of children with disabilities are faced with important situations that many parents might not otherwise encounter, so Katims's voice is not without merit. However, familial and clinical voices should not be taken for a substitute for informed experience. While this is not uncommon in popular culture, where writers and producers provide constructed realities for the public, it does little to represent disabled voices" (2013, 8).

Issues of authenticity are further complicated when the genre in question is not a documentary, biopic, or drama but a comedy. The intention here is not necessarily to inform or educate viewers, but to make them laugh. Additionally, the primary function of a comedy—entertaining the audience—could be disrupted by the inclusion of straight, factual representations or serious issues like mental health struggles (Nordahl-Hansen, Tøndevolda, and Fletcher-Watson 2018, 352). Scott Silveri, the creator of the network sitcom *Speechless* (2016–2019), has discussed this challenge. *Speechless* centers on the family of a nonverbal teenage boy with cerebral palsy; the show reflects Silveri's experience of growing up with a disabled brother. Silveri reports that his initial draft of the pilot script was "suffocating": "It's hard enough to make one of these things entertaining or funny, but when you're walking that line between therapy or comedy writing—you don't get paid for therapy" (quoted in Salud 2017). More broadly, humor is a fraught area when it comes to Otherness. The classic distinction between whether you are laughing with or at a character has deep stakes here, as does the line between accurate representation and mockery. One person's accurate impression is another's ableist caricature.

Such complexities of humor are further refracted within the realm of autism. Jason McCormick, a psychologist, has observed that people with ASD and their neurotypical peers tend to have different senses of humor, especially when elements like punch lines or the nuances of facial expressions come into play. This does not mean that autistic people lack a sense of humor. Instead, McCormick proposes, "rather than calling this finding a humor deficit, humor atypicality is perhaps more appropriate" (n.d.). Mc-Cormick's choice of words is strikingly appropriate for this chapter's case study. What might it mean to display, as well as to critique, the authenticity of atypicality in a television series, especially when the condition and the formats are so variable?

Atypical's Development Stage

Robia Rashid honed her writing skills in sitcom writers' rooms, starting her career on the final season of *Will and Grace* (1998–2006) and then becoming a staff writer on the short-lived sitcoms *The Loop* (2006–2007) and *Aliens in America* (2007–2008). She then climbed up the writing ladder to become a supervising producer on *How I Met Your Mother* (2005–2014), a consulting producer on *Bad Teacher* (2014), and then a co–executive producer on *Friend Me* (2012; never aired) and *The Goldbergs* (2013–). She signed an overall deal with Sony TV in 2013, under which *Atypical* was born (Andreeva 2019).

In writing *Atypical*'s pilot script and planning the first season's trajectory, Rashid was inspired to tell a relatable story about the challenges of dating and finding love, but from the unique perspective of someone who had grown up on the autism spectrum (Garofalo 2017; Fernandez 2017). She told a *Vulture* reporter: "That point of view seemed so interesting to me—and such a cool way to tell a dating story. You've seen the story of somebody looking for independence and looking for love before, but not from that specific point of view. I really was drawn to that. I was a little annoyed because it sounded really hard! I had to do a lot of research" (quoted in Fernandez 2017). As this indicates, Rashid had no immediate experience with autism other than a personal relationship that she has alluded to but has declined to reveal (Fernandez 2017). Most resonant in her research was a 2012 memoir by David Finch titled *The Journal of Best Practices: A Memoir of Marriage, Asperger Syndrome, and One Man's Quest to Be a Better Husband*, which she subsequently gave to every cast and crew member. She also retained a consultant for the series, Michelle Dean, from the UCLA Center for Autism Research and Treatment, who offered advice on scripts and episodes for accuracy, but not story suggestions (Garofalo 2017; Fernandez 2017). Importantly, though, no one working in a creative capacity on the series has (at the time of this writing) identified as autistic, a factor that became central to the contentious reception of season 1.

Rashid seemingly would have had such hiring freedom, given the creative control she was granted by the outlet that picked up the series. And because of her extensive network experience, it is telling that Rashid decided Netflix would be the best home for *Atypical*: "I guess it felt like a non-network show to me. [Netflix] felt like a place where creators had room to explore a little bit and I definitely knew that this show needed space. I don't ever want to fall into jokes or be too cutesy. I want there to be edge and heart, so I knew that a place where there's this freedom to explore with tone and content would be a great home for this show. Netflix always felt like that kind of place to me" (quoted in Fernandez 2017). As a half-hour comedy outside the broadcast-network model, *Atypical* can reflect a greater generic freedom in which a predominance of dramatic elements over jokes is acceptable. The television critic Alan Sepinwall (2017) described *Atypical*'s first season as being "like one of those Showtime half-hours circa 2011 that were labeled comedies more for their running time than for how funny they were." But *Atypical*'s particular mix of comedy and drama raised concerns for some reviewers, particularly regarding Sam's behavior.

Most controversial in this regard is that Sam is played by an actor who does not self-identify as autistic. Rashid auditioned autistic actors for the part, one of whom she liked so much that she created a minor role for him as a family friend (Garofalo 2017). But the lead role went to the neurotypical actor Keir Gilchrist. Two of Gilchrist's major roles before *Atypical* were characters with mental health issues, and in interviews publicizing *Atypical* he opened up about his struggles with depression and anxiety. He said that he is probably attracted to such roles "because they're important and it opens up a conversation that does not happen very often" and could thus potentially help end stigmas around mental health struggles (quoted in Fabian 2009). But in the US television industry, in which only around 20 percent of characters with disabilities are played by actors with those disabilities (Nissim and Mitte 2018), some questioned the ethics of Gilchrist accepting the role of Sam.

The Contentious Reception of Season 1

Before *Atypical*'s premiere, Rashid made it clear that the series was not intending to provide a definitive portrait of autism: "We're telling a very specific story, Sam's story, and not trying to speak for every person on the spectrum" (quoted in Rowe 2017). She also insisted that although she did make the series partly for those who were experiencing autism firsthand and yearned for greater representation of such perspectives on television, she wanted the show to reach a broader audience, one that would identify with

Sam and the family beyond any autism-specific aspects (Garofalo 2017). Initial reviews indicated that general audiences would likely enjoy the series. Noel Murray (2017) wrote, "The average viewer will likely find *Atypical* easy to watch," and Leslie Felperin (2017) said the series would probably be "incredibly illuminating for those who don't know much about the condition." For some of those who do, however, it was not an easy watch (O'Keefe 2017), particularly as they seemed to be expecting something more like a definitive portrait.

For reviewers who identified themselves either as autistic or as a parent of an autistic child with emotional investment in representations of autism, the most glaring problem in the first season of *Atypical* stemmed from the belief that Sam was written too much like the standard autistic characters seen in numerous films and TV series, especially recent ones (Rozsa 2017). As Haley Moss (2017) wrote in the *Huffington Post*: "[Sam is] totally the stereotypical higher functioning autistic character, except he isn't obsessed with trains. Otherwise, he's a perfect stereotype." Sam's opening scenes feature him describing himself in a way that perfectly aligns with the familiar *DSM-5* traits (Nordahl-Hansen 2017), and Leslie Felperin (2017) laments:

> Often it feels like *Atypical*'s writers have combed through the literature—
> the many academic accounts, memoirs and so on—and extracted, intensi-
> fied and amplified all the most obvious autistic behaviours, particularly
> those that would have been described as signs of Asperger syndrome before
> that latter diagnosis was brought in under the autism umbrella by the latest
> edition of the Diagnostic and Statistical Manual of Mental Disorders. So
> Sam is basically a human whiteboard illustrating the triad of impairments.
> He talks in a somewhat rat-a-tat monotone voice (demonstrating atypical
> verbal development), can't understand social cues and takes everything very
> literally (social and emotional difficulties), and has obsessions (imaginative
> restriction or repetitive behaviour), which manifests [*sic*] in his case as an
> all-consuming interest in Antarctica and the Arctic and all the fauna of
> those environments, especially penguins.

Felperin also complains of "tons of clunky exposition and autism 101 lectures shoehorned in, especially among characters who would surely know this stuff by now," which are evident throughout the series. Certainly, some of this would be needed for the broader audience, thus calling into question the fairness of this critique, but the frustration stems from having these aspects bracketed off in ways that seem separated from plotlines rather than being more integrated with them.

By exhibiting such a slim collection of archetypal character traits, Sam also lacks the complexity that many of these reviewers yearned to see on-screen. The *AV Club* reviewer John Hugar (2017) wrote:

> The show goes so far in making Sam seem as autistic as possible that he winds up being nothing like an actual person with autism. All the traits on the spectrum are turned up to the absolute max, to the point of parody. Sam doesn't merely miss social cues from time to time, he does it in *every single scene*. He doesn't just occasionally say something awkward in the middle of a conversation, that happens in just about every line of dialogue he has. You'd think a show that makes an autistic character the protagonist rather than part of a supporting cast would have led to a deeper, more nuanced portrayal, but you'd be wrong.

Haley Moss (2017) was similarly frustrated by the lack of nuance underlying Sam's miscues and missteps—"With autism, it isn't always this obvious," while Noel Murray (2017) lamented that Sam has a singular goal throughout the first season, to obtain a girlfriend, but isn't supplied with the dialogue or plot situations needed to put that goal into a sufficiently personal or cultural context to make him seem like a real-world character.

A related concern was that Sam's primary autistic traits are mobilized less to define him as a character than to function as plot contrivances when provocative, boldly entertaining moments are needed. Matthew Rozsa (2017) points to incidents such as Sam suddenly punching a girl at the start of a romantic encounter or telling his girlfriend in front of her whole family that he doesn't love her: signs that he will be "inept, bumbling and awkward when the plot demands it." Suzanne Garofalo (2017) shares a teenage autistic viewer's complaint that the constant oversight of Sam's relatively high-functioning life by his mother, Elsa (Jennifer Jason Leigh), is more melodrama than reality. Sam's obsession with his therapist, culminating in him breaking into her house, received the most complaints. Rozsa writes of such absurd moments: "These aren't classic signs of autism—they're violent, creepy, cruel and make the autistic character seem like a monster. When the show then shifts gears to make us feel sorry for Sam, the characterization becomes *more* offensive. Arguing that those with neurological conditions shouldn't be held accountable for hurting others is as patronizing as it is socially irresponsible" (2017). Other reviewers similarly found that Sam came across as so oblivious of others as to be an unlikable jerk rather than a character with complex nuances (Hugar 2017). Noel Murray, on the other hand, just finds the character flat: "Sam is too much of a fictional construct, deployed for easy comedy and melodrama. . . . I can't deny that to me, Sam always felt 'written,' not lived." Murray, who is not an especially strident reviewer of this show, clearly had unfulfilled expectations.

The "easy comedy" generated by Sam's behavior in season 1 was a particularly contentious issue. In a review, Alan Sepinwall (2017) relays his opinion that the series never crosses the line into laughing at Sam's quirky traits, but some reviewers disagreed and identified that very factor as the show's major comedic flaw (O'Keefe 2017; Rowe 2017; Moss 2017; Gilbert 2017). Many of Sam's funny lines come because he has observed something in a matter-of-fact, emotionless way, not because he is witty or even trying to be funny. Jack O'Keefe conveyed concern in his overview of the show's backlash that such moments would encourage the audience to laugh at Sam, because "the show frames Sam in a way that him not acting normal is supposed to be hilarious." Humor is also frequently tied to the discomfort that other characters feel around Sam when his behavior gets outlandish. The autistic actor Mickey Rowe comments:

> Throughout the show, Sam's autism manifests in how he simply makes the people around him incredibly uncomfortable. In one scene, he tells his counselor, "I can see your bra. It's purple," seemingly unaware that this isn't a socially acceptable thing to say. In another, he just repeats the word "twat" over and over for no apparent reason. As he does each of these things, it feels like the audience is supposed to laugh at how weird and different Sam is. This is the crux of *Atypical*'s comedy, but there's nothing that funny about turning someone's disability into a punchline.

These critiques of Sam's portrayal illustrate not just frustration with the series but also the fundamental challenge of judging any portrayal of an autistic character. Autism is a heterogenous condition, no two individuals necessarily have the same experience with it, and parents cannot know what their autistic children experience.

Recalling Nordahl-Hansen's observation "If you have met one person with autism, you have met *one* person with autism," one could say that if you have seen one TV series with a character identified as autistic, you have seen one character, not autism. As noted previously, Rashid explicitly stated that *Atypical* was not made to speak for all autistic people, but critics for whom such representations are deeply relevant to their personal lives may not be satisfied with this intention or accept it at face value. This makes criticism of *Atypical* as complex a representational object as the series itself.

At the root of many of these purported problems onscreen, insist many critics, is the lack of creative input from anyone on the spectrum as a writer, director, producer, or lead actor (Rowe 2017; Rozsa 2017; O'Keefe 2017; Arky 2017). Mickey Rowe acknowledges Rashid's efforts to do research and speak with the parents of autistic children in order to glean insights, but argues, "That isn't the same as talking to an autistic person about how they view the world and giving them the platform to present their point of view—an opportunity that is so rarely granted to them." And Matthew Rozsa insists the problem isn't just one of representational equality: "It's hard to imagine a series like this being effective if the voice it aims to capture isn't among those telling the story" (2017). Of course, there may be unavowed autists on the production staff.

Notably, praise is offered when the season does get certain small details and gestures right, and these are most frequently the kinds of moments that the reviewers experienced personally or through family members. Suzanne Garofalo (2017), the mother of an autistic boy, recognizes Elsa's Post-it note reminding Sam to put on deodorant, and Noel Murray (2017) notes that Sam's failed attempt at an inviting grin reminded him of his own autistic son, and both reviewers comment on the literalization of terminology they hear from their boys. In addition, Murray appreciates specific details that take viewers into Sam's tactile experiences, like the annoyance of a squeaky leather jacket, and he praises times when Sam gets to narrate his own experiences, which, Murray says, "are generally the moments when it presents him most as a complicated person and not a collection of textbook ASD tendencies." Importantly, these are not necessarily moments that advance the plot or tie in with the central premise of Sam's goal to find love, indicating that character and story details help define Sam and his condition as much as any major plot point. Murray perceptively notes, "In a well-told story, the specific can open up to become more universal, if those specifics are unique, personal, and carefully chosen. Too often, *Atypical* defaults to the typical."

In some reviews, one can feel personally invested writers yearning for greater understanding of their experiences. These reviewers appreciate the good intentions behind the series, but they also lament such a rare opportunity coming up short (Felperin 2017; Hugar 2017; Rozsa 2017). In a typical example, John Hugar cynically writes that *Atypical*'s attempt to depict autism in a picture-perfect way makes it something like *Autism Speaks: The Sitcom*:

> *Atypical* desperately wants to be the show that *gets* autism. You can see this right in the promotional poster for the show, which tells us that "normal is

overrated," which is the type of quick-fix sentiment that seeks to heal, but is only capable of pandering. This show wants to be to autism what *You're The Worst* is to depression, or perhaps even what *Transparent* is to being transgender. Unfortunately, it trips over its feet at just about every turn, and the fact that the show so clearly thinks it's handling the topic the right way just makes it more irritating whenever it gets things wrong.

In addition to a lack of creative input from autistic people, some critics indict Rashid's intention to foreground the themes that no one is really normal and everyone can relate to the struggle to find love; thus, Sam is just like all of us (Fernandez 2017; Kennedy 2017). While this stance is well intentioned, it may be the main thing that leads to a problematically clashing mix of tones across episodes, which numerous reviewers take issue with. In the *Atlantic*, Sophie Gilbert (2017) writes, "It's hard to tell whether its inconsistency is due to a blurry conception of what tone it should strike, or whether producers simply wanted to appeal to as broad a swathe of potential viewers as possible—the show skews so wildly from slapstick to gritty drama to teen soap to family sitcom that it should come with Dramamine." And Mickey Rowe (2017) pinpoints this tonal inconsistency as the point where the show's laughter at Sam's differences fosters a disconnection with its aim to illustrate that his problems are universal and relatable.

Changes and Revaluations in Season 2

Atypical was renewed for a second season less than a month after its Netflix premiere. Netflix does not release viewership figures, but *Deadline*'s characterization of the decision as "a quick renewal" indicates that *Atypical* had a strong initial viewership and that any negative response to the show's representations of autism did not hinder it (Andreeva 2017). This vote of confidence could have encouraged Robia Rashid to stay the course in season 2, but she told the *New York Times*, "[I] definitely heard the criticism and it was a guiding principle for me in Season 2" (quoted in Luterman 2018). While no autistic writers or producers were added to the creative team, Rashid went a step beyond having her crew read David Finch's book by adding him as an adviser to the series (Ali 2017). She also made a concerted effort to increase gender diversity behind the scenes, and women made up half the members of the writer's room and seven of the ten directors in season 2 (Reynolds 2018).

Most notably, six actors with autism were cast to play members of a peer support group whose meetings Sam regularly attends. The actors were re-cruited from the Miracle Project, an arts program in Los Angeles for dis-abled youth that offers training and professional development workshops in theatre, film, and the expressive arts (Patton 2018). That the charac-ters they play are diverse in identity, personality, and abilities helps drive home the point that Sam is indeed just one character with autism that view-ers have met. While these characters are almost exclusively contained in the support-group scenes and thus don't get story lines of their own, their scenes display their individual senses of humor, each quite distinctive from Sam's, while they earnestly discuss topics of great import, such as the em-ployment struggles for autistic people. The autistic journalist Sara Luter-man (2018) especially appreciated that these new characters display an ar-ray of professional aspirations, including dentist and EMT: "I have an MFA in creative writing—most of us aren't Bill Gates or Sheldon Cooper of 'The Big Bang Theory,' and it was nice to see that acknowledged here." Given the predominance of white men as film and television characters with autism, it is important to note that there are women and people of color in the group.

In addition to this casting expansion, Sam's goals and interests widen in season 2, giving many viewers the greater nuance and complexity in his character and story lines that they were pining for. While there is still a ro-mantic angle to some of Sam's efforts, he is more focused on the broader fu-ture as he approaches the end of his senior year. In particular, he considers the possibility of college, choosing a major, and handling the opportunity and challenge of greater independence. *TV Guide*'s Megan Vick (2018) notes that the goal for any second season of a TV series should be to expand the narrative world and deepen the character portrayals. But more is at stake in this case, given the dearth of prominently featured autistic characters on television and the limited stereotypes tied to them.

Thus, it is important to note the specific ways in which Sam is further developed in season 2, especially elements uncommon in past portrayals of autistic characters. About Sam's focus on college, Vick writes, "The newness of his situation not only pushes him to grow, but allows him to be better at asking for help and appreciating the people around him who offer it. Sam's quest to set out on his own ironically makes him more open to the world around him" (218). Kayla Cobb (2018), writing in the *Decider*, likewise notes that Sam is handed more mature challenges to deal with in season 2, such as losing the everyday presence of his older sister at school, and he moves forward on his own more than he did in season 1. Notably, the academic pursuit that Sam ends up finding most engaging is not a science, technol-ogy, engineering, or mathematics major, a divergence from the predominant math and science savant image of fictional autistic characters. Instead, he is drawn to the arts and professional drawing, albeit with a scientific-design bent, given his love of penguins. As the columnist Gabbi Calabrese (2018) argues, "That duality is partly why Sam is such a dynamic character. His autism might explain how he processes the world, but it is not the only quality that defines him. He's not a walking compilation of symptoms, he's a person with hobbies, relationships and fears." The comedy in season 2 is noticeably less tied to Sam's behavioral patterns. Cobb praises the season for "both easing back on the Sam punchlines and giving Gilchrist more to work with while leaning into the darker comedy that was always lurking in this show."

These changes make Sam less a human whiteboard for the autism triad and more the kind of broadly relatable character that Rashid insisted she had intended for season 1. Writing in *Vulture*, Jen Chaney (2018) appreciates the revised Sam: "[His] place on the spectrum is treated less like an issue with a capital-I this season and more like just one aspect of the busy, complicated life of a family. In some ways, that's a positive and feels more reflective of the way actual families function. When a child has special needs, every day at home doesn't suddenly turn into a Very Special episode of television. It's just another regular day, and *Atypical* innately understands that." The expectation that a television show should reflect everyday life is problematic, but this comment harks back to the concern expressed by Leslie Felperin (2017) about season 1, bracketing off educational lessons from the plot. By doing this less, season 2 is able to give more narrative space to the rest of the family, especially Sam's sister Casey (Brigitte Lundy-Paine), a critic's favorite in both seasons. Ironically, adding more expertise about autism to the series seemingly decentered the focus on the condition in the larger narrative world, which in turn helped naturalize its depictions.

There were fewer reviews of the second season than of the first, which is to be expected, since the nature of television criticism prioritizes a show's first season. And some frustrated viewers might not have been willing to continue watching the series. But Matthew Rozsa, a *Salon* writer with autism who was highly critical of season 1, returned to review season 2, and while he still found flaws, he was impressed by the show's growth and the wider range of experiences granted to Sam (2018). Rozsa contacted two others with autism who had been critical of season 1, and they agreed that the changes equaled small but impactful improvements. Alex Plank, an autism advocate, believes the addition of David Finch as a consultant helped improve the writing, and he appreciated Sam's more three-dimensional personality: "Sam gained a lot more agency and became less of a caricature and I think he acted in ways that were more in line with what one should expect from an autistic high schooler" (quoted in Rozsa 2018). And Mickey Rowe, who wrote a widely quoted review of season 1 that called it "a major disappointment," offered a "loving challenge" for Rashid, based on his appreciation of season 2's improvements: "Keep listening, keep slowly making progress towards representation, diversity, and equity. And thank you for the small changes you made this season. You got this. Now keep going" (ibid.).

Atypical has kept going, as has the critical appreciation of it.[1] The third season sees Sam attend a nearby university and grapple with making new friends, managing college courses, and deciding whether to use the campus disability services. Part of his conundrum is whether he sees himself as "disabled." In an assessment of the season, notably titled "*Atypical*'s Journey to Authentic Disability Representation," Charlotte Little (2020) praises the latter story line in particular: "It's refreshing for audiences to be introduced to a narrative that acknowledges disability services, enabling viewers to conclude that there's no shame in asking for help as it's there for a reason. Disability is no indication of limited capabilities, and education should be accessible to everyone." Such thoughtful messages were arguably less likely to be found in season 1, because of its more narrowly focused premise and Sam's more limited characterization; the show's narrative expansion has thus served representational needs. And this change had evident creative payoffs. One could contend that *Atypical* became a better show after season 1, with more complex and nuanced characters, more compelling story lines, and more consistent tones. One article about season 1 contains the subheading "Accuracy versus good storytelling" (Garofalo 2017), which reflects a common conception that providing an authentic representation of autism has to come at the expense of entertainment. But the evolution of *Atypical* illustrates that this is a false binary. Striving for more accurate representation in the series improved it as a piece of television storytelling.

But it should be stressed that there is no such thing as a truly authentic singular representation of autism, because of the complexities outlined in the first part of this chapter. The criticisms of season 1 illustrate the weight of expectations placed on a series that never claimed to offer a definitive portrayal of autism. Therefore, a worthy goal is to push for a wider and more voluminous range of representations of autistic characters in film and television. Anders Nordahl-Hansen, Magnus Tøndevold, and Sue Fletcher-Watson conclude their *Psychiatry Research* analysis of twenty-six film and TV portrayals of ASD with the statement: "For portrayals of ASD on screen to have true value in developing public understanding of the condition, a larger and more varied number of autistic characters need to be included in the cultural canon" (2018, 353). The problem isn't just that Sam may not be an authentic representation of a person identified as autistic; it is that Sam is the *only* representation of a person identified as autistic in a leading role in a television comedy right now. Jennifer Laszlo Mizrahi, president of the disability advocacy organization RespectAbility, likewise stresses the importance of having character representations that focus on aspects of individual lives and humanity: "The only way to create authenticity within entertainment television is if characters with obvious and hidden disabilities are included within every script and story line, just as they are found within the diversity of our everyday lived experience. All too often, these characters are featured when there is a focus on disability within the script; when in reality, characters with disabilities should be included in the vast majority of roles that are non-descript and have nothing to do with a particular disability" (quoted in Kennedy 2017).

Finally, unless people with autism are in the writers' room, portraying autistic characters, standing behind the camera, and making decisions from the executive suite, autistic voices will continue to be marginalized and their representations limited. Mickey Rowe (2017) expressed this in his critique of season 1: "The point of storytelling is to connect us with people we otherwise wouldn't come in contact with, to bring us life experiences we don't already have. That is why diversity in the arts and media matters. Inclusion in the media matters because it leads to inclusion in life. If even a show about autism can't include autistic people thoroughly and directly, we have some good work still to be done." In that regard, *Atypical* is still all too typical.

Note

1. While one can question the reliability of scores from review aggregator sites, the IMDb and Rotten Tomatoes scores for the series grew in season 2 and into season 3. The series was renewed by Netflix for a fourth and final season, which was released in 2021.

CHAPTER 12

Community's Human Laugh Track: Neurodiversity in a Metamodern Sitcom

JOSHUA SCHULZE

Following a set of characters lovingly carved from recognizable arche-types, *Community* (2009–2015), Dan Harmon's community-college-set sit-com, ably strikes a balance between familiar comedic story lines and more self-contained, high-concept fare across its 110 episodes. With a principal cast comprising the quite literally too-cool-for-school reluctant hero Jeff Winger (Joel McHale); the overly keen Goody Two-Shoes Annie Edison (Alison Brie); the football jock Troy Barnes, who self-imposes a fall from grace (Donald Glover); the outspoken feminist and activist-who-ruins-everything Britta Perry (Gillian Jacobs); the devout Baptist divorcée and as-piring professional baker Shirley Bennett (Yvette Nicole Brown); the local neighborhood entrepreneur Pierce Hawthorne (Chevy Chase), predictably old, white, racist, sexist, and homophobic; and Abed Nadir (Danny Pudi), the neurodiverse pop-culture obsessive, *Community* plays out a penchant for metafiction mainly channeled through Abed, the only character who repeatedly shows an awareness that he exists in a television sitcom.

In the very first episode ("Pilot"), Jeff tells Abed, "You have Asperger's Syndrome." Although it is never explicitly stated beyond this, it has been widely acknowledged that Abed falls "somewhere on the autistic spectrum" (Tansley 2014, 219). In critical writing on the subject, however, few have satisfyingly considered the complexity with which *Community* approaches the topic of neurodiversity, particularly on a formal and structural level. That is the purpose of this chapter. In addition to its self-awareness, its acute understanding of the mechanisms of genre, and its metamodern oscillation between postmodern pastiche and hopeful sincerity, much of *Community*'s appeal comes from its contemporary mobilization of the idea that television is an object both "comfortable and comforting" (Corner 1999, 99), whose address to the audience provides companionship and "relaxed sociality" (26). This mobilization, I argue, is inextricable from the portrayal of autists. Virtually every textual nod to the audience is communicated through Abed, and so rather than holding the audience at a postmodern distance, the show brings it closer to a character whose condition might have otherwise presented an obstructive challenge. The audience is offered an ongoing sense of companionship facilitated by Abed's notable cognizance of "living in a television sitcom" that he is watching along with the viewers at home. He watches himself as we watch him watching.

Here a creative spin is put on the antiquated convention of the laugh track, another tactical weave of viewer and program content, a spin that in turn contributes to the audience's growing affinity with and understanding of a neurodiverse character. To explore this further, I want to first establish how *Community* both earns and negotiates its sitcom credentials before considering how it updates and reworks these conventions to accommodate its portrayal of a character with autism. I then assess how this reworking of convention aligns with more contemporary notions of televisual complexity and the important figure of the showrunner before thinking about how *Community* navigates such issues and brings cinematic genre to the forefront, not to boast some superior cinephilic knowledge but instead to demonstrate precisely how and why genre fascination is important to Abed as a character.

"Is That Even a Sitcom Staple?"

Community's appellation as a sitcom has been the subject of much discussion, and often disagreement, in part because of its awareness of the tropes it frequently deploys. Indeed, several writers have outlined how the show revises or subverts the traditional sitcom formula: some argue that it "embraces, acknowledges and critiques the artifice inherent in the sitcom form and its own status as a sitcom" (Barnett and Kooyman 2012, 114), while others describe its "movement away from sitcom convention and toward metafictional consideration of the contemporary destabilization of identity" (Walker 2014, 188) and the ways that it "upsets the viewer's expectations and disrupts our assumptions for how a sitcom plot 'should' transpire" (Kuechenmeister 2014, 132). Nettie Brock takes a more extreme stance on its categorization as sitcom: "If it is just the simulacrum of a sitcom, can it still actually be called a sitcom? . . . The sitcom reality is becoming aware of itself and elevating into hyperreality" (2014, 49). Evidently, something about *Community*'s self-awareness as a sitcom complicates the ease with which critics can categorize it as one.

This has led some academics to ponder instead how the program exhibits postmodern tendencies. Rekha Sharma, for instance, outright dubs *Community* a "postmodern sitcom" (2013, 183), while Kuechenmeister claims that "the depthlessness of form and shallowness of content is another hallmark feature of the show, as well as of postmodernism" (2014, 135). Here there is a clear invocation of Fredric Jameson's understanding of postmodernism, which highlights the "waning of affect" (1991, 10) as a principal symptom. Yet contrary to Kuechenmeister's characterization, others have explicitly highlighted *Community*'s ability to sustain a tonal warmth and sense of compassion that would ostensibly be incompatible with postmodernism. For instance, it has been categorized as a "metamodern sitcom . . . defined by a specific comic tonality" (Rustad and Schwind 2017, 137) by authors drawing upon the definition of metamodernism outlined by Vermeulen and van den Akker: "[Metamodernism] oscillates between a modern enthusiasm and a postmodern irony, between hope and melancholy, between naïveté and knowingness" (Vermeulen and van den Akker 2010, 5–6).

Others have suggested that at its core *Community* still colors inside the lines of the sitcom more than it subverts them. For instance, Shannon Wells-Lassagne writes of how it "both reifies sitcom conventions and links them back to the spectator's own lives" (2012, 24). Surprisingly, though, almost none of the writing that discusses *Community* in these terms considers it especially necessary to turn to more canonical work on the sitcom as a genre, even though, I argue, the explicitness with which *Community* defines and refers to itself as a sitcom is ultimately crucial to our appreciation of its portrayal of Abed as a neurodiverse character.

Brett Mills offers a canonical definition: "Sitcom can be most usefully defined as *a form of programming which foregrounds its comic intent*" (2009, 49; original emphasis). In other words, for Mills there must be clear textual markers in order for a sitcom to be categorized as such. It is probably fair to suggest that *Community* takes this requirement to extreme levels; the number of times "the sitcom" is diegetically referred to seems designed to foreground the show's self-definition as one. For example, in "Football and Nocturnal Vigilantism" (3:9), when Annie, after breaking Abed's special-edition DVD of *The Dark Knight* (2008), suggests buying a new one and not telling him, Troy responds: "Do you know how many sitcoms have done the fake replacing of the irreplaceable item?" Similarly, in "Herstory of Dance" (4:9), Abed arranges to take two dates to the same event, leading him to exclaim, "Which means I can do the classic two-dates-in-one-night sitcom trope!" These instances exemplify the more straightforward sensibility that Sallie Maree Pritchard identifies; for her, *Community* "follows the sitcom format in the way it uses its artificial nature to alert audiences that it is a comedy. If one of the features of the sitcom is to be clear and obvious in its purpose, the series also uses this artificiality to provide comment on film and television itself" (2014, 154).

Bearing this observation in mind, one of the ways we might try to explain how *Community* modernizes well-worn generic conventions is by pointing to those it ostensibly abandons. Given that both the main cast and the primary location remain relatively fixed throughout, the most interestingly absent sitcom feature is the laugh track (which the majority of contemporary sitcoms have omitted from their production). In its traditional deployment, however, the laugh track is a device that "attempts to remind audiences that they're not laughing at this stuff alone" (Mills 2005, 142) and functions as "the electronic substitute for collective experience" (Medhurst and Tuck 1981, 45). As a substitute, it is an essential component of the medium's "relaxed sociality." We might also note the naturally self-aware quality that a laugh-track sitcom often possesses. For Lawrence Mintz, sitcoms "usually have an element that might almost be metadrama in the sense that since the laughter is recorded (sometimes even augmented), the audience is aware of watching a play, a performance, a comedy incorporating comic activity" (1985, 114–115). Mintz offers a particularly useful lens through which we can understand *Community*'s metafictional sensibility. Several scenes feature Abed offering a commentary on the narrative, in a way that invites a sense of alignment between him and the audience through mutual recognition of the program's religious adherence to convention. It is doubly significant that Abed, a neurodiverse half-Palestinian character—the kind of person who is often the butt of the joke in American television—is frequently given such power, prevalence, and superior knowledge over the narrative. Abed is something of a replacement for a laugh track.

The Human Laugh Track

If in fact *Community* retains its rapport with the audience through Abed as a character in place of the traditional laugh track, it represents a significant modernization of established tropes for progressive purposes, particularly when he appears to offer evaluative commentary on the program's conformity to the sitcom genre, thus turning into what Pritchard describes as the program's "perceived representative, within the series, of the audience" (2014, 159). In his discussion of the diminishing prominence of laugh tracks in contemporary sitcoms, Mills writes: "We cannot see the movement towards sitcoms without laugh tracks as evidence of audience empowerment because the fact that a programme doesn't incorporate its audience into the text in no way shows that it doesn't offer a single position from which the comedy can be best understood" (2009, 105). As the following examples demonstrate, *Community*'s positioning of Abed as the central connecting vessel between the audience and the text represents not an abandonment of the laugh track but a reworking of it that has significant implications for the series's depiction of neurodiversity.

There is, in fact, a single use of a laugh track in *Community*, in the cold opening of "History 101" (4:1), although the laughing audience is later revealed to be inside Abed's head, an example of how the program understands and uses such conventions. In the first season, the will-they-or-won't-they romance between Jeff and Britta is frequently compared to Ross (David Schwimmer) and Rachel's (Jennifer Aniston) relationship in *Friends* (1994–2004), as though no one would be watching the present show except committed viewers of the earlier one. For instance, in "Communication Studies" (1:16), Abed compares the scenario of Britta having drunk-dialed Jeff to being "in a sitcom where one character sees the other one naked," a blunt reference to the *Friends'* episode "The One with the Boobies" (1:13), in which Chandler (Matthew Perry) accidentally walks in on Rachel when she is naked. Remarks like Abed's prepare audiences for and contextualize a significant moment that occurs later on, in the first episode of the second season, "Anthropology 101" (2:1), in which Abed expresses his desires for the direction he would like the program to take. Jeff asks Abed why he is mining his personal life for classic sitcom scenarios, and Abed tells him, "I guess I'm just excited about the new year, looking for ways to improve things. I'm hoping we can move away from the soapy relationship-y stuff and into bigger, fast-paced, self-contained escapades."

Abed's commentary represents the program essentially managing its own tensions, following certain rules—"Nothing that has happened in the narrative of the previous week must destroy or even complicate the way the situation is grounded" (Eaton 1981, 33)—while simultaneously demonstrating the newfound complexity that allows modern comedies, following the likes of *Arrested Development* (2003–2006), to "selectively engage serial norms" (Mittell 2013, 22). Mills acknowledges these changes, but also argues that "all of these comedies of distinction maintain significant links with narrative and aesthetic conventions developed in the early days of the genre, even if they go out of their way to suggest that they don't" (2009, 142). The difference in *Community* is that these conventions are constantly repurposed to foster a sense of identification with Abed.

Consider an especially fascinating sequence from the cold opening of "Football, Feminism and You" (1:5). Here is a moment worthy of attention for the way in which it plays on the notion that the laugh track provides a sense of collective experience and actively includes the audience in its construction of comedy. As Jeff, Britta, Troy, Shirley, Pierce, Annie, and Abed congregate around the study table, Troy approvingly fist-bumps Pierce after he cracks a juvenile penis joke. Abed intervenes with the following assessment, typically muttered to himself in a voice loud enough for the world to hear: "Pierce and Troy didn't get along at first, but now they're bonding through mutual adolescence." (He is openly remembering earlier episodes of the show.) Such a line seems designed to function primarily as a way of "including its audience in the text" (Mills 2009, 104), managing to offer a perspective on events that takes their seriality into account, reminding the audience of earlier episodes just as Abed is reminded of them, and charting the progression of relationships within the central group. Oddly, the other characters take issue with Abed's observations and heckle him for making them. In a strange way, these responses encourage an identification with Abed that stems from pure rationality: he is the only one who appears to understand that *Community* is a television sitcom, and so he stands out to the audience as saner and more logical than anyone else we see.

In these instances, Abed's role is predominantly narrational and supplementary to the action. His presence provides viewers with "running commentary," giving the impression that someone is watching the program alongside them, which, as others have demonstrated, is a staple of the sitcom as a genre usually provided by the soundtrack of a studio audience. In doing so, *Community* strikes a far warmer tone than many have given it credit for. Wells-Lassagne, for instance, describes the self-awareness as "defamiliarizing and distancing" (2012, 11), taking a point of view that neglects not only the genre's history of self-awareness but also its potential to be comforting rather than alienating.

There are even occasions when Abed's meta-lens and commentary are used to elicit emotional responses that might not have been possible through more naturalistic means, in ways that manage to articulate his hopes and desires with an unprecedented sense of directness. For instance, in "Basic Sandwich" (5:13), Jeff and Britta brazenly announce their sudden engagement. While the other characters congratulate them with forced enthusiasm, Abed expresses an anxiety toward the possible direction of the program. He accuses them of wanting to start their own spin-off and declares that the series belongs to everyone else as much as it does to them. While framing events through the lens of sitcom conventions—the spin-off, the division of characters between central and marginal ones—he expresses a sincere desire for the group to remain together and for the core makeup of the series to remain untouched.

In this way, he encapsulates the pain of television fans when favorite actors leave a series, even when it is to gain their own shows (the classic case being Valerie Harper, whose *Rhoda* [1974–1978] sprang from *The Mary Tyler Moore Show* [1970–1977]). Walker has argued that *Community* exemplifies the changing expectations of viewership in the modern era of media convergence, and that the show especially keeps the internet in mind in order to "invite the engaged viewer to occupy the vacant eighth chair at the study table that is the center of its universe" (2014, 183). In worrying about the consequences if Jeff and Britta leave, Abed provides recognition of how the audience engages with television as a medium, in both a historical and a contemporary sense. As a consequence, reciprocal recognition gradually cultivates an affinity between Abed and audience whereby both parties take comfort in "watching the same sitcom" together.

"I'm Not Knocking It, It Works": Operational Aesthetics and the Pleasures of Genre

Returning to the opening moments of "Football, Feminism and You," we find an instance involving Abed that both marks a significant update in sitcom form and poses a potential problem in its clash with the show's otherwise progressive reinterpretation of the laugh track. At their study table, Britta and Jeff are trading playful insults with each other, and these become increasingly crass and sexual. The two are framed in over-the-shoulder compositions and edited in a standard-shot/reverse-shot style, with Abed creeping slightly into the frame behind Britta. After Britta calls Jeff a pig, suddenly the camera noticeably pans left, reframing Abed in a central position. He remarks, presumably to himself, "Will they or won't they? Sexual tension . . ." Abed can be seen to embody the laugh track in providing the audience with companionship and a sense of collective viewing. But in this moment we also have a visual joke: Abed encroaches on the frame with an eye-rolling sense of inevitability, since his comment closely follows his remark about Pierce and Troy's adolescent bonding. The gag largely succeeds because as the camera pans, the audience expects nothing other than to see him. His appearance actively calls visual attention to not only his intervention but also his very presence, in much the same way that an overbearing laugh track announces itself aurally, signaling both that an "audience" is "there" and that the audience finds this funny.

This camera move and the associated character action exhibit characteristics of "complex comedies" (Mittell 2013, 21) in the sense that attention is shifted away from a particular actor (here, Jeff) and aimed instead at the writer or showrunner. Historically, the sitcom has largely been thought of as a genre that foregrounds the spectacle of the comic performer, but most of *Community*'s jokes are devised in a way that calls attention to the skill of their construction rather than the skill of their delivery. This new emphasis is taken to extreme lengths when Abed's involvement in an episode is sacrificed for a self-reflexive joke about television writing. Following Abed's scrutiny of Jeff and Britta's progress as a will-they-or-won't-they couple, Jeff expresses his exhaustion with Abed's relentless critiquing, and angrily retorts: "Abed, it makes the group uncomfortable when you talk about us like we're characters in a show you're watching." Abed is clearly the only character in this show who knows he is a character in a show. He responds: "Well, that's sort of my gimmick. But we did lean on that pretty hard last week. . . . I can lay low for an episode." (We: my buddy the showrunner and I.) Sure enough, for the rest of the episode, Abed hardly features in the narrative. Harmon and his collaborators effectively remove Pudi's contribution to the program for an entire episode for the purpose of making a joke based on Abed's awareness of sitcom tropes and his compulsion to examine and comment on how *Community* handles its conventions as a television sitcom.

Yet even when Abed's screen time is sacrificed, it is still his superior awareness of convention that is foregrounded, even in jokes that call attention to their own construction by the writers. One example, especially suggestive in its simplicity, merely points to the existence of a structural device that, although ubiquitous, is likely to have gone unnoticed by most viewers who are not television writers themselves. To establish the closing scene of the sixth season's paintball episode, "Modern Espionage" (6:11), we cut straight to Abed telling the punch line of a joke, after which he immediately apologizes for not being able to remember the rest of it. Jeff, typically, responds with sarcasm, explaining to Abed that, based on the punch line alone, he is sure it was a funny joke.

Cutting to a conversation in which a character is finishing a speech is a well-worn structural device in television—particularly following commercial breaks—as a way of indicating that time has passed and creating the impression that we are rejoining the cast after a brief interlude. This is something the majority of viewers would probably not have identified as a prominent device, and it is likely to be more familiar to television writers than television watchers. Working as it does here in *Community*, the trick accentuates and draws attention to the writers' knowledge and mastery of television structure, momentarily emphasizing the script and the editing more than the actors. But since Abed remains the primary source of this reflexivity and the ultimate purveyor of laughs that poke fun at sitcom convention, it is still fair to consider this metasensibility as a reconditioning, rather than a total abandonment or reinvention, of traditional methods.

The emphasis on construction is highly characteristic of an "operational aesthetic," in which "a program flexes its storytelling muscles to confound and amaze a viewer" (Mittell 2013, 43). Much of *Community*'s deployment of an operational aesthetic comes from its well-documented acknowledgment and subversion of sitcom formulas. While such constant mobilization of an operational aesthetic might well begin to come off as overly assertive in its foregrounding of the creative genius behind the camera, it should be noted that the homages in *Community* tend to exhibit a love and respect for the genre, which can be connected back with Abed as an aid to our identifying with how he sees the world. Across the show's six seasons, it covered numerous generic styles: stop-motion animation in "Abed's Uncontrollable Christmas (1:10), a space adventure in "Basic Rocket Science" (2:4), a conspiracy thriller in "Conspiracy Theories and Interior Design" (2:9), a *Law and Order* parody in "Basic Lupine Urology" (3:17), a platform video game in "Digital Estate Planning" (3:20), a haunted house in "Paranormal Parentage" (4:2), an animated *G.I. Joe* parody in "G.I. Jeff" (5:11), and several others.

In each of these, the program moves through the motions of the genre in question with a relatively straight face, deploying "Harmon's encyclopedic knowledge of popular culture and his affection for genre television permeate the show, with characters making pop culture allusions as a means of making sense of their lives" (Barnett and Kooyman 2012, 110). I would take this a step further by arguing that genre is deployed to specifically demarcate how Abed makes sense of the world. This is particularly evident in "Critical Film Studies" (2:19), in which Abed stages a dinner with Jeff, explaining his desire to transcend the referential, pop-cultural lens through which he sees the world. The dinner turns out to be just another reference, of course, and an homage to Louis Malle's *My Dinner with Andre* (1981). In her analysis of the episode, Pritchard delineates its operation as a game and suggests that Abed invites the audience to participate in his deceit of Jeff and the rest of the study group: "The audience gains from this play by elevating their status, both among the *Community* audience and the film and television viewers" (2014, 160).

Even when it threatens to damage his relationship with the rest of the group, Abed's love of television and film genres serves the purpose of encouraging the audience to identify with his worldview. For Bridget Julie Hanna, he "highlights the reworking of genre, opening the discussion between audience, texts and creator through his role as parodic mediator" (2014, 150). True enough: in the more explicit parodies of genre, Abed is almost always the character to announce or recognize whatever genre organizes a particular episode—most famously in "Cooperative Calligraphy" (2:8), which he diagnoses as the "bottle episode,"[1] or in "Epidemiology" (2:6), when, upon the outbreak of an uncontrollable virus, he shouts, "Zombie attack!" with more enthusiasm than fear, thrilled in the knowledge that the show is keeping within specific genre territory and that it is still just that: a television show.

"Let's Face It, I'm Pretty Adorable": Working through Neurodiversity

This ultimately heartfelt outlook, and the sense of reaching out to the audience through the television set, is what has made *Community*'s popularity enduring. Without a doubt, this sense of hope is principally channeled through Abed. And although he is frequently deployed as a device, one through which the skill and wit of the showrunner is repeatedly alluded to, it would be erroneous to separate Abed's wit from his non-neurotypical condition. As mentioned, Abed effectively modernizes a traditional sitcom sensibility by providing a feeling of companionship and reliable comfort through his running commentary on events. To close, then, we might turn to some corners of television theory as a way of identifying what we can give *back* to a character intent on sharing his enthusiasm for pop culture with us. Abed openly describes himself as having been "raised by TV," and through his direct address to the audience, we are encouraged to share his love of television. In addition to allowing the audience to be a part of the joke, to adopt a love of genre and popular culture, and even to "join" the study group itself, *Community* does something more classically televisual by celebrating the conventions of television comedy as a source of companionship.

One could go as far as to posit this as a metamodern reaction to the scathing commentary by David Foster Wallace on the viewer's relationship to television: "The more time spent watching TV, the less time spent in the real human world, and the less time spent in the real human world, the harder it becomes not to feel alienated from real humans, solipsistic, lonely" (1993, 163). Indeed, through constant reminders that Abed struggles to make "ordinary" social connections and maintain human relationships, *Community* increasingly accentuates his dependency on television and, by extension, us, the audience he is putatively drawing in. At one point, in "Anthropology 101" (2:1), he tells Jeff, "I can tell life from TV. TV makes sense. It has logic, structure, rules, and likable leading men. In life we have this. We have you."

Here we might invoke the concept of "working through," a process that capitalizes on television's capacity for longevity, one "whereby material is continually worried over until it is exhausted" (Ellis 2002, 79). In particular, the more optimistic invocation by Jimmy Draper and Amanda Lotz, who describe "texts that attend to the contested nature of ideological positions, often through the depiction of nonidealized, nonstatic characters that struggle to reconcile their outlooks with those of their community" (2012, 523), is instructive for reading Abed as a character. *Community*'s ultimate goal of pushing viewers to locate themselves both in and with Abed manifests as a strangely metamodern "working through" over the course of the series. We watch *Community* alongside him, and he gives us the impression that we are not alone. In exchange, we are guided to recognize him as the only *real* person on the program, and the only one who understands how things work—something that cannot be achieved in the space of a single episode.

Over time, *Community* uses Abed's love of the medium to, in a quite revolutionary act, gradually displace Jeff, the painfully cool, handsome, popular white man, from the position of protagonist. It is Jeff with whom the audience initially identifies, having followed his perspective in the pilot episode. The series shifts between the type of reflexive, postmodernist sensibility that evades criticism by providing its own brand (the enigmatic closing voiceover by Harmon in the final episode, which reflects openly on the program's successes and failures, is particularly emblematic of this) and a more hopeful (thus metamodern) outlook. It maintains a nostalgic attitude toward television as the friendly object in the room, one that Abed himself admits to having shared, since he preferred television to the diegetic living folk around him. With its cast of familiar faces in a location that never changes and the recognizable tropes and genres it pays homage to, *Community* is a sitcom, but it is one whose representational project is unquestionably a noble one: to repurpose the comforting sound of collective laughter and the familiar mechanisms of genre via commentary by a neurodiverse character who is finally able to reveal how a person like him—if there are any other persons like him—sees the world.

Note

1. A familiar sitcom trope, derived from *The Outer Limits* (1963–1965), involves numerous disparate characters "trapped" or "bottled" in a restricted single space.

CHAPTER 13

Portrait of the Autist as a Young Man

FINCINA HOPGOOD

In 2007 a network ensemble comedy about four scientists working at the California Institute of Technology premiered on CBS. Over the course of the next decade, *The Big Bang Theory* became one of the most watched shows worldwide, a landmark pop-culture product with a dedicated fan base that heralded the age of "geek" or "nerd" culture. For Vlad Dima, writing in the *Bright Lights Film Journal* in 2012 during the show's fifth season, the series was "a paradigm shift of big-bang proportions": "The show's main achievement . . . is to create an [*sic*] universe in which the outcast scientists, the *nerds*, function as leading men" (original emphasis).

Dr. Sheldon Cooper—the self-appointed "leader" of this group of nerds— has been regarded by many viewers as exhibiting traits associated with the autism spectrum.[1] These traits include Sheldon's strict adherence to routine and his distress when his routine is disrupted; his difficulty in relating to other people and understanding their emotions; his physical clumsiness and social awkwardness; his lack of affect in vocal and facial expressions; and his obsessive interests in science and "geek" popular culture, such as comic books and science-fiction TV shows. In 2009, Paul Collins noted similarities between Sheldon's features and those commonly associated with autists, quoting responses published online in forums and blog posts as evidence of a shared recognition. The widespread speculation and media reports about Sheldon's characterization prompted the show's cocreator Bill Prady to disavow a clinical diagnosis: "We write the character as the character. A lot of people see various things in him and make the connections. Our feeling is that Sheldon's mother never got a diagnosis, so we don't have one" (Holverstott 2011). Prady is referring here to one of Sheldon's oft-quoted lines: "I'm not crazy; my mother had me tested." Prady—who also served as executive producer and head writer on the series—argued that a diagnosis would place an unreasonable burden on the writers to portray autism accurately, and that the other characters would seem cruel in mocking Sheldon's eccentricities if these traits were given a medical label. Prady explained that he based Sheldon's personality on computer programmers with whom he used to work (Sepinwall 2009). As chronicled by Steve Silberman in *NeuroTribes*, the Silicon Valley tech boom provided an opportunity for many programmers and other "geeks" to find a safe haven for their skills and talents in a supportive work environment: "[The] culture of these places had opened up social possibilities for men and women on the Spectrum that had never before existed in history" (2015, 10–11).

Despite Prady's insistence otherwise, the perception that Sheldon is on the spectrum, or can at least be viewed through the lens of autism, has remained. Jim Parsons (the actor who plays Sheldon) is frequently asked in interviews about his character's autistic traits: "It's a difficult question. . . . Very early on I was asked by a reporter whether Sheldon had Asperger's. I wasn't sure what that meant. I asked the writers and they said no. He has [autistic] traits. But their saying that took away a social responsibility" (Clarke 2015). In the absence of a confirmed diagnosis within the show's diegesis, Sheldon Cooper has been the subject of speculative, or "armchair," internet diagnoses (Heilker 2012). Select episodes of *The Big Bang Theory* have even been used as a teaching tool at Rutgers University's Robert Wood Johnson Medical School to illustrate the features of autism (Tobia and Toma 2015). Residents in training analyze Sheldon's social interactions, traits, and behavior according to the new diagnostic criteria for Autism Spectrum Disorder (ASD) in the fifth edition of the *Diagnostic and Statistical Manual of Mental*

Disorders (2013), which absorbed the label "Asperger's Disorder" while retaining its defining features in the diagnostic criteria for ASD.

Among autists publishing online, opinion is divided about whether Sheldon's portrayal in *The Big Bang Theory* is a positive or regressive development in media representations of ASD. The author and advocate Kerry Magro, who has autism, works with the entertainment industry to ensure realistic portrayals of autists in film and television. In a 2014 guest post for the Autism Speaks website, Magro wrote a blog titled "Why Our Autism Community Loves Sheldon Cooper," reflecting on the widespread popularity and impact of *The Big Bang Theory*. In a follow-up article published on his personal website in 2016, Magro suggests, "Even though [Sheldon is] not on the autism spectrum, because it may not fit into the storyline of the show, he's still very relatable for our community."[2] The author Jacqueline Koyanagi, who was diagnosed with autism as an adult, is more critical of the show. She argues, interestingly, that while Sheldon is "obviously coded as autistic," the decontextualization of his autism—due to the lack of a diegetic diagnosis and the statements of denial from the show's creators—is irresponsible, since it leads to caricature rather than accuracy of representation: "Eschewing labels does not equate dodging responsibility" (2015; see as well the chapter by Christine Becker in this volume). When asked about Sheldon's diagnosis, Mayim Bialik, who plays Amy (Sheldon's girlfriend, then wife) responded: "All of our characters are in theory on the neuropsychiatric spectrum . . . What should not be lost on people is we don't pathologize our characters. We don't talk about medicating them or even really changing them. . . . It doesn't always need to be solved and medicated and labelled" (Gill 2015).

Sheldon's portrayal on *The Big Bang Theory* has been the subject of academic analysis from scholars working in cultural studies, disability studies, English, linguistics, and psychology. These analyses employ diverse theoretical frameworks, including neoliberalism (Stratton 2016a, 2016b), rhetoric (Heilker 2012; Walters 2013), eccentricity and creativity (Winston 2016), impoliteness theory (Bednarek 2012), humor theory (Walters 2013), and whiteness and ethnicity (Heilker 2012; M. Matthews 2019). While I am mindful of the divergent views and strong opinions on the question of Sheldon's diagnosis, in this chapter I offer a reading of the character Sheldon Cooper across two series, *The Big Bang Theory* and its spin-off, *Young Sheldon*, through the lens of autism and from the discipline of screen studies. Using a close analysis of promotional material and select scenes from *Young Sheldon*, I focus primarily on Sheldon's experience of childhood and the influence of comic books, superheroes, and science fiction on his identity formation. This reading is informed by wider discussions about autism and the work of writers such as Stuart Murray and Steve Silberman, who reframe aspects of autistic subjectivity and experience as productive and enabling rather than limiting and disabling. Inspired by Mark Osteen's urging for empathetic scholarship—"a particularly valuable model for non-autists who hope to represent authentically and accurately what it means and how it feels to be autistic" (2008b, 8)—my reading of Sheldon is also shaped by my experience of viewing these shows as a parent of an autistic child. For pre-teen and adolescent viewers on the spectrum such as my son, Sheldon offers a rare point of identification and aspiration in popular culture: a heroic protagonist whose superpower is his brain.

Every Legend Has a Beginning

"EVERY LEGEND . . . HAS A BEGINNING." So declares the promotional trailer for *Young Sheldon* in announcing the series premiere on CBS September 25, 2017. Marketed as both a spin-off and a prequel to *The Big Bang Theory*, *Young Sheldon* focuses on the prepubescent years of Sheldon Cooper while he was growing up in East Texas—where he lives with his parents, Mary and George; his older brother, George Jr. (or "Georgie"); and his twin sister, Missy—and his experiences in high school, which he attends early, from the age of nine, because of his "intellectual gifts." The idea for the series originated with Jim Parsons, who pitched it to *The Big Bang Theory*'s cocreator and executive producer Chuck Lorre. Lorre worked with Steven Molaro, another executive producer on *The Big Bang Theory*, to create the series. All three *Big Bang* alumni are executive producers on *Young Sheldon*, along with Todd Spiewak (Parsons's husband).

A spin-off is designed to capitalize on the success of a popular series by featuring characters from the parent show. In serialized narratives such as comic books and the cinematic universes they inspire, it is common practice to create a prequel or series of prequels that provide the backstories to established popular characters and narrative events. In the case of superhero narratives, the protagonist's origin story—how she or he became a superhero—carries particular weight and cultural significance. Some iconic origin stories, such as the origins of Superman, Batman, and Spider-Man, are continually retold and recycled across comics, feature films, animation, and television shows. Indeed, both Superman and Batman have inspired origin stories in the form of television series, *Smallville* (2001–2011) and *Gotham* (2014–2019), respectively. While these retellings of a superhero's origins vary somewhat, the fundamental defining features of the characters and a recounting of their transformation into superheroes remain largely unchanged.

For *Big Bang* fans and (especially) acolytes of Sheldon Cooper, *Young Sheldon* offers pleasures like those of a superhero origin story: the pleasure of recognizing key character traits, paired with the promise of gaining deeper knowledge and insight into a beloved character. Elements of Sheldon's upbringing are established in anecdotes told across episodes of *The Big Bang Theory*. Before the first episode of *Young Sheldon* premiered, fans of the parent series knew that as a "once in a generation" mind and child prodigy, Sheldon graduated high school early, at the age of fourteen; that he grew up in Texas, one of three children; that he is very close to his mother, despite her Christian faith clashing with his atheism; and that when Sheldon was a teenager, his father died of weight-related health issues. This is the established family tree, the scaffolding on which the writers of *Young Sheldon* would flesh out the architecture of the Cooper home.

The first-look promotional trailer for CBS's *Young Sheldon* offers a five-minute preview of scenes from the pilot episode. The pilot was directed by Jon Favreau, who had an established track record in superhero origin stories as the director of the first movie in the Marvel Cinematic Universe, *Iron Man* (2008), and its sequel, *Iron Man 2* (2010). Close analysis of the trailer for *Young Sheldon* reveals how the spin-off was promoted to fans of the parent series.[3] The trailer employs a range of textual and aesthetic strategies to frame *Young Sheldon* as the origin story of an intellectual superhero. Opening with an image of outer space accompanied by a grand orchestral score that mimics the triumphal strains of Richard Strauss's *Also sprach Zarathustra* (1896) (thereby alluding to Stanley Kubrick's sci-fi epic *2001: A Space Odyssey* [1968]), the trailer presents a montage of images of the adult Sheldon Cooper from key moments in *The Big Bang Theory*: Sheldon dressed in black tie, cradling a glass of brandy, and imitating the smooth sophistication of James Bond as he delivers the line, "Well, hello!"; Sheldon wearing denim overalls and bandana, driving a steam train; and Sheldon in his preferred "uniform" of a colored T-shirt over a long-sleeved shirt, standing in front of a whiteboard as he ponders complex mathematical calculations. This final image of Sheldon "in his element" is preceded by the onscreen text "EVERY LEGEND" in all-caps and styled like the font used in the opening credits of Superman movies from the 1980s. Poised in front of the whiteboard as though ready to strike, and accompanied by timpani, Sheldon narrates his thinking process aloud, speaking in the style of a sports commentator: "A hush falls over the crowd as Sheldon Cooper studies the board. He makes his move"—at which point he starts to scribble on the board, and trumpets announce his breakthrough before his monologue resumes—"and he solves the equation! Crowd goes wild: 'Nobel! No-bel!'" An audience laugh track is included, a defining feature of the multicamera ensemble comedy, signaling the "audience's pleasure" and shared celebration of Sheldon's breakthrough, as well as their amusement at his self-aggrandizing commentary.

The superhuman feat of Sheldon's intellectual achievement is emphasized by the return of the Superman-style text onscreen: "HAS—A—BEGIN-NING." The words appear onscreen one at a time, beneath three successive images that show Sheldon gesticulating wildly and "freaking out"; Sheldon dressed as the android Data from *Star Trek: The Next Generation* (1987–1994); and an awkward Sheldon trying to dance seductively (therefore humorously) in his black-tie outfit from the beginning of the montage. The orchestral score surges and then stops abruptly for one more scene excerpted from *The Big Bang Theory*: Sheldon seated on the couch with Amy, both facing the camera as if to address the audience, when he suddenly turns to look offscreen and commands, "Howard, flashback sounds!" His Caltech friend Howard (Simon Helberg) dutifully responds by playing a repeated arpeggio motif on an electronic keyboard, a sound bridge, as the scene dissolves into an image of Earth seen from space. We zoom in toward Earth and then transition to a map of Texas before another dissolve reveals an aerial view of a suburban district. This sequence of rapid transitions from a macro- to an increasingly microscopic viewpoint finally comes to rest on a close-up of a model train set, the shift in tone and setting signaled by the country music "twang" of the opening strains of "The Yellow Rose of Texas." The text "East Texas" and "1989" is superimposed over shots of the miniature railway, accompanied by the distinctive tones of the adult Sheldon declaring in voiceover, "I've always loved trains." A young boy (Iain Armitage) suddenly appears in the background of the shot, popping up into the frame from beneath the train set. As an inserted title card informs us, this is Sheldon Cooper, age nine.

As we watch Armitage gleefully playing with his train set, setting a Ping-Pong ball into a holder on one of the cars, Parsons continues his narration as the adult Sheldon. Parsons's ongoing narration is a crucial point of continuity between the two series, and his voiceover features in every episode of *Young Sheldon*. This device encourages the viewer to recognize traces of the adult Sheldon in his younger self, as we watch Armitage press a button that launches the ball into the air while the train is moving: "When I figured out that trains allowed me to prove Newton's first law *[the ball lands back on the train]*, I felt like Neil Armstrong on the moon: alone and happy." This statement neatly encapsulates Sheldon's superior intellect, his love of science, and his preference for solitude—key characteristics familiar to *Big Bang* fans. The scenes excerpted from *Young Sheldon*'s pilot and edited together in this promotional trailer serve a dual function: enticing viewers to watch a brand-new show, regardless of their familiarity with *The Big Bang Theory*, and rewarding fans of the parent series with glimpses of trademark "Sheldon-y" traits and behaviors in a new onscreen incarnation. Seated around the family dinner table, the younger Sheldon is—like his adult self—a germaphobe who insists on wearing mittens to hold hands with his father (Lance Barber, in the sequel series) and brother while his mother says grace. He also demonstrates the same sense of intellectual superiority, manifested in cruel mockery of his siblings, as his adult counterpart typically shows toward his friends: over dinner, Sheldon speaks in derogatory tones to his older brother ("Think, monkey, think") and his twin sister ("Good luck with your finger painting") as he gloats at the prospect of starting high school. When the family dinner is disrupted by bickering between the siblings, food throwing, and the mother's futile attempts to restore order, Parsons's voiceover returns with a typically snarky comment from the adult Sheldon to accompany this scene of chaos: "Jane Goodall had to go to Africa to study apes. I just had to go to dinner."

Beyond its role in connecting the two series and establishing the authorial "presence" of Parsons as both star and executive producer, the narration in *Young Sheldon* is one of the key signifiers of the spin-off's shift away from the parent series in tone and style. The broad comedy of *The Big Bang Theory*'s ensemble format, filmed in front of a studio audience with an augmented laugh track added in later, is replaced by a more naturalistic and intimate mode of performance filmed on location and on a closed set with a single camera. This single-camera format was the preferred style of comedy shows such as *Modern Family* (2009–2020), *The Office* (US version, 2005–2013), and *Parks and Recreation* (2009–2020). While these comedies tend to pair single-camera setups with mockumentary interviews showing the characters commenting on narrative events, *Young Sheldon*'s narration provides a retrospective commentary that recalls other nostalgic comedy series about growing up, such as *The Wonder Years* (1988–1993) and *Malcolm in the Middle* (2000–2006). The closed set creates a performance environment more supportive for child actors than the high-pressure demands of recording episodes in front of a studio audience.

Importantly, this format allows *Young Sheldon* to provide greater insight into how Sheldon sees the world. The camera offers intimate shots that bring the viewer closer to the subtle play of emotion on Armitage's face, and

Parsons's voiceover gives privileged access to Sheldon's thought processes and feelings in that moment, even if this narration is being performed as a recollection several years after the events portrayed onscreen. An example is that comment of the adult Sheldon's over the chaotic family dinner in the pilot, comparing himself to Jane Goodall observing apes. He conveys his sense of being an outsider in his family, displaying an emotional detachment typical of scientific observation. He adopts the role of an anthropologist observing the foibles of human behavior, Temple Grandin's metaphor for autistic subjectivity that inspired the title of Oliver Sacks's *An Anthropologist on Mars* (Silberman 2015, 465). As a representation of autism onscreen, and perhaps especially of the older Sheldon's astonishing visual memory, *Young Sheldon* is able to employ a greater range of aesthetic devices in sound and image than its predecessor, producing a potentially richer, more nuanced portrait of the autist as a young man.

Sheldon as Superhero: "A Mighty Little Man"

In both shows, Sheldon is portrayed as a man-child. As an adult, he is emotionally immature, behaving childishly and petulantly when he doesn't get his way. With his brightly colored logo T-shirts over long-sleeved tops, Sheldon dresses more like a teenager than the eminent theoretical physicist he has become. Combined with his love of comics, superheroes, and *Star Trek*, the adult Sheldon embodies Murray Pomerance's concept of the "man-boy": "the man who never quite abandons his boyhood" (2005, 137). As a child, he speaks with a formal tone and an extensive vocabulary that bewilders his peers and intimidates his elders, and his preference for bow ties with buttondown collared shirts and slicked-down hair projects his self-image as a "little man." This conception of Sheldon as a man-child is apparent from the opening title sequence for the first two seasons of *Young Sheldon*, in which his signature outfit of short-sleeved shirt-*cum*-bow tie is accessorized with a briefcase and—incongruously—leather cowboy boots, to tout his loyalty to Texas. The sequence opens with a close-up of these cowboy boots striding confidently across tumbleweeds and dirt before a rapid pullback reveals a wide shot of a young boy alone against a vast, rural landscape. Sheldon assumes a heroic stance, with his chin upturned and gaze aloft. The assertiveness of this pose is undercut by a cow entering from the left of frame, unsettling Sheldon and forcing him to shuffle sideways as the cow moves closer. This sequence acts as a visual motif for Sheldon feeling "out of place" in Texas and conveys his sense of being an outsider or misfit, which (as season

1 progresses) leads him to identify with the superhero mutants from *X-Men* comics ("A Therapist, a Comic Book, and a Breakfast Sausage," 1:3) and Spock from the original *Star Trek* (1966–1969) ("Spock, Kirk, and Testicular Hernia," 1:8). Sheldon's heroic self-image—of superhuman potential as an intellectual "giant" despite his small stature—is encapsulated in the lyrics of the title song, "Mighty Little Man" by Steve Burns:

> Nobody else is stronger than I am
> Yesterday I moved a mountain
> I bet I could be your hero
> I am a mighty little man.

Viewers of *The Big Bang Theory* know the importance of superheroes and comic books in Sheldon's adult life. The Comic Center of Pasadena is a key location for the characters of *Big Bang*, functioning much like the coffee shop in ensemble comedies such as *Friends* (1994–2004) and *Seinfeld* (1989–1998). This store, owned by their friend Stuart (Kevin Sussman), provides a social space and a sense of community for nerds, geeks, and social misfits. Sheldon's rotating costume of superhero T-shirts is a constant visual reminder of his comic book fandom and the role that it plays in his sense of identity, along with his special interest in and expert knowledge of science fiction, particularly the original *Star Trek* series. In addition, comic books provide Sheldon with a social script that facilitates his interactions with his peers and gives him a sense of belonging. Comics are pop-culture texts that figure prominently in both geek culture and in the lives of many autists, with annual conventions bringing fans together to socialize and share their expertise (Silberman 2015, 506–507).

Young Sheldon takes viewers back to the character's induction into the world of comics in "A Therapist, a Comic Book, and a Breakfast Sausage" (1:3), an episode that has been described as "Sheldon's superhero origin story" (B. Travers 2017). Initially, he looks down on comic books, telling Tam, his sole companion in high school, "You do understand those are for children?" Tam (Ryan Phuong) is a Vietnamese immigrant who, like Sheldon, is socially isolated, and in subsequent episodes the boys regularly eat lunch together in the school library rather than in the noisy, crowded cafeteria. In this episode, Sheldon develops a phobia of eating solid food, triggered by an incident in which he nearly choked to death on a breakfast sausage. His parents take him to a family psychiatrist, who encourages him to read some comics in the waiting room while he consults with Mary and George. As Sheldon starts to read, Parsons's voiceover narration cues the audience to the significance of this moment: "As fate would have it, the comic I picked up was called *X-Men*: young mutants with incredible powers who were feared and misunderstood by the entire world." Sheldon's eyes light up as he declares aloud to the empty waiting room: "Hey, it's about me!" The next scene shows him walking alone past a row of shops, having evidently abandoned the psychiatrist's waiting room, while Parsons narrates his character's motivations: "I was on a mission. I had gotten my first taste of serialized superheroes and I needed more."

This pilgrimage brings Sheldon to King Kong Comics, where he finds Tam seated on the floor, surrounded by comics, chewing a licorice strip while reading. In the conversation that follows, we see the nascent friendship between these two social outcasts develop, with Tam reminding Sheldon, "I thought you said comic books were for children," and Sheldon observing, "You challenge me. I like that." Sheldon then fixates on the red licorice Tam is chewing, and Tam offers him one. Parsons's voiceover resumes to share with us Sheldon's thoughts at this point: "I didn't have to read many comic books to understand that every superhero had a weakness, something they had to overcome through an extraordinary act of courage." After recalling the obstacles overcome by the *X-Men* mutants Cyclops and Rogue, he continues: "For me, it was food that required chewing. So if I truly was a mutant, I would have to do the same." Immersing the viewer in Sheldon's imagination, the orchestral score builds the suspense of this moment as the close-up on Sheldon's face is intercut with single comic book panels showing a boy superhero with a determined expression chomping down on a licorice strip: "Ker-chomp!" The episode concludes with a triumphant Sheldon reflecting on the number of scientists in comic books who are supervillains. He warns Tam: "If the world doesn't respect me, I might change sides."

Throughout the series, *Young Sheldon* continues to explore the increasing importance of comic books and superheroes to Sheldon's sense of identity as he approaches puberty. Another season 1 episode, "A Mother, a Child, and a Blue Man's Backside" (1:17), depicts Sheldon's conflict with Mary over whether comics such as *Watchmen* and *The Flash* are appropriate for his age. For season 3, a new opening-title sequence was produced, with alternate versions showing Sheldon dressed in the iconic costumes of Spock (his Vulcan ears and blue uniform) and the Flash (his red supersuit and mask). The Flash is one of the adult Sheldon's favorite superheroes: in *The Big Bang Theory*, he often wears a T-shirt with the Flash logo, and he dressed up as the Flash in "The Justice League Recombination" (4:11). In other versions of the opening titles, young Sheldon appears dressed as some of his real-life heroes: Albert Einstein (a brown suit and wig of disheveled gray hair) and Neil Armstrong (his spacesuit).

Equally significant in this new title sequence is the inclusion of Sheldon's family, his support team. While he remains centered in the group composition, other family members stand close to him, with his grandmother's hand sometimes resting on his shoulder. As the cow enters from left of frame in the same movement as it did in the title sequence from seasons 1 and 2, the family moves as one, stepping to the right of frame and then copying Sheldon's heroic pose of upturned chins and upward gazes. The season 3 title sequence highlights the importance of the family both within and beyond the narrative universe of *Young Sheldon*. In television industry practice, it recognizes the increased profile of the actors who perform the characters of Mary (Zoe Perry), George Sr. (Barber), George Jr. (Montana Jordan), Missy (Raegan Revord), and Connie, or "Meemaw" (Annie Potts), Sheldon's grandmother. In the show's portrayal of Sheldon's autism, this sequence draws attention to the crucial role of family members as supporters, carers, and advocates for children on the spectrum. Even superheroes need allies.

Everyday Autism and Mental Health

The Big Bang Theory's portrayal of Sheldon Cooper as "an ersatz superhero" (M. Matthews 2019) has been criticized by disability scholars, who rightly question the dominant framing of people with ASD as "shiny autistics": a term used by some in the autism community to describe high-profile figures with remarkable gifts and intellectual achievements, such as Temple Grandin, who are held up as unrealistic examples of "what autistics should be" (Heilker 2012). Greta Thunberg is a recent example on a list of contemporary and historical figures who have been identified as having autism and celebrated for their achievements. The public fascination with these high achievers contributes to a misleading and ultimately damaging stereotype—one that is sustained by fictional representations such as Sheldon Cooper—that conflates autism with giftedness. This popular misconception may bear little resemblance to the experience of autism as it is lived by many on the spectrum and their families (Anderson and Francey 2019).

Stuart Murray's idea of "everyday autism"—"the daily business of a life lived being autistic" (2012, 16)—offers a different perspective from these grand narratives focused on achievement rather than experience. Murray reminds us that autism is always present and that this lived experience shapes the autist's encounters with family, work, school, and community. Despite

Sheldon's formidable intellectual gifts, *Young Sheldon* includes moments of "everyday autism" that provide insight into his experiences of perceptual and sensory difference, of social exclusion and isolation, and of difficulties relating to the people around him. Superhero origin stories sometimes reveal moments when heroes are anything but "super": on the journey toward realizing their true potential, they may at times be lost, angry, confused, or vulnerable, such as when Peter Parker (aka Spiderman) is bullied in high school. These moments of vulnerability make superheroes relatable rather than exceptional. While very few autistic children have the intellectual capacities that Sheldon displays at age nine, many encounter the same hostility, misunderstanding, and social isolation that he experiences in high school and in the wider community.

Within the confines of a network sitcom with an average running time of twenty-two minutes per episode, the writers of *Young Sheldon* must navigate a delicate balance between Sheldon's exuberant joy and pleasure when he is immersed in intellectual activity, and the sobering realities of how he is perceived and treated by others. Sheldon is often oblivious of the puzzled looks and snide comments of adults, teachers, and peers who do not understand him or feel intimidated by his intellect. The series treads lightly around the issue of bullying, avoiding any scenes that depict actual or threatened violence, instead representing these indirectly through Parsons's narration. For example, when explaining his "impressive ability to wait for things," the adult Sheldon recalls the time he was left in a locker for over four hours. All we see onscreen is an empty locker room, with young Sheldon's voice (presumably from the locker) politely calling out, "Hello . . . anyone there? That's OK, I'll wait" (3:17).

It falls to Sheldon's parents, especially Mary, to defend him from intolerance and disapproval in the community, and to advocate for his social inclusion. In the pilot episode, when Sheldon talks about puberty during a church sermon, a woman turns to Mary and asks accusingly, "What is wrong with him?" The otherwise pious Mary reveals her angry side: "Nothing is *wrong* with him. Now turn around before I knock your lights out!" The Coopers' next-door neighbor Brenda Sparks (Melissa Peterman) openly calls Sheldon "a weirdo," and in "A Party Invitation, Football Grapes, and an Earth Chicken" (3:9), Mary is incensed when Brenda invites Missy—but not Sheldon—to her son Billy's birthday party. Mary confronts Brenda and insists on Sheldon being invited, even though he doesn't like birthday parties. Sheldon reluctantly attends, wearing his Spock costume and adopting Spock's persona (copying Leonard Nimoy's voice and interviewing guests with his tricorder) as a way to cope with a social custom he does not enjoy.

In contrast to scenes such as Billy's birthday party, when Sheldon's idiosyncrasies and "odd" behaviors are presented for our amusement, there are moments when manipulated images, music, and narration align us with his perception of events, encouraging the viewer to empathize with his experience. Distorted sounds, tense music, and shots framed from Sheldon's point of view are frequently employed to portray situations as unpleasant or threatening. The series's intention of aligning the viewer with Sheldon's view of the world is signaled early on: two scenes in the pilot episode use close-ups and sound amplification to show the Coopers' suburban neighborhood and Sheldon's high school as places of noise, chaos, and potential danger. These scenes effectively convey the perceptual and sensory differences experienced in "everyday autism." When Mary sends Sheldon outside to play in their front yard, the sounds of a barking dog and a lawnmower combine in a harsh cacophony, and a chicken looms large as it is thrust by Billy (Wyatt McClure) toward the camera—placed at Sheldon's height. Similar audiovisual techniques are used during Sheldon's first day of high school when a stuffed wolf (the school mascot) is photographed from his viewpoint. The camera zooms forward toward the wolf's sharp teeth while ominous music and the sound effect of a roar combine to express the boy's anxiety in this new environment.

While the rise of the neurodiversity movement means there is now greater awareness than ever about autism, Steve Silberman cautions there are still considerable mental health issues for people on the spectrum, who are at greater risk of anxiety, depression, and suicide because of bullying, social isolation, and workplace discrimination (2015, 532–534). The writers of *Young Sheldon* included a story line spanning seasons 2 and 3 that explores mental health through the character arc of Sheldon's mentor and friend, the college professor John Sturgis (Wallace Shawn). Connie becomes romantically involved with the eccentric professor and recognizes the similarities between John and her grandson: both are incredibly smart and passionate about science, but each has difficulty with interpersonal communication and navigating social situations. Realizing that he will never win the Nobel Prize for his work, John becomes despondent, suffers a psychotic breakdown, and needs to be hospitalized. His absence is keenly felt by Sheldon, who describes John as "the one person in Texas who understands me" (3:5).

The writers use John's discharge from hospital as an opportunity to stage a conversation about mental health around the Cooper family dinner table. Despite Mary's instructions to avoid the topic, Sheldon and his siblings are eager to ask John questions about his time in hospital, to which he happily responds: "The best way to destigmatize something is to talk about it" (3:5). Although John reluctantly ends his relationship with Connie out of his desire to protect her from his mental health problems, he remains a recurring character in subsequent episodes and develops a friendship with Sheldon's father, George. Through the portrayal of John's recovery, his return to lecturing, and his friendship with the Coopers, this plotline engages with contemporary conversations about mental health (despite the series being set three decades ago) and further strengthens the show's embrace of neurodiversity.

The Big Bang Theory concluded its twelve seasons in 2019 with Sheldon's greatest intellectual triumph: he and Amy jointly receive the Nobel Prize in Physics. Sheldon Cooper reached his true superhero potential, finally achieving the goal he had dreamt of as a young boy. Sheldon's career aspirations are written into *Young Sheldon* in a poignant scene at the end of the season 2 finale, "A Swedish Science Thing and the Equation for Toast" (2:22): a forlorn young Sheldon mourns the fact that he does not have any friends to join him in listening to the radio announcement of that year's Nobel Prize winners. As the camera pans away from a tearful Sheldon, a series of slow panning shots cut together reveals three boys and three girls of similar ages, each in their bedrooms. *Big Bang* fans would instantly recognize these children as Sheldon's future friends, with each character identifiable from key visual signifiers associated with their adult selves, such as appearance (Leonard's glasses), books (Amy reading *Little House on the Prairie*), or hobbies (Howard's magic kit and rocket). The combined pathos and optimism of this moment is encapsulated in the lyrics of "Someday We'll Be Together" (performed by Diana Ross & the Supremes), which accompanies the montage. This foreshadowing of Sheldon's future continues in the season 3 episode "Pasadena" (3:16) when George Sr. takes Sheldon to hear Stephen Hawking give a lecture at Caltech. The episode's final scene shows father and son at the cafeteria that would become a significant location in the adult Sheldon's professional and social life, the place where he finds "his tribe":

SHELDON: Imagine all the stimulating conversations that must go on at these tables.
GEORGE: I bet.
SHELDON: I can see myself going here one day.
GEORGE: I think you'd fit right in.

If all this sounds like a fairy tale or, indeed, a superhero origin story, perhaps this is part of the appeal of *Young Sheldon* for autistic people and their families, especially younger viewers. As I watch this series alongside my son, we both know that Sheldon Cooper is a fictional character, just as we know Clark Kent (Superman), Bruce Wayne (Batman), and Peter Parker (Spiderman) are fictional characters, too. But this does not mean we cannot enjoy this superhero's tales of triumph as he realizes his true potential. Nor does it prevent us relating to Sheldon's struggles as he faces his fears, overcomes challenges, and finds his place in the world.

Notes

1. Autists publicly identify themselves in several ways, using terms such as "on the spectrum," "has a diagnosis of autism," "with autism," or "autistic." When quoting from written works, I use the term that each author adopted. In other cases, I use identity-first language (e.g., autistic person or autist) to align with the position taken by Amaze, the authoritative advocacy group for autistic people and their supporters in Victoria, Australia (Anderson and Francey 2019).

2. The post has been republished on Magro's personal blog; see Magro 2016.

3. The first-look promotional trailer for *Young Sheldon* can still be viewed on *The Big Bang Theory*'s fandom wiki site, which is an encyclopedic resource created by the show's fan community: www.bigbangtheory.fandom.com/wiki/Young_Sheldon.

CHAPTER 14

Due Diligence: Exploring ASD in *Nightcrawler* and *The Accountant*

DOMINIC LENNARD

Complications of social cooperation dominate fictional landscapes, just as they dominate our real world. We are constantly meeting people very unlike ourselves, indeed even strange, in our view, with whom we sense the need to cooperate and converse. But learning is crucial in such encounters, and fiction provides a safe yet intriguing avenue to facilitate this. Brian Boyd writes that the story "increases the range of our vicarious experience and behavioural options . . . without subjecting ourselves to actual risk" (2009, 193). Narratives frequently focus on challenging interpersonal relations, lingering on questions of trust, safety, friendship, betrayal, status, freedom, duty, and romance. Joseph Carroll points out that the interplay of social and personal power is "an active theme in most literature. In many great works, it is the central theme" (2006, 144). Like all organisms, we are genetically predisposed to prioritize our individual interests, but we have spent our natural history living in small tribal coalitions (that come with their own demands), and there has never been any escape from the perpetual awareness and negotiation of competing interests and attendant trade-offs. David Barash argues that fiction's persistent theme of individuality versus the social, "self versus group, selfishness versus altruism, callow youth versus responsible adulthood, individual needs versus society's expectation," prevails because "it is a conflict that may reside, literally, in our genes" (2004, 201).

Recently, there has been a rise in cinematic depictions of individuals with autism as awareness has been raised around the condition and diagnoses have increased. Stuart Murray refers to autism as "the condition of fascination of the moment, occupying a number of cultural locations that reflect a spectrum of wonder and nervousness—the allure of potentially unquantifiable human difference" (2008b, 5). Little as most viewers might know about spectrum disorders, they likely know that such things are characterized by problems with interpersonal communication: difficulty understanding nonverbal cues, joint attention, and social reciprocity (Garner, Harwood, and Jones 2016, 152). Interpreting communication is indispensable to successful social interaction and mobility, and it thereby lies at the heart of the "wonder and nervousness" of the "potentially unquantifiable" difference Murray describes. As Steven Pinker points out, "[We] mortals can't read other people's minds directly. But we make good guesses from what they say, what we read between the lines, what they show in their face and eyes, and what best explains their behavior" (2005, 330), and it is in this area of "mind reading" (more technically, "empathic accuracy") that those with Autism Spectrum Disorder (ASD) are particularly prone to be challenged (Demurie, De Corel, and Roeyers 2011; Ponnet et al. 2008, 905). It is unsurprising then that the appearance of high-functioning autistic characters in fiction might have a strong "exploratory" focus, evoking uncertainties in our strategies of social interaction, especially our ability to read and predict the moods, thoughts, and intentions of others.

With a few exceptions, Hollywood cinema has not been greatly interested in centralizing adult characters with severe neurological or cognitive impairments. Such people are easily pigeonholed into unhelpful categories: they do not pose a question. But the "question" provoked by high-functioning autistics is not simply a product of some categorical uncertainty (which itself explains nothing). I suggest that those with profound deficits are not perceived as agents of mutually beneficial social exchange and thus may be safely (though cruelly) ignored in both culture and media—understanding them is not a great priority. In contrast, we are aware that adults with ASD are frequently independent and high-functioning members of society, often demonstrating high-value abilities; consequently, they more easily provoke interest in how neurological difference, social interaction, and understanding can be beneficially navigated. Nevertheless, perhaps the interest in media representations of those with high-functioning ASD can help gradually expand our acceptance of difference more generally, prompting broader conversations about social value. Such a hope, though, suggests that attention should be devoted to the autistic characters that we already have. Those with ASD in the real world are a distinct minority—approximately 1.68 percent of the population (Centers for Disease Control and Prevention 2020).

Thus, most people are more likely to encounter those with ASD through fictional media, where representations are less likely to be balanced, diluted, or dispelled through everyday interactions than in real life. Autistic characters play into fiction's allure as a potential learning experience. In the rest of this chapter, I examine two films, *Nightcrawler* (2014) and *The Accountant* (2016), as examples of an exploratory interest in ASD beyond earlier perceptions of a "narrow stereotyping of autistics in media accounts as freakish and mentally defective" (Robertson 2009, 12). These two films place characterological ambiguity at their center, both focusing on talented but mysterious—even potentially dangerous—adult males. Both films, I suggest, invite us to exercise a kind of due diligence around highly capable neurodivergent protagonists, ultimately arriving at different perspectives on the relationship between neurological difference and social belonging.

Nightcrawler: Intrigue and Caution

Dan Gilroy's acclaimed thriller *Nightcrawler* provokes us to wonder, by fits and starts, what exactly is up with the man at its center, a petty criminal named Lou Bloom (Jake Gyllenhaal). As the opening credits appear, we see static shots of predawn downtown LA, accompanied by mellow electric-guitar strumming, suggesting a harmonious readiness for production and life. Then we see Lou at work: he is clipping through a chain-link fence on an industrial avenue. A security officer approaches; Lou puts his bolt cutters away, wearing a placid smile of expectation, even mild enthusiasm. Recognizing the officer as an employee of a private company, Lou parries, with curious amiability, the guard's request for identification. Suddenly, Lou is distracted by the gleam of an incongruously expensive Breitling Chronomat on the guard's wrist. We cut to a rear wide shot as he lunges at the guard; the shot then retreats to an even greater distance, at which the men are no longer visible. A train arrives somewhere close by: the scene has reverted to the detached and docile tone of the opening credits. Lou's act is despicable, but the camera's evasion of its violence seems to avoid labeling the perpetrator. In the next shot, we see Lou driving away placidly, a roll of chain link in his trunk and the Chronomat on his left wrist.

He drives to a scrap processor and pitches the fencing and a couple of stolen manhole covers to a surly supervisor, haggling over a price to which his buyer grudgingly agrees. But Lou doesn't understand conversational nuance. He begins presenting himself as a job seeker, with an incongruous pitch that suggests he has no sense of context. He doesn't get the job. Soon, after a chance encounter at an accident scene, Lou immerses himself in the world of stringers: private videographers who chase crime scenes and accidents, selling the footage to news networks (in the tradition of Arthur "Weegee" Fellig). He listens to police-scanner reports, rushing to crime scenes to nab his new commodity. The income allows him to upgrade his equipment and, eventually, his car—a Dodge Challenger that sweetly whisks him to his targets, often before the police—and he is able to command great prices for his increasingly lurid wares. He also takes on an assistant, Rick (Riz Ahmed), and strikes up a relationship of sorts with a hard-nosed late-night news producer, Nina (Rene Russo), who relies on him to produce the sort of sensationalism that will be her rescue in a ratings war.

Lou is provided no backstory, which piques viewer curiosity and speculation through onscreen action, especially given the incongruity of his early behavior, framing our approach to him as voyeuristic surveillance. Any "condition" he has is never explicitly labeled, yet during his progress through his new occupation, his insensitivity to social nuance is extensively demonstrated, compounding a reading of him as autistic. Lou is able to do well as a stringer (and make his breakthrough sale) because of his seeming ignorance of unspoken rules, as when he gets right in the face of a bloodied, dying victim. Even other shameless stringers have internal guidelines that cap the degree of obscenity they are willing to capture, guidelines that Lou cannot seem to understand as he wanders right up to a dying victim being swarmed over by EMTs, hoisting his camera overhead. In conversations, Lou garrulously signposts his interest in and study of business management and economics, an exclusive intensity suggesting a neurodivergent restrictive focus. As it happens, this mode of thinking benefits his career, but it is a doctrine to which he adheres utterly and without any sense of perspective.

What little we see of Lou's outside life compounds our sense of his atypical psychology: his tiny apartment is pedantically spotless, and later we see him engaged in the conscientious cleaning that maintains its minimalism. In another scene there, Lou assiduously memorizes police radio codes in order to speed up his response times. Early in his run as a stringer, Lou encroaches too much on the scene of an accident, provoking a police crackdown on photographers. This restriction raises the ire of a competitor: "Get the fuck home. There's people trying to do their fucking jobs." The fellow stringer walks away, phoning his boss, yet Lou, attempting to learn more of the profession, hovers in awkwardly intimate proximity, as if oblivious of both the man's aggression and appropriate social distance. His inappropriateness extends to his romantic life (or attempts at one). Trying to woo the television producer Nina (a scenario that requires great sensitivity to nonverbal cues), Lou artlessly blurts out: "I like the dark makeup on your eyes. I also like the way you smell." Lou's opportunistic criminality is apparent early, but the film makes no real attempt to couch this in socioeconomic woe or a malicious nature. Instead, what we see is an obsessive and domain-specific interest and an incapacity to grasp the subtleties of communication.

A counterpoint to Lou's persona is Rick, the twentysomething assistant he takes on, at a measly thirty dollars a night, to navigate and shoot with him. South Asian American, underskilled, and underequipped for the cutthroat LA bustle around him, Rick is a familiar down-and-out big-city straggler. Yet despite similarities in their social stations, Lou and Rick could hardly be more different, and as Lou's ambition surges into criminality, Rick is dragged along, but only with obvious moral reluctance. This character also has the effect of highlighting Lou's communicative oddness. After Rick gets Lou to agree to increase his paltry pay, in a rare moment that approaches acknowledgment of him as a fellow partner in the business, he encourages Lou to strive further in these steps toward connecting with others: "You gotta bring people in, Lou, seriously—you gotta talk to them like they're fuckin' human beings. I'm saying this for you, dude, for the future, to help you. Because you got a seriously weird-ass way of looking at shit. You know you do! You know what your trouble is, man? You don't fuckin' understand . . . *people*. Okay?" This isn't the kind of reproach one gives to a predator—or even just a prick—but is apt, rather, for a person in whom one senses a genuine deficit that might be remedied.

Yet Lou remains incapable of understanding people. His only technique for navigating relationships is his economic template, structured by bargaining power, market values, hardball negotiation, and careerist maxims—a fixed system that a personality such as his can use to process interactions and achieve confidence. Lou is young, good-looking, and upwardly mobile, thanks to his talent for obsessive engagement. Yet his deficits in monitoring nonverbal feedback and predicting or interpreting social responses—implicated as they are in his criminality—make him inherently unpredictable, and he thereby commands attention. While never expressly identified, Lou's nature betrays enough for us to recognize his neurodivergence, presenting him as one who wheels and deals but whose idea of the game is not the same as ours and whose gambits we have yet to grasp.

By promoting our curiosity about Lou, even curating his moral ambiguity, *Nightcrawler*, toward its conclusion, seems to attempt to dispose of much of the viewer's uncertainty. Lou convinces Nina to join him for a date, during which he discourses on his career goals and goes so far as to blackmail her into sleeping with him. Unmoved, she politely rebuffs him. He immediately plays the same hardball game he does over the sale of his footage, garrulously touting his economic value as a content producer, indifferent to the obscenity of his sexual coercion. Shortly afterward, having lost a scoop to a rival outfit and receiving a dressing-down from Nina, Lou gazes at his reflection in a cabinet mirror before screaming in frustration and smashing the reflection before him—a somewhat clichéd signal pointing to an already frayed moral identity that finally "breaks."

From this point, Lou's driven nature accelerates through all ethical obstacles. He enters the scene of a home invasion before the police in order to film the gory aftermath, snagging the most attention-grabbing kind of footage: bloody white middle-class corpses. His most stunning transgression, and point of irredeemability, comes during an extended scene in which, having located the armed culprits, Lou waits for them to enter a late-night restaurant before calling the police, hopeful of filming a bloody arrest that will endanger those nearby. Several people are killed, and the perpetrators escape, tailed by the police—with Lou in pursuit. The scene culminates with Lou's orchestration of Rick's murder, deliberately luring him into the firing line of one of the fleeing killers. Lou films the dying Rick as a casualty of the event, just as he would any other victim. As Rick gazes up at Lou in shocked betrayal, Lou spouts more of his banal corporate-speak about "not jeopardizing his business." If Lou did in fact hear Rick's earlier plea about relating to his fellow humans, he heard it only through his obsessive lens of economic conflict, his solution to which was to turn Rick into just another bloody piece of business.

By the end of the film, Lou has become "monstrous," a character from whom we are—finally—able to distance ourselves in bewilderment and disgust. This transformation allows him to better serve the film's broader critique of media parasitism. In himself, Lou is not terribly important, perhaps: he is enabled by a broader system, in a well-worn comment on capitalism as a promoter of psychopathy. In interviews around the film's release, the writer-director Dan Gilroy promoted this interpretation. When asked by Slash Film about his goals for the character, he replied that his intent was to communicate "that people like Lou are increasingly rewarded for what

they do. I feel that in today's world you will often find people with some sociopathic tendencies who are succeeding on a corporate level. . . . It allows
him to thrive, and to fully embrace the uber-capitalist concept, the ultimate
hyper-free market. Which I feel is increasingly the world that we live in"
(Fischer 2014).

For his part, Gyllenhaal was more willing to complicate the idea of our
reading Lou that way, telling the *Guardian*, "I don't like to call him a sociopath . . . The reason he doesn't become unwatchable is because there's this
great innocence to him" (Barnes 2014). Indeed there is: when misty-eyed
Lou rambles about his career dreams to Nina, the score plays a gentle synth
melody that accents his innocence. Seconds later, his attention is snagged
by the stage set for a breakfast show: an enormous static photo of nighttime
LA on the backdrop behind the hosts' vacant desk, not (as Lou had apparently assumed) a live feed. "Wow," he sweetly ponders, "on TV it looks so
real!" In a later Q&A, Gilroy, maintaining the same line on Lou's empowerment by a morally bankrupt culture, seemed to admit that Lou's character
was not merely sociopathic but also autistic: "somewhere on the spectrum of
those things, and they were intersecting" (Gilroy and Gilroy 2018).

While many reviewers (writing in a genre in which shorthand hyper-
bole tends to dominate) glossed him as a "sociopath," the question of what
was up with Lou spawned intrigued viewer commentary online. The *Sociopath World* blog suggested that he is "autistic with antisocial traits," and several commenters concurred; a blogger named Stay Smart replied, "There is
no sugarcoating when it comes to an autistic person, and there are certain
nuances that escape him/her. And speaking of this particular protagonist,
once again, the autistic analysis fits him—not a sociopath or a psychopath
at all" (*Sociopath World* 2014). A poster to Reddit's movies message board
noted how clear it is that Lou is autistic, highlighting the conspicuously exacting neatness of his apartment (in opposition to the messiness of most
psychopaths' [see, for example, Lynam and Derefinko 2006, 142; Paulhus
and Williams 2002, 559]) as well as his obliviousness of social cues and his
garrulous speaking style (Reddit 2014). Another poster confidingly agreed:
"I think it was definitely on the higher functioning side of the spectrum."
He continued: "From the moment he spoke, I instantly knew [he was au-
tistic], and throughout the entire movie I was just reminded of something I
might have done or said that I just suddenly realized was really bad."

Despite the obvious attempt to steer Lou's characterization toward psychopathy as the film goes on, as viewer and reviewer commentary attests,
Nightcrawler was hardly capable of erasing perceptions of his earlier disposition. Lou tells Rick, recalling an earlier conversation, "What if it's not that

I don't understand people; it's just that I don't like them." This bald and apparently revelatory confession of misanthropy is clumsily at odds with the rest of the film: the viewer has seen ample evidence that Lou really *doesn't* understand people—his awkward approach to job seeking, his interactions with his date, his inability to simply know when he is walking too close to someone. While Lou's behavior transgresses the boundaries of taste and ethics, the film invests heavily in depicting an otherwise incongruent naïveté in his interactions, which undermines attempts to pigeonhole him as a cunning, and thus self-aware, predator. While the Lou-as-psychopath turn may come as a relief in a cultural landscape nervous about stigmatizing images of autism, it raises further questions. It might indeed be the case that Lou has both autistic and psychopathic traits. While this is diagnostically possible, in such rare occurrences ASD and psychopathy are thought to be distinct disorders rather than implicated in each other (Rogers et al. 2006). Since Lou's behaviors go unlabeled until he is finally placed in a relatively stable characterological category that prompts viewers' fear and repugnance, I suggest that the film melds his ASD traits into those of a darker and more antisocial malaise.

I am not of the school of thought that assumes that characters should be depicted, or necessarily taken by viewers, as models of their "type" (however identified)—for example, that female politician characters should (favorably) represent female politicians broadly. This paradigm logically concludes with disallowing villains drawn from any currently or historically disadvantaged social group. Such a perspective implies that works of art have a moral duty to do double service as advocacy. It is also anathema to the very idea of individual characters. Nevertheless, given the relatively new interest of audiences in characters who are autistic, or are read as such, reflection is warranted on how characters with conspicuously neurodivergent traits and behaviors are handled within their texts' internal logic. In *Nightcrawler's* case there certainly appears to be an otherwise incongruous dovetailing of recognizable characteristics of autism and monstrousness: once Lou's psychopathy is brought into definitive relief, his autistic traits are positioned to be read in line as early symptoms of predacity. In short, if the film does encourage us, as its director seems to imply, to watch "people like Lou" with caution, what clues are we supposed to be cautiously looking for?

Adjusting for Difference in *The Accountant*

Whereas *Nightcrawler* is evasive about its antihero's condition, Gavin O'Connor's 2016 thriller *The Accountant* centers its protagonist's neurodivergence almost immediately. As the film opens, we see a man—his identity unclear—arriving on the scene of a gangland shooting. He attempts to intercept its perpetrator, but finds himself outmaneuvered and at the killer's mercy. After this cryptic fragment, we flashback to a warmly furnished semi-residential neuroscience clinic in 1989. A mother and father seek advice on their preteen son, who assiduously completes a jigsaw puzzle nearby, becoming distressed when he cannot locate the final piece. The therapist identifies familiar ASD symptoms but tells the parents: "I don't like labels." This realignment of normative modes of identity becomes a crucial focus of the film. After the consultation, the father elects for his son not to stay at the clinic: despite his difficulties, it is the broader world, he says, where the boy must learn to live.

Later we see this boy, Christian Wolff (Ben Affleck), working in a low-profile accounting practice. Visibly rigid and soft-spoken, yet having achieved much success in overriding the impulses that make communication a challenge, Christian rescues an aging couple from financial ruin and earns their great fondness through a series of clever tax deductions that indicate his talent for systemization. After work, he returns to a presentable yet barely furnished suburban home, prepares a simple dinner alone, with plated morsels precisely separated and eaten in specific order. His life is isolated, emphasizing his individuality and, foremost, his lack of social connections. We see that he has the kind of hypersensitivity to touch common in those with ASD (Kaiser et al. 2016), which he attempts to mitigate by using a regular, punishing routine of self-stimulation (running a length of wood along the exposed skin of his leg), blasting music, and exposing himself to a strobe light in his bedroom.

In such a moment, we are urged to sympathize with Christian's struggles. And yet this man also checks the live feed of security cameras during his consultations and speaks to a mysterious voice on speakerphone as he drives: he is obviously involved in some kind of illegal activity. Attempting to avoid scrutiny, he accepts a job doing forensic accountancy for a high-tech robotics outfit, the junior in-house accountant Dana (Anna Kendrick) having detected a discrepancy in its records. In a post-financial-crisis cultural landscape, there is as much corruption in this apparently unselfish prosthetics manufacturer as in the criminal underworld of which Christian is an indistinct participant. A major embezzlement is detected, with inventory fraud having been used to inflate the company's valuation before an initial public offering. Christian is already being tracked by a group of US Treasury agents, but after the fraud is detected, a group of highly financed hit men are set loose, charged with eradicating anyone who threatens to expose it, including Christian and Dana.

The noirish plot that unravels is convoluted (sometimes implausibly so) beyond efficient summary, yet worth attention is the way in which the film positions the cryptic man at its center in relation to our frames of expectation. In his accounting, Christian demonstrates talent—"nothing short of supernatural" according to one of his recommendations for the position—beyond that of any neurotypical peer, signaling his exceptional usefulness, analyzing fifteen years of financial records in one night, whereas it took Dana two weeks. His character thus adheres to the stereotype of savantism that surrounds autistic representation (S. Murray 2008b, 97), since his skills are not statistically typical of those on the spectrum. But some people with ASD do in fact demonstrate remarkable talent in detail-oriented areas. And it is hardly uncommon for Hollywood films to focus on remarkable people, neurotypical or otherwise. Aside from its narrative purpose, Christian's skill allows the film to maximize the enigma around autism by underscoring spectrum disorders' subversion of perceptions of ability and disability. For Mark Osteen, such autistic representations threaten to depict the autistic as "more a puzzle than a person" (quoted in Loftis 2016, 4). Christian is indeed a mystery, the emphasis on the jigsaw puzzle in the film's opening scene paralleling a discussion of how he will fit into society.

The puzzle motif is also complemented by the taxing number of twists in the film's plot, a puzzling metatextual strategy that doubles for the "puzzle" of its central character. We eventually discover that "Christian Wolff" is an alias, one of many this man has used in the past, derived from the names of famous mathematicians. (Christian Wolff [1679–1754] was a German polymath.) His dichotomized or at least unresolved character is enhanced for the audience. We might even say that Christian's shadowy, seemingly criminal nature and his autism overlap, one becoming a kind of metaphor for the other, at least concerning the ambiguity they inject into his social compatibility. In any case, while possessed of skills of great social value, Christian is also a figure of a social dissonance who invites investigation, who must be figured out. Yet the adult Christian's altruistic behavior in connection with an ordinary couple facing financial ruin means we receive an early assurance of his innate goodness. The film may generate uncertainty and unfamiliarity around him, but it never seriously suggests to us that he will turn out to be a villain.

The Accountant takes significant steps to build audience identification with Christian beyond simply provoking curiosity about his cultural categorization. It renders him relatable despite his difference, suggesting that in his unique way, Christian is but one of many individual puzzle pieces overwhelmed by a world where finding one's fit is a challenge. For instance, Christian's lonesome and spartan home routine is especially isolated and peculiar. But it is overlaid with the wistful strains of Jim James's melancholically down-tempo "State of the Art (A.E.I.O.U.)" on the soundtrack, with lyrics of isolation:

I use the state-of-the-art technology,
Supposed to make for better living
Are we better human beings?
We got all our wires all crossed, tubes all tied
JAMES OLLIGES JR.

The song insinuates that Christian is a representative of a shared state of sterile modernist disconnection.

Perhaps the main way in which he becomes more readable (and relatable), however, is through an emphasis on his childhood (which also implies a sympathetic innocence within this adult character). In a painful flashback, we see his mother's leaving the family, attributed to the child Christian's difficulty; ASD aside, the guilt that surrounds this episode is common among children of divorced parents. The childhood flashbacks also intensify viewer identification through a focus on what is for everyone a seminal stage of awareness and negotiation of conflicts between self and other, autonomy and social belonging. Christian's father enforces on him an especially brutal program of martial arts training, which explains his combat skills throughout the film. But the impetus for the lessons is no different from what inspires many millions of children: after Christian becomes a target of bullies, self-defense training allows him to assert independence against threats of subjugation to group demands. The philosopher René Girard has written: "No culture exists within which everyone does not feel 'different' from others. . . . There exists in every individual a tendency to think of himself not only as different from others but as extremely different" (1986, 21). Despite the difficulties of this particular child, childhood generally in *The Accountant* is positioned as a common ground of tenuous belonging and a locus of difficulties in social integration. In short, Christian's autism is placed on a continuum of individuality in which it becomes relatable for its stark manifestation of what we might call the "otherness" of selfhood.

This focus on childhood as the most poignant space-time of social belonging is reinvoked as the adult Christian and Dana meet while eating lunch outside the corporate building on Christian's first day. During their brief, earlier encounter, when Dana handed over the company records, they had each put the wrong foot forward in their attempts to communicate; now Dana sits nearby as Christian carries his lunch to an out-of-the-way concrete step. We are both amused and endeared by his diagonal responses to his new colleague's small talk. Not put off by his awkwardness and lack of eye contact, Dana brings her lunch closer to him and continues her introduction. She inadvertently stumbles into mutual conversational territory, earning interested responses; a few placid smiles from the usually rigid Christian indicate that however halting the conversation is by conventional means, the two have had a pleasantly reciprocal moment, have encountered each other's humanity. The scene, with the loner Christian and junior Dana, resembles a first day at school, in which one braves connection with a fellow pupil.

The icebreaking continues in the "classroom": Dana enters the meeting space where Christian has been working and marvels at his whiteboard financial analysis (which covers almost every exposed surface). The two delight in the puzzle before them, sharing smiles and muted camaraderie, twice repeating each other's sentences. Later in the film, on the run from the hit squad, Dana and Christian are holed up in a hotel, and the film's emphasis on youthful connection is underlined, appealing to us through its poignancy. When Christian tells Dana of his difficulty with socializing, despite his desire to do so, she relays an anecdote about struggling to purchase a prom dress. She snags Christian's interest by mentioning in passing the math club—a social niche in which Christian would have thrived. The point of the dress for Dana was not materialism but social acknowledgment: "I was trying to belong; I was trying to connect," she confides. "I think no matter how different we are, we're all trying to do the same thing." While Christian explains his autism to Dana, he speaks of its cognitive and behavioral manifestations, affirming one kind of difference while affirming her supposition of common ground: "I'm not unique." The autistic isn't simplistically a symbol of modern isolation for a neurotypical audience. Rather, neurotypical viewers can recognize themselves in someone with whom they share characteristics—even if in a less amplified way—eroding barriers to understanding and integration.

Christian's criminality, especially its involvement in brutal violence, presents an obstacle for us to overcome in perceiving him as a reliable social actor, but his autism seems to offer an assurance rather than a liability. Stuart Murray has written that despite a "potential for violence within autistic behavior, stemming from frustration or misunderstanding, ideas of aggression are largely infrequent in the various fictional accounts of the condition" (2008b, 156). *The Accountant*, however, at least sharpens our awareness of potential violence. Agents investigating the mysterious slaying depicted at the start of the film eventually isolate a sound sample, picked up by a bug in the gangsters' enclave, in which the killer monotonously murmurs a nursery rhyme to himself over and over. Torben Grodal points out that "one of the central clichés of crime fiction is the serial killer that repeats certain rituals that have to be performed obsessively and compulsively" (2010, 69). Yet it turns out that the rhyme is a calming strategy that Christian—who was indeed the gunman—has used since he was a child. Moreover, the slaying was payback for the far more grisly and inhuman torture-murder of a nonviolent mentor who had helped Christian immeasurably in his social communication and was supposed to be under federal protection.

We learn that Christian's violence is as accurate and discriminating as his accounting, and he attacks only those who breach a personal ethical code that spares the innocent. Indeed, he has aided the police in apprehending offenders who took things beyond the moral pale. Any violence he commits is precise, readable, morally codified, and therefore "safe" for the viewer— a precision exemplified in his hobby of long-range shooting, which rewards the patient calculation of variables. Given this slant, his autistic nature gives us confidence that his violence is subject to the same intense systematization as his other routines. When he is drawn into physical combat, Christian is robotically composed, resembling Schwarzenegger's programmed-to-protect cyborg of *Terminator 2: Judgment Day* (1991). Autism in this context is therefore not a liability but instead an assurance against extravagance and bloodlust. In fact, Christian's nature in this respect is juxtaposed with that of his neurotypical brother Braxton (Jon Bernthal), who turns out to be the leader of the hit crew hunting him and Dana. Braxton, fanciful in his predacity, threatens the rape of one victim's wife before confessing, "I just say shit": in other words, his violence is not calculated, but whimsical and imaginative and the more frightening for being so.

Having confirmed for us Christian's nature and identified his shared desire for connection, *The Accountant* concludes by maintaining his difference, not seeking to corral the autistic into conventional frames of expectation. After Dana's protection by Christian leads to moments of tender confession and closeness between the two, they seem poised for romance. Yet it is not to be: at the film's conclusion, Christian drives off into the distance, his Airstream trailer in tow, having sent Dana a marvelous gift, signaling his contentment in the friendship they forged. The two are together through crosscutting (as she unwraps her present) but not more so. Like the hero of a western (towing a "wagon" of sorts), Christian rescues but does not marry the girl; he helps repair society while retaining his autonomy. This skillful use of genre convention allows an ending that is satisfying in its formalism while dodging neurotypical expectations, opening us up to what we might call a positive "mythology of difference."

The protagonists in *Nightcrawler* and *The Accountant* are high functioning and socially mobile, yet their sometimes stark psychological difference positions them for our curiosity and, implicitly, investigation. But reading other people is difficult. For all the emphasis on autists' difficulty in reading other people, we struggle to read them just as much, maybe even more. In *Nightcrawler*, ASD—never mentioned explicitly—is strongly signaled, only to be remystified or at least evaded: Lou's mind-reading deficit is blended with a wanton moral illiteracy, finally distancing us from him as a soulless agent of media exploitation. By contrast, in *The Accountant*, the negotiation of independence and connection becomes our common thread while difference is both maintained and dignified. Christian is not "cured," but happily and autonomously rides on.

CHAPTER 15

Mind the Gap: Autistic Viewpoint in Film

ALEX CLAYTON

I think in pictures. Words are like a second language to me. I translate both spoken and written words into full-color movies, complete with sound, which run like a VCR tape in my head.
TEMPLE GRANDIN, *THINKING IN PICTURES*

How might art evoke the outlook of someone with autism? When well-known spokesperson for autism Temple Grandin reports that she thinks in moving images, we might readily imagine that film would be the medium of choice. It is a long-standing hope of art that it might bring us to see the world differently, to shake our habitual ways of seeing and to apprehend familiar things in new ways. Viktor Shklovsky ([1919] 2016, 217) and T. S. Eliot ([1933] 1986) saw this potential in poetry. George Wilson (1998) and Gilberto Perez (1989) found it in movies. Among a small handful of other theorists and critics, they showed how movies are able to realize complex points of view through the patterning of events and the perspectives from which these events are shown. Wilson and Perez took their cue from V. F. Perkins, who was the first to really demonstrate the significance of the fact that films do not merely give views of things but also embody the viewpoints from which those things are seen. Perkins shows that "what we see [in the organization of a fiction film] is, primarily, a way of seeing: the direct registration and embodiment, in a 'secondary world', of a point of view" ([1972] 1986, 119–120). That is to say, the things of a movie are always exhibited from a particular angle, and the location and nature of that perspective are part of what is exhibited. From the selection of what is included and excluded in a shot, and what is given more or less prominence in the image and on the soundtrack, a movie starts to assemble its range of perspectives. The global, more-or-less-coherent point of view constructed need not be thought of as that of the director or even of the wider filmmaking collective, but may be more usefully considered the viewpoint of the film itself. Some theorists have taken this idea a step further and proposed that it is useful to consider whether films "think" (Frampton 2006; Mulhall 2016). If, in keeping with Gilles Deleuze's provocation, "the brain is the screen" (1988, 48), if cinema in its movements and connections exhibits a kind of thought, then we could start to wonder whether, and how, films might model autistic thinking.

Fiction films regularly seek to evoke how a particular character experiences the world, and doing so may be an important possibility for movies that centrally depict a person with autism. The need to imagine how the world manifests "through" autism is pressing for those of us with friends and relatives on the spectrum, with whom conversation may not yield the vividness of insight we crave into the condition as lived. Part of the lived reality of autism as a condition is its production of a "consciousness gap" that can be distressing for parties on both sides of the divide. People on all points of the spectrum commonly struggle to express their feelings and convey their thoughts in ways that satisfy them. On the other side, those without the condition are less able to use standard methods of behavioral detection to grasp from the outside what the other person is feeling, since the body language of people with autism is often perceived to be geared more toward coping than communicating (whether or not it is). Although vexed questions of accuracy and representativeness immediately arise, and must be conceded, it is tempting to wonder whether the extraverbal, thinking-in-images nature of film might help provide a bridge, a stimulus to the imagination. It might make the condition more appreciable. More importantly, by expanding the range of possibilities of seeing the world, film has the capacity to enrich our understanding of human consciousness.

This is a grand ambition, and we must first take baby steps. One of the most concerted attempts I know of to bridge the gap through a personal account is the facilitated testimony of a thirteen-year-old Japanese boy with severe autism and limited verbal communication skills, translated into English by K. A. Yoshida and David Mitchell and published as *The Reason I Jump* (2013). With disarming directness and reflexivity, Naoki Higashida addresses a series of questions that he imagines someone without autism would want to ask. Here he is, for example, on why people with autism sometimes echo questions back at the asker:

> Firing the question back is a way of sifting through our memories to pick up clues about what the questioner is asking. We understand the question okay, but we can't answer it until we fish out the right "memory picture" in our heads. (25)

On why people with autism often cup their ears:

> There are certain noises you don't notice, but that really get to us. The problem here is that you don't understand how these noises affect us. It's not quite that the noises grate on our nerves. It's more to do with a fear that if we keep listening, we'll lose all sense of where we are. (81)

On why people with autism often don't make eye contact when talking:

> What we're actually looking at is the other person's voice. Voices may not be visible things, but we're trying to listen to the other person with all of our sense organs. When we're fully focused on working out what the heck it is you're saying, our sense of sight sort of zones out. (43–44)

Finally, Higashida seeks to relay how he believes people with autism see differently from neurotypical people:

> You may be looking at the exact same things as us, but *how* we perceive them appears to be different. When you see an object, it seems that you see it as an entire thing first, and only afterwards do its details follow on. But for people with autism, the details jump straight out at us first of all, and then only gradually, detail by detail, does the whole image sort of float up into focus. (91–92)

We need to acknowledge the strong tendency to generalize here, which risks denying the considerable variation between different autistic behaviors and brain types. There is no one single way that people with autism see things. Nevertheless, the clarity with which this account is offered, and the overlap with other first-person descriptions of the condition, may make it a useful starting point for considering how film might evoke perceptions and modes of engagement that are characteristic of autism. I want to keep these snippets of testimony in mind as I consider how they might relate to film style, and in particular to common movie conventions.

What prompted my interest in these matters was a recent realization that I have a brain condition that makes me incapable of generating mental imagery. I had observed this difference from others for many years, but didn't suppose it was that unusual and didn't have a name for it until recently learning that "aphantasia," blindness of the mind's eye, affects approximately 1–2 percent of the population. I was often mystified, for example, when friends could relay in detail how they imagined a character in a novel to appear, consult a visual memory to recall what someone was wearing yesterday, or summon an image of a relaxing beach for meditative purposes. I can do none of that. I seem to be on the other end of the spectrum of "thinking in pictures" from Temple Grandin, although I don't believe it affects my imaginative ability or capacity to engage with imagery. I even wonder whether it is what draws me to cinema, with film supplying the phantom pictures I cannot produce for myself.

At any rate, it dawned on me that this condition might explain why I find myself somewhat resistant to certain common movie conventions, especially those that simulate thinking as visual recall and hallucination. Such tropes generate a kind of friction for me that others seem not to experience. Top of the list is the subjective flashback, when a character recalls an event by summoning it to mind visually and we are offered the recollection in exquisite visual detail. That is just not the way I remember. Admittedly, the flashback is a strange convention that diverges from all human memory, in that typically the scene is replayed in the third person and the level of visual detail transcends what anyone could or would care to recall. In practice, it isn't usually an image of memory so much as a mechanism for showing what happened. Nonetheless, people do commonly report having flashbacks and speak of memory as images (perhaps especially autists: recall Higashida's reference to the "memory picture" [2013, 25]). The flashback seems to have a natural connection with the way most people remember.

This makes me wonder whether other formal conventions might chime with some neurological dispositions more than others, perhaps even whether some ways of seeing and modes of thinking may be "baked in" to certain standards of filmic expression. As a medium addressing a mass audience, cinema had to develop its repertoire based on presumptions about the "average viewer." Filmmakers need to get in sync with what a typical person might gather, desire, predict, and assume. That raises the question, how does the standard "language" of film form relate to a condition such as mine, and then, more pressingly for me here, how does it relate to a condition such as autism?

One dominant way in which films tend to construct space and tell stories, for instance, is through eyeline matching and the use of shot-countershot editing. It has come to seem perfectly "natural" that if characters should glance or gaze offscreen, we should next see what they are looking at (though not necessarily from their spatial position). Moreover, in most films, the rhythm and formal logic of a face-to-face dialogue scene is motivated by the exchange of responsive glances between characters. Medium close-ups are bounced back and forth in such a way as to place emphasis on minute facial "tells." Each cut is typically timed to take in or "stand for" a character's reaction at the instant of understanding the content of an immediately preceding utterance or behavior. This formal system puts behavioral anomalies doubly under the microscope through literal magnification (close-up) and the channeling of responses through a character (reaction shot). In this way, the film models a manner of attentiveness to its world. Through reverse-field editing, the film dramatizes the reciprocal mind reading of the characters (often fabricating a rapport between actors who, at the moment of shooting each half of a dialogue scene, may not even be in the same space or know each other). The film responds "on behalf" of a viewer whose disposition to scrutinize eyes and mouth is assumed. Returning to the comments from Higashida, above, we can see how this fluid reciprocal exchange, and particularly the emphasis on facial detail, is at odds with the ways in which people with high-functioning autism more typically navigate a conversation. They would pick out a detail or two, but maybe not the "right" ones.

It is also through the meaningful or searching look that movie characters become narrative subjects rather than mere objects of the camera's gaze. As Hitchcock knew, and as film theorists have long observed, aligning the viewer with a character's look creates the possibility for making him or her a kind of audience surrogate. Insofar as it cues the next shot, a triggering glance offscreen gives the beholder a share of narrative agency, as if they were leading the movie's investigation. For this reason, one suspects that a scene following a standard-shot/reverse-shot procedure between one character with autism and one without would tend to be asymmetrical, favoring the latter, since the avoidance of eye contact would provide fewer opportunities to cue the next shot in the chain of facial close-ups. Partly for this reason, movies that seek to align viewers with a character on the spectrum tend instinctively to avoid "tennis match" cutting and instead show a preference for point-of-view cutaways, shots from his or her optical perspective of objects in the immediate environment.

Raymond's Point of View

To take a well-known example, *Rain Man* (1988) is peppered with insert point-of-view shots from the position of Raymond (Dustin Hoffman). These include, for example, the traveling shot of patterns created by the struts of a suspension bridge, the shock zoom into the running faucet during Raymond's panic attack, and the shot of toothpicks spilling to the floor in a roadside diner. Even this brief list indicates a range of different techniques offering degrees of access to Raymond's inner life. The shock zoom on the faucet is a highly psychologized use that breaks optical realism in order to evoke Raymond's distress. The high-angle shot of the tumbling toothpicks, by contrast, while matching Raymond's spatial position, is unable to emulate the unique *way* that he sees them, owing to his savant ability to count them in the split second after they land. (It is difficult to know how that could be conveyed visually, short of a crude *Sherlock*-esque gimmick that was unavailable for use in 1988.) The passing point of view of the bridge struts, on the other hand, marks an attitude, not merely to show what Raymond is looking at but also to indicate his mindset while looking. It is an example of what Jason Jacobs, in an insightful account of the film focusing on Dustin Hoffman's performance, calls Raymond's "aesthetic feeling" (2018, 216), the wonder and sensitivity with which he attends to features of the world around him.

We find this aesthetic feeling most boldly declared in the slideshow of photographs that accompany the film's end credits, ostensibly taken by Raymond during the car journey, which are effectively deferred point-of-view shots, since nothing indicates that they are intended for exhibition but are principally an illustration of "what caught Raymond's eye." Jacobs finds that these "do not give us any deeper insight into Raymond's mind or thoughts" (2018, 213), although this may overstate things a touch. While there are no new revelations in this coda, we observe a tendency for canted and tilted angles, motion blur, sky-heavy compositions, and the tight cropping of details. And we note the choices made about what to isolate in the viewfinder: a pair of feet, a line of cars, the shapes made by a bridge, the shadow lines cast by railings. There is a palpable interest in the ephemeral, in structure and pattern, in numeric design, and in things that recall the 1950s, the era of Raymond's childhood. These all confirm what we may have gathered about Raymond already, but they also give a little more shape to the *nature* of his aesthetic responsiveness. None of this undermines Jacobs's wider argument about the film. As he describes it, Hoffman's achievement is to "communicate . . . a soul" while at the same time refusing to convey "a legible interior" (214, 213). This understanding works in support of the film's moral lesson, which is "to take on the responsibility for accepting people whoever and whatever they are, and *as* whatever and whoever they are" (216). If Jacobs is right, the film has undertaken to strike a delicate balance. It needs to show *that* Raymond thinks and feels and to convey something of the *nature* of that thinking and feeling, but without unduly defining it. As Jacobs demonstrates, Hoffman holds this line admirably. I merely add that the point-of-view shots play their part in this balancing act by offering glimpses of interiority without overdetermining or presuming to know too much.

One such point of view that grants access without definition appears at the outset of the restaurant scene that culminates in the toothpick counting. We move from a standard exterior establishing shot of a new location, a restaurant on a busy intersection, to a more unusual, low-level shot of the restaurant's tiled floor illuminated by shafts of light that rest and move across its surface. Traffic noises are now more muted, voices burble in the background, and we hear the chiming of a cash register. This shot is followed by a medium close-up of Raymond, seated next to his brother Charlie (Tom Cruise), intently watching the floor. What is notable here is the reversal of the standard glance-object structure of shots, whereby we would tend first to see someone looking offscreen and then cut to what they see. In this case, we see the object of the gaze first and only afterward have it confirmed as Raymond's optical view via the cut to Hoffman. Further instances of restructured points of view, leading to more radical dislocations, are considered later in this chapter. The advantage of the reversal in this instance is simply to allow us to witness the way light falls across the floor, to study its emerging pattern as a phenomenon in itself, and only afterward to discover that we share that interest with Raymond. Bracketing the shot more conventionally would have placed it merely as an illustration of something that has taken his attention and need not be relevant to ours.

Moreover, by omitting an initial wider view of the restaurant interior, which would have located Raymond and Charlie firmly in their newfound spots, the choice to cut straight into a point-of-view shot and then to a medium close-up of Raymond provides a mild dose of disorientation akin to what Raymond must be feeling at this moment, having been wrenched from his familiar surroundings, yanked out of his treasured routine, and plonked into this strange and beautiful place. This last point suggests that another long-standing building block of so-called film grammar, the establishing shot, may also play a part in the construction of a character's viewpoint. Notwithstanding the delayed interior master shot, it is worth noting that we do get a conventional exterior shot: an unremarkable brick building on a busy crossroad, marked by the sign "Restaurant." This shot is ostensibly there to let us know where the next scene will take place, although it is redundant for these purposes: surely all the relevant information is carried by the décor of the point-of-view shot, with its tables and chairs, and the soundtrack, with its cash-register chime and dulled traffic noises.

Why do we need an establishing shot at all? The convention of using wide shots to launch scenes appears to be a hangover from the development of analytical editing in the mid-silent era, when scenes were still thought of as tableaux that needed to be shown first, before they would yield to a series of closer views. This practice was consolidated, I suspect, when detailed screenplays became a standard tool in preproduction and the initial entry for every new scene (e.g., EXT. ALLEYWAY—OUTSIDE THE THEATRE—EVENING) seemed implicitly to propose an establishing shot for the opening of every scene. In Hollywood, it became almost an article of faith, or common sense, that every shift of locale required one. *Rain Man* is no exception. As Charlie and Raymond travel across the country, almost every new scene and stop along their journey begins conventionally with a building exterior or a wide view. For instance, when Charlie and Susanna (Valeria Golino) go in search of Wallbrook, the institution where they later find Raymond, an image displaying the brick steps and exterior of a grand building announces that they have arrived. Above the neoclassical entrance, one word is carved in stone: WALLBROOK. This shot, like that of the restaurant, is principally iconic: it stands for something. It is true that a later scene unfolds on and near these brick steps, but the orientation is quite unnecessary. The main things for viewers to gather are the building's associations of grandeur and formality. Like the exterior establishing shot of the restaurant, above, this is a shot of place-as-concept.

Built into the standard establishing shot, one might say, is a disposition to "see an entire thing first" (Higashida 2013, 91). The initial view of Wallbrook is of a type that would strike a visitor such as Charlie, not a resident such as Raymond. Although it is doubtful that the bullish Charlie would have lingered outside even so long as this brief shot, it matches his first rough impression of Wallbrook as imposing and inconveniently anti-quated. The film would have been significantly different if we had started with Raymond in his familiar habitat, carrying on with his comforting routines, and had encountered Wallbrook first via him. For one thing, the road trip would strike us more forcefully as a kidnapping. But the film's project is for us to encounter Raymond *through* Charlie. Although Charlie is depicted as a jerk from the outset, he is the narrative's apprentice figure: the figure who learns and with whom we learn (see the chapter by Daniel Sacco in this volume). And so the regular establishing shots that initiate each new locale chime with Charlie's way of seeing. This correspondence happens principally because he is the one charting the journey: these shots are almost like place markers on the route he is plotting. But they also evoke the mind-set of someone inclined to presume to know the general notion of a place—institute, motel, restaurant, casino—or, for that matter, the general notion of a type of person, and only later to deal with the particulars, as necessary. By contrast, Raymond, in Hoffman's realization, is rarely seen looking up or out at a wider view. He tends to find himself in the midst of things, in the absence of regularity, seeking orientation through calculation and scrutiny, as in a study of how light falls. The brothers' profound mismatch of perspectives is expressed in that cut from wide-shot restaurant exterior to the shot of the tiled floor. As Higashida says, "The details jump straight out at us first of all, and then only gradually, detail by detail, does the whole image sort of float up into focus" (92).

Autistic Bresson?

The director Robert Bresson, in his gnomic advice to filmmakers collected as *Notes on Cinematography*, insists that fragmentation of the visual field into details "is indispensible if one does not want to fall into REPRESENTATION. To see beings and things in their separate parts. Render them independent in order to give them a new dependence" (1977, 46). As Harun Farocki observes, "Bresson almost never uses long shots *and* never in order to give an overview of something before the details have been examined" (2012, 471). In the same account, one finds the following: "Continuously looking at the importance of speaking people (with words and with facial gestures) is unbearable. . . . Before Bresson shows a close-up of a face, he shows the close-up of a hand [or] concentrates on the actions of the head (or the foot)" (476). That word "unbearable" is telling, recalling Higashida's account of why those with autism may be inclined to divert their gaze when faced with "speaking people." Higashida implies that attention is difficult to sustain partly because the face is seen to generate an unhelpful surfeit of data. Bresson's instinct is similarly to limit communication channels that compete or otherwise create noise through amplification. "When a sound can replace an image," he advises, "cut the image or neutralize it."

Noa Steimatsky has even been moved to claim that Bresson's "modes of composition, visual and poetic rhetoric, framing and editing, the organization of movement and temporality, and certainly his notorious direction of the actor/model—all seem poised to harness or deny expression, to withdraw the potentialities of the face in a move so drastic as to evoke a strangely vivid relation to autism" (2012, 160). Steimatsky's supporting textual examples for this thesis, insofar as they are developed, are rather opaque, and the claims ostentatious. For example, she points to a moment from Bresson's *Au hasard Balthazar* (1966) when the film enigmatically cuts from a conversation between Marie (Anna Wiazemsky) and Jacques (Walter Green) to a shot of the titular donkey, and asks us to see this as "a questioning of the extent to which face-to-face reciprocity within the spatiotemporal continuity can 'communicate' at all" (164). It is beyond the scope of the present chapter (and the talents of the present author) to untangle what that means, exactly, but I suspect the general intuition would reward further study.

Notwithstanding these potential affinities between Bresson's style and the inclinations of autistic perception, it is not evident that any of Bresson's characters could confidently be confirmed as autistic. One may have a hunch about Mouchette, perhaps, although this would be difficult to isolate given the many other issues that affect her (*Mouchette* [1967]). Moreover, Bresson is not the least interested in the kind of verisimilitude that would allow for diagnosis. Perhaps it could be considered strangely fitting that an evocation of the autistic gaze should float free from any rooted perceiving subject. Regarding Bresson's films in this way may be a helpful way to understand his distinctive approach to filmmaking. But it would presume too much, and risk a circular argument, to seek an understanding of autism through Bresson.

Ricky Underground

A film that *does* seek to evoke the perspective of a character with autism, and that achieves this more evocatively than any other film I know, is a little known low-budget movie entitled *Stand Clear of the Closing Doors* (2013). It follows an autistic teenager named Ricky (Jesus Sanchez-Velez), who stays away from home for a series of days and nights in the New York City subway system. The film moves between Ricky's odyssey through this underworld and the experience of his distressed mother (Andrea Suarez Paz) as she deals with his absence at ground level. Ricky's initial motivation for venturing into the subway is to follow a stranger with the motif of a dragon on his jacket. (We have already encountered Ricky's identification with this mythical creature.) His reasons for remaining down there, however, riding the rails for days on end, are ambiguous, even to himself. His lack of water, food, and company is grueling. We may wonder whether he is testing himself or hoping for the dragon to reemerge or searching for a beacon to help him reorient himself and find his way home. Perhaps all of these. He entertains himself with wordplay and through detached observation of the flow of life underground.

We experience this subterranean world through Ricky in ways that complicate traditional point-of-view structures and sometimes verge on abstraction. Spots of different colors and intensities drift across the black screen before a shot resolves as a view from the front of the train. An extreme close-up of subway-car doors closing becomes a blur of lines and shapes. The letter *A* flickers in and out of sight, and we glimpse some passengers in a parallel car. We hear Ricky repeating, "A-Train, A-Train . . . a *train*." (The A train is a Manhattan subway route under 8th Avenue.) More kaleidoscopic spots of colored light and blurred arrival vistas. On the soundtrack, the speaker finds pleasure, or takes solace, in what emerges from his repetitions: "I-Train, I-Train . . . I *train*." (The New York subway has no I train, but Ricky may be misperceiving a "1," the train that runs beneath Broadway.) Only then, after this montage of shots, do we see Ricky attending the front window of the passenger car as if teaching himself, *train*ing himself, to receive and accept the disorder of whatever will emerge around the next corner of track. The phantom voice accompanying the imagery allows us to grasp the preceding half-dozen shots as fragments of Ricky's optical perspective, but only with the capping shot of him watching is the structure formally resolved. Whereas conventional point-of-view structure, with its bracketing of vision, tends to affirm the self as searchlight, the arrangement here places a different emphasis, on the self as receptor, collector of impressions.

Hands at work and at rest; shoes crisscrossing the station floors; curiosities of behavior; indistinct gestures; the textures of plastic seats, woolen bags, and mosaic tiles; the sight of others absorbed in thoughts or devices: these are among the things that catch Ricky's attention and the film's. And indeed, the empathic bond forged between the viewer and Ricky, with the manner of his outlook, is there from the movie's first shot. On fade-in, we find this young man in a purple hoodie at Rockaway Beach, throwing scraps in the air for seagulls. On the soundtrack we hear the harmonic pulsation of bagpipes. Beneath that, lower in the sound mix, is Ricky muttering quite happily to himself or perhaps to the birds. The camera is placed directly behind him and tilted up so that only his unfocused head and shoulders are visible at the bottom center of the frame against a homogenous grey sky, which is flecked intermittently by sporadic hovering gulls and sliced across at one point by a single jet plane. The low angle aligns our view with Ricky's upward attention while omitting the customary reverse shot of his face. The framing crops out all details (railings, lamppost) that would anchor the space as a place. Above all, what we sense in this opening shot is an ambivalent relation between order and noise, chaos and calm. The emergence and movement of seagulls is riotous, random, and yet predictable. The airplane cutting arbitrarily, rudely across the sky: there it is, on schedule, following its preordained flight path. Bagpipes to some, like the self-mutterings of people with autism, may sound like a relentless drone, but from another perspective, the constancy of the sound is white noise: cushioning, self-sustaining.

It is difficult to say which is the stronger: Ricky's wish for cocooned isolation from the world or his willingness to receive its neglected and forgotten shards. Both may be characteristic of autism. Both may be served by cinema.

CHAPTER 16

Performative Restraint and the Challenges of Empathy in *Being There* and *Phantom Thread*

MATTHEW CIPA

Hal Ashby's *Being There* (1979) opens with a presentation of the film's central protagonist, Chance the Gardener (Peter Sellers), and his morning routine. Chance is coaxed out of sleep by the comforting sound of a television that functions in some ways as his alarm clock. Unlike an alarm clock, though, the TV performance of Schubert's Eighth Symphony is allowed to continue playing as Chance begins his day. Stiffly, mechanically, and purposefully, he brushes his hair and rotates some small plants in his bedroom before moving outside to water select parts of the garden while still in his pajamas. Having moved into the garage, he dusts a vintage car with grand and extended gestures. Chance conducts the orchestrated world he has created and now inhabits—a world that is protected and insular.

Paul Thomas Anderson's *Phantom Thread* (2017) offers viewers something slightly different before presenting its own version of its central protagonist—the dress designer Reynolds Woodcock (Daniel Day-Lewis)—and his customary start to the day. In a firelit conversation between a woman whom we eventually learn is Alma (Vicky Krieps), Woodcock's wife, and Dr. Robert Hardy (Brian Gleeson), a young physician who attends to Woodcock, spectators hear not just of Alma's devotion and gratitude to her husband but also of his stringency. The unsettling and dissonant electronic sounds that introduced the film's title give way to silence as we see Alma's face in close-up, informing us, as much as the doctor, of how she has given every piece of herself to her husband—a "most demanding man," they both agree. A brief, swirling musical phrase is replaced by a cascading, romantic, and more fully pianistic score as the camera cuts, introducing us directly to Woodcock.

Through a series of close-ups, we see Woodcock fastidiously apply shaving cream to his face, buff his black dress shoes to a level of satisfaction, trim his nose and ear hairs, cleanse his face, tame his hair through confident strokes of dual-wielding brushes, fold his socks down, and begin methodically tucking his shirt into his trousers. While he goes about his mannered and precise preparations, his sister Cyril (Lesley Manville) begins opening the large folding wooden shutters of their expansive home so that white morning light can complement the artificial lights glowing on the walls and mirror frames within. A long queue of assistants waiting outside in the cold are allowed into the impressive mansion, and they then slowly make their way up the large spiral stairs. Pleasant, simple strings are introduced to the score, and the camera tracks forward and tilts directly upward in the center of the staircase, allowing us to briefly make out the patterned movements of the assistants ascending to their place for the start of the day, some beginning to busy themselves with their duties, others awaiting the emergence of the man of the house, who has made his way, sketchbook in tow, to have his breakfast.

I am focusing on the morning routines of the two characters—scenes that also function as our direct introduction to them—because of how these moments provide a sense of each man's mental life. For each, the world that he has created is representative not just of the way his mind works but also of the conditions that it requires—order maintained, expectations met, and habits continued—so that it can function undisturbed. Part of what I consider in this chapter is the importance of the externalization of Chance's and Woodcock's minds. These moments are critical to our experience because of what I call "performative restraint," a term that refers to how the demands of the characters—specifically, their interactional troubles—require each performer to hold back or hold in the usual means of performance across gesture, voice, and facial expressions. As Stanley Cavell notes in relation to cinematic performance, the "screen performer explores his role like an attic and takes stock of his physical and temperamental endowment; he lends his being to the role and accepts only what fits; the rest is non-existent" (1979, 28). The challenge of performative restraint reflects just how much is usually lent to a performance by way of bodily and aural expression that is left out, given the requirements of the character.

The externalization of each character's mind in his habits of life, the structure and design of his local environment, and the objects and people in the surround constitute one way that both films look to balance the spectator's engagement with Chance and Woodcock against the interpretive challenges created through restrained performance. Another way is indicated by the preface in *Phantom Thread*, that conversation between Alma and Hardy. While the spectator's direct introduction to Woodcock occurs after this brief but important moment, it is appropriate for two reasons that our first understanding of him comes secondhand. First, *Phantom Thread* is Alma's story as much as Woodcock's, giving attention to a couple tumultuously, intensely, yet keenly in love. Second, and of greater interest to the present concerns of this chapter, along with the behavioral externalization of their minds, the performative restraint involved in the creation of Woodcock and Chance means that spectators must rely on the experiences, reactions, and engagements of other characters to help guide their own experience and engagement with the two central ones. Because of the particular challenge involved in knowing or understanding Woodcock and Chance, a difficulty created by performative restraint, one finds an obstruction or complexity in empathizing with them.

In an extended preamble to his analysis of *Being There*, the anthropologist Douglas Hollan notes how empathy is "a type of understanding that is neither purely cognitive and imaginative nor purely emotional, but a combination of both the emotional and experiential part of the response guiding and providing an emotional context for what one imagines about the other's experience" (2008, 475). Importantly, as Hollan notes, "empathic understanding unfolds over time" (476). In adopting a similar understanding in regard to film experience, Jane Stadler emphasizes that cinematic empathy is "an emotional process that occurs when audience members perceive, imagine, or hear about a film character's affective and mental state and, in so doing, vicariously experience a shared or congruent state" (2017, 317). Because performative restraint limits the usual means of expression, there are fewer human cues—bodily, gestural, and aural—to help shape and inform the spectator's engagement with Chance and Woodcock. Therefore, if we are to empathize with either character, we must look to other means. The externalization of their minds is one of those means, and so we can track how the control that Woodcock and Chance have over their worlds develops or is disrupted across the duration of the films. Another means is the close attention paid to the experiences and engagements of characters surrounding the central two. As these shift across the duration of each film, our understanding of Chance and Woodcock becomes more nuanced and more detailed, yet still remarkably incomplete.

A Tally of Symptoms

As required by the narrative worlds they inhabit, the characters created by Sellers and Day-Lewis can be considered broadly autistic. While my aim is not to provide a diagnostic analysis of either character, tracking how closely each aligns with clinical criteria for an autistic person and looking to the language used to describe the hallmarks of an autistic person is helpful in fleshing out how performative restraint is central to each characterization and how performative restraint underpins the features central to our experience of each film—the externalization of Woodcock's and Chance's minds, and the spectator's reliance on the experiences and reactions of other characters. In many cases, a diagnosis of autism is reached through reference to the current edition of the *Diagnostic and Statistical Manual of Mental Disorders (DSM-5)*, whose diagnostic criteria rely heavily on behavioral markers that, helpfully for us, dovetail with the particular performative challenges faced by Lewis and Sellers in their work.

The *DSM-5* defines autism by identifying deficits across three broad categories: social-emotional reciprocity, nonverbal communicative behaviors, and developing, maintaining, and understanding relationships. Such deficits feature distinctively in Woodcock and Chance. Regarding reciprocity, *DSM-5* notes the one-sided nature of conversation for those with autistic traits, in which there is a tendency for labeling, requesting, or demanding as opposed to a sensitivity to the back-and-forth exchange central to conversation. This feature is readily seen in *Being There*: Chance's clipped and incomplete sentences involve either requests for a television set or pathos-tinged statements involving gardens and gardening. These latter declarations are usually interpreted by Chance's interlocutors—including Ben and Eve Rand (Melvyn Douglas, Shirley MacLaine), a wealthy couple who take him in after he was forced to leave his home, and "Bobby," the president of the United States (Jack Warden)—as deeply intuitive analogies of genius in the areas of political governance and the economy, as well as veiled romantic counsel regarding Eve and Ben's faltering relationship.

In *Phantom Thread*, Woodcock's use of speech is nuanced. He does share feelings, as in the first breakfast scene with Cyril when he declares that he has "an unsettled feeling." After his and Alma's relationship begins to deepen later in the film, he offers a sensitive—though flawed—understanding of himself and marriage: "Marriage would make me deceitful, and I don't want that," he states, adding, "I think it is the expectations and assumptions of others that cause heartache." Even when fitting the heiress Barbara Rose (Harriet Sansom Harris), an enormously wealthy client who is concerned about how ugly she looks in his latest creation, Woodcock attempts to be consoling (in his own way): "Barbara, I am trying to make you a beautiful dress. I need your help."

In the context of the film's treatment of Woodcock, however, such moments are attempts not so much to express feelings, to sympathize, or to empathize with others as to fix problems. His declaration regarding his unsettled feeling is less an expression of his state of mind than an indirect request to his sister to make the feeling go away. His imploring of Barbara is less to reassure her of her appearance than to do justice to the garment he has created, an activity so intertwined with his sense of self that he states in the same scene: "This is what I do. This is my place here." As the film critic A. O. Scott (2017) notes in his review of *Phantom Thread*, each garment contains "invisible traces of his hand": "His dresses are more than luxurious commodities. They are works of art, obscurely and yet unmistakably saturated with the passion and personality of their creator." For Woodcock, it is a central tenet of belief that his designed and created dresses are the ordered world he looks to maintain.

Restraint in the content of Woodcock's and Chance's speech is intertwined with restraint in delivery, which is covered by the second diagnostic criterion, concerning not only the use of language and speech intonation but nonverbal communication too: eye contact, bodily movements and gestures, and facial expressions. Chance's delivery of his speech is tonally narrow, trancelike and slowed, suggesting not so much depth of consideration as lack of surety. Woodcock's vocal delivery is richer and even-toned, his intonation strained to the point of ghostliness. Each syllable is pronounced with care and ponderous consideration.

A subcategory of nonverbal communication involves the sensitivity and repertoire of gestures that can be asynchronous or uncoordinated with the use of speech. Therefore, in interactions with others, autistic persons may appear overly exaggerated in the use of bodily gestures or else steer toward the other extreme and act in a restricted, wooden way. This aspect afflicts Chance more than Woodcock. In one scene toward the end of *Being There*, Chance is in his bedroom inside the stately Rand home, where he has been living. Sitting on the end of the bed, he is watching a romantic scene of two people kissing on television. Eve enters, upset. He stands up and starts kissing her, imitating what is unfolding on the television and simultaneously bringing Eve's latent romantic desires to the surface. As the camera starts swirling around the televised scene being watched by Chance, he responds by circling himself and Eve as they continue kissing each other. Once the scene ends, Chance becomes wooden and unresponsive, his arms move from being wrapped around Eve and drop to his side, and Eve is left confused and somewhat embarrassed.

Sobbing, her head dropping and defeated, she exclaims that she doesn't know what he likes. Misunderstanding the question, Chance replies that he likes to watch. Misunderstanding his answer, Eve ends up writhing on the floor while Chance, who is seated on the edge of the bed and watching television again, completely oblivious of her attempts to please him as she pleases herself, eventually mimics the elaborate stretching now displayed in an exercise routine on the screen. This example highlights his inability to understand relationships. Chance's behavior is not just alternately limited and exaggerated. Underscored by the fact he mimics what he sees on television rather than responding to the particularities of the social interaction, his behavior exemplifies the deficit in his capacity to act in a way appropriate to the social context in which he finds himself.

This fraught connection with context is one of the hallmarks of *Being There*. The orderly world he created for himself was devastated by the death of his old benefactor, so Chance was forced to enter an unfamiliar, untamed zone where he has a series of encounters that leads to his meeting Eve via a fortuitous car accident, befriending and advising her dying husband, Ben, and offering his counsel and mentorship to Ben's friend, the US president. As Mary Lazar notes, other characters "continually interpret Chance's behavior and pronouncements according to their own needs. Through his imitations of their speech and mannerisms, they see themselves reflected and are free to manipulate those reconstructed images" (2004, 101). Throughout the film, encounter after encounter sees Chance remarking about gardens or television, and each person with whom he interacts—the Rands, the president, ambassadors, young gang members, or lawyers—overcomes Chance's incapacity to speak and act in accordance with the social context, through adventurous interpretation and application of his words to their own particular circumstances.

Captured by the Camera

Woodcock has a better sense of acting in accordance with context, but in only a limited number of contexts and only to the degree that he is involved with aspects of his personally designed world. For example, he is comfortable when ordering meals—as he does when he first meets Alma, a waitress in a countryside hotel where he has decided to take breakfast. Having taken his coat off and folded it over a chair, he hikes his trousers up from the thighs, sits down, and takes his customary posture, all with a practiced, familiar, obviously quotidian rhythm.

In identifying the important connection between film style and performance, James Naremore notes that the "camera's mobility and tight framing of faces, its ability to 'give' the focus of the screen to any player at any moment, also means that films tend to favor reactions" (1988, 40). It is not just Day-Lewis's realization of Woodcock in this important moment that helps us discover something about him, but also the way the camera works in tandem with the performance. In close-up, Woodcock sits with a neutral expression on his face, head tilted down and cocked ever so slightly to one side, his gaze penetrating nothing in particular. It is difficult to tell whether he is lost in thought or simply waiting, but nevertheless the gaze shifts at the sound of movement, his eyes lifting first and then his head. The shot cuts to a rare point-of-view shot as he tracks the quickly moving figure of Alma, whose own gaze briefly meets that of the camera/Woodcock/spectator before she missteps and half stumbles, briefly looking up again as a broad smile breaks across her face. Laughing sheepishly, she drops her head too far, looking to escape attention as she clears a nearby table. Woodcock looks on, a thin, tight smile written inscrutably on his lips.

They make a date, have dinner together, and at the end of the evening arrive at Woodcock's countryside manor. Sitting opposite each other in front of the fire, the two are silent, staring at each other. Woodcock's face is neutral, but a slight smile develops before he shifts his posture. Alma responds, sitting back in her chair, quietly defiant and playfully combative: "If you want to have a staring contest with me you will lose." Woodcock's smile stretches further, and he grunts and nods in agreement. Soon afterward, they find themselves in Woodcock's fitting room. Bilge Ebiri (2017) describes the scene well: "Reynolds is taking her measurements, and the seriousness of purpose with which he does so—and the coolness with which he calls out the numbers [to his sister, who is assisting] that delineate her physical presence in the world—suggest that Alma only exists for him to the extent that he can quantify and categorize, and maybe even mold, her." The necessary proximity and intimacy required in the fitting and measuring of a new dress are tempered by the object of Woodcock's attention, which is not Alma. As Ebiri hints, Woodcock's delicate and precise movements are directed toward the nascence of a new means of self-expression—that is, a new garment at the moment of imaginative creation—rather than at wooing Alma, who, although inspiring something in Woodcock, stands at this moment as a human mannequin.

This example highlights how, in the early stages of *Phantom Thread*, Woodcock's relationships are in service to the fashion world of his creation, an ordered and highly controlled world that conditions the expression he achieves by designing singular and beautiful dresses. Alma disturbs and interferes with this world. Sheila O'Malley (2018) sees "a hermetically sealed world, where Alma tries to throw open the windows." As the loving tumult of Woodcock and Alma's relationship deepens, the externalization of Woodcock's mind, the world he has worked to create in order to afford himself a means of living in a particular way, becomes upset and unstable. Lacking the familiarity of that world, he must struggle to adjust to new social contexts and relationships.

Manifold challenges are posed by the performative restraint required for the creation of Chance and Woodcock. Both characters eschew the caricatured representations of autism that ordinarily populate mainstream American cinema, not only because they are ambiguously autistic but also because they are complex and rich despite the restraint required in such creation. As Murray Pomerance notes, for performances of mental disturbance of various kinds: "[The] symptom is not only visible but inherently fascinating. And the performance is often a concatenation of credible symptoms, to the detriment of personality. Thus we find twitching, screaming, extremity of muscular exertion, paralyzed stillness, preposterous claiming, shadowy withdrawal, and so on" (2019, 284). Pomerance connects the extremity of the typical performance of symptoms with the "mental" component of mental disturbance, whereby "the mind does not openly 'perform' to camera, this leading audiences and performers alike to conviction in, and emphatic display of, symptoms" (ibid.). Such insights can be connected with what Susanne Rohr identifies as the three typical ways in which "madness" is present in American culture: as "benign . . . wise fools embodying some kind of wisdom or deep knowledge about eternal human truths"; the opposite of that, whereby "the insane are seen as wayward, animal-like savages"; and madness as being "associated with certain special mental talents, above all a heightened creativity or clairvoyance" (2015, 233). While the first has some resonance with Chance, and the third with Woodcock, both characters in their performative creation evade such easy and one-dimensional descriptions.

Pomerance's comments on the performance of symptoms and the complexity of the characters being portrayed combine to suggest that performative restraint requires a particularity relative to the world the character inhabits rather than just the kind of presentation emblematic of broad types. Furthermore, the symptoms of each character involve certain negatives, identified by an absence of or deficits in expressions of various kinds, so it is worth turning now to a consideration of the craft of performance to better understand how these characters complicate the spectator's capacity to empathize with them.

In his treatment of the fluency of film performance, Andrew Klevan writes that as "each action flows fluidly into the next or as one move integrates with another, they make it difficult for us to isolate or crystallize meaning" (2012, 35). In Klevan's account, it is a lack of discreteness in the parts of performance that makes for a spectator's difficulty in identifying individual gestures and thereby drawing out meaning. Performative restraint achieves similar ends—a difficulty in isolating or crystallizing meaning—but by means that work notwithstanding the holding in of fluency. The spectator's capacity to isolate or crystallize meaning in the performances of Day-Lewis and Sellers is made difficult through a scarcity of the ordinary evocative and gestural ways in which performers realize their characters. The opacity, narrowness of expression, and confinement of gesture that are required for Woodcock and Chance establish a complex challenge to reading, for both other characters and spectators.

Another effect of fluent performances suggested by Klevan involves the sense of satisfaction achieved by the successful identification of a meaningful, isolated gesture: "Any piece of their [the performer's] behavior, no matter how slight, may arise out of sympathy with the dramatic environment and contain significance. Yet this behavior might appear as incorporated (in the fictional world) rather than presented (to the viewer), so noticing it feels like the discovery of a secret" (2012, 37). In the two films I consider here, the reverse can be true, whereby the spectator is presented with an aspect of the character that seems intended for us rather than the diegetic world. Rather than discovering a diegetic secret, the viewer is the recipient of a special gift. In this, the interaction of performance, cinematography, and mise-en-scène is crucial, since performative expression and restraint are woven together to position us in various ways in relation to the character, guiding our attention to notice fine details (or not), to be given opportunities to achieve a connection with the character that other characters are not afforded (or perhaps are). When expression and restraint are in place, they resonate with what Richard Dyer calls interiority, in which the performance and its context in the film give (or are meant to give) some sense of the character's inner life, thoughts, emotions, feelings, and so on (1998, 118–120).

I Know a Character Who Knows a Character . . .

The separation between the audience's knowledge and the knowledge imputed to other characters underpins the entirety of *Being There*, since we know more about Chance than do any of the characters with whom he engages, excluding the maid of the old man's house, who knows him better even than we do. Spectators understand that Chance's ruminations on gardens and seasons derive from his role as a gardener, for example, rather than being the sagacious expressions of wisdom that other characters take them to be. In this instance, despite the extent of Chance's deficits in verbal and nonverbal communication and his lack of understanding of social context, we know him more than the other characters, yet as a result, we paradoxically find his words less meaningful.

In *Phantom Thread*, the performative restraint required to show Woodcock's personality frustrates not just the spectators' capacity to draw out meaning but also the same capacity in other characters. In a scene early in Alma's inclusion in the household, when her role as muse and love interest is still ambiguous, she is sitting at the breakfast table with Woodcock and Cyril. Alma engages in seemingly ordinary actions: she shifts slightly in her seat and butters her toast. But the sound of these actions is boosted to signal Woodcock's way of hearing. The sounds intrude on the orderly world he has created. He chastises Alma: "Please, don't move so much, Alma. It's very distracting. It's as if you just rode a horse across the room." Having had enough, Woodcock storms out of the room, and as does Alma, spectators require an explanation from another character—in this instance, Cyril—to help us interpret the problem. Cyril is informative: "His routine, when he's in it, is best not shaken. This is a quiet time. Not to be misused. If breakfast isn't right, it's very hard for him to recover for the rest of the day." The world of order that he has taken such pains to create and safeguard has been disturbed, disrupted, perhaps destroyed. What could otherwise easily be heard as simple sounds, entirely disregardable, now explodes into cacophony and interruption.

Such moments of expression—even contemptible frustration, as in the present example—are impactful because of the context of general performative restraint in which they are situated. Drawing on the work of Cavell, Klevan notes how "a viewer's engagement with a performer depends on him or her communicating aspects of their character's consciousness. Such an understanding should remind us again that our disposition towards a narrative is not necessarily tied to our identification with character—however elegantly refined—but lies equally with appreciating the performer's capacities for revealing *and* withholding aspects of the character's sensibility" (2005, 9). As might be expected, given how I have characterized performative restraint, the central characters in *Being There* and *Phantom Thread* are more often concerned with withholding than with revealing. There is some revelation of character in how Chance and Woodcock look to externalize their sensibilities in the ordered worlds they created for themselves. Failing to grasp the autists' expressions, spectators can align themselves with surrounding characters in hopes of extracting meaning from, or understanding expression by the help of, those who are more in the know—characters like Cyril, for example. Furthermore, as demonstrated in *Being There*, the structure can be inverted, with audiences positioned to have greater knowledge of the origins and meaning of a character's words than other characters have; the other characters' misunderstandings arguably function as the source of the film's comedy. We find Chance's "pithy epigrams" less meaningful than do Eve, Ben, or the president, and we see how they can be interpreted in a wholly other way. A further interesting dynamic can be seen in *Phantom Thread*: spectators witness characters sharing a moment, represented through gestural performance—even restrained gestural performance—and suspect that meaning is present, but without being certain, without possessing the certainty about meaning that, in this case, is shared between Alma and Woodcock.

In one of the final scenes of *Phantom Thread*, Alma stands in the kitchen, making Woodcock a mushroom omelette. The omelette is her own expressive act of creation. It is given the same kind of close-up, as it cooks in rapidly melting golden butter, as Woodcock's dresses received earlier in the film. Her methodical, careful, and thoughtful attention to the dish mirrors the methodical, careful, and thoughtful process that is the hallmark of her husband. The mushrooms are significant. Earlier in the film, after a particularly hurtful exchange, she foraged some poisonous mushrooms, ensuring that Woodcock would ingest just enough to make him ill without endangering his life (and thereby introducing him to the doctor who is sharing with us, the spectators, Alma's retelling of her and Woodcock's story that frames the entire film). This current meal, prepared by Alma with such love, features the same poisonous mushrooms. As Woodcock sketches while waiting to eat, he occasionally looks up at Alma, who is preparing and cooking with broad, noticeable gestures—allowing the egg mixture to drip from a great height into the pan, for example. A slow tension builds alongside an aimless piano on the soundtrack: the meal sizzling, Woodcock sketching and looking, Alma crafting the omelette, poking at the half-cooked meal as it sits in the pan. Woodcock's glances seem increasingly pensive and skeptical, though of course we cannot be sure what thoughts are being turned over behind his impassive face. Alma brings the omelette to the table, scoops it out of the pan with a spatula, and slides it onto the plate that sits in waiting. She removes her apron. She visibly irritates Woodcock by imitating her egg gestures, pouring glasses of water from a pitcher that she lifts up as the water falls until it is high above the table. She sits down next to her husband, and they wait in silence, looking at each other.

This moment toward which we have slowly progressed mirrors the earlier one when Alma and Woodcock sat across from each other on the evening of their first date. While that scene had a spark of possibility lit beneath the challenge of their stares, here the mood is heavier, indicating the weight, present behind each gaze, of accumulated arguments, disagreements, and hurtful fights. Woodcock inspects the meal with his nose, bringing the plate to his face and looking up at Alma after inhaling. He expressively and elaborately slices a portion of the omelette and rests it on his fork, extending his arm out and eventually consuming the food. The prolongation of each gesture by each performer—temporal stretching as much as physical extension—provides spectators the time to reflect back on that earlier staring contest, and on Alma's declaration that she would not be beaten. She wasn't beaten then, and she isn't beaten in this scene either.

The gestures and glances serve to reinforce how little understanding we have of the couple, and especially Woodcock. We might contemplate all the moments left out of Alma's tale, and the meaning attached to them, all the lessons learned in her firsthand experience of and involvement with Woodcock. We can detect the gestures, we know what repeated surprise lurks in the folds of her omelette—we might even reasonably presume that by the time he takes his bite, Woodcock knows, too—and we can even grasp the significance of their little connubial dance: he gets uppity, she feeds him tricky mushrooms, he gets ill, she lovingly tends to him—the whole thing allowing for the most demanding man to be tamed and subsequently cared for by his wife, allowing their relationship to hold together. Spectators can only look on at these glances and the movements, so elegantly designed one for the other, persistently aware that something greater, something more significant rests within each look and gesture but not knowing what that something is.

Being There concludes with Ben's funeral, the magnate having finally been overcome by his long fatal disease. As the president offers a heartfelt eulogy, Chance wanders off through the nearby woods and happens upon a lake. The iconic final moments of the film show Chance testing the water and then walking across its surface, demonstrating to us the water's depth with an adventurous prod of his umbrella, despite his confident stance on the face of the lake. Christopher Beach considers the character in the frame of these final moments as follows: "Chance is not a messiah or even a saint, but he may have reached a point of tranquility within the 'garden' of his own mind in which the laws of the natural universe no longer apply" (2009, 117). As the president utters Ben's motto—"Life is a state of mind"— Chance walks with his same stiff, mechanical, but purposeful stride across the lake and into the distance. Whether or not Beach's interpretation is accurate, the life of the mind—the garden of the mind, in Chance's terms— is one of the key sources of expression that is ultimately concealed in performative restraint.

By restricting spectators' access to ordinary expressions of thoughts, feelings, and emotions, as required by the demands of the characters, Chance and Woodcock highlight how performative restraint poses a problem for empathy. To counter this difficulty, spectators can connect the character with the world by paying attention to how the life and habit of each man's mind is externalized in his ordered existence. We can also look to the experiences, engagements, and reactions of others around them to guide us in seeing through such opaque characters. The notable orderliness of the characters' lives and the way people around them interpret it allow us to peek over the fence and into the "garden of the mind," offering us incomplete glimpses of meaning and understanding that can only hint at the growth and change of seasons that lie at its center.

CHAPTER 17

"A Spoonful of Sugar": Watching Movies Autistically

MARK OSTEEN

The more Mary Poppinses the better.
P. L. TRAVERS, *MARY POPPINS*

On a Monday in February 2009, I was scheduled to drive my autistic son, Cameron, back to his boarding school, ninety miles away. It was 12:15, but he hadn't budged from his kneeling position in the corner of the living room since 10:30, despite my offers of a DVD, music, and food. He was wise to the game: we were going back to school, and he didn't want to go. But his father was determined to stay on schedule.

Suddenly, Cam became agitated. "Shopping! Shopping!" he shouted, pounding on the dining room table. He is seldom able to speak, so when he does, it's meaningful.

"We can't go shopping right now, buddy; you have to go back to school." Then he landed on a favorite. "Raffi!"

A Raffi fan since he was a toddler, at nineteen my son still regularly watched videos of the legendary children's star. I looked around: the folks at school had sent home his mini DVD player, but *not* the tried-and-true Raffi DVDs. Oh-oh.

"Rafffiiii! I want Raffi!" At first plaintive, he had become vehement.

"Cam, we don't have Raffi on the DVD. We have *Poppins*, though. How about *Poppins*?"

"Raffi!!"

If I gave in, we would be stuck here for another hour, making him late to school and me late getting home. I held my ground. Cam sprang up and bounded into the kitchen. I followed him as he pulled open the snack cupboard and rummaged; finding Cheez-Its, he opened the bag as I retrieved a bowl.

"Just a minute, son."

He couldn't wait: he clutched my sweatshirt front and started gnawing on it.

"Cam, calm down. Dad will put on *Poppins*, and you can sit here as long as you want."

"Poppins!" he exclaimed, releasing his grip and plunking down on a kitchen stool. I hastily slapped in the *Mary Poppins* DVD. Within ten minutes he had relaxed; five minutes later, we were out the door and in the car.

The soundtrack of my son's early life consisted of children's music videos and Disney movies, which he watched incessantly. The same videos, the same foods, his beloved white shoelaces, the same schedule: these routines kept him anchored, as if without them he might become lost in time.

But Cam's favorite movie, hands down, was *Mary Poppins* (1964). He watched "Poppins" every day—whether at school or at home—for twenty years. Every. Single. Day. Sometimes more than once. My wife, Leslie, and I have seen it a thousand times. I am not exaggerating. We've marched for miles around the house to "Step in Time," taken scores of jolly holidays with Mary, and downed so many doses of meds to "A Spoonful of Sugar" that the song's first few notes now reliably trigger my gag reflex.

But thank heavens for that marvelous nanny (Julie Andrews)! Whenever Cam was mad or sad, refusing to move from the kitchen or a doorway, we would offer "Poppins." He would repeat the word and quickly go to wherever he could view the movie. The word was as magical as the character. The movie was even more entrancing, depicting a fabulous world outside of schedules and demands. It offered blessed respite—a spoonful of sugar in our sometimes unsavory lives.

By his late teens, Cam began to tolerate non-Poppins films: first, other Disney movies (*Pinocchio* [1940], *Aladdin* [1992], *Mulan* [1998]); a couple of years later, superhero movies like *Spider-Man* (2002) and his current favorite, *Guardians of the Galaxy* (2014), joined his pantheon. But "Poppins" was still number one.

One evening in 2013, Cam watched all of *Toy Story 3* (2010) with us. Afterward, hoping to retire to the den to watch a television program, Leslie and I put the movie back on for him. Within a few minutes we heard shouting, then "No!" followed by wordless yelling. Soon I noticed that I couldn't hear his TV, so I checked on him. Cam was kneeling in front of the set, pushing a white shoestring against the screen. He had turned off the cable box. The message was clear: no more *Toy Story 3*! In case I didn't understand, he clarified: "Poppins."

My son clearly agrees with the narrator of P. L. Travers's novel, who declares, "The more Mary Poppinses the better" ([1934] 2016, 36).

Such repetitive watching is common among autists, and they don't merely watch. Ron Suskind's *Life, Animated* (2014) recounts how his autistic son, Owen, learned to speak by watching Disney movies and repeating memorized phrases (see the chapter by Rebecca Bell-Metereau in this volume). David Karasik, the subject of his siblings' memoir *The Ride Together* (2003), committed to memory dozens of episodes of the *Adventures of Superman* and reenacted them daily for years. Both books reveal how watching becomes acting through an elaborate form of echolalia that Julia Rodas dubs "ricochet" (2018, 6). Although Cam is a less elaborate echoer than these champion ricochet artists, he can sing the songs and recite dialogue from his favorite videos (including "Poppins"); for years, these scripts were virtually his sole verbal utterances. Reiterations of the same story, characters, and visuals provide order and stability in a world that often seems to make no sense to him. *Mary Poppins* was Cam's aural-visual comfort food, a focal point amid a threatening surround.

One of Cameron's home aides, a young man named Jon, was raised with an autistic sister. If for Cam the greatest movie in history is *Mary Poppins*, for Jon's sister it is *The Wizard of Oz* (1939).

"My other sister and I were talking one day, and we decided we'd seen it ten thousand times," Jon told me.

"I know the feeling. But it could be worse," I said. "One of Cam's school-mates is still obsessed with Barney, the super-saccharine purple dinosaur, at age twenty."

We discussed why autistic folks become fixated on a single video or movie. I suggested that the habit exemplifies "local coherence": the idea that autists, who struggle to fit components into a large context, find meaning in the smaller bits themselves. Jon pointed out that his sister notices details that he misses. I wondered: do autistic viewers discover something new each time, so that what seem to neurotypicals like repetitions are, to the highly focused eyes of an autist, not the same at all? Do they find nuances in the nooks and crannies of the story or mise-en-scène with each viewing? Jon commented, "It's familiar and new at the same time." This is one key idea that I want to explore in this chapter.

Again

> BERT (Dick Van Dyke) to the audience:
> I feel what's to happen
> Has all happened before.

The well-documented autistic love of repetition is manifest in a variety of ways, from a compulsion to maintain routines (which can sometimes slide into a paralyzing rigidity) to "stimming"—those "repetitive and restricted behaviors" that typify autism (Alderson 2011, 71), such as hand flapping, rocking, and, in my son's case, constant fiddling with strings. Long frowned on by clinicians, these behaviors are undergoing reassessment, in part because articulate autistic people have explained their value as soothing and centering activities. But is that all there is to it? Are there other reasons for repetitions, for watching the same movie over and over?

A further explanation involves sensory differences. It is widely known that autistics' sensory perceptions often differ dramatically from neurotypicals' (Bogdashina 2003, 2010). Many autists struggle to distinguish salient sounds from background noise and cannot rely on consistent perceptions from one day—even one hour—to the next (Bogdashina 2003, 46). Hyper-vision and hyperhearing may alternate with hyposensitivity (54). The autistic writer Tito Rajarshi Mukhopadhyay observes, "There are components in the environment that I can miss due to the overindulgence of one sense or an overindulgence toward one component of the environment." Once, as he watched a film in a theater, "while [his] senses were caught in the activity of drawing diagonals across the ceiling, [he] missed the whole movie" (2008, 121).

Nor is narrative the same for autists as for neurotypicals. The neuroscientist Matthew K. Belmonte proposes that we should view the autistic tendency to perceive the world in parts as a disruption of narrative organization (2008, 168-170).[1] This theory could help explain Cam's obsession with fragments: unable to make sense of lengthy stories, he gravitated to the excerpts in sing-along videos. Because of his sensory inconsistency and unreliable perceptions, he needed multiple viewings to piece together the narrative puzzle of "Poppins." As he has aged and his perceptions have become more reliable, he can follow longer stories and welcomes more novelty (but not too much: he still watches his favorites). Repetition, then, promotes coherence.

Or perhaps, repetition itself is the attraction. Research on autism and music suggests as much. Adam Ockelford, a music educator who has worked with dozens of autistic youngsters and adults, suggests that "music, with its reliance on repetition, could have been especially devised for those on the autism spectrum" (2013, 99). Autistic people, he posits, process all sounds "as though they were inherently musical, and in terms of musical structure (repetition)"; in this light, echolalia is merely "the organization of language . . . through musical structure" (240, 239)—that is, through patterned repetition.

A great deal of evidence also bears out Jon's insight that autists can discern patterns and details where neurotypicals cannot (Bogdashina 2010, 167; Grandin 1995a, 44). The famed autistic author and scientist Temple Grandin proposes that her attention to detail frees her from the "global bias that gets in the way of top-down thinkers" (2013, 124). This ability to "look long and deep"—as when my son studies the intricacies of a white shoelace, examining each of the filaments one by one, like Walt Whitman's patient spider—is both a "stim" and a skill (Rodas 2018, 59).[2] Likewise, Ockelford notes, autistic musicians may hear more in a sequence each time it is played or hear it "afresh on each occasion" (2013, 240). What strikes neurotypicals as tedious sameness may yield unending novelty to an autist's penetrating eyes and attentive ears. Every repeated melody or movie thus presents itself as at once comfortingly familiar *and* wonderfully new.

A truly autistic movie, then, would appeal to a neurodivergent mind in its own terms by using repetition and musical structures.[3] Why did Cam love *Mary Poppins* so much? Because it is organized around musical structures— emotional crescendos and diminuendos, repeated melodic motifs that offer sameness with variation—and because, as I discovered when I viewed the movie one more time, it celebrates neurodivergent ways of thinking, feeling, and communicating.

A Song

He knows a song will move the job along.[4]

The movie's story is not that of the source novel; nor is the title character the same. Travers's Mary Poppins, unlike Julie Andrews, *needs* a spoonful of sugar, for she is a supremely tart character. Vain and fond of admiring herself in the mirror, she is also brusque, impatient, and irascible, much like P. L. Travers herself, if we can trust *Saving Mr. Banks*, the 2013 film about the making of *Mary Poppins*. An abbreviated list of adverbs modifying Mary Poppins's speech paints a prickly picture: she answers "contemptuously" and "rudely" (33, 34), asks a question "snappily" (42), replies "haughtily" and "scornfully" (55), converses "crossly" (101), and (my favorite) dismisses bad ideas "uppishly" (150). In short, she "never waste[s] time in being nice" (166). Yet she is also magical, able to talk with animals, carry kids around the world with her compass, host a tea party while hovering in the air, and speak to a star in the Pleiades.

A few scenes from the first novel appear in the Disney film. The Banks children's visit to the hilarity-addicted Uncle Albert is there, as is the lady who implores, "Feed the birds. Tuppence a bag" (95). The medicine-taking scene is present in the novel, albeit sans sugar (21). But in the novel the Bankses have four kids, not two, and none of them accompany Bert (not a chimney sweep or a one-man band but a "match man") and Mary on their jolly holiday.[5] The parents are little more than clueless ciphers, Mr. Banks present mostly as a nose poking around a ubiquitous newspaper and the nameless mother (no suffragette, she!) ineffectual when she isn't absent. Static and episodic, the novel lacks a narrative thread, and neither Mary Poppins's arrival nor her departure is explained. Richard Sherman, who, with his brother Robert, wrote all the movie's songs, points out in a documentary celebrating the movie's fortieth anniversary, *Supercalifragilisticexpialidocious* (2004), that the novel has "no story line; it [is] a series of adventures": Mary Poppins flies in for no apparent reason and flies away for no apparent reason.

The Disney team—the Shermans, the writers Don Da Gradi and Bill Walsh—created a batch of lively, memorable songs that advance the story and deepen the characters. In fact, the screenplay was written *around* the songs: the Shermans decided which scenes to include by underlining chapter titles in red crayon, then wrote a song for each one. Music organizes the movie like a unified composition, each movement calibrated for emotional effect and narrative momentum. Disparate scenes are connected through musical motifs. Hence, for example, "The Life I Lead," Mr. Banks's theme song, is later transformed into Bert's lament about the father's woes; and "Chim Chim Cheree" echoes Bert's opening busker number. It has all happened before.

As I prepared to write this chapter, I asked myself: who else watches the same movies repeatedly? Many small children and some adults enjoy revisiting familiar films to appreciate favorite scenes and reacquaint themselves with beloved characters. Who else? Neurotypical film critics, myself among them. Most of us have taken to heart David Thomson's caution to be "wary of ourselves and that first viewing," for we may get caught up in the story and miss a great deal (2015, 57). Repeated viewing has become not merely possible but essential as generations of film critics have enjoyed the luxury of rewatching, rewinding, and pausing to catch every last nuance. Are we as attentive as my son and other autistic viewers? Is our attraction to repetition like theirs?

Can we learn something from autistic watching?

Surely, I told myself, I do not need to watch *Mary Poppins* ever again: I know every song by heart and can recite the dialogue along with the characters. But to answer the questions asked above, as well as to perform due diligence—to view the movie as a sedulous critic rather than as a beleaguered dad—I decided to watch *Mary Poppins* one more time. As the theme from "Feed the Birds" began, I felt an overwhelming nostalgia. But within a few minutes, I grasped that I had so long treated the movie as aural-visual wallpaper that, in important respects, I had not really watched it at all.

A Mirror

Happiness is bloomin' all around her.

After his solo concert in the park, Bert guides us to No. 17, Cherry Tree Lane, home of George Banks and family. Our visit starts with a bang, or rather a boom—the bombastic (and hard-of-hearing) Admiral Boom, a farcical emblem of masculine authority and punctuality, shoots off his cannon at every hour (always on the dot!), sending tremors through his neighbors' home. Boom's obsession with order is shared by Mr. Banks (David Tomlinson), who, upon returning home from his banking job, delivers an ode to male complacency, "The Life I Lead"—"It's grand to be an Englishman, in 1910 / King Edward's on the throne, / It's the age of men"—especially men who run a tight ship and rule with a "firm, but gentle hand." Although smugly satisfied with a routine in which his children are "scrubbed and tubbed" and "adequately fed," at the moment he has no idea where they are. His wife, Winifred (Glynis Johns), knows little more, having just returned from a suffragist rally to find their nanny exiting in a huff, disgusted by the children's repeated disappearances. Winifred boisterously sings "Sister Suffragette," a hymn to feminism—"Though we adore men individually / We believe that as a group they're rather stupid"—but her devotion is skin deep: she meekly submits to her husband's plan to hire a new nanny who will fit his fantasy version of himself as "a general" who can "give commands."

Jane (Karen Dotrice) and Michael (Matthew Garber) have different ideas, which they relay to their parents in a touching advertisement for a nanny with a "cheery disposition," "rosy cheeks," and "no warts," who will play games and never "scold or dominate" them. Harrumphing, George tears up their ad and throws it into the fire; hence, he is baffled when Mary Poppins (having floated in on her umbrella) reads it back to him. She further flummoxes Mr. Banks by displaying precisely the authoritative nature he thought he wanted. After the children tidy up the nursery with the help of Poppinsian magic—the other Mary Poppins, who appears in a mirror during "A Spoonful of Sugar," isn't merely a reflection; she adds an embellishment (technically, a cadenza), after which the "real" MP calls her "cheeky"—a suspicious Michael refuses to take his medicine, upon which the new nanny sings "A Spoonful of Sugar." As I watched this scene, I recalled that my son has taken medications daily since he was ten, resisting often enough that we have often wished a Mary Poppins could assist us, with or without sugar.

Other elements, I noted for the first time, also mirror my son's life. When Cameron was young, we maintained a home-education program to supplement his regular school. That meant he was visited every day by one or more of a cast of (mostly young, female) therapists and teachers. Perhaps he hoped one of them would one day produce unexpected items from a bottomless bag or move objects by merely thinking about them. Moreover, as Andrews comments in the making-of documentary, Mary Poppins "fixes things." So does Cam's mother, who, although perhaps not "practically perfect in every way," is supremely competent and, like the beloved MP, makes up songs to sing to her child. Mary Poppins indeed represents an avatar of what Travers elsewhere calls the Great Mother, one of the mythic constructs she explores in essays such as "If She's Not Gone, She Lives There Still" (1978, 47). Like Mary Poppins, the Great Mother never dies; she merely retreats and then returns in a new guise.[6]

Cam's mother has also taken him on many jolly holidays, but none as delightful as the one to which Mary Poppins treats the Banks children after they jump through Bert's chalk drawings. "Happiness is bloomin' all around [Mary]" and Bert, who behave like a couple in love, served by animated penguins. This sequence captures one of the novel's primary themes: that imagination can transform mundane reality and take us to places we have only dreamed about. As Cristina Pérez Valverde observes, Mary Poppins's magic allows the children to "gain access to a supra-sensual reality inaccessible to adults, and their parents in particular" (2006, 267). No doubt this theme also appealed to my son. I can almost hear him thinking: "Poppins pulls me out of my cramped house to a place where my body does what I ask. She lets me sing, travel, float, laugh, and, for once, be myself."

A hint of adult sexuality creeps in as Bert launches into a list of the women he has known—ending the roster of twenty (!) with praise for MP as "cream of the crop, tip of the top." A love of lists is common among some autistic people, whose strong systematizing impulses compel them to relish the "catalogic and taxonomic" (Rodas 2018, 57) and to enjoy compiling (and sometimes regaling others with) such data dumps.[7] Here, then, *Mary Poppins* begins to address the viewer in autistic terms.

A (Non-)Word

You'll always sound precocious.

An even more autist-friendly moment follows. After their carousel ponies win a race, Mary Poppins is asked to express her feelings about the victory. "There probably aren't words to describe your emotions," acknowledges the host. But there *is* one word. This word is actually a nonword, an aggregation of syllables that means nothing and is celebrated (and therefore meaningful) for that very quality. Iiiiiit's supercalifragilisticexpialidocious!! In the song with that title, Bert recalls his father's punishing him for his shy refusal to speak. But when young Bertie uttered this word, he was miraculously cured: you merely "summon up this word and then you've got a lot to say." My son, who can seldom call up words and whose apraxia prevents him from forming them, surely identifies with Bert's condition. Although the word is meaningless in itself, in context it means a great deal, signifying that the speaker rejects the requirement to say what the listener wants to hear and resists the convention of making sense. Indeed, "Supercalifragilisticexpialidocious" perfectly exemplifies what Rodas (among others) has described as a key characteristic of autistic speech—its ejaculatory properties, the "tendency to speak in bursts, eruptively, a verbal practice abounding in possibility" (2018, 7). While Cam cannot actually pronounce this tongue twister (though he has tried countless times), he regularly injects his own nonwords—for example, deafening howls of "Eeeeeeeeeeeeeee!"—into conversations to express glee, gain attention, or contribute to a convivial mood. His falsetto squeals may not impress "dukes and maharajas," but they're precocious enough to make Frankie Valli turn green with envy. He also "speaks" through his body, particularly via an entire lexicon of claps. These handmade interjections function like the movie's nonword, attracting attention, adding punctuation, drowning out anyone who annoys him. Mary Poppins promises that her word can "change your life," but it can do so only if other people appreciate its value as a disrupter, a protest, and a token of the beauty of nonsense. Semantically empty but emotionally laden, this word exemplifies autist language.

The next morning (a diminuendo following all that riding, dancing, and singing), Mr. Banks can't even pronounce the word, but insists that he doesn't need to, for he "always know[s] what to say." Despite his scorn, Bert, Mary Poppins, and the kids experience another autist-friendly encounter, this time with Uncle Albert (Ed Wynn). Midway through his song "I Love to Laugh," MP and Bert list six types of laughing, each one funny itself (and true). Here is another instance of autistic expression. As I watched this scene again, I suddenly comprehended that the song may have inspired Cam to invent the "ha ha" game, which he and I have played for many years. It goes something like this:

CAM: Ha ha!
DAD: Ha ha ha!
CAM: Ha HA!
DAD: Hee, hee, hee!
CAM: (*Bemused look*)

When the elated kids describe their hovering, hilarious tea party, however, their dad brings them down by explaining why they should be practical and save their money. To the tune of "The Life I Lead," he lauds the British bank as an emblem of "tradition, discipline, and rules," dismissing

Poppinsian activities as useless because they fulfill "no basic need." This man gets his thrills not from racing imaginary horses or floating on the ceiling but from "totting up a balance book." Michael will deposit his tuppence in the Dawes, Tomes, Mousely, Grubbs Fidelity Fiduciary Bank. On the way there, however, the kids encounter a woman who beseeches them, "Feed the birds. Tuppence a bag." Her candid pleas present a vision of altruism at odds with their father's individualist, utilitarian credo. Essentially a gospel song, complete with plagal ("amen") cadences, "Feed the Birds" is an altar call for Mr. Banks, an invitation to convert to the bird woman's charitable doctrine. But Mr. Banks, as usual, is not listening.

A Gentleman

A father can always do with a bit of 'elp.
BERT, TO JANE AND MICHAEL

The children are bullied by the bank executives, especially the senior Mr. Dawes (Dick Van Dyke, who pointedly plays both Bert and his polar opposite, both father figures), a "giant in the world of finance" who, along with Banks and his other minions, delivers a paean to finance capital. By putting his meager coins into an account, Michael will help build "Railways through Africa / Dams across the Nile, . . . / Majestic, self-amortizing canals" and to grow "plantations of ripening tea." These imperialist enterprises yield "Bonds! Chattels! Dividends! Shares! Bankruptcies! Debtor sales! Opportunities!" Daddy Dawes (like Admiral Boom, partly deaf) then extends his claw—the (non)invisible hand of predatory capitalism—snatches the boy's tuppence, and welcomes Michael to their "family of investors," a family consisting entirely of older men who preach George's patriarchal, domineering, order-obsessed dogma.

But Michael mutinies, causing a run on the bank. Fleeing from the bank, the kids encounter Bert, now transformed into a chimney sweep. In "Chim Chim Cheree," he again offers an ethos opposed to the bankers', one in which happiness matters more than money, and beauty trumps propriety. Fittingly, the song features more nonsense syllables that challenge the Banksian obsession with utility, suggesting, perhaps, that the bankers would benefit from learning to speak Autistic. To the children's surprise, however, Bert sympathizes with their father, who, they are convinced, hates them. No, replies Bert, he is a "fine gentleman, and he loves ya," but is trapped by "cold, heartless money." "They make cages in all sizes and shapes," he points out. "Bank shapes, some of 'em, carpets and all." Their dad takes care of them, but who cares for their dad? Nobody. (Winifred seems forgotten.) Yet he "pushes on at his job, uncomplaining, alone and silent." "A father," Bert acknowledges, "can always do with a bit of 'elp."

In the "Jolly Holiday" sequence, Bert served as surrogate father, embodying a style of masculinity starkly different from that of George Banks. The chimney sweep episode fleshes out the traits of this Other Father: he is nonthreatening, fun loving, and artistic, willing to take risks and dispense with his schedule; he is empathetic and wise—but not judgmental—and he listens to children. To underscore his empathy and to highlight the contrast between himself and George, Bert sings this song to the tune of Mr. Banks's theme, "The Life I Lead," transposed into a minor key.

At this point in my viewing, I was struck by a recognition that I should have made decades ago: this movie is not about the children or even about Mary Poppins. It is about the father. That is the argument of *Saving Mr. Banks*, which presents *Mary Poppins* as a biographical allegory restaging Pamela Travers's relationship with her own father. The film dramatizes how Walt Disney (Tom Hanks) and his team struggled to persuade Travers (Emma Thompson) to sign over the adaptation rights. Thompson's Travers is even more prickly than her famous nanny: snobbish, stubborn, and awkward, she is impossible to work with, objecting to the casting of Van Dyke and dismissing singing as "frivolous" ("A Spoonful of Sugar" is "enormously patronizing"). As Andrews comments in the making-of documentary, Travers was a "pretty crisp lady." Disney's blandishments and promises not to "tarnish" a story he loves soften that crispness enough that Travers tentatively agrees to collaborate. These events are juxtaposed with flashbacks to Travers's Australian childhood with her troubled, ne'er-do-well father, Travers Goff (Colin Farrell; her given name was Helen Goff). An alcoholic and unsuccessful bank manager, Goff died when Helen was a child. A "germinal moment," as she calls it elsewhere, his death "strongly fix[ed]" her memories of him—embellished by a daughter's idealizing fantasies (1965, 239).

As the Shermans audition their bank song for her in *Saving Mr. Banks*, Travers recalls a drunken speech her father gave (using many of the song's phrases) and explodes: "He was not a monster!" She protests that they have made Mr. Banks (viewers know that she is conflating him with her own father) "unspeakably awful" and insists that they change his character. When seeing the dancing penguins in the "Jolly Holiday" sequence sends her back to England in a huff (she had stipulated that there be no animation), Disney is forced to follow her there and use all his paternal charms to win her back. Having grasped that Travers's entire authorial career, including her name, amounts to a tribute to her father, he recalls how his own father, Elias, employed eight-year-old Walt in his newspaper delivery business in Kansas City, even in the winter, when the boy had no warm shoes, keeping him in line with a strap. But Walt is no longer in thrall to those memories. "Don't you want to . . . let it all go, have a life that isn't dictated by the past?" he asks her. Then he purrs, "It's not the children she comes to see. It's their father. It's your father, Travers Goff." If she permits them to complete the movie, he promises, everyone who views it "will see George Banks being saved." In movie houses around the world, Mr. Banks (along with Mr. Goff and perhaps even the senior Mr. Disney) "will be redeemed . . . in imagination." She gives in, and the writers make amends by creating a redemptive trajectory for George Banks.

His upward arc begins after the banking scene when, to the tune of "The Life I Lead," he laments to Bert how Mary Poppins has brought him to "rack and ruin before his time." She has administered not a spoonful of sugar but a "bitter pill." Bert replies with a sympathetic but subtly chiding song about how Banks has never had time to dry his tykes' tears because he has been forced to "Grind, grind, grind at that grindstone, / Though childhood slips like sand through a sieve." Banks gets the message, yet Bert's words offer little solace as he trudges to the bank to face his fate. Upon learning that he has been fired, however, he erupts with "Supercalifragilisticexpialidocious!" and giddily yells at the befuddled executives, "There's no such thing as you!" Then he repeats one of Uncle Albert's silly jokes. Old Dawes doesn't understand it, or perhaps even hear it. Indeed, it cannot be an accident that all three oppressive paternalistic characters—Admiral Boom, Daddy Dawes, and George Banks—are literally or metaphorically deaf. But Mr. Banks, at last, has begun to listen, and Daddy Dawes, too, eventually gets the joke: we learn later that he died laughing at it. Mr. Banks has learned to think and speak autistically, freeing himself from his cage, rising from his grindstone, and discarding his obsessions with punctuality and utility.

The movie concludes with everyone flying kites and singing the kite song as Mary Poppins departs, her job complete: George Banks has remembered how to be a child, which will make him a better parent. Presumably, her final assessment of Mr. Banks echoes that of Travers herself, who, after the credits roll in *Saving Mr. Banks*, is heard on a tape recording (she insisted that all story conferences be taped) observing that Mr. Banks has "always been sweet, but worn out with the cares of life." No longer. He has completed the process that Travers describes elsewhere as "re-storying," learning to reconstitute his childhood, "relive intentionally what was organically

lived by the blood" (1983, 141), and thereby rediscovering a "radical innocence" (1965, 237). In so doing, he fulfills the primary purpose, as she sees it,
of the mythic hero: the recovery of "a treasure that was lost . . . his own self,"
and with it "the reinstatement of the fallen world" (1976, 16). Mr. Banks's
redemption saves his family and, as indicated when the bank executives join
their kite-flying escapade, changes the world.

A Message

> Every time I see the film, I think it's better and better.
> GLYNIS JOHNS, IN *SUPERCALIFRAGILISTICEXPIALIDOCIOUS*

As the movie ended, I was flooded with guilty questions. Am I like George
Banks? Is this what my son has been wanting to tell me? As I recalled the
episode with which I began this chapter, I recognized, with a cringe, the
similarities: fixated on my schedule and determined to grind at my grindstone, I didn't hear what my son was trying to say. I then recollected the
many times I've worked instead of spending time with him, the occasions
when I have been annoyed by his autistic speech instead of apprehending
his intentions and appreciating his intonations. I had interpreted his love of
Mary Poppins as a symptom, not a signal. And although I had watched this
movie a thousand times, I had never before watched it autistically, attending to every detail, and hence had never discerned its celebration of autistic
thought and expression. I had not grasped that for Cam, I was Mr. Banks!
Perhaps *Mary Poppins* was my son's "spoonful of sugar," his way of spoon-
feeding me a medicinal message. If so, I never swallowed it. Cam may have
needed many repeated viewings to understand the movie, but I needed even
more viewings to understand him.

Of course, my obliviousness was not the only reason for his obsession
with "Poppins"; he had motives that had nothing to do with me. But my
reencounter with the movie has convinced me that we—film critics, parents, neurotypicals—should train ourselves to watch more autistically. Autists' attention to detail and patterns should prompt us to look more closely,
to prize the beauty of familiarity, and to appreciate how much small differences matter. Watching autistically may help us fashion more flexible definitions of value; reject reductive utilitarian ideas about work, productivity,
and language; and recognize the importance of joyful nonsense. Let us not
emulate Mr. Banks. Let us not dismiss children's or neurodiverse people's

desires and modes of expression before we have tried to understand them on their terms. If watching autistically can teach us how to speak Autistic, it can also make us better critics and, more importantly, better human beings.

Now I must ask you to excuse me. I need to watch *Mary Poppins* again: I know I missed something.

Notes

1. In "Narrating Autism" (2013), I explore the challenges involved in reconciling the conflict between the lure of repetition and the requirements of linear narrative in autism stories.

2. In *One of Us* (2010, 153–156), I discuss my son's string obsession in greater detail. It is worth noting that many autistic visual artists also display a fondness for repetition and use it creatively in their works. For further analysis, see my article "'Grow Your Brain!': Contemporary Art on the Autism Spectrum" (forthcoming).

3. In "Narrating Autism" (2013, 276–277), I note that the documentary *George* (1996) is one movie that briefly presents the world through an autistic boy's point of view.

4. Lyrics from *Mary Poppins* are by Robert B. Sherman and Richard M. Sherman.

5. The filmmakers adapted the kite episode and chalk art scenes—along with the merry-go-round material in the "Jolly Holiday" sequence—from the sequel, *Mary Poppins Comes Back* (P. Travers [1935] 2016, 7–13, 222–227). In fact, at the beginning of the second novel, Michael's kite reels the nanny in (11-12).

6. In "If She's Not Gone, She Lives There Still" (1978), might Travers have been influenced in some way by James M. Barrie's books *The Little White Bird* (1902) and *Peter and Wendy* (1911) or his 1904 play *Peter Pan: or, The Boy Who Wouldn't Grow Up*?

7. Rodas (2018) terms this cataloguing trait "discretion," and though her discussion is illuminating, the word seems less than apt.

CHAPTER 18

David and Lisa:
The Healing Power of the Group

R. BARTON PALMER

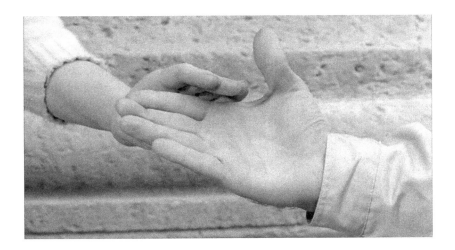

Modern man no longer communicates with the madman. . . . There is no common language: or rather, it no longer exists; the constitution of madness as mental illness, at the end of the eighteenth century, bears witness to a rupture in a dialogue, gives the separation as already enacted, and expels from the memory all those imperfect words, of no fixed syntax, spoken falteringly, in which the exchange between madness and reason was carried out. The language of psychiatry, which is a monologue by reason about madness, could only have come into existence in such a silence.

MICHEL FOUCAULT, PREFACE TO *MADNESS AND CIVILIZATION*

Adapted for the screen from a best-selling short story by Dr. Theodore I. Rubin, and directed by Frank Perry from a screenplay by his wife, Eleanor,

David and Lisa (1962) poignantly dramatizes an at least partial therapeutic success in the treatment of two adolescents suffering from autism, their major symptoms being different forms of obsessive-compulsive behavior, schizophrenic ideation, communication difficulties, and, most importantly, a lack of interest in initiating or maintaining social relations (for the published text, see Rubin [1961] 1998). The story (one-third of a best-selling collection of three fictional case histories) and its subsequent screen adaptation were lent considerable authenticity by the writer's reputation (for biographical information about Rubin, see Carey 2019). Rubin was then one of New York City's most respected therapists as well as a popularizer of psychotherapy well known to American culture at large through his best-selling self-help books and frequent contributions to the *Ladies' Home Journal*.

David and Lisa was the debut project of the writing-directing pair, who were associated not with the Hollywood establishment but, loosely, with the iconoclastic, vaguely leftist New York school, whose members included John Cassavetes, Sidney Lumet, and less well-known figures such as Shirley Clarke and Jerry Schatzberg (Lennard, Palmer, and Pomerance 2020). The authenticity of the film's dramatization of residential treatment for mental illness—as autism was classed at the time—was enhanced considerably by Eleanor Perry's extensive work in psychiatric social work, an area of study in which she had earned a graduate degree. Considerable box-office and critical success with *David and Lisa* gave the Perrys national prominence, and their reputation increased when this very small independent film was nominated for Academy Awards for best director and best adapted screenplay in a year of outsize prestige productions, most notably David Lean's *Lawrence of Arabia* (1962), which dominated the awards. At a time when the social-problem film was enjoying widespread popularity (Cagle 2016), *David and Lisa* struck a responsive chord with the American public, which was then more willing, perhaps, than in previous generations to accept and sympathize with the "abnormal" behavior of the autistic. In two of its most tear-jerking sequences, the film in fact advocates that the "afflicted," whose behavior was shown to be unconventional but harmless, be treated with more tolerance by the public at large.

With its unembarrassed promotion of the value of psychiatry, this independent film is very much of a piece with similarly themed releases from the first two decades of postwar Hollywood filmmaking; these are numerous enough to constitute a cycle of sorts (Gabbard and Gabbard 1999). On this era's screens, the practitioners once known somewhat darkly as alienists came to be depicted as securely established within the ever-expanding ambit of Western medicine, this trend reflecting emerging patterns of practice in the wider culture as psychotherapy became more widely accepted and intellectually respectable, even as the main concepts of Freud, like those of Marx, became subject to revisionist critiques that, somewhat paradoxically, only increased their cultural value. Deeper, perhaps disabling attacks on Freudian "truths," like the debunking that the entire psychoanalytical project later received at the hands of thinkers such as Frederick Crews and Todd Dufresne, were then intellectually unimaginable (Crews 2017; Dufresne 2003).

At least metaphorically, psychiatrists in the 1960s were seen in life and on the screen as donning the same white clinical coats worn proudly by their colleagues in other medical specialties. Their supposed ability to produce dramatically sudden cures, largely through facilitating recovered memory, turned them into heroes of considerable cultural power. The vexed therapeutic goal of "normality" and contested definitions of what constituted a "disorder" (a struggle that in 1952 had generated the *Diagnostic and Statistical Manual of Mental Disorders*) later in the decade made for a darker fictionalization of psychiatry, most notably in Miloš Forman's *One Flew Over the Cuckoo's Nest* (1975). In *David and Lisa*, autism (never labeled as such, but clearly referred to in Rubin's story) is understood not only to create difficulties for those experiencing it but also to reveal qualities—especially the capacity for fellow feeling—worthy of being nurtured.

The film dramatizes not cure but adjustment, as measured by the freedom gained gradually by David (Keir Dullea) and Lisa (Janet Margolin) from the restricting aspects of the condition, which is shown as particularly affecting sociability. Any possibility that either might leave the treatment center and resume life is passed over in silence. This puts the film at odds not only with other entrants in the psychiatric cycle but also with its source, since the attainment of normality for both David and Lisa is clearly the goal of the treatment chronicled in Rubin's downbeat, theory-rich account of the "condition," which is juxtaposed with an uplifting narrative that ends with them joining hands, thus overcoming at least for a moment their previous resistance to physical intimacy. In his dialogues with David, Dr. Alan Swinford (Howard Da Silva) shows a distaste for psychoanalytical theorizing, a subject with which the young man, after years of therapy and study, is quite familiar. Like Rubin, Swinford insists on a plain-language, commonsense approach. Writing in the *New York Times*, Bosley Crowther (1962) observed that "the psychiatric definitions are vague and elusive in this film, and, therefore, the whole situation of conflict must be taken on verbal trust." The film's refusal to define autism does not, in the critic's view, mar but enhances its portrayal of the healing friendship of the two main characters. This plot trajectory reflects time-honored industry formulas by focusing on a personal relationship that is not overly medicalized.

The developing, unplanned connection between David and Lisa also emphasizes the healing energies of residence-centered group therapy, in which the authoritative, professional voice plays a smaller role than in traditional psychotherapy (and in screen versions of traditional psychotherapeutic practice). Of this "odd little boy-meets-girl romance," Crowther points out that "their growing curiosity and attachment in the midst of a cheerless institute is specifically and touchingly presented *by them*—and that's the sum and substance of the film" (emphasis added). Crowther is badly mistaken, however, that this relationship, which is void of sexual energy, can be called romantic. To reduce it to this most banal of stock themes is to mischaracterize the major focus of the filmmakers, which is not directed on the individuals as much as it is on the transpersonal energies of the group. Moreover, the treatment center provides a nurturing, domestic alternative to both the family home, which is shown to be the source of developmental discontents, and the public institution, notorious for being an emotional wasteland, as depicted, for example, in Anatole Litvak's 1948 exposé, *The Snake Pit*, which is based on the autobiographical account of Mary Jane Ward (see the materials collected in Frith 1991).

The dramatization of mental struggle in Perry's film seems quaint, perhaps antiquated, at times clichéd, with its unbridled endorsement of the effectiveness of residential "milieu" therapy and mildly directive psychoanalytical dialogue. Suffused with the energies not only of Rubin but also of the practitioner-researcher Jacob L. Moreno, the film movingly captures the energies and hopes for the therapeutic amelioration of autism in young adults, a concern that dominated the United States in the 1950s and early 1960s. In any archaeology of what was such a prominent element of early postwar American culture (especially among coastal urban elites and the country's intelligentsia), *David and Lisa* is of unmatched evidentiary value. The film's continuing popularity in the new millennium (in July 2020 it enjoyed an 83.9 percent rating on *Rotten Tomatoes*) likely exposes a vein of nostalgia for a prepharmacological, humanistic approach to the easing of the more disabling aspects of autism. Filmgoers in 1962 had already caught a glimpse of these therapeutic practices and their unanticipated but welcome result two decades earlier in Irving Rapper's *Now, Voyager* (1942), based on the fiction of Olive Higgins Prouty. In *David and Lisa*, Perry brought to the screen with greater realism an updated version of the gentle, noninvasive approach shown there, which is currently gaining a renewed foothold in US mental health practice.

David and Lisa is most notable for challenging the then-established paradigm of films that celebrated heroic psychiatric success by shifting the focus from the therapist-analysand relationship to the aleatory dynamics of mutual healing. Interactions between the patients that produce therapeutically valuable insights seem to occur spontaneously, within and through a thoughtfully designed and "managed" residential treatment center and school. Individual psychiatric sessions, most of them unplanned, remain only a part of what is by design a loosely organized regimen. The move back to a version of the reformed asylum approach from individual therapy is significant, and in Rubin's text the two approaches to therapy are interestingly juxtaposed. Freud's methodological advance had enabled the treatment of patients in the office, obviating for many with mental troubles the horrors of confinement and separation from society. But the value of separation might be enhanced by the presence of similarly afflicted others, especially in a minimally regimented and restricted environment. For a view of the office-therapy model, taken to some dramatic extremes, note Hitchcock's *Spellbound* (1945) (Pomerance 2004).

Residential group therapy as theorized by Moreno (1953)—whose ideas were widely adopted in the United States—promoted the notion of the treatment center, an idealized version of which is at the center of Perry's film. This emphasis on physical setting marks a major departure from Rubin's story, in which the unnamed site of healing is never described, its very presence in fact only implied. In the manner of postwar locative realism, *David and Lisa* focuses on the complex relationship between place (here a found site, not a set) and the people shown living therein (see Palmer 2016 for a full discussion of the extended production trend that includes Perry's film). An interesting precursor to *David and Lisa* is offered by Fred Zinnemann's *The Men* (1950), which depicts the rehabilitation of paraplegic veterans in a military residential clinic, with the Birmingham General Hospital in Van Nuys, California, serving as the "real" setting where informal group healing (with some actual patients among the actors) supplements conventional medical rehabilitation.

With its unplanned interactions between patients and staff, as well as occasional talking-cure sessions in which Dr. Swinford assumes control of a sort, the residential treatment center in the film promotes a hybrid approach, as did other such centers in the United States at the time. Perry's film, in short, offers itself as being very much *dans le vent* of current practice, even as it rejects the resort-in-the-country model presented in earlier Hollywood representations of these institutions, notably the sanitarium "Cascade" in *Now, Voyager*, based on the Austen Riggs Center in Stockbridge, Massachusetts. Interestingly, among the patients at Cascade is an adolescent girl, Tina (Janis Wilson), who seems to be suffering from autism and whose difficulties with social interaction (seemingly explained by a so-called refrigerator mother) are significantly relieved by her experience with group residency, especially with her fellow patient Charlotte Vale (Bette Davis), who, assuming the role of her caretaker, becomes something of a substitute parent in a narrative trajectory that recalls the growing relationship between Lisa and David. In *David and Lisa*, however, the treatment center is presented as a site completely self-contained, isolated not only from town and city but also from the larger medical community, with which it seems to have no connection, an important aspect of the film's establishment of its fictional space.

Rubin's Version

In an important way, *David and Lisa* differs considerably from Rubin's original text, which, like "Jordi" and "Little Ralphie and the Creature," the two other pieces that complete the collection, is, strictly speaking, more than a story. "Lisa and David" (the title shift for the film being a marketing move) consists of two sections: an episodic narrative and two medical files that provide detailed records of treatments, which differed in the approach taken for each. In the story, David and Lisa are characters; in the medical reports, they are patients. The bulk of the text consists of a series of forty-one disconnected but chronologically ordered vignettes, of varying lengths, in which their experiences at the treatment center are recounted. In this fiction, Rubin deploys noncharacter narration, with occasional focalization that permits the description of characters' mental states (e.g., "David listened and wondered what she meant. He finally gave up and thought about a big calendar clock he had seen a year ago" ([1961] 1998, 18). Such a fictional text offers interior (and also sympathetic) access to the characters—whose actions and mental states can both be perfectly known and then chronicled in detail by a narrator who, in the manner of classic realism, speaks with the voice of God. In the story section of "Lisa and David," the narrator aligns with the characters and does not judge them; he is not associated with Dr. Swinford, to whose thoughts the story affords no access. Unobtrusive, the narrator has at his disposal no psychiatric insights that would signal an intellectual or a professional separation. He evinces no Conradian urge to render visible the world in which these events unfold. The focus here is on the movements of the inner life, which are largely inaccessible to an outside observer, including even the most perspicacious psychoanalyst.

A quite different kind of knowledge of these two characters is provided by the "Notes" that follow Rubin's narrative. These texts offer what Foucault terms a "monologue by reason about madness." If in the story the characters are subjects, in the notes they become the objects of medical analysis and surveillance, with a narrative imposed on them that leads, in the Hippocratic style, from diagnosis to prognosis. The moments of the story, loosely chronological in their succession, lack specific indications of time and space; the entries in the notes are carefully dated. These overflow with information, much of which is irrelevant to the deeper, less quantifiable truths that the story is determined to convey. What does it matter that David is a slightly built fifteen-year-old, always neat and formally dressed, or that Lisa, dark complexioned, does not always comb her hair? She weighs ninety-eight pounds, precisely thirty-three less than David, but is this an important measure of the difference between them?

Only the story's narrator seems interested in the granularity of character in the deeper sense of the term, reporting, for example: "Lisa lay in bed and thought about the snow. She pictured the sky opening up and tons of it falling down all at once. . . . She remembered the smell of John's coat" (Rubin [1961] 1998, 53). Only the narrator, a presence distinct from the therapist, can be a witness to such movements of the mind in which autism displays itself. Only in a rudimentary sense can either the vignettes or the brief narratives of progress be said to constitute a plot, but this is in accord with the unplanned, aleatory nature of the group-therapy experience. The story does have a through line, however, as it traces how both characters in their different ways come to will themselves toward self-awareness and a meaningful connection with each other. In the final vignette, Lisa comes to the realization that the malignant presence haunting her waking life, whom she calls Muriel, is an aspect of her own self, and so is not to be feared. Recognizing the importance to his friend of this moment of clarity, David takes her hand, overcoming for the first time the aversion to physical touch that had kept him angrily isolated from others for much of his life. What passes between them through this gesture is private and fleeting, but nonetheless of the greatest significance. A moment inaccessible to the writer of the notes.

In the film, this quiet, small-scale moment of mutual triumph becomes a dramatic rescue, but with much of its original meaning intact. Lisa feels jealous and hurt when David seems more interested in one of the other students and angrily tells Lisa to go away. Desperate for some connection, she runs off from the treatment center and somehow makes her way to the city museum, which the group had earlier visited, and where she had found herself deeply drawn to the sculpture of a family group and curled up like a baby in the lap of the mother figure. When Lisa is discovered to be missing, the staff tries desperately to find her, fearing for her safety, but only David remembers the incident with the sculpture. Perhaps, needing comfort, she went to the museum. Swinford drives him there, but the museum is now closed, and they find her collapsed on the steps. Leaving the psychiatrist behind in the car, David runs to her and, apologizing, takes her hand. The gesture acknowledges both the responsibility and the affection he feels for his friend, whose flight from the center had put her in danger. This concern for another, inculcated in him by the group experience at the treatment center, allows him to ignore his fearfulness, whose origin, thanks to treatment, he now understands. Perhaps most importantly, in assisting the staff to locate Lisa, he takes effective action, responding to his best instincts and revealing a growing independence that is only hinted at in the film's source.

In general, *David and Lisa* renders faithfully the optimistic, celebratory, de-dramatized tone of the episodic story, eschewing the distanced medicalism of the notes, whose tone is uninvolved, cautious, conscious of the need to be professionally correct in the analysis of behaviors identified as autistic. Careful commentary in the notes anticipates the scrutiny of other colleagues. The story constructs a quite different reader. With a triumphant poignancy, the last vignette ends with David taking Lisa's hand as he overcomes his previously disabling isolation. None of this appears in the final update in his record, in which he is simply said to be "veering away from the borderline of schizophrenia," but still "anxiety-ridden" (Rubin [1961] 1998, 74). Do these two accounts connect? Similarly, according to her final update, Lisa "continues to be hyperactive" and to "demonstrate inappropriate affect." Her "hiding in closets" has not diminished (68), but the notes do not reflect that in talking to David, she made clear her understanding that the split selves of her schizophrenia are both "her," a signal advance in her rejection of the invading schizophrenic thoughts that forced her into mindlessly repetitive behavior intended to keep them at bay.

Absent from the notes is any mention of the other breakthrough moments prominently featured in the story. This intimate knowledge of the characters and their struggles is available only to the story's omniscient narrator, who is, as it were, "with them." Though deploying a considerable command of the facts that to him are relevant, and though making use of appropriate professional discourse, the reporting psychiatrist responsible for the notes shows himself ignorant of what is most human and uplifting in the characters' experience. His monologue about madness hardly connects with the "fictional" accounts, which, as Rubin surely means us to think, have more truth in them or, perhaps better, have more of a truth that most readers would find engaging and uplifting. Rubin's intent in juxtaposing these jarringly different texts can hardly have been other than to problematize the value of the facts and reasoned inferences uncovered by the medical gaze, which he himself deployed in his hospital work, an interesting account of which he provides in *Shrink! The Diary of a Psychiatrist* (1974). As he confesses, "There are times I feel that scientific diagnostic categories are mainly used to separate and protect doctors from feeling like patients" (130). Just so, "Lisa and David" incorporates his doubts about a psychiatry that was too concerned with taxonomy and professional distance.

The Perrys' Version

In contrast to the story, *David and Lisa* abjures Rubin's critique of his own professionalism by ignoring it. In Rubin's formally complex version of the characters, they occupy a liminal space between two opposed ways of accounting for who they are. The film, in contrast, provides access to their private moments while locating them securely in an anti-institutional institution that is more home than asylum, a space where comity can do the work that, in Rubin's view, therapists can only assist, never direct. The place of collective refuge assumes a concrete form that it does not have in the source text, and, suiting the mild antiauthoritarianism of the treatment offered there, it speaks a fierce oppositionality to the Stalinist functionalism of the "modern" medical center.

The community of fellow sufferers, brought together by chance, plays a thoroughly unscripted role even more crucial than that of the genial and unassuming therapist, who is satisfied by his roles as concerned bystander and occasional source of insight in one-on-one sessions, both formal and informal. In the manner of an international art film, and closely following the story portion of its source, *David and Lisa* offers a study in character, with major Freudian themes (the death instinct, the castrating mother, transference) making predictable appearances, to provide atmosphere rather than intellectual depth. Lisa is too isolated in her repetitive behaviors and fear of Muriel to participate in therapy with Swinford, but when David shows a polite interest in her, she is immediately drawn to him. Largely nonverbal and trapped in childlike repetitive behaviors, including speaking in rhymes (a regime she imposes on others talking to her), she attracts only limited dramatic interest, given the absence of a narrator who can chronicle and explain her inner life. Her most affecting scenes are largely silent. Perry's camera observes her discovery that masturbation can be soothing, in a scene that is tasteful but unambiguous, a faithful version of the story's exploration of how Lisa comes to know herself.

An explanation of sorts for her illness emerges in two other sequences.

As the group from the center waits in the local station for a train to take them to the city museum for a field trip, Lisa engages with a young child who is sitting on a bench with her parents. In so doing, she violates the unwritten social law about keeping her distance. Her conduct is inappropriate but not threatening; she does not understand the family's discomfort at her intrusion, and a staff member must gently get Lisa to move away. Turning toward the patients as he retreats outside with his wife and daughter, the father viciously blurts out, "Bunch of screwballs ruining the town," giving them the chance, angrily and defiantly, to taunt him with his own words, thus affirming the solidarity of the group. Later that day, at the museum, fascinated by the life-size statue of a family group, Lisa curls up onto the mother's lap and must be gently removed by treatment center staff. A desire for maternal comfort, even if the parent is cold stone, prompts her unauthorized return, as mentioned above, providing David the opportunity to rescue her and, with the same gesture, assert control over his own fear.

Intelligent, voluble, and combative, but well mannered when he chooses to be, David is by far the more focused character. The story of the treatment center begins with him when he arrives, accompanied by his mother, and, with some fearfulness, manages to settle into a new routine. His courage is mixed with no little desperation, as eventually becomes clear. David is forced to return home some months later by his mother, who resents that he is finally learning how to stand up to her. But unable to stand the emotional blankness of life at home, he soon runs off back to the center. At first he is isolated by the rage he barely holds in check, expressed not only in sudden outbursts when he feels threatened but also in off-putting arrogance with his peers and the staff. His superior intellect gives him no comfort, however, and in a private moment after a particularly haughty outburst, he floods out into bitter weeping. A series of scenes with his parents (an addition to the screenplay) shows him at the mercy of an overbearing mother (Neva Patterson) and a father (Richard MacMurray) who, after having been emotionally absent during his childhood, now has no idea how he might connect with his son. Swinford helps David understand how his anger is positive, an expression of his healthy desire to be free of his mother. It is easy enough to criticize these themes and representations as simplistic and barely connected with what is now received scientific opinion about autism. On one level, in fact, *David and Lisa* can be read as yet another screen representation of Momism, the notion, popularized by Philip Wylie in the 1940s, that a national cult of overbearing motherhood was impeding the maturation of the nation's young men (Wylie 1942). What is clear, however, is that the film reflects the general project of 1950s neo-Freudianism's optimism about human possibility.

With Swinford's help, David comes to realize that his fears of intimacy are linked with the horror he feels at the prospect of his inevitable death, while his desire for control finds expression in a repetitive dream in which he executes his enemies with a bladelike "hand" as their heads show through a clock face. Fortunately, this treatment center is where "the language of psychiatry" becomes more than "a monologue by reason *about* madness." "Imperfect words" about mental illness can indeed be spoken there, and in the context of an untheorized discourse that focuses on feelings and actions, never pretending to a dominating knowledge (Foucault 1967, xix). The film's elliptical, unstructured style perfectly matches the center's loosely supervised, unmedicated (even though mood-altering chlorpromazine had been introduced in 1950), family-style treatment, designed for a small cadre of adolescents (the sons and daughters of privilege, with the exception of one on financial aid). All suffer from the range of schizophrenic symptoms that only fifty years before (1911) had been labeled collectively as autism by Eugen Bleuler. The Swiss psychiatrist coined the term (*aut* = "self") to emphasize the isolating social dysfunctionality that was the condition's most notable and damaging symptom. The film features no discourse about autism, its diagnosis, or treatment. The condition is presented by indirection.

A Therapeutic Milieu

Rubin's imagination of such a therapeutic milieu, as it had come to be formally known by the 1950s, is very much in line with, and surely in some sense dependent on, the theories that had been developed since the early 1930s by Moreno, who saw human nature as defined more deeply by spontaneity and creativity than by the instinctual forces adduced in Freudian theorizing or the materialist "facts" promoted by Marx. For Moreno, whose reformulation of the Freudian therapeutic paradigm led him to theorize and promote both group therapy and psychodrama, successful living is possible only through love and compassion, a view of human possibility—and free will—that his most recent biographer admires equivocally as hopelessly utopian (see Moreno 1947 for a discussion of his social utopianism; see Nolte 2014 for a detailed discussion of his critique of Freudian instinctualism). In Moreno's concept of human nature, the "now" and the personal, the feeling-inspiring encounter is all, with spontaneity providing the creative energy for self-fashioning, which is decontextualizing (or identity shedding), and not only for instincts or economic relations. Being is a continual discovery in Moreno's view, with true community as the ultimate, admittedly idealistic goal, as he argues in an intellectually ambitious monograph, *The Future of Man's World* (1947). The psychodrama that Moreno pioneered as a form of individual and group therapy (in which improvisation plays a crucial role) gave patients the opportunity to reimagine themselves spontaneously and free of the material facts of their lives. Their identities abandoned, if only temporarily, participants could work out their conflicts in another form and then, as it were, put themselves together again.

A similar decontextualization shapes Perry's evocation of the therapeutic milieu in *David and Lisa*, compromising the film's relationship to screen realism. On one hand, the Perrys adopt a documentary approach—the film's principal location was a more or less unprepared existing building. (The use of a real property was to some degree a reflection of the project's very limited budget.) This approach, however, afforded access to only what could be dramatized. A different aesthetic choice was made in the presentation of several notable dream sequences that make use of elaborate special effects and a noirish stylization in framing, lighting, and sound and music accompaniment. Overall, however, the film is largely shot in the plain black-and-white style of other dramas of the period from the New York school, and it compares interestingly to Shirley Clarke's *The Cool World* (1963) and Sidney Lumet's *The Pawnbroker* (1965), as well as to Frank Perry's own *Lady Bug Lady Bug* (1963). Paradoxically, though, the fictional world that the film creates, using the "real" as material, is emptied of any detailing that would fix its identity in social space and time.

David and Lisa opens with a striking and complex establishing shot that presages the movement the narrative will take away from the paralyzing mental disorder (a fact of individual nature) toward the coziness of compassionate community (in which concern for others can emerge). Over the credits, Perry's restless camera executes a long upward pan through winter-bare hardwood trees, finding their twisted branches black and mysteriously threatening as they are framed by a bleak and cloudless sky and the eeriness of Mark Lawrence's atonal score. This free-floating image then discovers a specific location, as what comes into view in the distance are the upper stories of a Victorian mansion, perhaps a century or more old. The camera tilts down to reveal the building's considerable architectural heft. Its elaborately decorative exterior, the work of stonemasons and carpenters, was once meant to impress, but in the context of the film's early-1960s moment appears anachronistic, a legacy from a bygone era whose relevance in the film's present moment emerges only when the building's repurposing is revealed as the residential treatment center where the story's action unfolds.

Though made present, this striking building is neither named nor identified by an onscreen chyron. It is not shown to be part of a residential neighborhood. No fence surrounds it. Reached by a complex camera movement and not by characters who start out from somewhere, it occupies a kind of narrative no-place that can be defined by the interactions of patients and staff. With its perhaps sinister musical accompaniment, this image seems a deliberate evocation of the horror genre and its recent, startling reinvention in Alfred Hitchcock's *Psycho* (1960), a film in which a lonely Victorian house, haunted by unusual avenging spirits, becomes the scene for the continuing murderous reenactment of toxic family relations. If in this opening sequence of *David and Lisa* there is at first a continuity in tone between the wild woods and the isolated ancient house, that sense of its fearfulness is soon dispelled, since the house is located within the larger ambit of what Foucault calls the "great confinement," the officially sanctioned separation of those deemed mentally ill from society at large that occurred at the beginning of the modern age. The house does not present as part of any organized system of separation, however. No signage is visible, and not one of the characters ever gives this place a label that might point toward affiliation, institutional purpose, or ownership. Once the camera is afforded access to its interior spaces, the house shows itself to be a home of sorts, with a lived-in, homey ambience that stands in stark contrast to the antiseptic aura of the modern hospital. Even its general location, beyond placement in a fictionalized version of US space, remains unrevealed throughout the film (although the curious viewer can judge that from its old-money, Gilded Age aura, this house is to be found in some Main Line suburb).

This abstractionism, it is clear, can only be seen as carefully intentional, an attempt to avoid the "true story" resonance of Hollywood's most famous previous presentation of psychiatric success, Nunnally Johnson's *The Three Faces of Eve* (1957), which enjoyed a substantial success at the box office and with the critics. In its attempt to render plausible a tale of multiple personality disorder, *Eve* summons up an onscreen witness, the journalist Alistair Cooke, whose cultural authority was beyond reproach and who enthusiastically attests to the truthfulness of the story that follows. Cooke affirms that this perhaps unlikely tale of multiple personality disorder is based on an accurate version of an actual case, whose details he briefly describes, anticipating its carefully documented dramatization, with some sequences shot in the relevant "true" locations. Converted from master of ceremonies to voice-of-God narrator once the story proper begins, Cooke comments at regular intervals throughout to identify the date, time, and place of the events being dramatized, stitching together a complex story whose medical twists and turns he carefully explains, providing the ostensibly accurate detail that one might expect of an actual case history, which in fact it is.

The source of *Eve*'s script was a case study written by Johnson in collaboration with the two psychiatrists who worked on the case, Hervey Cleckley and Corbett Thigpen (Thigpen and Cleckley 1957). With the director's help (he even provided the very unscientific title), they turned the case study into a best-selling book, whose screen rights Johnson had obtained before it was even finished. In a later and unanticipated reality effect, "Eve" unmasked herself, eventually publishing three accounts offering the therapeutic victory she had in some sense won, and attesting to the general truth of the book and screen versions. Importantly, the former patient filled in some of the story's darker corners, particularly the sense of the "cure" that Johnson's script somewhat distortingly provides in service of Hollywood's need for a credible and satisfying happy ending. We might add that Eve's embrace of self-actualization and her choice of a healthy relationship with others as she abandons an abusive marriage to couple with a more supportive and socially appropriate partner—goals for the direction of her life that emerge from therapy—suit perfectly both the neo-Freudian agenda of the therapeutic moment and Hollywood's need to confirm conservative social values. The film promotes marriage as the social arrangement best suited for the satisfaction of female sexuality, countering the disturbing revelations of Kinsey's report on American women, which was released to great controversy in 1953 while the film project was in the early stages of development (for further discussion, see Palmer 2020).

In complete contrast, the script for *David and Lisa* does not claim that the story is true, that it is based on an actual case (which it is not), although the original story presumably makes use of Rubin's clinical experience. So powerful is Perry's documentary stylization and use of actual locations that some viewers might have been led to believe that *David and Lisa* is a lightly fictionalized version of Rubin's own founding of, and work for, an innovative treatment center for autistic adolescents. But this space of healing is not based on an actual institution, as is the case in *Eve* (which includes location footage of the Medical College of Georgia, in Augusta, where Cleckley and Thigpen taught and whose facilities they used for their private practice).

To be seduced by the formal realism of *David and Lisa* is to ignore the film's carefully curated essential quality: its abstract aura, achieved by the total suppression and, one presumes, excision of context-orienting details, those markers of the real known to narratologists as "effects," which, in their apparently accidental randomness, attest to the not completely planned nature of the story world. The treatment center is not connected with the outside except in regard to those connections that must be acknowledged. A patient must have parents, and they must appear if their effect on his mental health can be calibrated by the viewer. But where is their house? If the group of patients is to go on a field trip, the destination must be some seemingly significant somewhere. Beyond these slight acknowledgments of some sort of social space beyond the front porch of the treatment center, however, the film depicts a world of almost complete mystery. No television provides orienting updates. No radio plays the songs of the moment, because there is no moment for them to reference. The film's "scene" is the American present, to judge from clothing, hairstyles, and accents as well as other marks of the perdurable real. A film must reference a "now," but in this vision of healing togetherness, the present is of the most minimal sort that the filmmakers might manage to confect. Contemporary events or people in the news rate no mention. The conversations in the treatment center do not include even an offhand comment about the local world that must lie beyond the empty sector dominated by the house, and from which the patients and staff have in some sense come. Even the Museum of Art, one of Philadelphia's most famous landmarks, is not identified;[1] exterior shots of the building avoid its signage and the distinctive staircase leading to the main entrance, thereby refusing to place it in its distinctive urban setting or to detail how the group of students makes its way there after arriving by train from an unmarked station. Such ellipses are so thoroughgoing that they demand a deeper aesthetic explanation. Like the house, the museum and the train station are self-evidently real, as the camera bears witness, but the film's suppression of what we might call locative or reportorial truth, though it does not rob these realia of authenticity, renders them general rather than particular. The effect is to turn the story into something like a fable, enabling it to convey something beyond the limits of the veridical, since viewers are asked to believe that the spirits of the mind can be quieted, even if not dismissed. The screenwriter and the director found such decontextualizing generalization so effective that they deployed it again in *The Swimmer,* their 1968 adaptation of a John Cheever short story, a poignant recounting of moral deterioration and mental collapse in which the withholding of orienting locative details blurs for the viewer the shifting line that separates delusion from sanity.

"Lisa and David" trades in the same kind of referential haziness prominent in the film version's affect—a sense of time out of time in a fictional space that merits little if any description and whose particularity is thus, by implication, dismissed as having no real importance. The screen adaptation promotes a kind of context-free idealization of a reality-derived diegetic world where there might be staged fantasies of "cures" for autism. If fiction can dispense with setting, film must deploy images within a place, which must be more than implied. This venerable dwelling, then, is yet another mystery, located at the edge of some woods where barren and randomly shaped limbs speak some kind of message, but where no other signs of human habitation are seen. Though never named, the house is quickly established as an asylum, that is, a place inviolable, safe from violence, beyond the reach of other authorities, never identified by the semiotics of a fully professionalized medical establishment.

It is nonetheless a place where specialized knowledge can be applied to bodies and minds in need of healing. But in tone and practice, in the kinds of relations that it creates and fosters, this repurposed residence offers a domestic ambience suited to the therapeutic purpose the film has been assigned.

The postwar psychoanalytic films (and this one is no exception) inevitably reflect the neo-Freudian atmosphere of early-1960s American theory and practice. In its revisionist deployment of Freudian ideas, this nexus of theory and increasingly widespread practice was heavily influenced by Karen Horney's emphasis on social rather than instinctual accounts of human nature, which could be transformed into advice for living that was made available to the general reader. In a number of books, Rubin contributed to this popularizing professional initiative. The most important of these was *The Angry Book* (1969), with its meditations on the avoidance of the "sick emotional climate" characteristic of modern, especially American, culture (Rubin [1969] 1998, 24).

Horney's best-selling *Self-Analysis* (1942) advocated forcefully for the kind of individual adjustment that David is shown achieving. Her work reflected and recapitulated themes and modes of analysis and self-healing that have been prominent in Western thought from Lucretius to St. Augustine, Marcus Aurelius to Descartes, a project in which she was followed by other theorists and practitioners in the United States during the 1950s and 1960s, including two of the Frankfurt school's most notable exponents, Erich Fromm and Herbert Marcuse. This Pelagian vision of an untrammeled, self-directed human drive for fulfillment needs to be awakened and nurtured in those hampered by many sorts of psychological dysfunction, of which autism, with its thwarting of the natural drive toward sociability, would be most challenging to overcome. Jacob Moreno and his acolytes, including Theodore Rubin, imagined group therapy, and its ancillary forms such as psychodrama and the residential milieu, as sites of dynamic interaction that would give full play to spontaneity and creativity, in the process fostering a health-restoring drive for interpersonal connection. In the film's finale, that goal is movingly symbolized by the joining of hands as

David and Lisa find in each other a solace not provided by their dysfunctional families.

No film Hollywood produced during the period offers a more comprehensive picture of the neo-Freudian project than *David and Lisa*, with its optimistic dependence on the informed self (a heritage from the Enlightenment and, more distantly, from philosophical traditions like Stoicism) to effect, if not a cure for the painful isolation and fearful loneliness that torment the autistic, then at least an amelioration of symptoms, and this to be achieved with no pharmacological intervention. In the film, sociability is not only the means, but also the end of the therapeutic journey, with acceptance of separation from the family (and its predictable lack of nurturance) understood as the sign of maturity even as another form of comity, born from the group experience, takes its place. This happy ending, however, is achieved through a significant silence. If the impression of that final scene, from which the psychiatrist is excluded, is that the young man has taken charge of Lisa and himself, the fact remains that they will presumably need to return to the treatment center, where their prospects for anything like a cure (whatever form that might assume) are less than certain, but must inevitably flow from the application of science.

Theodore Rubin composed a text in which the wish for therapeutic victory could be figured, as it is in the film, through an empathetic narrative that collapses the necessary distance between doctor and patient, but that account was juxtaposed with the medical judgment that any achievement of normality for the two was at present unimaginable. The film makes no room for this sobering reality, which measures the sad distance between therapeutic desire and the facticity of disorder, which is at some level simply the human condition. Finally, what we are given is a dream that things are better.

Note

1. Recent exhaustive attempts to find records there (and at Philadelphia's Rodin Museum) of the sculpture that Lisa climbs onto have proved fruitless.

CHAPTER 19

Jesse: Torture That Autist

MURRAY POMERANCE

This is an attempt to point out some interesting features of a visual narrative for which a collaboration was made to offer a portrait of a central autistic character over and above the already exciting plot. The plot is a conventional type, while the autist is not. The point of the program material I analyze is, bluntly, that the distinctive qualities of the autist are at least as important to consider as, if not more so than, the story points—which make clear that this person as a person comes first. That is also the deep point of this chapter: no matter what the discursive mind might like to say about them, autists and their experience must be understood as paramount, in the same sense and in much the same way that anybody and their experience should take precedence over calculating theorizations. It happens that the show received raves from widespread audiences, this alone suggesting that a form of visual narrative with the courage to frame but then step aside from a plot need not be considered a failure in advance.

.   .   .

There is a chasm between the appearance we make to others and the feeling we keep to ourselves. At each instant, we sense and know ourselves to be what we are, while others read us through the logic of their own experience. Could I somehow share aspects of another person's experience, my reading of him might gain considerable sympathy. But when reacting to an autist, most observers do not share his internal world. He has inexplicable trouble with "things" that non-autists don't even notice, his reactions and hesitations are off-key, he is especially prone to being thought "strange," "not like us," "extreme." But when an autist is central to a visual narrative, his experience must be made accessible through image and sound, lest he be nothing more than a moving lacuna. Autism then becomes a collection of (sometimes repeated) signals, whereas for the autist it is experience, plain and simple.

Autistic persons frequently have extreme sensitivity to sound (especially high-pitched treble), and are virtually incapable of not hearing (while many people filter sound effortlessly). Echoes, loud music, and even persistent, possibly rhythmic small local sounds—all these can be unneglectable, sometimes painful. Autists require pattern, order, and stability around them, in the way that fish require water; garble, confusion, chaos, discoordination, logical inconsistency—all these are disarming and confusing on a very deep level. Autists tend to have a compromised ability (if any at all) to decipher ambiguities or latent subtleties of meaning, to follow tacit "game rules" salient to others: they may thus be unable to perceive sarcasm, sly wit, nuances of etiquette. And there is often—especially among high-functioning autists—notable visual talent, because they organize their perceptions and thoughts as pictures. In not reading between the lines, autists can easily appear to have social difficulties. Some autists have trouble looking other people in the eye (see Robison 2008). Most people who have neither been diagnosed as autistic nor taken such a diagnosis into their worldview systematically fail to see how a situation they think "normal" could give someone trouble. Yet autism is no affliction, no disability, no disease: it is a condition of life susceptible to the press of an unfavorable prevailing social organization.

Just as the autist's experience is elusive for friends and associates, dramatic depictions of it can elude the viewer. Even when achieved with the most exacting care and sensitivity, a portrait may not register with non-autistic audiences who don't notice what autists in the same audience see immediately. Discussion of an autistic representation in film or television, or on the stage, can involve two discrete levels of appreciation: What does the autist's behavior signify about his or her experience that would not be retrieved absent the signification? And how does the portrayal advance a state of affairs, sequence by sequence, so that a plot can unfold?

I choose to look carefully at a central character in six opening scenes of Shelley Birse's 2014 Australian police thriller *The Code*. How does the series show an autistic life? Series dramas tend to use characters as motors for moving audiences through a plot, but *The Code* is unique in its profoundly revealing portrait of Jesse Banks, limned far beyond the precincts of the central story. Ashley Zukerman's portrayal of what Birse carefully scripted is a brilliant, indeed superlative example of how an autistic personality can be dramatized. (Zukerman, an Australian born in Los Angeles, won the Australian Academy of Cinema and Television Arts award for best actor for it.) Numerous pointedly difficult challenges for the autist are set out for nuanced exposition in the show. A further twist on my exploration: by communicating with the writer and more fully with the performer, I was given the opportunity to move past the filmed surface of Jesse Banks's being toward the private territory of his sensibility—to whatever extent the actor who plays him *is* the character being played (for more on this topic, see Pomerance 2019).

· · ·

Ned and Jesse Banks (Dan Spielman, Ashley Zukerman) live in a small house in Canberra. Jesse is about twenty-six. His brother has been caring for him since the boy was diagnosed as being on the spectrum (long before we meet them). Ned sticks by Jesse's side, morally and geographically, tending to his brother's needs whenever Jesse becomes so tied up in a project that he forgets about the everyday world. Ned is employed as a reporter for *Password*, an online news publication, a job perhaps beneath his merit. Jesse, who, for unexplained reasons, is forbidden to surf the net, has a job serving food out of a kebab truck. Spielman offers Ned as thoughtful, gentle, sincere, affectionate, and committed to his brother. Jesse is blazingly intelligent, wry, keenly analytical, and passionate, not to say purposive, as well as innocently attractive (a clear love interest as well as a clear mystery). At the keyboard he is a genius. The computer is his teddy bear. In the story, his interpretations of screen data show him at a most advanced level of competence.

I move here to set out scenes and provide analytical comment, occasionally interpolating comments from Shelley Birse and Ashley Zukerman taken from my conversations with them in May and June 2020. I break the scenes with flag numbers that match the comments below each.

Episode 1: Jesse's First Scene—The Brothers

Across the Molonglo River on Canberra's Waterloo Bridge, Ned is chauffeuring Jesse to work, as always. Jesse fiddles with an air vent: [1] "There's a leaf in there. It's making a very . . . like a phft, phft, phft. It's really, I don't know, disconcerting." Momentarily distracted, [2] Ned misses an exit; Jesse stews; and Ned, warning, "Just this once you're gonna have to be late," heads for the capitol instead. Jesse is red faced with self-containment, [3] fearing to be late for his job under any circumstances. Parking, Ned issues a [4] very explicit instruction:

> NED: Don't get out of the car. Don't talk to anyone. Just stay in the car.
> [5] JESSE (robotically): "Don't get out of the car. Stay in the car." You're making the same point twice. Not ideal in your line of work.
> NED: Stay in the car.
> JESSE: One more for good luck.

Alone now, Jesse withdraws from his knapsack a sealed box addressed to Dr. Enid Shore in Canberra and loaded with postage stamps. He is determined to get this out of his hands. [6] "Dr. Enid Shore. Enid Shore. Enid Shore. Thing. Sure thing, Enid. To be sure, Enid." Box in hand, he steps out of the car.

Ned is summoned from his press conference because outside, armed police have surrounded Jesse, screaming that he should put his hands on his head and put down the box. The situation rapidly escalates. Ned seizes the thing—"Sir!! Do not touch the box!!!"—and empties it: pills, pills, and pills. Jesse is on his knees, trembling. Back in the car together:

> [7] JESSE (straightforwardly): You're angry at me, aren't you.
> NED: I told you to stay in the car, didn't I? Didn't I say that, "Stay in the car"?
> JESSE (straightforwardly): Yeah.

Ned touches his brother [8] affectionately on the back of the neck while Jesse gets his breath, calms down. Why has Jesse decided to send his medication back? "I don't like it."

> NED: [9] Haven't we been through this a hundred times? You can't just decide to stop taking it.
> JESSE (meekly): Yeah. . . . Are you finished? . . . I'm 67 minutes late for work.

Here and throughout, the script is written to both motor the story line forward without neglecting Jesse's condition in his relationship with Ned. Birse: "I passionately wanted, as much as possible, the characters to drive and the plot to follow." Plot clues are dropped periodically, with accelerating tempo, as Jesse becomes clearer, to a depth. Birse's pledge was to not sacrifice Jesse's character in maintaining the narrative logic. "We rarely spoke to one another," Zukerman said. "It was her writing that spoke to me." The design of the show is that instead of being "shown" autism (through a character's or narrator's diagnostic vision), we live with it. What can we learn, living through this scene, by which I mean, what can we pick up if, like an autist, perhaps, we are attentive?

- [1] Fluttering vent. Jesse's attentiveness is fastidious and acute (one leaf, conventionally negligible, focuses him). He is easily irritated by the "insignificant," muttering his complaint with a quiet confidence. In typical dramatic scriptings, autistic characters stress their oddity, proclaiming themselves unique, but Zukerman gives Jesse expressive boldness only when he is in extremis.
- [2] "Just this once." Ned is intimating that he stretches a long way to make sure Jesse is never late for anything. (Jesse is forever time sensitive.) The message doesn't seem to get across.
- [3] Late. Being late for work is a limiting act for Jesse. To play this anxious instant and others, Zukerman (who is not on the spectrum, as far as he knows) found himself developing a deep commitment to the order and structure that he knew autists want. For him, "That went in parallel but not intersecting with an incredibly complicated six-episode show in a nine-week shooting schedule. The fact that it was a thriller made it very clear to me that every scene had to lead to the next scene." He needed for his part of the production to have order. "It was through that that I drew this map of the entire show." Birse remembered "visiting him in his trailer some way into the production and finding it wallpapered with every single moment, in every single scene of every single episode." Zuker-

man said, "I took photographs of the set and inhabited it as we were shooting. *This is all just too big for my mind.* I had these six scripts that I carried around with me, and I had a very limited time to get my head around the whole story."

- [4] "Stay in the car." Clarity and precision, not condescension: the direct and unambiguous speech that Jesse requires.
- [5] Ned's repetition: "Don't get out . . . stay in." Repetition not because Jesse needs emphasis—he knows the routine. It is Ned's neurotic tic, which Jesse here "echoes" with affectionate mockery. Ned may not be autistic, but he also isn't perfect. Jesse knows Ned is speaking out of compulsiveness, not because he thinks Jesse is forgetful. "Don't talk to anyone": a script hint at Jesse's easy distractability, as with the fluttering leaf. His magnetized attention can be drawn by anything. Zukerman said, "I was always occupied by whatever was most intriguing. I can notice that enough in myself that I can exploit it in Jesse."
- [6] Enid. Jesse plays, especially with verbal construction. "Sure thing, Enid." "Enid," instead of "Dr. Enid Shore": no obsequious respect for authority here.
- [7] Angry at me: An angry Ned would certainly disturb Jesse, certainly touch a nerve. "I entered the series thinking Ned was the protagonist and I'm the antagonist, and that aided me in being able to feed off him. And I thought that his journey was one of needing to grow . . . For Ned, Jesse was both the problem and the solution, and Jesse needed Ned to be free of that. There's something going on for Ned that I [Jesse] don't understand. . . . He's going through conflict about me, he's held up his own career . . . he uses Jesse as an excuse. . . . I don't understand why *I* have to bear the burden of Ned's frustration."
- [8] Touch. The vital need between the brothers for concrete, wholly unambiguous, unmissable signals of affection, coupled with agreement and comprehension, such as the neck rub. Jesse *feels* Ned's feeling, proximity, and assurance. Zukerman on working with Spielman (whom he knew before the show but had not worked with): "We made a decision, the second day if not the first day, to *never touch.* Touch was something Ned instinctually wanted to use (to control or to convey information) and I instinctively repelled touch as the sensation was too strong. He keeps trying to touch me in the show." The specific touch was soothing—Zukerman and I agreed, perhaps a stimming from when Jesse was young.
- [9] Meds. It isn't really a hundred times they have been through this: Ned, the writer, is a language user, able to exaggerate for making a point. The drug prescriptions and Jesse's dislike of the side effects are a

frequent topic of conversation. (Jesse has been on and off drug therapy for a considerable time. "For anxiety disorder," said Zukerman, "there's no meds.")

In this scene, then, we catch Jesse's attitude to his medications while catching his marshaled anxiety, linguistic precision, sensitivity to sound, and penchant for rational order. A very complex character. A relatively brief scene.

Episode 1: Jesse's Second Scene—The Job

Jesse is serving at the food truck when Hani (Adele Perovic) approaches the window, smiling his way. "No—this is not good. You can't be here. . . . More specifically, [10] I'm not allowed to talk to you." (Clearly, Hani is part, perhaps a key part, of Jesse's "before.") Behind her a man interrupts. He wants a wrap with light cheese:

JESSE (helpful and direct, though still drawn to Hani, to whom he "cannot" talk): We have ordinary cheese.

MAN: I can't have ordinary cheese. I'm on a strict regime.

JESSE (still helpful, then dismissive): [11] Perhaps you don't need cheese at all??? Or even the kebab?

MAN: I beg your pardon, fuckhead!

JESSE (in riposte): Well perhaps you and all those people who asked for light cheese on your stupidly [12] unhealthy kebab on Thursday need to wake up and pass on the experience altogether . . . [13] fuckhead. (*Jesse is taken aside by the owner and summarily fired.*) (*To the owner, calmly:*) I do [14] everything my contract says I'm required to do.

OWNER (calmly): Yeah, but it doesn't [15] say in your contract that you can tell people what they should and shouldn't eat.

JESSE (fighting both the tension of the situation and confusion about the prevailing "rules of the game"): [16] Am I meant to lie to them? Because I don't remember it saying that.

OWNER (with some embarrassment): I'll need the . . . uniform . . . back. (*Jesse strips off the T-shirt.*) I . . . I didn't mean right now.

JESSE (placidly): [17] Well, it doesn't make sense that I would wear it home in order to take it off then bring it back. (*Offering his hand without rancor:*) I'm sorry I wasn't able to meet your expectations. (*The owner is worried that Jesse won't be allowed on the bus dressed like that, but Hani offers a T-shirt of hers.*)

CUT TO the Banks house, where, entering, Ned sees objects flying around this way and that and discovers Jesse in serious consternation (and wearing Hani's T-shirt, which is small on him):

JESSE: Where is it??? I lost my job tonight. Not directly but ultimately as a result of your lateness. And for some reason (*He is spitting out his words in desperation, red faced, strained to the maximum.*), I can't even begin to get my head around the idea of losing my [18] stupid moronic, could-be-done-by-a-fucking-monkey job! And having to look for another stupid, moronic, could-be-done-by-a-fucking-monkey job is making me feel stressed. . . . As you well know, Ned, stress is the enemy of . . . calm.

NED (a simple fact): You can't have the modem, Jesse.

JESSE (crying): Why are you being an arsehole, Ned. You know that half an hour online, [19] doing something real, and the stress will be gone. (*Touches his chest and shoulder.*)

Informative content:

- [10] No talking to Hani. The writer knowingly doesn't say how Jesse was involved with this girl and why he has been enjoined from talking to her about specific matters. Hani might be dangerous for Jesse, at least under some conditions; Jesse may have been in trouble with the law. Who is not doing the allowing, we have not yet learned.

- [11] Perhaps no cheese? As a cook and a server, Jesse is being entirely polite and servile, merely helping a customer with a dietary requirement. But his pleasant smile and direct (sincere) gaze are (far too easily) misread as insolence, resulting in a sneering rejoinder in which he is called a fuckhead. (A fuckhead: someone who has no active intelligence; someone whose only concern is mindless pleasure. For Jesse, this is a contextually confusing insult.)

- [12] Unhealthy kebab. Offering back a less aggressive insult, Jesse generalizes to "you and all those people," suggesting that even though the man's food order is not very healthy, he is there to serve it.

- [13] "Fuckhead." But then, as ornamentation (for the viewer, delightfully unexpected), he volleys back the insult verbatim. Effectively: "I speak English, too, and also jargon, and I can use the word 'fuckhead' just as well as you can, which means, let's subtract that out and see what this conversation is really all about."

- [14] Everything my contract says. Jesse isn't denying responsibility; he is calmly affirming the legal arrangement that he agreed to in taking the job, the "rules," as he understands them, and showing that he realizes how, even with a low-level service job like this one, fundamental human relations are in play and that people make arrangements (formally or casually) in getting involved with one another. He signed a contract, and a contract means something.

- [15] Doesn't say in your contract. The owner shows real respect for Jesse's intelligence, a serious commitment to speaking to him on equal terms—in effect, acknowledging that yes, you are doing what you are told to do, but you are also, right now, going beyond what you were told to do. Going beyond could be seen as violating the contract.
- [16] To lie? Jesse won't give up yet. He knows that pumping out unhealthy kebabs could be seen as baiting and luring an innocent public, even though the customer "is always right" and he misspoke.
- [17] T-shirt. Jesse exhibits impeccable logic in giving over the shirt, but he will have trouble on the bus. Jesse sincerely doesn't catch the logic—beyond the spurious modesty of covering oneself (in a subtropical climate)—in trundling all over the place just to remove a shirt inside his home (and then, worse, having to come back to this now somewhat unpleasing site to hand it back). Solve the problem now, here, one-two-three, and be done with it. (Hani both helps him and comes on to him just a little when she puts her shirt on his body.)
- [18] Stupid, moronic, could-be-done-by-a-fucking-monkey job. Built-up anger at the blunt stupidity of the social arrangements we often make. Not, "I am smarter than this," but instead, "Nobody should have to put up with this kind of nonsense." Jesse has felt this anger before. It has stewed.
- [19] Doing something real. For Jesse, surfing is real; fixing kebabs isn't.

A scene showing intolerance of ambiguity in language; a refusal to accept reading between the lines of a contract or a conversation; a grudging recognition of the existence of "official" though invisible rules; having a serious work ethic. A formal game is in play in this scene, but Jesse isn't playing. (And it isn't a game about Jesse and Hani and romance: there were plenty of other ways she could have been introduced.)

Episode I: Jesse's Third Scene—The Video

A road accident has occurred in the outback town of Lindara, and Ned has been sent a corrupted video file taken by a victim. He stands behind Jesse, who is at the computer: "Can you open it?"

Jesse says [20] there might be an error in the video compression. He might be able to fix it, [21] "but I would need to get online." An anxious face as he takes Ned's thumb drive: "It would be easier for me if you'd . . . [22] go to another room."

All Ned wants is a hint of their chances: "Snowflake's chance in hell, or better than even?" Jesse, in an especially calm—his edgy—voice: "I don't know yet, [23] Little Ted." Give him an ice block (a Popsicle or ice pop) and he will get to work [24]. "And fish cakes. I want fish cakes, too." [25] Thumb thoughtfully in mouth, then fingers racing on the keys, with appropriately incomprehensible codes flashing onscreen. Visual garble. More fingers, more garble. [26] Still more fingers, garble separating into red, green, and blue layers. Examining the pixel ratios in all three: "Ned, um . . . , there's still a chunk in the middle missing, but—."

They watch, breath suspended.

A teenage girl in a vehicle, talking to a camera—possibly held by her boyfriend. A crash from behind. Ned's face freezes. "No!" she's screaming, "No! Please, stop it!" She can't feel her legs. Static. Boy's voice: "Run! Run! Run!" Ned is glued to the screen but Jesse has turned away in revulsion. "Please don't hurt me!" Jesse looks down [27], sharpening his hearing. Screen static. "Please! Please don't hurt me!" Static. "No! No, please stop! Let me out! Let me out!" Static, then a blue image of the girl trapped, then more static.

Ned gets up to email the file to his editor, but Jesse grabs the thumb drive. "I want a [28] reward. Thirty minutes, free play." Ned, forever the shepherd: Do you get what happens if they catch you again? "I get to spend some time in the big house with the bars on the windows. I won't hack. Cross my heart and hope to die. [29] I will surf. I will frolic in the cyber waves. I will be a virtual porpoise." Earnest expression, eyes open in supplication. His sweater has a patch of sea blue running from the top of each arm across the chest beneath his collar bone, so that as he sits before the screen his head vaguely appears to be popping out of the waves.

The series will offer much more to discover about the road accident, but it is Jesse who made our early viewing possible. He is no slaphappy computer nerd, but someone able to "clean up" a video record. That the accident is clearly a case of probable murder makes Jesse's *attention* a bridge between the "accident" and him as "cybergenius." If he is caught up with, even stunned by, the movie (the movie as series plot encapsulated), Jesse finds the computer itself far more vital.

- [20] Error in the video compression. The action could progress as written without Jesse noting this, but it is an upfront—and unboastful—

announcement of his prowess. "Video compression" is a professional term. Ned doesn't go to Jesse just out of brotherly love, then, but also because he is an unaccredited pro. From Birse's perspective, showing professional fingers on the keys prepares us to see codes and color separations and then the sketchy film itself, in a dramatic buildup.

- [21] "Need to get online." "Need" has a double meaning. Jesse isn't expressing taste or preference or curiosity; he is showing what he considers a natural drive. (He has made the computer universe a part of himself, his nervous system, his flesh.) But "need" also means, bluntly and technically, "I cannot help you unless I do it online; therefore, I will need you to get me online." A sidelight: Jesse means he is intending to use an online technology not available widely, to which he has special (password or hacked) access and which can accomplish digital maneuvers far beyond "normal" people's talent. Legal or not, he has a specific, dramatically irreplaceable skill, one embedded in his personality, regardless of its utility in this case of emergency. Jesse's personality and the series plot unified.

- [22] "Go to another room." Keyboard action is a kind of masturbation for Jesse or a stimming: self-generated limitless pleasure. To play with a mechanism so closely connected that one can feel it as embodied. For Jesse, being cut off from the keyboard (for any reason at all, however bound to legalities) is surgical.

- [23] "Little Ted." Affectionate put-down, a name he—probably he alone—feels free to use, it being clear that Jesse does not see his older brother as little at all. For Zukerman, "So much of what Jesse does is in aid of achieving a goal." Wordplay again: "little" = "big." Ted = Theodore = Ned. Ned recognizes the sarcasm but doesn't react; it is brotherly love. For Jesse, the delicacy of the sarcasm clarifies, but does not emphasize, its bite, increasing the chances that Ned will take the hint and leave the room.

- [24] Fish cakes. Jesse orders an ice block and fish cakes, junk food. Zukerman imagined Jesse thinking, "Not only did I get access to the Internet, I will now eat all the bad food I want." In short, "Jesse now has the power."

- [25] Thumb in mouth. A coup de grâce move. In many representations, the autist is infantilized; and computer savvy is thought the property of the very young. But Jesse uses self-touching for concentration, not regression. Jesse is feverishly embroiled in the programming tricks that will save the day here. Importantly, the show wants, in Birse's words, to "honor the skills of a different kind of heroism."

- [26] Color separations. Making color separations and checking their technical quality are very sophisticated actions. The separations make for a striking image, saturated and bright, the kind of presentation that would appeal to Jesse's penchant for pictures even as it hurls us forward with our penchant, too.
- [27] Looking away. Jesse knows that the image will be qualitatively worse than the soundtrack (bad video compression: his diagnosis), so he concentrates on the sound. Since he has trouble isolating stimuli—the world floods in—he blocks off what might otherwise, fruitlessly, be seen. Were he to see visual garble, he would hear garble, too: synesthesia.
- [28] Reward—free play. Zukerman reflected to me on the lure of the internet for Jesse: "He can completely interface to the full extremes of his mind. Full interaction, but not with people." Yet he knows, too, that although having worked hard, he has still not quite succeeded. "A seed was planted in his mind that this video had clues that didn't make sense, and he thought he could still figure out more. Finishing the task is more important to him than just the keyboard time."
- [29] Porpoise. A carefully chosen word (and for Jesse a semantic fillip): the porpoise is notably peaceable but also outstandingly intelligent, a perfect dream avatar—a balletic swimmer that effortlessly speeds forward in a vast area of freedom.

This scene shows Jesse's technical genius, highly elaborated visual sense, open admission of profound desire, and belief in a fair quid pro quo. It dramaturgically opens the "secret code" on which the show revolves, by way of Jesse's qualities and concerns. For a spectator, watching and listening to Jesse making his way through this puzzle on his screen, with his hungry eyes bulging and bright, is far more captivating than wondering what happened in Lindara.

Episode I: Jesse's Fourth Scene—The Port Scan Attack

As Ned urges his editor to publish an exclusive about the car crash, Jesse is alone at home, keyboarding with [30] lightning-fast fingers. Various red ACCESS DENIED flags. Then a blue ACCESS GRANTED. He moves forward [31] but soon sees a Network Alert sign: "Port Scan attack is logged." [32] He pauses, in macro close-up, steadfast concern on his face. "What the fuck?" (An assertion, not a question.) More typing, urgent. "Virus Alert. Antivirus has detected Trojan Backdoor on your system. The file was deleted." Deflation: "Oh shit, [*matter-of-factly*], they've got me." Typing anxiously now. [33] "Come on, come on, come on, come on, sometime today, please!" The screen shows a "Terminal/Bash" readout with a timeline racing rightward. He has snagged a file called Physanto. He quickly shoves his USB drive in ([34] camouflaged as a red Lego piece) and starts to copy the Physanto material. From the door behind him, suddenly: "Thirty minutes, uh?" Jesse swivels and [35] screams in shock:

JESSE: Why would you do that to me?

NED: This is your idea of being a virtual porpoise, is it? . . . Nothing to say?

JESSE (shouting): [36] These are all rhetorical questions, are they not? . . . (*While Ned sips a glass of water.*) Those kids in the car, they hit a truck. (*The two of them are watching the screen as the film plays back.*) I imported it using a different program which lets you advance a single frame at a time. (*We are paused on a close shot of a license plate: Y05963.*) You can see, uh, the license plate, so I went looking.

NED (in an assertive tone): You traced the truck?

JESSE: I did. Followed it back to a company in Canberra. That's who I was arguing with just now.

NED: What company?

JESSE: Um . . . Phs . . . Phs . . . Physinto? Physanto? [37]

NED: What do they do?

JESSE: I dunno. Research.

NED: Well, what research?

JESSE: I don't know. (*The copy is half-done.*) Come on!

NED: What are you doing?

JESSE (on the verge of tears): [38] When I was in there, in the system, someone, one of their security guys, saw me and somehow they managed to sneak into my hard drive and drop some malware.

NED: Why would they do that?

JESSE (in a questioning tone): To try and scare me. (*Talking faster and faster*) To have access to my computer, to track my activities. (*Ned frowns.*) So I gotta erase the whole system. (*Jesse bends over the keyboard, typing, but shakes his head.*) I don't feel so good. . . . Oh! (*He races into the kitchen and* [39] *throws up.*)

Ned rushes in behind Jesse, holds his head down patiently.

- [30] Fast fingers. Plot points and Jesse's autism come across together. He types program code at a whirlwind speed—this is both his physical experience revealing itself and a clue about how urgently forward progress is now needed. But the cue (in his posture) that we should heed the sound shares an important characteristic of Jesse's autism, his unparalleled acoustic sensitivity. We experience it. And soon it will become crucial.

- [31] Restricted access. Jesse has confronted access restrictions before (the reason for his arrest before the story began?). He cruises through these like a pro.
- [32] Steadfast concern. But something is beyond the kind of blocks he has encountered before. Plot point: he is facing an unconventional denial of access. Character point: he has taught himself to hack firewalls, but now that skill is thwarted. He is disabled, not just as a hacker but also as a person who wants shapes to be discernable and whole.
- [33] "Sometime today, please." At Jesse's speed, even a few seconds seem an eternity. (He moves at the speed of film, hitting twenty-four buttons a second.)
- [34] His Lego USB. Plot point: The USB is disguised, and may remain so for some time. Character point: A playful type and a genius, Jesse acquired the perfect key ring. Where better to secrete a USB than inside a toy, a red Lego piece? Easy to spot, but apparently nothing but a treasured keepsake. As for Jesse, we can easily imagine him as a child building spaceships out of Lego.
- [35] Shocked scream. Hypersensitive to sound, Jesse can't tolerate surprise. Do not approach him from behind.
- [36] Rhetorical questions. Snarky in a brotherly way, yet also irritating, since his diligent involvement in helping Ned far exceeded the ridiculous thirty-minute limit.
- [37] Physinto . . . Physanto. A musical mind in action: even the erroneous one has a structural similarity to the right name. But also a mind trusting that the file name will be available after the transfer. We might not have caught the name when it flashed, so the file name is for us.
- [38] The malware. This little speech has an entirely plot-centered function, since until this moment viewers less computer literate than Jesse have needed to be told what all those screen codes, warnings, and threats were. Some of the language was plain English—"Access Denied"—and some was computer-geek lingo—"Port Scan is logged." Since Jesse is the resident expert, his account of what happened is to be taken seriously. The broader plot depends on our grasping that Jesse has identified Physanto; Jesse has identified a license plate; and Physanto has found him. But we still don't move away from Jesse's Jesse-ness: his clear sense that he is now trapped in a complex web of potential malevolence, an awareness made visible and audible by his shifting around and shifting lin-

guistic focus while actually not shifting at all. Action to keep the parts in motion.

• [39] The vomit. Jesse's desperate nervousness because Big Brother and big brother are both surveilling him. The trap he is caught in might lead to prison. And in any event, he has expended all his energy and he collapses.

Ned flies off to see the Lindara situation for himself. Jesse is left alone in the house for the very first time. When Ned's taxi has pulled away, Jesse is abruptly attacked and thrown into a van. This marks the end of episode one, in which a hint of a very complex, nefarious conspiracy is caught by a diligent autist, but in such a way that the autist and his fate remain, by far, more interesting than the hint. He is now seriously threatened.

Episode 2: Jesse's First Scene—Torture Begins

A too-bright, empty, high-ceilinged room with what seem like concrete walls. Jesse (in close shot) is bent over, hooded, whimpering. Rock music plays at an excruciatingly loud volume—in fact, for Jesse, even much, much louder than that—then suddenly stops. An interrogator is with him.

INTERROGATOR: Shall we sit? (*He draws up a metal chair behind Jesse, who is now shown to be* [40] *completely unclothed.*) (*Politely:*) Sit down, Mr. Banks. (*As Jesse continues whimpering, the hood is yanked off. His mouth is taped. As the tape is ripped away, he screams in pain.*) There is . . . a . . . spot on the wall . . . just below the air conditioner. (*Jesse looks up.*) Can you see it, Mr. Banks? (*Cut to black spot on white wall.*) (*Jesse grimaces.*) That is *your* spot. Do not look away from it. Do you understand?

JESSE (whimpering): No. [41] I don't understand why I'm here or why I would look at that spot. There's no conceivable reason for me to look at that spot. (*The hood is thrown back on.*) (*Screaming:*) All right! All right! All right! I'm looking at it! I'm looking at it! (*The hood comes off. Jesse looks up, lips clenched tightly.*)

INTERROGATOR (Patiently): I told you to look at the spot. That is your reason. (*Steps behind Jesse.*) I'm going to ask you some questions.

JESSE (desperate): [42] I want Ned. I wanna call Ned.

INTERROGATOR: Ah, no, you don't get to make calls. You get to cooperate. You go to the movies. I'm sure you understand the benefits of cooperation.

JESSE (quickly, stammering): I don't. [43] I don't go to the movies. It's too much for me. The sound, the surround sound, and the screen's too big.

INTERROGATOR (chuckling): You have no idea how much trouble you're in, do you? (*Mocking:*) The little . . . the little [44] *Rain Man* act. You, my young friend, have fucked up in a profound way.

JESSE (crying): I don't know what you're talking about.

INTERROGATOR: Really? You hacked into a system last night and stole some files that do not belong to you. I want to know why. I want to know who you're working for, and I want to know where the files are now. (*Jesse is crying silently.*) Those questions will not be changing. So have a good old think. Time is no object here. (*Walking away, he kicks the chair out from under Jesse, who collapses to the floor.*)

Exceeding discomfort, probably terror for Jesse, the conditions geared to augment anxiety and bring desperation out of control. Here was "an evil system of grisly torture and terror . . . terror was the central tool of the free-market transformation," as Naomi Klein wrote in *The Shock Doctrine* (2007, 117), a book that Birse and Zukerman both read.

- [40] Naked. The interrogation is staged as if taking place in a total institution. (Zukerman was thoroughly briefed on Jeremy Bentham's panopticon.) In *Asylums*, Erving Goffman describes "mortification of self" ([1961] 2009, 21): the dignity, integrity, and identity of the inmate are systematically reduced through enclosure without garments in a room with a transparent door. Here, interrogators come close to Jesse—what Edward T. Hall called "intimate social distance" ([1959] 1990, 170)— fully clothed while he is fully not. Since we know something of Jesse's sensitivities and vulnerabilities, we can recognize how he must be agonized. The featureless room and interrogators' glibness show this as a systemic process that has likely been applied to countless victims, there being no special awareness of Jesse as distinct, let alone unique. (We are moved to feel a special double sympathy for him: he's treated badly, but also as though he has no unique troubles.)
- [41] Why look at the spot? Jesse is entirely rational. The spot on the wall has no value whatever. The instruction not only makes no logical sense, but partakes of the nature of an authoritarian command. Unaccustomed to brutality, Jesse is elementally confounded. Why would he be here, indeed! And why would anybody demand without reason that he look at that spot? What is the secret reason hiding "between the lines"? Zukerman knew Jesse to be "immune to the system," in that "he retains logical

power": a balm for us, particularly if we can see and somehow enjoy how logical he is being.

- [42] Wanting Ned. Jesse has never been away from Ned's proximity and guidance, and hasn't the self-confidence for withstanding a pummeling by unfeeling strangers.
- [43] The movies. Jesse recognizes that most "normal" people go to the movies (and watch movies like this one!), and he wants to clarify what exactly about the medium is troublesome for him. Here (in the context of Birse's action-adventure) we learn how—and why—action cinema, full of extreme sound and movement, is lethal for autists (at least autists like this one).
- [44] The *Rain Man* act. Pure mocking deprecation, yet also a compliment, since, as he is told, even if he were acting, he would be at least as accomplished as Dustin Hoffman. The agent's intent is to dismiss and demean. But Jesse is a collector of facts: there is a movie called *Rain Man*, and whether or not he knows the film, he is being seen as pretending to have a condition, instead of actually having one; and presumably, his pretense takes *Rain Man* for an instructive model. He knows he isn't doing any sort of an act, and is confounded, not insulted, by the comparison. He's acting brilliantly but also, he's not acting.

Episode 2: Jesse's Second Scene—Torture Continues

Jesse is naked at a window with a new questioner confronting him. A third interrogator enters. "Did you speak to anyone about your hack into Physanto?" Jesse is humming to himself. A shot of his face shows red eyes, tears, and concentrated gaze.

> NEW (SECOND) INTERROGATOR: "Are you listening, shithead? . . . (*snaps fingers*) ENOUGH OF THE FUCKIN' HUMMING!!!!!" ([45] *Jesse uncontrollably urinates.*)
> THIRD INTERROGATOR (a quiet command): Maybe you want to take a little break, Dean. (*When Dean has gone:*) I see he left your undies here just to piss you off. (*Calmly*) Some people enjoy their work just a little bit too much, don't they. (*Bending down, he gently* [46] *helps Jesse don the underwear.*) Is that better?
> JESSE: Mmm.
> THIRD INTERROGATOR: You okay? You all right?
> JESSE (quietly imploring): [47] Could you put your hand on the back of my neck?

THIRD INTERROGATOR (complying): Like this? Is that all right? (*Bending over and sobbing, Jesse nods.*)

THIRD INTERROGATOR: This is all a bit of a bloody mess, isn't it? Hmm? Okay, listen to me, Jesse. Now, you don't know me, and you've got no reason to take my advice. But if I were you, I'd think very strongly about doing whatever it is that they ask. (*Jesse blinks.*) Do you understand what I'm saying?

JESSE: Mmm.

- [45] *Urination.* The second interrogator stands close to Jesse, almost touching the young man's nakedness, and screams at the top of his lungs (like a drill sergeant). The situation alone could trigger an autonomic response.
- [46] *Underwear help.* This third interrogator means to show kindness and consideration, as well as common respect for Jesse's manhood. Yet there is no avoiding furthering Jesse's discomfort, shame, and humiliation in dressing him, Jesse's hands still being bound. We might hope for calmness once the underpants are on, but we don't really find it.
- [47] *The back of the neck.* This, we know, is Jesse and Ned's private calmdown signal, to be used in adverse circumstances only. Jesse is converting the interrogator into a Ned substitute, so that at least Ned will "be there" with him, even if only through substitution.

Not long later, we find Jesse on the cold floor, lying in a fetal position while rock music blares at him torturously through the loudspeaker. He is curtly hooded again and led away. Next he is free on the lawn in front of Ned's ex-girlfriend, still virtually naked. She is tender to him, but distant.

.   .   .

Typically in series drama, central characters and plot teasers are shown at the very beginning. Characters stand out by virtue of their action in the story, to the extent of their involvement. The character is the propulsive action he initiates. Outside the story "cage," we aren't invited to meet the characters as persons, persons such as we would take ourselves to be. Jesse, however, eclipses the action.

While plot complications in *The Code* are designed to fit the show's length, drawing the viewer inexorably forward to find the "hidden secret" that explains disparate events with coherence, Jesse Banks's personality and fate are given extensive, highlighted portrayal independently. We sometimes learn details of Jesse's personality, but only when they bear upon dramatic happenings. A great deal is shown of him that is tangential, even marginal, to the story line. Thus:

- We discover elements of his unique autism beyond what the story requires for explication, even loosed altogether from the story line. Jesse's plot-relevant actions never take precedence over his autism, even when he hacks Physanto.
- Yet even while devoting itself to him, the program forwards its story, Jesse clearly being even more a key player in the show than a key player in the events. He belongs to the show frame, so *The Code* is both indicative and recursive. As unfolding events prod us to want more plot-relevant information about Jesse, already at the beginning we want to know him as a charming person, thus to know him in a special way. His autism doesn't rationalize, motor, or help decode the plot.

For the interested viewer (for any viewer willing to allow the actor to engage his interest), watching Jesse is far more an aesthetic fascination than an exercise in typification. It would be only on reflection, on second thought, that one might put together some of the characteristics one had perceived and wonder whether they form a syndrome and deserve a label. With a great elegance of economy, his every gesture and act provides information about his particular way of being in the world, his self. Jesse is not given to us fully or roundly as a story-relevant player at any point: nor is Ned, even though peopling television dramas with story-relevant players is the definition of televisual reality. Even as a part of a television serial drama, Jesse "doesn't fit the parameters of the normal." Diegetic and extradiegetic autism together, in unison.

Works Cited and Consulted

Alderson, Jonathan. 2011. *Challenging the Myths of Autism: New Perspectives, New Strategies, New Hope.* Toronto: HarperCollins.

Ali, Lorraine. 2017. "Sharp, Quirky and Empathetic, the Second Season of Netflix's 'Atypical' Grows with Its Characters." *Los Angeles Times*, September 7. latimes .com/entertainment/tv/la-et-st-atypical-netflix-season-2-20180907-story.html.

Anderson, Rebekah, and Shona Francey. 2019. "MythBuster—Autism Spectrum Disorder: Fighting Myths with Evidence." Orygen, the National Centre of Excellence in Youth Mental Health, Australia. orygen.org.au/Training/Resources /Neurodevelopmental-disorders/Mythbusters/Autism-spectrum-disorder-Fighting-myths-with-evid.

Andreeva, Nellie. 2017. "'Atypical' Renewed for Season 2 by Netflix." Deadline, September 13. deadline.com/2017/09/atypical-renewed-season-2-netflix-1202169360.

———. 2019. "'Atypical' Creator Robia Rashid Re-Ups Overall Deal with Sony Pictures TV." Deadline, April 10. deadline.com/2019/04/atypical-creator-robia -rashid-renew-overall-deal-sony-pictures-tv-1202593268.

Arendt, Hannah. (1945) 1994. "Nightmare and Flight." In *Essays in Understanding, 1930–1954: Formation, Exile, and Totalitarianism*, edited by Jerome Kohn, 133–135. New York: Harcourt Brace.

Arky, Beth. 2017. "Netflix's 'Atypical' Splits Autism Community." Child Mind Institute, August 15, 2017. childmind.org/blog/netflixs-atypical-splits-autism -community.

Asperger, Hans. (1944) 1991. "Autistic Psychopathy in Childhood." Translated by Uta Frith. In *Autism and Asperger Syndrome*, edited by Uta Frith, 37–92. Cambridge: Cambridge University Press.

Baker, Anthony D. 2008. "Recognizing Jake: Contending with Formulaic and Spectacularized Representations of Autism in Film." In *Autism and Representation*, edited by Mark Osteen, 229–243. New York: Routledge.

Baker Street Babes. 2015. Podcast. "Episode 63: Robert Doherty." May 11. https:// podcasts.apple.com/us/podcast/episode-63-robert-doherty/id446383728?i =1000341914947.

Barash, David P. 2004. "Biology Lurks Beneath: Bioliterary Explorations of the Individual versus Society." *Evolutionary Psychology* 2, no. 1: 200–219. journals.sage pub.com/doi/full/10.1177/147470490400200125.

Bargiela, Sarah. 2019. *Camouflage: The Hidden Lives of Autistic Women*. London: Kingsley.

Bargiela, Sarah, Robyn Steward, and William Mandy. 2016. "The Experiences of Late-Diagnosed Women with Autism Spectrum Conditions: An Investigation of the Female Autism Phenotype." *Journal of Autism and Developmental Disorders* 46:3281–3294. doi.org/10.1007/s10803-016-2872-8.

Barnes, Henry. 2014. "Jake Gyllenhaal on Nightcrawler: 'I'm a Bit Strange, You Know?'" *Guardian*, October 31. www.theguardian.com/film/2014/oct/30/jake -gyllenhaal-nightcrawler-interview.

Barnett, Tully, and Ben Kooyman. 2012. "Repackaging Popular Culture: Commentary and Critique in Community." *Networking Knowledge* 5, no. 2: 109–134.

Baron-Cohen, Simon. 2010. "Empathizing, Systemizing, and the Extreme Male Brain Theory of Autism." *Progress in Brain Research* 186:167–175.

Beach, Christopher. 2009. "I Like to Watch: Shampoo and Being There." In *The Films of Hal Ashby*, 96–117. Detroit: Wayne State University Press.

Bednarek, Monika. 2012. "Constructing 'Nerdiness': Characterisation in The Big Bang Theory." *Multilingua* 21:199–229.

Belcher, Christina, and Kimberly Maich. 2014. "Autism Spectrum Disorder in Popular Media: Storied Reflections of Societal Views." *Brock Education* 23, no. 2 (Spring): 97–115.

Belmonte, Matthew K. 2008. "Human, but More So: What the Autistic Brain Tells Us about the Process of Narrative." In *Autism and Representation*, edited by Mark Osteen, 166–179. New York: Routledge.

Bishop, Rudine Sims. 2003. "Reframing the Debate about Cultural Authenticity." In *Stories Matter: The Complexity of Cultural Authenticity in Children's Literature*, edited by Dana L. Fox and Kathy G. Short, 25–36. Champaign, IL: National Council of Teachers of English.

Blume, Harvey. 1997. "Autistics, Freed from Face-to-Face Encounters, Are Communicating in Cyberspace." *New York Times*, June 30. nytimes.com/1997/06/30 /business/autistics-freed-from-face-to-face-encounters-are-communicating-in -cyberspace.html.

———. 1998. "Neurodiversity." *Atlantic*, September. https://archive.is/2013010500 3900/http://www.theatlantic.com/doc/199809u/neurodiversity.

Bogdashina, Olga. 2003. *Sensory Perceptual Issues in Autism and Asperger Syndrome: Different Sensory Experiences, Different Perceptual Worlds*. London: Kingsley.

———. 2010. *Autism and the Edges of the Known World: Sensitivities, Language and Constructed Reality*. London: Kingsley.

Bolaño, Roberto. 2008. *2666*. Translated by Natasha Wimmer. New York: Farrar, Straus and Giroux.

Boyd, Brian. 2009. *On the Origin of Stories: Evolution, Cognition, and Fiction*. Cambridge, MA: Harvard University Press.

Bresson, Robert. 1977. *Notes on Cinematography*. Translated by J. Griffin. New York: Urizen.

Brock, Nettie. 2014. "Greendale Hyperreality." In *A Sense of "Community": Essays on the Television Series and Its Fandom*, edited by Ann-Gee Lee, 36–50. Jefferson, NC: McFarland.

Bryant, Michael. 2005. *Confronting the Good Death: Nazi Euthanasia on Trial 1945–53.* Boulder, CO: University Press of Colorado.

Brynjolfsson, Erik, and Andrew McAfee. 2016. *The Second Machine Age: Work, Progress, and Prosperity in a Time of Brilliant Technologies.* New York: Norton.

Cagle, Chris. 2016. *Sociology on Film: Postwar Hollywood's Prestige Commodity.* New Brunswick, NJ: Rutgers University Press.

Calabrese, Gabbi. 2018. "Why Everyone Needs to Be Watching Netflix's 'Atypical.'" *Study Breaks Magazine,* September 19. studybreaks.com/tvfilm/everyone -needs-watching-netflixs-atypical.

Campbell, Joseph. 2008. *The Hero with a Thousand Faces.* 3rd ed. Novato, CA: New World Library.

Carey, Benedict. 2019. "Theodore Isaac Rubin Is Dead at 95; Popularized Psychotherapy." *New York Times,* February 20. nytimes.com/2019/02/20/obituaries/dr -theodore-rubin-dead.html.

Carroll, Joseph. 2006. "The Human Revolution and the Adaptive Function of Literature." *Philosophy and Literature* 30, no. 1: 33–49. muse.jhu.edu/article/199379 /pdf (subscription required).

Cavell, Stanley. 1979. "Audience, Actor, Star." In *The World Viewed: Reflections on the Ontology of Film,* rev. ed., 25–29. Cambridge, MA: Harvard University Press.

Centers for Disease Control and Prevention. 2020. "Prevalence of Autism Spectrum Disorder among Children Aged 8 Years: Autism and Developmental Disabilities Monitoring Network, 11 Sites, United States, 2016." *Surveillance Summaries* 69, no. 4: 1–12. cdc.gov/mmwr/volumes/69/ss/ss6904a1.htm?s_cid=ss6904a1_w.

Chaney, Jen. 2018. "Atypical Season 2 Widens Its Perspective, but Loses Some Charm." Vulture, September 4. vulture.com/2018/09/atypical-netflix-season-2 -review.html.

Chavisory's Notebook (blog). 2018. "The Shape of Love: Cupid and Psyche and Other Considerations of Monstrosity in 'The Shape of Water.'" March 11. https:// chavisory.wordpress.com/2018/03/11/the-shape-of-love-cupid-and-psyche-and -other-considerations-of-monstrosity-in-the-shape-of-water.

Chew, Kristina. 2013. "Autism and the Task of the Translator." In *Worlds of Autism: Across the Spectrum of Neurological Difference,* edited by Joyce Davidson and Michael Orsini, 305–317. Minneapolis: University of Minnesota Press.

Clarke, Donald. 2015. "Jim Parsons: 'I Am Quite the Opposite of Unapproachable.'" *Irish Times,* March 20. irishtimes.com/culture/film/jim-parsons-i-am-quite-the -opposite-of-unapproachable-1.2145657.

Cobb, Kayla. 2018. "'Atypical' Season 2 Is More Cynical, Less Self-Congratulating, and Better." Decider, September 7. decider.com/2018/09/07/atypical-season-2 -review.

Cohen, Jeffrey Jerome. 2007. "Monster Culture: Seven Theses." In *Gothic Horror: A Guide for Students and Readers,* edited by Clive Bloom, 198–216. Basingstoke, UK: Palgrave Macmillan.

Collins, Paul. 2009. "Must-Geek TV: Is the World Ready for an Asperger's Sitcom?" Slate, February 6. slate.com/culture/2009/02/is-the-world-ready-for-an -asperger-s-sitcom.html.

Collins, Rosemary. 2016. "Saga Norén, the Autistic Superwoman of 'The Bridge.'" *The Toast* (blog), June 27. https://the-toast.net/2016/06/27/saga-noren-the-autis tic-superwoman-of-the-bridge.

Corner, John. 1999. *Critical Ideas in Television Studies*. Oxford: Oxford University Press.

Crews, Frederick. 2017. *Freud: The Making of an Illusion*. New York: Holt.

Crowther, Bosley. 1962. Review of *David and Lisa*. *New York Times*, December 27. nytimes.com/1962/12/27/archives/screen-david-and-lisa-odd-romance-involves -mentally-ill-children.html.

Czech, Hedwig. 2018. "Hans Asperger, National Socialism, and 'Race Hygiene' in Nazi-era Vienna." *Molecular Autism* 9, no. 29. doi.org/10.1186/s13229-018-0208-6.

Deleuze, Gilles. 1995. *Negotiations, 1972–1990*. Translated by Martin Joughin. New York: Columbia University Press.

Deleuze, Gilles, and Melissa McMuhan. 1988. "The Brain Is the Screen: Interview with Gilles Deleuze on 'The Time-Image.'" *Discourse* 20, no. 3 (Fall): 47–55.

Demurie, Ellen, Maaike De Corel, and Herbert Roeyers. 2011. "Empathic Accuracy in Adolescents with Autism Spectrum Disorders and Adolescents with Attention-Deficit/Hyperactivity Disorder." *Research in Autism Spectrum Disorders* 5:126–134. sciencedirect.com/science/article/pii/S1750946710000279 (subscription required).

Dent, Shirley. 2007. "Don't 'Diagnose' Fictional Characters." *Guardian*, April 4. theguardian.com/books/booksblog/2007/apr/04/dontdiagnosefictionalcharac.

Dima, Vlad. 2012. "'I Am Not Insane. My Mother Had Me Tested': The Mothers of the *Big Bang*." *Bright Lights Film Journal*, January 31. www.brightlightsfilm.com /i-am-not-insane-my-mother-had-me-tested-the-mothers-of-the-big-bang.

Dowdy, Katie. 2013. "Representations of Autism in the Media: Perspectives in Popular Television Shows." Rehabilitation, Human Resources and Communication Disorders Undergraduate Honors Thesis, University of Arkansas, Fayetteville. scholarworks.uark.edu/rhrcuht/4.

Doyle, Arthur Conan. (1890) 2009. *The Sign of the Four*. In *The Penguin Complete Sherlock Holmes*, 89–158. London: Penguin.

Draaisma, Douwe. 2009. "Stereotypes of Autism." *Philosophical Transactions of the Royal Society B* 364:1475–1480.

Draper, Jimmy, and Amanda D. Lotz. 2012. "'Working Through' as Ideological Intervention: The Case of Homophobia in *Rescue Me*." *Television and New Media* 13, no. 6: 520–534.

Dufresne, Todd. 2003. *Killing Freud: Twentieth-Century Culture and the Death of Psychoanalysis*. London: Continuum.

Dyer, Richard. 1998. *Stars*. New ed. London: BFI.

Eaton, Mick. 1981. "Television Situation Comedy." In *Popular Television and Film*, edited by Tony Bennett, Susan Boy-Bowman, Colin Mercer, and Janet Woollacott, 26–52. London: British Film Institute.

Ebiri, Bilge. 2017. "With 'Phantom Thread,' Paul Thomas Anderson Stitches Together a Daringly Quiet Love Story." *Village Voice*, December 19. villagevoice .com/2017/12/19/with-phantom-thread-paul-thomas-anderson-stitches-to gether-a-daringly-quiet-love-story.

Eco, Umberto. 1984. *The Name of the Rose*. Translated by William Weaver. New York: Harcourt.

Eliot, T. S. (1933) 1986. *The Use of Poetry and the Use of Criticism: Studies in the Relation of Criticism to Poetry in England*. Cambridge, MA: Harvard University Press.

Ellis, John. 2002. *Seeing Things: Television in the Age of Uncertainty.* 2nd ed. London: Tauris.

Evans, Meg. 2020. "The Autistic Genocide Clock." In *Autistic Community and the Neurodiversity Movement: Stories from the Frontline,* edited by Steven K. Kapp, 123–132. London: Palgrave.

Fabian, Renee. 2009. "Actor Keir Gilchrist on 'Atypical' Season 3, Autism and Mental Health." The Mighty, November 11. themighty.com/2019/11/interview-atypical-star-keir-gilchrist-autism-mental-health.

Faden, Eric. 2007. *A Fair(y) Use Tail.* Posted to YouTube by Jas A, May 18, 2007. Accessed August 13, 2020. https://youtu.be/CJn_jC4FNDo.

Farocki, Harun. 2012. "Bresson, a Stylist." In *Robert Bresson Revised,* edited by James Quandt, 471–478. Bloomington: Indiana University Press.

Felperin, Leslie. 2017. "What Netflix Comedy *Atypical* Gets Right and Wrong about Autism." *Guardian,* August 14. theguardian.com/tv-and-radio/2017/aug/14/atypical-netflix-autism-spectrum-depiction-cliches.

Fernandez, Maria Elena. 2017. "*Atypical* Creator Robia Rashid on Autism: 'I Had to Do a Lot of Real Learning.'" *Vulture,* August 15. vulture.com/2017/08/atypical-showrunner-robia-rashid-interview.html.

Fiedler, Leslie. 1972. "On Remembering Freshman Comp." In *Unfinished Business,* 163–168. New York: Stein and Day.

Fischer, Russ. 2014. "'Nightcrawler' Director Dan Gilroy on Manipulation and Ditching the Character Arc," SlashFilm, October 31. slashfilm.com/dan-gilroy-interview.

Fitzpatrick, Michael. 2004. *MMR and Autism: What Parents Need to Know.* London: Routledge.

Foucault, Michel. 1967. *Madness and Civilization.* Translated by David Cooper. London: Routledge.

Fox, Jesse David. 2018. "How Funny Does a Comedy Need to Be?" Vulture, September 4. vulture.com/2018/09/post-comedy-how-funny-does-comedy-need-to-be.html.

Frampton, Daniel. 2006. *Filmosophy.* London: Wallflower.

Frith, Uta, ed. 1991. *Autism and Asperger Syndrome.* Cambridge: Cambridge University Press.

Gabbard, Glen O., and Krin Gabbard. 1999. *Psychiatry and the Cinema.* 2nd ed. Washington, DC: American Psychiatric Press, 1999.

Garfinkel, Harold. 1967. "Good Organizational Reasons for 'Bad' Clinic Records." In *Studies in Ethnomethodology,* 186–207. Englewood Cliffs, NJ: Prentice-Hall.

Garland-Thomson, Rosemarie. 2002. "The Politics of Staring: Visual Rhetorics of Disability in Popular Photography." In *Disability Studies: Enabling the Humanities,* vol. 1, edited by Sharon L. Snyder, Brenda Jo Bruegemann, and Rosemarie Garland-Thomson, 56–75. New York: MLA.

Garner, Andrea, Valerie Harwood, and Samantha C. Jones. 2016. "Discourses of Autism on Film: An Analysis of Memorable Images That Create Definition." In *The Palgrave Handbook of Adult Mental Health,* edited by Michelle O'Reilly and Jessica Nina Lester, 151–166. London: Palgrave Macmillan.

Garofalo, Suzanne. 2017. "Autism—How Important Is It for 'Atypical' to Get It Right?" *Houston Chronicle,* August 11. houstonchronicle.com/entertainment/tv/article/Autism-how-important-is-it-for-Atypical-to-11751540.php.

Gilbert, Sophie. 2017. *"Atypical* Is So Close to Great." *Atlantic*, August 13. theatlan
tic.com/entertainment/archive/2017/08/atypical-review-netflix/536538.

Gill, James. 2015. "Is Sheldon Autistic? The Big Bang Theory Actress Mayim Bialik Gives This Brilliant Response." *Radio Times*, June 15. www.radiotimes.com/
news/2015-06-15/is-sheldon-autistic-the-big-bang-theory-actress-mayim-bialik
-gives-this-brilliant-response.

Gilroy, Dan, and Tony Gilroy. 2018. "Nightcrawler Q&A with Dan Gilroy and
Tony Gilroy." Posted to Youtube.com on August 29, 2018, accessed May 27,
2020, but now unavailable.

Girard, René. 1986. *The Scapegoat*. Translated by Yvonne Freccero. Baltimore: Johns
Hopkins University Press.

Goffman, Erving. (1961) 2009. *Asylums: Essays on the Social Situation of Mental Patients*. New Brunswick, NJ: Aldine.

Grandin, Temple. 1995a. *Thinking in Pictures: And Other Reports from My Life with
Autism*. New York: Doubleday.

———. 1995b. "How People with Autism Think." In *Learning and Cognition in Autism*, edited by Eric Schopler and Gary B. Mesibov, 137–156. New York: Plenum.

———. 2013. *The Autistic Brain: Helping Different Kinds of Minds Succeed*. With
Richard Panek. Boston: Houghton Mifflin Harcourt.

Grandin, Temple, and Catherine Johnson. 2006. *Animals in Translation: The Woman
Who Thinks like a Cow*. London: Bloomsbury.

Grant, Carrie. 2019. "Raising the Voice of the Lost Girls." In *Girls and Autism: Educational, Family and Personal Perspectives*, edited by Barry Carpenter, Francesca
Happé, and Jo Egerton, 26–33. London: Routledge.

Greenfield, Mat. 2014. "We Shouldn't View Sherlock as an Autistic Savant." *Huffington Post*, July 1. huffingtonpost.co.uk/mat-greenfield/sherlock-not-autistic_b
_4548520.html.

Grodal, Torben. 2010. "High on Crime Fiction and Detection." *Projections* 4, no.
2: 64–85. berghahnjournals.com/view/journals/projections/4/2/proj040205.xml
(subscription required).

Grodin, Michael A., Erin L. Miller, and Johnathan I. Kelly. 2018. "The Nazi Physicians as Leaders in Eugenics and 'Euthanasia': Lessons for Today." *American
Journal of Public Health* 108, no. 1 (January): 53–57. ajph.aphapublications.org/doi
/abs/10.2105/AJPH.2017.304120?journalCode=ajph.

Hacking, Ian. 2009a. "Humans, Aliens & Autism." *Daedalus* 138, no. 3 (Summer
2009): 44–59.

———. 2009b. "How We Have Been Learning to Talk about Autism: A Role for
Stories." *Metaphilosophy* 40, nos. 3–4 (July): 499–516.

Haddon, Mark. 2003. *The Curious Incident of the Dog in the Night-Time*. New York:
Vintage.

Hall, Edward T. (1959) 1990. *The Silent Language*. New York: Anchor.

Haller, Beth. 2019. "Authentic Disability Representation on U.S. Television Past
and Present." In *The Routledge Companion to Disability and Media*, edited by
Gewrrard Goggin, Katie Ellis, and Beth Haller, 88–100. New York: Routledge.
Proquest ebook.

Haney, Jolynn. 2015. "Autism, Females, and the DSM-5: Gender Bias in Autism
Diagnosis." *Social Work in Mental Health*, October. researchgate.net/publica

tion/283467413_Autism_Females_and_the_DSM-5_Gender_Bias_in_Autism
_Diagnosis.

Hanna, Bridget Julie. 2014. "'That's So Meta!': Allusions for the Media-Literate
Audience in *Community* (and Beyond)." In *A Sense of Community: Essays on the
Television Series and Its Fandom*, edited by Ann-Gee Lee, 138–151. Jefferson,
NC: McFarland.

Happé, Francesca. 2019. "What Does Research Tell Us about Girls on the Autistic Spectrum?" In *Girls and Autism: Educational, Family and Personal Perspectives*,
edited by Barry Carpenter, Francesca Happé, and Jo Egerton, 10–15. London:
Routledge.

Heilker, Paul. 2012. "Autism, Rhetoric, and Whiteness." *Disability Studies Quarterly* 32, no. 4. www.dsq-sds.org/article/view/1756.

Henderson, Rob. 2019. "'Luxury Beliefs' Are the Latest Status Symbols for Rich
Americans." *New York Post*, August 17. nypost.com/2019/08/17/luxury-beliefs
-are-the-latest-status-symbol-for-rich-americans.

Hendrickx, Sarah. 2015. *Women and Girls with Autism Spectrum Disorder: Understanding Life Experiences from Early Childhood to Old Age*. London: Kingsley.

Higashida, Naoki. 2013. *The Reason I Jump: The Inner Voice of a Thirteen-Year-Old Boy
with Autism*. Translated by K. A. Yoshida and D. Mitchell. London: Sceptre.

Hollan, Douglas. 2008. "Being There: On the Imaginative Aspects of Understanding Others and Being Understood." *Ethos* 36, no. 4: 475–489.

Holton, Avery. 2013. "What's Wrong With Max? Parenthood and the Portrayal of
Autism Spectrum Disorders." *Journal of Communication Inquiry* 37, no. 1 (February): 1–19.

Holverstott, J. 2011. "Aspie or Not, What Sheldon Cooper Brings to TV." *A Shade
unDifferent: Examining ASD from an NT World* (blog), January 16. www.jholver
stott.wordpress.com/2011/01/16/aspie-or-not-what-sheldon-cooper-brings-to-tv.

Horney, Karen. 1950. *Neurosis and Human Growth: The Struggle toward Self-Realization*.
New York: Norton.

———. 1942. *Self-Analysis*. New York: W. W. Norton.

Howell, Paul. 2015. "From *Rain Man* to *Sherlock*: Theological Reflections on Metaphor and ASD." *Practical Theology* 8, no. 2: 143–153. www.tandfonline.com/doi
/abs/10.1179/1756073X15Z.00000000064 (subscription required).

Hugar, John. 2017. "The More *Atypical* Tries to Get Autism 'Right,' the More
Things Go Wrong." The AV Club, August 11. tv.avclub.com/the-more-atypical
-tries-to-get-autism-right-the-more-1798191910.

Jacobs, Jason. 2003. *Body Trauma TV: The New Hospital Dramas*. London: British
Film Institute, 2003.

———. 2018. "Dustin Hoffman in *Rain Man*." In *Close-Up: Great Cinematic Performances*, vol. 1: *America*, edited by Murray Pomerance and Kyle Stevens, 212–222.
Edinburgh: Edinburgh University Press.

James, Henry. (1881) 2002. *The Portrait of a Lady*. New York: Modern Library.

Jameson, Fredric. 1991. *Postmodernism: or, The Cultural Logic of Late Capitalism*.
Durham, NC: Duke University Press.

Kaiser, Martha D., Daniel Y. J. Yang, Avery C. Voos, Randi H. Bennett, Ilanit
Gordon, Charlotte Pretzsch, Danielle Beam, Cara Keifer, Jeffrey Eilbott, Fran-
cis McGlone, and Kevin A. Pelphrey. 2016. "Brain Mechanisms for Processing

Affective (and Nonaffective) Touch Are Atypical in Autism." *Cerebral Cortex* 26, no. 6: 2705–2714. doi.org/10.1093/cercor/bhv125.

Karasik, Paul, and Judy Karasik. 2004. *The Ride Together: A Brother and Sister's Memoir of Autism in the Family.* New York: Washington Square.

Kennedy, Greg. 2017. "Netflix Sitcom Atypical Challenges Prejudices on What Is 'Normal.'" *National*, August 9. thenational.ae/arts-culture/television/netflix-sit com-atypical-challenges-prejudices-on-what-is-normal-1.618114.

Klein, Naomi. 2007. *The Shock Doctrine: The Rise of Disaster Capitalism.* New York: Vintage.

Klevan, Andrew. 2005. *Film Performance: From Achievement to Appreciation.* London: Wallflower.

———. 2012. "Living Meaning: The Fluency of Film Performance." In *Theorizing Film Performance*, edited by Aaron Taylor, 33–46. New York: Routledge.

Kobie, Nicole. 2018. "The Questionable Ethics of Treating Autistic Children with Robots." *Wired*, July 18. www.wired.co.uk/article/autisim-children-treatment-ro bots.

Koyanagi, Jacqueline. 2015. "Context Matters: On Labels and Responsibility." Disability in Kidlit, April 17. disabilityinkidlit.com/2015/04/17/context-matters-on -labels-and-responsibility.

Kuechenmeister, Elizabeth Fleitz. 2014. "My Dinner with Abed: Postmodernism, Pastiche, and Metaxy in 'Critical Film Studies.'" In *A Sense of "Community": Essays on the Television Series and Its Fandom*, edited by Ann-Gee Lee, 125–137. Jefferson, NC: McFarland.

Kurchak, Sarah. 2017. "Film Review: The Shape of Water." Consequence, November 28. consequence.net/2017/11/film-review-the-shape-of-water.

Lai, Meng-Chuan, Michael V. Lombardo, Bhismadev Chakrabarti, Amber N. V. Ruigrok, Edward T. Bullmore, John Suckling, Bonnie Auyeung, Francesca Happé, Peter Szatmari, and Simon Baron-Cohen. 2019. "Neural Self-Representation in Autistic Women and Association with 'Compensatory Camouflaging.'" *Autism* 23, no. 5: 1210–1223.

Lattanzio, Ryan. 2019. "'Song of the South': 10 Fast Facts about Disney's Most Controversial Movie." IndieWire, November 3. www.indiewire.com/gallery /song-of-the-south-disney-you-must-remember-this/film-and-television-414.

Lazar, Mary. 2004. "Jerzy Kosinski's *Being There*, Novel and Film: Changes Not by Chance." *College Literature* 31, no. 2 (Spring): 99–116.

Lee, Marie Myung-Ok. "The Trouble with Autism in Novels." *New York Times*, February 4, 2019, 12.

Leitch, Thomas. 2007. *Film Adaptation and Its Discontents.* Baltimore: Johns Hopkins University Press.

Lenberg, Jeff. 2001. *Dustin Hoffman: Hollywood's Antihero.* Bloomington, IN: Iuniverse.

Lennard, Dominic, R. Barton Palmer, and Murray Pomerance, eds. 2020. *The Other Hollywood Renaissance.* Edinburgh: Edinburgh University Press, 2020.

Lifton, Robert Jay. 1986. *The Nazi Doctors: Medical Killing and the Psychology of Genocide.* New York: HarperCollins.

Little, Charlotte. 2020. "Atypical's Journey to Authentic Disability Representation: Shining a Spotlight on College Disability Services." Flip Screen, January 22.

flipscreened.com/2020/01/22/atypicals-journey-to-authentic-disability-repre
sentation-shining-a-spotlight-on-college-disability-services.

Loftis, Sonya Freeman. 2016. *Imagining Autism: Fiction and Stereotypes on the Spectrum.* Bloomington: Indiana University Press.

Lowry, Brian. "'Atypical' Explores Autism via Mostly Ordinary Netflix Show."
CNN.com, August 10, 2017. cnn.com/2017/08/08/tv-shows/atypical-review/in
dex.html.

Luterman, Sara. 2018. "How Season 2 of 'Atypical' Improves the Show's Depictions of Life as an Autistic Person." *New York Times,* September 11. nytimes
.com/2018/09/11/arts/atypical-season-2-autistic-depiction-improvements.html.

Lynam, Donald R., and Karen J. Deferinko. 2006. "Psychopathy and Personality."
In *Handbook of Psychopathy,* edited by Christopher J. Patrick, 133–155. New York:
Guildford.

Lyons, Viktoria, and Michael Fitzgerald. 2007. "Did Hans Asperger (1906–1980)
Have Asperger Syndrome?" *Journal of Autism Developmental Disorders* 37, 2020-
2021. https://pubmed.ncbi.nlm.nih.gov/17917805 (subscription required).

Magro, Kerry. 2016. "10 Things I Wish Our Entertainment Industry Knew About
Autism." *Kerry Magro* (blog), June 7. kerrymagro.com/10-things-entertainment
-industry-autism.

Maher, Theresa. 2017. "Robia Rashid—Writer and Producer, Creator of Atypical,
Calls for More Stories of Inclusion and Diversity." Respect Ability, November 18. respectability.org/2017/11/robia-rashid-writer-producer-creator-atypical
-calls-stories-inclusion-diversity.

Marini, Richard A. 2018. "Netflix Show 'Atypical' Recovering from Autism
Groups' Criticisms." *San Antonio Express-News,* September 26. expressnews
.com/entertainment/movies-tv/article/Netflix-show-Atypical-recovering-from
-13259510.php.

Matthews, Malcolm. 2019. "Why Sheldon Cooper Can't Be Black: The Visual
Rhetoric of Autism and Ethnicity." *Journal of Literary and Cultural Disability
Studies* 13, no. 1: 57–74.

Mayo, Elton. 1949. *Hawthorn and the Western Electric Company: The Social Problems
of an Industrial Civilisation.* London: Routledge.

McCarthy, Jay. 2018. "Rain Man at 30: Damaging Stereotype or 'The Best Thing
That Happened to Autism'?" *Guardian,* December 13. theguardian.com/film
/2018/dec/13/rain-man-at-30-autism-hoffman-cruise-levinson.

McCarthy, Kayla. 2019. "Remember Things: Consumerism, Nostalgia, and Geek
Culture in *Stranger Things.*" *Journal of Popular Culture* 52, no. 3: 663–677.

McCormick, Jason. n.d. "Asperger's Syndrome and Humor." Asperger/Autism
Network. Accessed May 28, 2020, aane.org/aspergers-syndrome-humor.

McDonald, Soraya Nadia. 2016. "Oscar-Winning Director Roger Ross Williams
Is Pushed to the Side No Longer." The Undefeated, July 8. theundefeated.com
/features/oscar-winning-director-roger-ross-williams-is-pushed-to-the-side-no
-longer.

Mead, Kit. 2018. "The Shape(s) of Narratives that Spill and Flow over Neat Lines
and Boxes." *Paginated Thoughts* (blog), March 5. kpagination.wordpress.com/tag
/the-shape-of-water.

Medhurst, Andy, and Lucy Tuck. 1981. "The Gender Game." In *BFI Dossier 17: Television Sitcom*, edited by Jim Cook, 43–55. London: British Film Institute.

Miller, Julie. 2017. "For Michael Shannon, the Clothes Made the Man in *The Shape of Water*." *Vanity Fair*, December 3. vanityfair.com/hollywood/2017/12/michael -shannon-getting-into-character-shape-of-water.

Mills, Brett. 2005. *Television Sitcom*. London: BFI.

———. 2009. *The Sitcom*. Edinburgh: Edinburgh University Press.

Mintz, Lawrence E. 1985. "Situation Comedy." In *TV Genres: A Handbook and Reference Guide*, edited by Brian G. Rose, 107–129. Westport, CT: Greenwood.

Mitchell, David T., and Susan L. Snyder. 2000. *Narrative Prosthesis: Disability and the Dependencies of Discourse*. Ann Arbor: University of Michigan Press.

Mittell, Jason. 2013. *Complex TV: The Poetics of Contemporary Television Storytelling*. New York: New York University Press.

Moore, Allison. 2019. "'He's Not Rain Man': Representations of the Sentimental Savant in ABC's *The Good Doctor*." *Journal of Popular Television* 7, no. 3: 299–316.

Moreno, Jacob L. 1947. *The Future of Man's World*. Psychodrama Monograph 21. Boston: Beacon House.

———. 1951. *Sociometry, Experimental Method, and the Science of Society: An Approach to a New Political Orientation*. New York: Beacon.

———. 1953. *Who Shall Survive? Foundations of Sociometry, Group Psychotherapy, and Sociodrama*. New York: Beacon House.

Moss, Haley. 2017. "My Autistic Opinion: *Atypical* is a Stereotypical Representation of Autism." *Huffington Post*, August 11. huffpost.com/entry/my-autistic-opinion -atypical-is-a-stereotypical-representation_b_598e2e04e4b0ed1f464c0abd.

Mukhopadhyay, Tito Rajarshi. 2008. *How Can I Talk If My Lips Don't Move? Inside My Autistic Mind*. New York: Arcade.

Mulhall, Stephen. 2016. *On Film*. Abingdon, UK: Routledge.

Mullan, Phil. 2017. *Creative Destruction: How To Start An Economic Renaissance*. Bristol, UK: Policy Press. Kindle.

Murray, Noel. 2017. "My Teen Son Has Autism. Here's what Netflix's New Dramedy Atypical Gets Wrong." *Week*, August 11. theweek.com/articles/716821/teen -son-autism-heres-what-netflixs-new-dramedy-atypical-gets-wrong.

Murray, Stuart. 2006. "Autism and the Contemporary Sentimental: Fiction and the Narrative Fascination of the Present." *Literature and Medicine* 25, no. 1 (Spring): 24–45.

———. 2008a. "Hollywood and the Fascination of Autism." In *Autism and Representation*, edited by Mark Osteen, 244–255. New York: Routledge.

———. 2008b. *Representing Autism: Culture, Narrative, Fascination*. Liverpool: Liverpool University Press.

———. 2010. "Autism Functions / The Function of Autism." *Disability Studies Quarterly* 30, no. 1. dsq-sds.org/article/view/1048.

———. 2012. *Autism*. New York: Routledge.

———. 2013. "Autism and the Posthuman." In *Worlds of Autism: Across the Spectrum of Neurological Difference*, edited by Joyce Davidson and Michael Orsini, 53–72. Minneapolis: University of Minnesota Press.

———. 2017. "Reading Disability in a Time of Posthuman Work: Speed and Embodiment in Joshua Ferris' *The Unnamed* and Michael Faber's *Under the Skin*." *Disability Studies Quarterly* 37, no. 4. dsq-sds.org/article/view/6104/4823.

———. 2020. *Disability and the Posthuman: Bodies, Technology and Cultural Futures.* New York: Oxford University Press.

Nadesan, Majia Holmer. 2005. *Constructing Autism: Unravelling the Truth and Understanding the Social.* New York: Routledge.

Naremore, James. 1988. *Acting in the Cinema.* Berkeley: University of California Press.

Neicu, Maria. 2012. "Prosthetics Imagery: Negotiating the Identity of Enhanced Bodies." *Platform* 6, no. 2 (Summer): 42–60.

Neufeld, Matt. 2016. Review of *Life, Animated*. Washington Film Institute, July 8. https://dcfilminstitute.org/film-review-life-animated.

Nissim, Hanna Shaul Bar, and R. J. Mitte. 2018. *Authentic Representation in Television, 2018.* rudermanfoundation.org/white_papers/the-ruderman-white-paper-on-authentic-representation-in-tv.

Nolte, John. 2014. *Theory and Methods of J. L. Moreno: The Man Who Tried to Become God.* London: Routledge.

Nordahl-Hansen, Anders. 2017. "Atypical: A Typical Portrayal of Autism?" *Lancet Psychiatry*, October. researchgate.net/publication/320685616.

Nordahl-Hansen, Anders, and Roald A. Øien. 2018. "Movie and TV Depictions of Autism Spectrum Disorder." In *Encyclopedia of Autism Spectrum Disorders*, edited by Fred R. Volkmar. New York: Springer. doi.org/10.1007/978-1-4614-6435-8_102247-1

Nordahl-Hansen, Anders, Magnus Tøndevolda, and Sue Fletcher-Watson. 2018. "Mental Health on Screen: A DSM-5 Dissection of Portrayals of Autism Spectrum Disorders in Film and TV." *Psychiatry Research* 262:351–353. researchgate.net/publication/319272810_Mental_health_on_screen_A_DSM-5_dissection_of_portrayals_of_autism_spectrum_disorders_in_film_and_TV.

Ockelford, Adam. 2013. *Music, Language and Autism: Exceptional Strategies for Exceptional Minds.* London: Kingsley.

O'Falt, Chris. 2016. "'Life, Animated': How Roger Ross Williams Captured the Insular World of Autism for a Touching True Life Story." IndieWire, July 11. indievwire.com/2016/07/life-animated-roger-ross-williams-interview-1201704032.

O'Keefe, Jack. 2017. "What Does The Autism Community Think about 'Atypical'? The Netflix Series Is Facing Some Backlash." Bustle, August 11. bustle.com/p/what-does-the-autism-community-think-about-atypical-the-netflix-series-is-facing-some-backlash-75533.

O'Malley, Sheila. 2018. "Love, after a Fashion." *Film Comment* 54, no. 1 (January–February). filmcomment.com/article/paul-thomas-anderson-phantom-thread-love-after-a-fashion.

Osteen, Mark, ed. 2008a. *Autism and Representation.* New York: Routledge.

———. 2008b. "Autism and Representation: A Comprehensive Introduction." In Osteen, *Autism and Representation*, 1–48.

———. 2008c. "Conclusion: Toward an Empathetic Scholarship." In Osteen, *Autism and Representation*, 297–302.

———. 2010. *One of Us: A Family's Life with Autism*. Columbia: University of Missouri Press.

———. 2013. "Narrating Autism." In *Worlds of Autism: Across the Spectrum of Neurological Difference*, edited by Joyce Davidson and Michael Orsini, 261–284. Minneapolis: University of Minnesota Press.

———. Forthcoming. "'Grow Your Brain!': Contemporary Art on the Autism Spectrum." In *The Routledge Companion to Art and Disability*, edited by Keri Watson and Timothy Hiles. New York: Routledge.

Otake, Tomoko. 2016. "IBM Big Data Used for Rapid Diagnosis of Rare Leukemia Case in Japan." *Japan Times*, August 11. www.japantimes.co.jp/news/2016/08/11/national/science-health/ibm-big-data-used-for-rapid-diagnosis-of-rare-leukemia-case-in-japan.

Palmer, R. Barton. 2016. *Shot on Location: Postwar American Cinema and the Exploration of Real Space*. New Brunswick, NJ: Rutgers University Press.

———. 2020. "Screening Multiple Personality Disorder in the Age of Kinsey: Lizzie and the Three Faces of Eve." In *Mind Reeling*, edited by Homer Pettey, 79–100. Albany: SUNY Press.

Patton, Rebecca. 2018. "Watch Young Actors with Autism Get Their Chance to Shine in 'Atypical' Season 2." Bustle, September 5. bustle.com/p/sams-peer-group-in-atypical-season-2-is-comprised-of-8-budding-actors-with-autism-video-11506867.

Paulhus, Delroy L., and Kevin M. Williams. 2002. "The Dark Triad of Personality: Narcissism, Machiavellianism, and Psychopathy." *Journal of Research in Personality* 36:556–563. doi.org/10.1016/S0092-6566(02)00505-6 (subscription required).

Perez, Gilberto. 1989. *The Material Ghost: Films and Their Medium*. Baltimore: Johns Hopkins University Press.

Perkins, V. F. (1972) 1986. *Film as Film: Understanding and Judging Movies*. New York: Penguin.

Pinker, Steven. 2005. *How the Mind Works*. London: Penguin Random House.

Poe, Charlotte Amelia. 2019. *How to Be Autistic*. Oxford: Myriad.

Pomerance, Murray. 2004. "A Bromide for Ballantine: Spellbound, Psychoanalysis, Light." In *An Eye for Hitchcock*, 58–91. New Brunswick, NJ: Rutgers University Press.

———. 2005. "The Man-Boys of Steven Spielberg." In *Where the Boys Are: Cinemas of Masculinity and Youth*, edited by Murray Pomerance and Frances Gateward, 133–154. Detroit: Wayne State University Press.

———. 2019. *Virtuoso: Film Performance and the Actor's Magic*. New York: Bloomsbury.

Poniewozik, James. 2017. "On 'The Good Doctor,' the Anti-Antihero Is In." *New York Times*, November 12. www.nytimes.com/2017/11/12/arts/television/the-good-doctor-freddie-highmore-abc.html.

Ponnet, Koen, Ann Buysse, Herbert Roeyers, and Armand De Clercq. 2008. "Mind-Reading in Young Adults with ASD: Does Structure Matter?" *Journal of Autism and Developmental Disorders* 38:905–918. link.springer.com/content/pdf/10.1007/s10803-007-0462-5.pdf (subscription required).

Porter, Lynette, ed. 2013. *Sherlock Holmes for the 21st Century: Essays on New Adaptations*. Jefferson, NC: McFarland.

Pritchard, Sallie Maree. 2014. "My Dinner with Andre / Our Dinner with Abed: Genre and the Audience." In *A Sense of "Community": Essays on the Television Series and Its Fandom*, edited by Ann-Gee Lee, 152–166. Jefferson, NC: McFarland.

Prizant, Barry. 2015. *Uniquely Human: A Different Way of Seeing Autism*. New York: Simon & Schuster.

Proctor, Robert N. 1988. *Racial Hygiene: Medicine under the Nazis*. Cambridge, MA: Harvard University Press.

Rafferty, Terrence. 2012. "So Which Borough Is Baker Street In?" *New York Times*, September 21. www.nytimes.com/2012/09/23/arts/television/jonny-lee-miller-as -sherlock-holmes-in-elementary.html.

Rapin, Isabelle. 2011. "Autism Turns 65: A Neurologist's Bird's Eye View." In *Autism Spectrum Disorders*, edited by David Amaral, Geraldine Dawson, and Daniel Geschwind, 1–10. London: Oxford University Press.

Rashkin, Esther. 2011. "Data Learns to Dance: *Star Trek* and the Quest to Be Human." *American Imago* 68, no. 2: 321–346.

Reddit. 2014. "Nightcrawler: One Thing I Noticed about Lou." In r/Movies, November 6. reddit.com/r/movies/comments/2lfuvv/nightcrawler_one_thing_i_no ticed_about_lou.

Reichelt, Susan. 2020. "A Mixed Method Analysis of Autism Spectrum Disorder Representation in Fictional Television." In *Telecinematic Stylistics*, edited by Christian Hoffmann and Monika Kirner-Ludwig. New York: Bloomsbury. Ebook.

Reynolds, Daniel. 2018. "Why *Atypical* Is Part of the Queer TV Revolution." *Advocate*, September 9. advocate.com/television/2018/9/09/why-atypical-part-queer -tv-revolution.

Roberts, Robin. 1999. *Sexual Generations: "Star Trek, The Next Generation" and Gender*. Urbana: University of Illinois Press.

Robertson, John W. 2009. "Informing the Public? UK Newspaper Reporting of Autism and Asperger's Syndrome." *Journal of Research in Special Educational Needs* 9, no. 1: 12–26. onlinelibrary.wiley.com/doi/pdf/10.1111/j.1471-3802.2009.01112.x (subscription required).

Robison, John Elder. 2008. *Look Me in the Eye: My Life with Asperger's*. Washington, DC: Three Rivers.

Rodas, Julia Miele. 2018. *Autistic Disturbances: Theorizing Autism Poetics from the "DSM" to "Robinson Crusoe."* Ann Arbor: University of Michigan Press.

Rogers, John, Essi Viding, R. James Blair, Uta Frith, and Francesca Happé. 2006. "Autism Spectrum Disorder and Psychopathy: Shared Cognitive Underpinnings or Double Hit?" *Psychological Medicine* 36, no. 12: 1789–1798. doi.org/10.1017 /S0033291706008853 (subscription required).

Rohr, Susanne. 2015. "Screening Madness in American Culture." *Journal of Medical Humanities* 36:231–240.

Rowe, Mickey. 2017. "Netflix's 'Atypical' Was a Major Disappointment for Autism Representation." *Teen Vogue*, August 8. teenvogue.com/story/netflix-atypical-au tism-representation.

Rozsa, Matthew. 2017. "Netflix's 'Atypical' Is Offensive, but That's Not Its Real Problem." Salon, August 7. salon.com/2017/08/07/netflix-atypical-review.

———. 2018. "Watching 'Atypical' with Autism: Still Flawed, but Season 2 Shows

Growth." *Salon*, September 22. salon.com/2018/09/22/watching-with-atypical -with-autism-still-flawed-but-season-2-shows-growth.

Rubin, Theodore I. (1961) 1998. *Lisa and David / Jordi / Little Ralphie and the Creature.* New York: Doherty.

———. (1969) 1998. *The Angry Book.* New York: Simon and Schuster.

———. 1974. *Shrink! The Diary of a Psychiatrist.* New York: Popular Library.

Russo, Vito. 1987. *The Celluloid Closet: Homosexuality in the Movies.* New York: Harper & Row.

Rustad, Gry C., and Kai Hanno Schwind. 2017. "The Joke That Wasn't Funny Anymore: Reflections on the Metamodern Sitcom." In *Metamodernism: Historicity, Affect, and Depth after Postmodernism,* edited by Robin van den Akker, Alison Gibbons, and Timotheus Vermeulen, 131–145. London: Rowman & Littlefield.

Sacks, Oliver. 1995. *An Anthropologist on Mars: Seven Paradoxical Tales.* New York: Knopf.

Salud, April. 2017. "'Speechless' Creator Scott Silveri on Writing from Experience: It's 'Really Liberating.'" *Hollywood Reporter,* July 2. hollywoodreporter.com /news/speechless-creator-scott-silveri-writing-experience-liberating-comedy -showrunner-roundtable-1011450.

Schmidt, Ulf. 2007. *Karl Brandt: The Nazi Doctor; Medicine and Power in the Third Reich.* London: Bloomsbury.

Schwartz, Karen, Zana Marie Lutfiyya, and Nancy Hansen. 2013. "Dopey's Legacy: Stereotypical Portrayals of Intellectual Disability in the Classic Animated Films." In *Diversity in Disney Films,* edited by Johnson Cheu, 171–194. Jefferson, NC: McFarland.

Scott, A. O. 2017. "Review: Daniel Day-Lewis Sews Up Another Great Performance in 'Phantom Thread.'" *New York Times,* December 24. nytimes. com/2017/12/24/movies/phantom-thread-review-daniel-day-lewis.html.

Sedgewick, Felicity, and Liz Pellicano. 2019. "Friendships on the Autistic Spectrum." In *Girls and Autism: Educational, Family and Personal Perspectives,* edited by Barry Carpenter, Francesca Happé, and Jo Egerton, 126–135. London: Routledge.

Sepinwall, Alan. 2009. "Reader Mail: Does Sheldon from 'Big Bang Theory' Have Asperger's?" *Newark (NJ) Star-Ledger,* August 13. nj.com/entertainment/tv/2009 /08/reader_mail_does_sheldon_from.html.

———. 2017. "Netflix's Charming 'Atypical' Gets to Know an Autistic Teen—and His Family." Uproxx, August 9. uproxx.com/sepinwall/atypical-netflix-review -jennifer-jason-leigh.

Shakespeare, William. (1594) 1997. *The Comedy of Errors.* Riverside Shakespeare. Boston: Houghton Mifflin.

———. (1595) 1997. *A Midsummer Night's Dream.* Riverside Shakespeare. Boston: Houghton Mifflin.

Sharma, Rekha. 2013. "Community Clip Show: Examining the Recursive Collaboration between Producers and Viewers of a Postmodern Sitcom." *Journal of Fandom Studies* 1, no. 2: 183–199.

Sheffer, Edith. 2018. *Asperger's Children: The Origins of Autism in Nazi Vienna.* New York: Norton.

Shildrick, Margaret. 2013. "Re-Imagining Embodiment: Prostheses, Supplements and Boundaries." *Somatechnics* 3, no. 2: 270–286.

Shklovsky, Viktor. (1919) 2016. "Art as Device." In *Viktor Shklovsky: A Reader*, edited and translated by Alexandra Berlina, 73–97. New York: Bloomsbury.

Silberman, Steve. 2015. *NeuroTribes: The Legacy of Autism and How to Think Smarter about People Who Think Differently*. London: Allen & Unwin.

Siskel, Gene, and Roger Ebert. 1988. Review of *Rain Man* on *At the Movies*. Posted to YouTube by cisio64123, July 9, 2009. https://www.youtube.com/watch?v=rdGn7ZNasKs.

Slagstad, Ketil. 2019. "Asperger, the Nazis and the Children: The History of the Birth of a Diagnosis." *Tidsskriftet den Norske Legeforening* 139, no. 9 (May 24). https://tidsskriftet.no/en/2019/05/essay/asperger-nazis-and-children-history-birth-diagnosis.

Snyder, Timothy. 2010. *Bloodlands: Europe between Hitler and Stalin*. New York: Basic Books.

Sociopath World (blog). 2014. "Nightcrawler." November 14. sociopathworld.com/2014/11/nightcrawler.html.

Solanas, Ferdinand, and Octavio Gettino. 1976. "Towards a Third Cinema." In *Movies and Methods*, vol. 1, edited by Bill Nichols, 44–64. Berkeley: University of California Press.

Sontag, Susan. 1978. *Illness as Metaphor*. New York: Farrar, Straus and Giroux.

Speaight, Robert. 1939 (1947). *Acting: Its Idea and Tradition*. London: Cassell.

Stadler, Jane. 2017. "Empathy in Film." In *The Routledge Handbook of Philosophy of Empathy*, edited by Heidi Maibom, 317–326. New York: Routledge.

Steimatsky, Noa. 2012. "Of the Face, in Reticence." In *Film, Art, New Media: Museum without Walls?*, edited by Angela Dalle Vacche, 159–177. London: Palgrave Macmillan.

Stein, Louisa Ellen, and Kristina Busse, eds. 2012. *"Sherlock" and Transmedia Fandom: Essays on the BBC Series*. Jefferson, NC: McFarland.

Stratton, Jon. 2016a. "The Price of Love: *The Big Bang Theory*, the Family and Neoliberalism." *European Journal of Cultural Studies* 19, no. 2: 170–187.

———. 2016b. "Die Sheldon Die: *The Big Bang Theory*, Everyday Neoliberalism and Sheldon as Neoliberal Man." *Journal for Cultural Research* 20, no. 2: 171–188.

Subbaraman, Nidhi. 2014. "Study on 'Extreme Male Brain' Theory of Autism Draws Critics." Spectrum, August 25. www.spectrumnews.org/news/study-on-extreme-male-brain-theory-of-autism-draws-critics.

Sullivan, Katy. 2018. "Paralympian Actress Katy Sullivan Chides Dwayne Johnson for Playing Amputee in 'Skyscraper.'" Deadline, July 16. deadline.com/2018/07/paralympian-chides-dwayne-johnsonamputee-skyscraper-casting-katy-sullivan-disabilities-1202427187.

Suskind, Ron. 2014. *Life, Animated: A Story of Sidekicks, Heroes, and Autism*. Glendale, CA: Kingswell.

Szasz, Thomas. (1974) 2010. *The Myth of Mental Illness: Foundations of a Theory of Personal Conduct*. New York: Harper Perennial.

Tansley, Laura. 2014. "'Six Seasons and a Movie!' Community, Creative Processes and Being Meta." In *A Sense of "Community": Essays on the Television Series and Its Fandom*, edited by Ann-Gee Lee, 211–224. Jefferson, NC: McFarland.

Thigpen, Corbett H., and Hervey M. Cleckley. 1957. *The Three Faces of Eve*. New York: Fawcett.

Thomson, David. 2015. *How to Watch a Movie*. New York: Vintage, 2015.

306 Works Cited and Consulted

Tobia, Anthony, and Annmarie Toma. 2015. "Rethinking Asperger's: Understanding the DSM-5 Diagnosis by Introducing Sheldon Cooper." *Journal of Communication Disorders, Deaf Studies and Hearing Aids* 3, no. 4. longdom.org/open-access/rethinking-asperger-s-understanding-the-dsm5-diagnosis-byintroducing-sheldon-cooper-2375-4427-1000146.pdf.

Townson, Rachel, and Carol Povey. 2019. "Run the World, Girls: Success as an Adult Autistic Female." In *Girls and Autism: Educational, Family and Personal Perspectives*, edited by Barry Carpenter, Francesca Happé, and Jo Egerton, 171–178. London: Routledge.

Travers, Ben. 2017. "'Young Sheldon' Isn't Just Better than 'The Big Bang Theory'—It's Funnier, Too." IndieWire, November 27. indiewire.com/2017/11/young-sheldon-better-than-big-bang-theory-funnier-1201901230.

Travers, P. L. (1934) 2016. *Mary Poppins*. London: HarperCollins.

———. (1935) 2016. *Mary Poppins Comes Back*. London: HarperCollins.

———. 1965. "A Radical Innocence." In P. L. Travers, *What the Bee Knows*, 235–241.

———. 1976. "The World of the Hero." In P. L. Travers, *What the Bee Knows*, 11–18.

———. 1978. "If She's Not Gone, She Lives There Still." In P. L. Travers, *What the Bee Knows*, 36–49.

———. 1983. "Re-Storying the Adult." In P. L. Travers, *What the Bee Knows*, 141–144.

———. 1989. *What the Bee Knows: Reflections on Myth, Symbol and Story*. Wellingborough, UK: Aquarian.

Treffert, Darold A. 2009. "The Savant Syndrome: An Extraordinary Condition; A Synopsis: Past, Present, Future." *Philosophical Transactions of the Royal Society of London, Series B, Biological Sciences* 364, no. 1522: 1351–1357. ncbi.nlm.nih.gov/pmc/articles/PMC2677584.

Valverde, Cristina Pérez. 2006. "Magic Women on the Margins: Ec-centric Models in Mary Poppins and Ms. Wiz." *Children's Literature in Education* 40:263–274.

Vermeulen, Timotheus, and Robin van den Akker. 2010. "Notes on Metamodernism." *Journal of Aesthetics and Culture* 2, no. 1. tandfonline.com/doi/citedby/10.3402/jac.v2i0.5677?scroll=top&needAccess=true.

Vick, Megan. 2018. "Atypical Remains the Most Surprising Family Comedy on TV," *TV Guide*, September 3. tvguide.com/news/atypical-season-2-review.

Wakeman, Nick. 2011. "IBM's Watson Heads to Medical School." *Washington Technology*, February 17. washingtontechnology.com/articles/2011/02/17/ibm-watson-next-steps.aspx.

Walker, Joseph S. 2014. "*Community*'s Communities: Bringing the Fan to the (Study) Table." In *A Sense of "Community": Essays on the Television Series and Its Fandom*, edited by Ann-Gee Lee, 181–196. Jefferson, NC: McFarland.

Wallace, David Foster. 1993. "E Unibus Pluram: Television and U.S. Fiction." *Review of Contemporary Fiction* 13, no. 2: 151–194.

Walt Disney Home Entertainment. 2006. "Treasures Untold: The Making of Disney's *The Little Mermaid*: Documentary Featurette." Bonus material on *The Little Mermaid*: Platinum Edition DVD.

Walters, Shannon. 2013. "Cool Aspie Humor: Cognitive Difference and Kenneth Burke's Comic Corrective in *The Big Bang Theory* and *Community*." *Journal of Literary and Cultural Disability Studies* 7, no. 3: 271–288.

Wells-Lassagne, Shannon. 2012. "Transforming the Traditional Sitcom: Abed in *Community.*" *TV/Series* 1 (May 15). journals.openedition.org/tvseries/1560.

Wilcox, Rhonda. 1993. "Dating Data: Miscegenation in *Star Trek: The Next Generation.*" *Extrapolation* 34, no. 3: 265–277.

Willey, Liane Holliday. 2015. *Pretending to Be Normal: Living with Asperger's Syndrome (Autism Spectrum Disorder).* New ed. London: Kingsley.

Wilson, George. 1998. *Narration in Light: Studies in Cinematic Point of View.* Baltimore: Johns Hopkins University Press.

Wing, Lorna. 1981. "Asperger's Syndrome: A Clinical Account." *Psychological Medicine* 11, no. 1: 115–129. cambridge.org/core/journals/psychological-medicine/article/aspergers-syndrome-a-clinical-account/D32E7EB0D467FD05D1A51D267B1F4A72 (subscription required).

Winston, Christine N. 2016. "Evaluating Media's Portrayal of an Eccentric-Genius: Dr. Sheldon Cooper." *Psychology of Popular Media* 5, no. 3: 290–306.

Wollen, Peter. 1985. "Godard and Counter Cinema: *Vent D'Est.*" In *Movies and Methods*, vol. 2, edited by Bill Nichols, 500–509. Berkeley: University of California Press.

Woudhuysen, James. 2020. "Nudging: An Elite Disease." Spiked, March 18. spiked-online.com/2020/03/18/nudging-an-elite-disease.

Wylie, Philip. 1942. *A Generation of Vipers.* New York: Rinehart.

Yehl, Joshua, and Scott Collura. 2019. "Star Trek: Seven of Nine's Jeri Ryan Shares How Her Character Has Resonated with Autistic People." IGN, July 24. ign.com/articles/2019/07/24/seven-of-nine-jeri-ryan-autism-star-trek-picard.

Photo Captions and Credits

p. 144   The objectification of Sonya (Diane Kruger) begins immediately with the camera focusing from behind on her long blond hair, in *The Bridge* (2013). Digital frame enlargement.

p. 159   In the first episode of *Atypical* (2017), Sam (Keir Gilchrist) wears headphones in a high school hallway to avoid being overwhelmed by sounds. Digital frame enlargement.

p. 174   Abed (Danny Pudi) intervenes in the narrative by commenting on the brimming sexual tension between Jeff (Joel McHale, not shown) and Britta (Gillian Jacobs) in *Community* (2009). Digital frame enlargement.

p. 186   *Left*: Sheldon Cooper (Iain Armitage) in *Young Sheldon* (2017); Sheldon Cooper (Jim Parsons) in *The Big Bang Theory* (2007). Digital frame enlargements.

p. 201   Dana (Anna Kendrick), a junior accountant, befriends the awkward but brilliant analyst Christian (Ben Affleck) in Gavin O'Connor's *The Accountant* (Gavin O'Connor, Warner Bros., 2016). Digital frame enlargement.

p. 215   Ricky (Jesus Sanchez-Velez), alone and at sea in the New York subway, in *Stand Clear of the Closing Doors* (Sam Fleischner, How Follows What, 2013). Digital frame enlargement.

p. 227   *Top*: The customary posture of Woodcock (Daniel Day-Lewis) in *Phantom Thread* (Paul Thomas Anderson, Focus Features, 2017) and Chance (Peter Sellers) in *Being There* (Hal Ashby, BSB/CIP, 1979). Digital frame enlargements.

p. 240   They've got a lot to say! Bert (Dick Van Dyke) and Mary Poppins (Julie Andrews) gleefully sing "Supercalifragilisticexpialidocious!" in *Mary Poppins* (Robert Stevenson, Walt Disney Productions, 1964). Digital frame enlargement.

p. 255   The final shot: an extreme close-up of David and Lisa joining hands for the first time in token of their friendship, in Frank Perry's *David and Lisa* (Lisa and David Company, 1962). Digital frame enlargement.

p. 272   Jesse (Ashley Zukerman) safe with his "teddy bear," in *The Code* (2014). Digital frame enlargement.

Contributors

BRENDA AUSTIN-SMITH is a professor in and head of the Department of English, Theatre, Film & Media at the University of Manitoba in Winnipeg, Canada. She teaches and publishes on cinephilia, screen performance, melodrama, film and emotion, cult films, adaptation, and film and the city.

CHRISTINE BECKER is an associate professor in the Department of Film, Television, and Theatre at the University of Notre Dame specializing in film and television history and critical analysis. Her book *It's the Pictures That Got Small: Hollywood Film Stars on 1950s Television* (2008) won an IAMHIST Michael Nelson Prize for a Work in Media and History. She has recently published anthology chapters about British actors on American television, BBC America's corporate strategies, and television programming during the US bicentennial. She also cohosts and coproduces the *Aca-Media* podcast for the *Journal of Cinema and Media Studies*.

REBECCA BELL-METEREAU, a professor at Texas State University, directs the film and media studies minor. She is the author of *Transgender Cinema* (2019) and *Hollywood Androgyny* (1985); the coauthor of *Simone Weil: On Politics, Religion and Society* (1998); and the coeditor of *Star Bodies and the Erotics of Suffering* (2015). Her essays appear in *Close-Up: Great Cinematic Performances, Volume 1* (2018), *The Many Cinemas of Michael Curtiz* (2018), *Critical Insights: Stanley Kubrick* (2016), *A Little Solitaire: John Frankenheimer and American Film* (2011), *Acting for America* (2010), *Cinema and Modernity* (2006), *American Cinema of the 1950s* (2005), *Film and Television after 9/11* (2004), *Bad: Infamy, Darkness, Evil, and Slime on Screen* (2003), and *Ladies and Gentlemen, Boys and Girls* (2001).

MATTHEW CIPA lectures in film and television studies in the School of Communication and Arts at the University of Queensland, Australia. His doctoral research examined how metaphysical concepts are artistically transformed through stylistic form and narrative across a range of films and television programs and are made sensible to spectators via the aesthetic experiences such works offer.

ALEX CLAYTON is a senior lecturer in film and television at the University of Bristol. He is the author of *The Body in Hollywood Slapstick* (2007) and *Funny How?* (2020).

INA RAE HARK is a distinguished Professor Emerita at the University of South Carolina and has been writing academically about *Star Trek* since 1978. She is the author of the BFI TV Classics volume on the series, as well as a dozen other articles and chapters. She has published more broadly on science fiction television and films and onscreen masculinity, historical epics, and Hitchcock.

BURKE HILSABECK is an associate professor of English and film studies at the University of Northern Colorado. He is the author of *The Slapstick Camera: Hollywood and the Comedy of Self-Reference* (2020).

FINCINA HOPGOOD is a lecturer in screen studies at the University of New England, Australia, where she teaches in the Media and Communications Program. A former editor of the online journal *Senses of Cinema*, she is currently writing a monograph on portrayals of mental illness in contemporary Australian film and television. Her research has been published in the journals *Screen*, *Adaptation*, the *Journal of Australasian Popular Culture*, *M/C: Journal of Media and Culture*, and the *Journal of Interdisciplinary Gender Studies*, and in several edited collections: *The Palgrave Handbook of Script Development* (forthcoming), *American-Australian Cinema: Transnational Connections* (2018), *Australian Screen in the 2000s* (2017), *Directory of World Cinema: Australia and New Zealand* (2010), *Australia: Who Cares?* (2007), and *Australian Film, 1978–1994* (1996).

JASON JACOBS is a professor of film and television studies in the School of Communication and Arts at the University of Queensland. He is the author of *David Milch* (2020), *Reluctant Sleuths, True Detectives* (forthcoming), and *The Persistence of Television* (forthcoming).

DOMINIC LENNARD is a teaching fellow in the predegree programs at the University of Tasmania. He is the author of *Bad Seeds and Holy Terrors: The Child Villains of Horror Film* (2014) and *Brute Force: Animal Horror Movies* (2019).

ELLIOTT LOGAN is a lecturer in media and communication at the University of Queensland. He is the author of *Breaking Bad and Dignity* (2016) and is associate editor of the journal *Series*.

DOUGLAS MCFARLAND is a retired professor of English and classical studies at Flagler College, Saint Augustine, Florida, where he taught Renaissance literature, Latin, and Greek. He has published on sixteenth-century English and French literature, as well as numerous articles and chapters on film. He is the coeditor of *John Huston as Adaptor* (2018) and *Patricia Highsmith on Screen* (2019).

MARK OSTEEN is a professor of English and director of the Center for the Humanities at Loyola University Maryland. Among his many books are a memoir, *One of Us: A Family's Life with Autism* (2010), and an edited essay collection, *Autism and Representation* (2008). His publications on film include *Nightmare Alley: Film Noir and the American Dream* (2013) and *Hitchcock and Adaptation* (2014). His book *Fake It: Fictions of Forgery* is forthcoming from the University of Virginia Press.

R. BARTON PALMER is an independent scholar based in Atlanta, Georgia. He has published widely in medieval literature, film, and adaptation studies, including coediting *Hitchcock's Moral Gaze* (2017).

MURRAY POMERANCE is an independent scholar living in Toronto and adjunct professor in the School of Media and Communication at RMIT University, Melbourne. He is the author of *Color It True* (forthcoming), *A Voyage with Hitchcock*, *The Film Cheat* (2020), *Virtuoso* (2019), *A Dream of Hitchcock* (2019), *Cinema, If You Please* (2018), and the BFI Film Classics monographs on *Marnie* (2014) and *The Man Who Knew Too Much* (2016). He is the editor of the Horizons of Cinema series published by SUNY Press and the Techniques of the Modern Image series published by Rutgers University Press.

DANIEL SACCO has published on the cinemas of Sam Peckinpah, Lucio Fulci, Vincent Gallo, and Andrew Jarecki. His writing has appeared in

Cinephile, the *New Review of Film and Television Studies*, and *Studies in the Fantastic*. He currently teaches screenwriting at the Toronto Film School at Yorkville University and is the Canadian representative in the Global Horror Studies Research Network at the University of Pittsburgh. His monograph *Film Censorship in National Context* is forthcoming.

JOSHUA SCHULZE is a doctoral student in the Department of Film, Television, and Media at the University of Michigan. His research interests revolve around cinema's relationship with space and place, and the material and environmental impact of film culture. More broadly, he is interested in the aesthetics of contemporary media. To date, his work has appeared in the *Quarterly Review of Film and Video*, the *Journal of Popular Film and Television*, and *Horror Studies*.

DANIEL VARNDELL is a senior lecturer in English literature at the University of Winchester, UK. He is the author of *Hollywood Remakes, Deleuze and the Grandfather Paradox* (2014), as well as publications on a range of film subjects, including, most recently, a journal article on *Shane* and book chapters on nostalgia and *Jaws*. His new monograph examines etiquette and torture in film performance.

CHRISTINA WILKINS is an interdisciplinary researcher with interests in adaptation, mental health, and identity across film and literature. She is the author of *Religion and Identity in Post-9/11 Vampire Narratives* (Palgrave), which spans such topics as adaptation, masculinity, and nostalgia, and the forthcoming monograph *Embodying Character: Adaptation and the Body* (Palgrave). She teaches at the University of Birmingham.

Index

Obama, Barack, 92
Ockelford, Adam, 244
O'Connor, Gavin, 208
O'Falt, Chris, 48
Office, The (TV, 2005–2013), 192
O'Keefe, Jack, 165, 167–168
O'Malley, Sheila, 234
One Flew Over the Cuckoo's Nest (Miloš
  Forman, 1975), 257
Osteen, Mark, 4, 10, 19, 33–34, 95–96,
  100, 132–133, 189, 210, 240–254
Otake, Tomoko, 77

Pagemaster, The (Joe Johnston and Mau-
  rice Hunt, 1994), 51
Palmer, R. Barton, 19–34, 255–271
Parenthood (TV, 2010–2015), 161–162
Park, Jae Sue, 83
Parks and Recreation (TV, 2009–2015),
  192
Parsons, Jim, 187, 189, 191–192, 195
Patton, Rebecca, 170
Paulhus, Delroy L., 207
Pawnbroker, The (Sidney Lumet, 1965),
  266
Paz, Andrea Suarez, 225
Pellicano, Liz, 140
Pennies from Heaven (Herbert Ross,
  1981), 141
People magazine, 55, 71
People's Court, The (TV, 1981–1993,
  1997–), 7
Perez, Gilberto, 215–216
Perkins, V. F., 216
Perovic, Adele, 278
Perry, Eleanor, 255–256
Perry, Frank, 34, 255–256, 258–259,
  263, 266, 268
Perry, Matthew, 178
Perry, Zoe, 196
Personal Shopper (Olivier Assayas,
  2016), 3
Peterman, Melissa, 197
Phantom Thread (Paul Thomas Ander-
  son, 2017), 33, 227–239
Philadelphia Museum of Art, 269
Phuong, Ryan, 194
Picardo, Robert, 40

Pinker, Steven, 202
Pinocchio (Ben Sharpsteen and Hamil-
  ton Luske, 1940), 242
Pitt, Brad, 84, 90, 93
Plank, Alex, 147, 171
Poe, Charlotte Amelia, 140, 142
Poésy, Clémence, 7
Poitier, Sidney, 1
Poltergeist (Tobe Hooper, 1982), 109
Pomerance, Murray, 1–18, 34, 123, 141,
  193, 234, 256, 259, 272–290
Poniewozik, James, 72
Ponnet, Koen, 202
Popular Mechanics magazine, 151
Porgy and Bess (Otto Preminger,
  1959), 1
Porter, Lynette, 104
Potts, Annie, 196
Povey, Carol, 131
Prime Suspect (TV, 1991–2006), 108
Pritchard, Sallie Maree, 177–178, 183
Prizant, Barry, 19, 26
Proctor, Robert N., 22
Prouty, Olive Higgins, 258
Psychiatry Research, 172
Psycho (Alfred Hitchcock, 1960), 267
Pudi, Danny, 174

Rafferty, Terrence, 105
Rain Man (Barry Levinson, 1988), 7,
  29, 59–70, 75, 96, 105, 108, 115,
  118–119, 220, 222, 287–288
Rainman Twins (Dave Wagner, 2008),
  49
Rapin, Isabelle, 63
Rapper, Irving, 258
Rashid, Robia, 160, 163–164, 167, 169,
  171–172
Rashkin, Esther, 40
Rassenhygiene (racial hygiene), 21–22
*Reason I Jump, The: The Inner Voice of a
  Thirteen-Year-Old Boy with Autism*
  (Naoki Higashida), 217
Rebel Without a Cause (Nicholas Ray,
  1955), 3
Reddit, 207
Reichelt, Susan, 160
Reid, Elwood, 147

CPSIA information can be obtained
at www.ICGtesting.com
Printed in the USA
LVHW100433150422
715934LV00006B/10/J